Employment Discr...

A Manager's Guide

DAVID P. TWOMEY
Professor of Law
Carroll School of Management
Boston College
Member of the Massachusetts and Florida Bars

WEST

WEST EDUCATIONAL PUBLISHING COMPANY

An International Thomson Publishing Company

Publisher/Team Director: Jack W. Calhoun
Acquisitions Editor: Rob Dewey
Development Editor: Mignon D. Worman-Member, Ohio and
    California Bars
Production Editor: Peggy K. Buskey
Marketing Manager: Scott D. Person
Production House: BookMasters, Inc.
Cover Design: Kim Torbeck, Imbue Design
Cover Photo: Copyright Photodisc, Inc.

Library of Congress Cataloging-in-Publication Data

Twomey, David P.
    Employment discrimination law : a manager's guide / David P.
Twomey.
        p.   cm.
    Includes index.
    ISBN 0–324–00082–0
    1. Discrimination in employment—Law and legislation—United
States—Cases.   I. Title.
KF3464.A7T96   1998
344.7301'133—dc21   97–53302
                                                     CIP

1 2 3 4 5 6 7 8 WE 4 3 2 1 0 9 8 7

Printed in Canada

International Thomson Publishing
West Educational Publishing is an ITP Company.
The ITP trademark is used under license.

Preface

Employment discrimination based on race, color, religion, national origin, gender, age, or disability is both unacceptable and illegal in our society.

When four executives of Texaco, Inc. were caught on tape making racist statements about minority employees and discussing how to conceal evidence sought by plaintiffs in a racial discrimination law suit, no argument could be made that such conduct was either legal or acceptable. Within two weeks of the release of the tapes, Texaco agreed to a $176.1 million settlement of the underlying lawsuit.

Top and middle management at Mitsubishi Motors Corporation may have been unaware of the hostile working environment faced by women at its production facility at Normal, Illinois; low-level managers may have been oblivious to such problems and some may have condoned this misconduct. However, in August of 1997, the company settled a sexual harassment law suit which had been brought against it by 27 female employees, effectively recognizing its responsibility for the improper activities allowed to transpire on its production lines.

Antidiscrimination laws are for the most part uncomplicated and straightforward, and management policies can deal effectively with discrimination and harassment issues and prevent employer liability if there is sufficient commitment by management, from the very top level down to supervisors on the plant floor. This book, a concise guide to antidiscrimination and related laws, is designed for managers and management students, to enable them to know the law and to provide the informed leadership necessary for a discrimination-free and harassment-free workplace.

Related Laws

When E. I. du Pont de Nemours & Co., Inc. terminated Louis Pettus for insubordination for failure to enroll in an inpatient alcohol treatment program, Pettus, an African-American with 22 years of service, filed suit against the company claiming race discrimination and retaliation in violation of Title VII of the Civil Rights Act of 1964. He also sued Du Pont and others, claiming breach of contract, wrongful termination in violation of public policy, unauthorized use of medical information, and invasion of his constitutional right to privacy under his state's constitution. He was successful in his claims for unauthorized use of medical information and invasion of privacy (*Pettus v Cole*, 57 Cal. Rptr. 2d 46). It is not unusual today for an employer to have to defend employment termination decisions against multiple claims, including claims under Title VII based on race, color, religion, gender, or national origin discrimination, as well as additional claims based on age or disability discrimination. Additional claims may be filed, as well, for breach of an employment contract derived from or implied in statements in personnel handbooks, or based on the public policy or the whistleblower exceptions to the employment-at-will doctrine. Further possibilities may include invasion-of-privacy or defamation claims. Other employment laws referred to in the text have indirect applications to employment discrimination law.

"Related laws" then are those laws often connected with antidiscrimination lawsuits, about which every manager should be informed.

Format

The language of court opinions is the language of lawyers and judges. The opinions presented in the text have been edited, and discussion of extraneous issues and nonessential procedural points have been eliminated. Questions have been added at the end of each opinion to direct attention to crucial facts, distinctions, and legal theories. Case problems derived from court and administrative agency decisions in real cases are presented at the end of each chapter and offer the opportunity to apply the legal principles set forth in the text to real-life situations. Citations at the end of each problem enable readers with access to a law library to research how the problem was actually resolved.

Instructor's Manual

The author provides comprehensive answers to all case questions and chapter problems and questions.

Employment Discrimination Case Updates on the Internet

The reader can bookmark **www.westbuslaw.com** and click to a continuing supply of new employment discrimination cases as they are issued by selected state and federal courts on the **West Educational Business Law Discipline Internet Page**. Each case is summarized to provide, in this dynamic area of the law, up-to-the-minute developments that can be incorporated immediately into classroom lectures.

Acknowledgments

I wish to thank all those who have helped make this book possible, especially the reviewers: John Allison, University of Texas-Austin; Karen J. Elwell, Bloomsburg University; Richard J. Hunter, Jr., Seton Hall University; Christine Neylon O'Brien, Boston College; Michael K. Fee Esq., Needham, MA; Kathleen M. Kyratzoglou, Newton, MA; and Rodrick Blacklock, Addison, VT.

Suggestions for improving this book will be cordially welcomed.

David P. Twomey
Carroll School of Management
Boston College
Chestnut Hill
Massachusetts

About the Author

David P. Twomey graduated from Boston College in 1962, earned his MBA at the University of Massachusetts at Amherst in 1963, and, after two years of business experience, entered Boston College Law School, where he earned his Juris Doctor degree in 1968.

While a law student, he began his teaching career serving as Lecturer in Finance and Marketing at Simmons College in Boston. He joined the faculty of the Boston College Carroll School of Management, in 1968 as an assistant professor and was promoted to the rank of professor in 1978. Professor Twomey has written 25 books and numerous articles on labor, employment, and business law topics. He has a special interest in curriculum development, serving three terms as chairman of his school's Educational Policy Committee. He is chairman of the Business Law Department.

Professor Twomey is a nationally known labor arbitrator, having been selected by the parties as arbitrator in numerous disputes throughout the country in the private and public sectors. In the context of impending nationwide rail strikes, his service includes appointments by Presidents Reagan, Bush, and Clinton to six Presidential Emergency Boards, whose recommendations served as the basis for the resolution of underlying labor disputes. Professor Twomey is a member of the National Academy of Arbitrators. He is also a member of the Massachusetts, Florida, and federal bars. He lives in Quincy, Massachusetts, with his wife Veronica and their three children, Erin, David, and Kerry.

Contents

CHAPTER 4—DISABILITY DISCRIMINATION LAWS:
          WORKERS' COMPENSATION

CHAPTER 5—EMPLOYMENT RELATIONSHIPS: CONTRACTUAL AND
          TORT THEORIES

CHAPTER 6—EMPLOYEE PRIVACY TOPICS

CHAPTER 7—DEVELOPING TOPICS

1
Discrimination Laws: Protected Classes Under Title VII and the Constitution

SECTION 1—INTRODUCTION

Numerous major federal laws regulate the equal employment rights of individuals. The Civil Rights Act of 1866, commonly referred to as a legal action under Section 1981, remedies discrimination based on race. Title VII of the Civil Rights Act of 1964, as amended by the Equal Employment Opportunities Act of 1972 and the Civil Rights Act of 1991, forbids employer and union discrimination based on race, color, religion, sex, or national origin. The Equal Pay Act of 1963 requires equal pay for men and women doing equal work. The Age Discrimination in Employment Act of 1967, as amended, forbids discriminatory hiring practices against job applicants and employees over the age of 40. The Rehabilitation Act of 1973 and Title I of the Americans with Disabilities Act of 1990 protect persons with disabilities from discrimination.

Additionally, Executive Order 11246, which has the force and effect of a statute enacted by Congress, regulates contractors and subcontractors doing business with the federal government. This order forbids discrimination against minorities and women, and in certain situations requires affirmative action to be taken to offer better employment opportunities to minorities and women.

This chapter and all subsequent chapters treat in detail, or in part, aspects of employment discrimination law. Coverage includes the above statutes and executive order, the U.S. Constitution, and the court decisions construing them.

SECTION 2—TITLE VII AS AMENDED

The general purpose of Title VII of the Civil Rights Act of 1964 is the elimination of employer and union practices that discriminate against employees and job applicants on the basis of race, color, religion, sex, or national origin.

Legislative Background

The Civil Rights Act of 1964 was passed in response to the civil rights movement in the early 1960s protesting racial segregation of black Americans. On June 19, 1963, President John Kennedy submitted a bill to Congress, which later became the Civil Rights Act of 1964. Title I was a voting rights proposal, which had already been submitted to Congress. Title II addressed the subject of public accommodation, dealing with the denial of full accommodation rights to all Americans at restaurants, hotels, and other public places. Title VII dealt with discrimination in employment, but the approach taken in the initial bill was quite modest in comparison to Title VII as ultimately enacted in 1964. In 1963, then Vice President Lyndon Johnson advised President Kennedy to go to the source of the opposition to the bill—the South—and present the bill as a question of simple morality. Johnson believed that the people in the South were good people who knew that what was happening to black Americans was just not right.

On November 22, 1963, President Kennedy was assassinated while the bill was being considered by the Congress. The president's death gave impetus to passage of the bill, and was considered by many to be a legislative monument to him. Title VII had been amended by opponents of the legislation, who added the word *sex* to the forms of prohibited discrimination, hoping that such an amendment would kill the entire legislation. However, the legislation was an idea whose time had come for Congress and President Johnson, and the bill was signed into law on July 2, 1964.

As Title VII is studied, it will become evident that this law has been the driving force in shaping fair employment practices in our society, and ridding society of unfair practices whereby otherwise qualified workers are impeded from competing on an equal basis with fellow citizens for employment and promotional opportunities.

Prohibited Practices and Coverage

Title VII forbids discrimination in hiring, terms or conditions of employment, union membership and representation, and the referral of applicants by employment services. Title VII specifically forbids any employer to fail to hire, to discharge, to classify employees, or to discriminate with respect to compensation, terms, conditions, or privileges of employment in any way that would deprive any individual of employment opportunity due to race, color, religion, sex, or national origin. Title VII also prohibits retaliation against persons who file charges with the Equal Employment Opportunity Commission (EEOC) or participate in EEOC investigations.[1]

Title VII covers private employers, state and local governments, and educational institutions that have 15 or more employees. The federal government, private and public employment agencies, labor organizations, and joint labor-management committees for apprenticeship and training also must abide by the law.

The employees of the U.S. Senate, the U.S. House of Representatives, and the executive branch are covered by Title VII, the Age Discrimination in Employment Act, and the Americans with Disabilities Act. However, each branch has its own enforcement procedures and remedies, and considerations of party affiliations, domicile, and political compatibility in employment decisions are not to be considered unfair employment practices.[2]

The Equal Employment Opportunity Commission

The Equal Employment Opportunity Commission was created by Title VII. It is a five-member commission appointed by the president and confirmed by the Senate. Members are appointed for five-year staggered terms. The five-member commission makes equal employment opportunity policy, and approves all litigation. The members do not "decide" individual cases under an administrative law system which is similar to the adjudicative procedures of the National Labor Relations Act. However, the general counsel to the EEOC is responsible for conducting EEOC enforcement litigation in the courts.

The EEOC administers Title VII of the Civil Rights Act of 1964, the Equal Pay Act of 1963, the Age Discrimination in Employment Act of 1967 (ADEA), Section 501 of the Rehabilitation Act of 1973 (which prohibits federal-sector discrimination against the handicapped), and Title I, the employment provisions of the Americans with Disabilities Act (ADA) of 1990.

EEOC Procedures

Where a state or local agency has the power to act on allegations of discriminatory practices, the charging party must file a complaint with that agency. The charging party must

---

[1] Charges filed with the EEOC during FY 1995:

Category	Number of Charges	Percent
Race	29,986	34.3
Religion	1,582	1.8
National Origin	7,035	8.0
Sex	26,181	29.9
Retaliation	15,342	17.5
Disability	19,778	22.6
Equal Pay	1,273	1.5

Source: Equal Employment Opportunity Commission National Database, Mar. 10, 1997.
[2] See Government Employee Rights Act of 1991, Pub. L. 102-166, Nov. 21, 1991, 105 Stat. 1088, 2 U.S.C. 1201.

wait 60 days or until the termination of the state proceedings, whichever occurs first, before filing a charge with the EEOC. The commission then conducts an investigation to determine whether reasonable cause exists to believe that the charge is true. If such cause is found to exist, the EEOC attempts to remedy the unlawful practice through conciliation.

The EEOC undertakes investigative and conciliation responsibilities through its regional offices. Figure 1–1 outlines the process. The charging party is interviewed by an equal opportunity specialist, who counsels the charging party on EEOC procedures and assists in the writing of the charge. The charging party is asked to complete a questionnaire providing information such as the name, address, and telephone number of the employer; the name of the supervisor; the date that the alleged discrimination occurred; and the nature of the discrimination.

The EEOC classifies incoming charges by letter-designated priorities, designating "A" charges as worthy cases for immediate handling, "B" charges as those requiring further investigation, and "C" charges as those that have a low likelihood of success. Cases where a restraining order may be deemed appropriate or where the charging party may be dying are placed in the highest-priority A category, as are cases that appear to be litigation worthy, have a potential for class action status, or present a new or novel legal issue. Cases that appear to meet a high standard of proof are also classified in the A category. Cases where further investigation is required are classified as B cases. Examples of low-priority C cases are cases where the charge is filed after the 300-day time limit for filing charges, or the employer has too few employees to be subject to Title VII, or the offending party is not an employer.

After a charge is filed, the employer is notified and a fact-finding conference is convened. At this conference both the charging party and the employer present evidence before the equal opportunity specialist, who tries to work out a settlement, if appropriate, satisfactory to both sides.

If the EEOC finds that there is reasonable cause to believe that discrimination has occurred, but is unable to conciliate the charge, EEOC attorneys will consider the complaint for possible litigation. If the EEOC decides to litigate the case, a lawsuit will be filed in federal district court. If the EEOC decides not to litigate the case, a right-to-sue letter will be issued that permits the charging party to take the case to court. The fact that the EEOC does not choose to litigate a case does not mean that the case is without merit. The EEOC does not have funding to litigate all arguable cases. If successful, the charging party will recover attorney's fees from the defendant.

Time Limits

The time limitation for filing charges with the EEOC is 180 days after the occurrence of the discriminatory act.[3] When the charging party is required to file first with a state or local agency, the time limit for filing charges is increased to 300 days after the occurrence of the discriminatory act or 30 days after receiving notice that the state has

---

[3] 42 U.S.C. Section 701(e).

FIGURE 1–1   EEOC Charge Processing

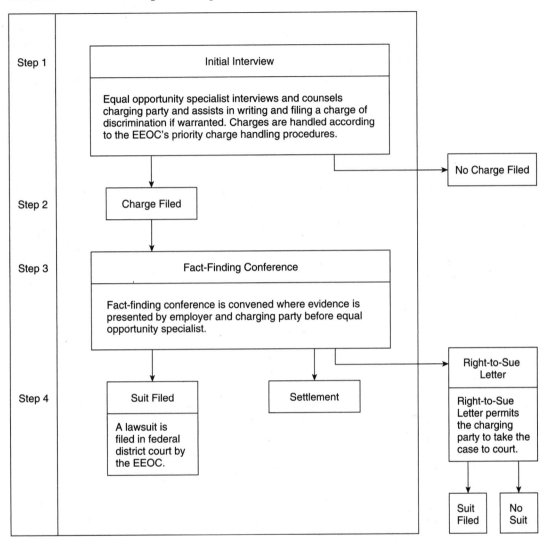

terminated its processing of the charge, whichever is earlier.[4] After the conclusion of proceedings before the EEOC, an individual claiming a violation of Title VII has 90 days after receipt of a right-to-sue letter from EEOC to file a civil lawsuit in a federal district court.[5] If an aggrieved individual does not meet the time limit of Title VII, the individual may well lose the right to seek relief under the Act. Limited exceptions exist

---

[4] 42 U.S.C. Section 706(e).
[5] 42 U.S.C. Section 706(f)(1).

where the time limits are considered "tolled" or suspended for equitable reasons. For example, in *Crown Cork & Seal Co. v. Parker*,[6] the Supreme Court decided that the 90-day limitation period for filing a court action after receiving a right-to-sue notice from the EEOC was tolled because of the filing of a class action suit by others where Parker was a member of the class.

Covered Employees

In *Robinson v. Shell Oil Co.*,[7] the oil company fired Charles Robinson. Shortly thereafter, Robinson filed a charge with the EEOC alleging that he had been discharged because of his race. While that charge was pending, Robinson applied for a job with another company, and that company contacted Shell for an employment reference. Robinson claimed that Shell gave him a negative reference in retaliation for his having filed the EEOC charge; he then filed a retaliation charge with the EEOC based on this postemployment incident. Both the district court and the *en banc* Fourth Circuit agreed that the term *employees* in Section 704 (a) of Title VII referred only to current employees, and therefore Robinson did not have a claim cognizable under Title VII based on retaliation. A unanimous Supreme Court disagreed with the lower courts, and held that a former employee is included within Section 704 (a)'s coverage. The Court stated that to cut former employees off from Title VII protection would undermine the effectiveness of the law.

Theories of Discrimination

The Supreme Court has created and the Civil Rights Act of 1991 has codified two legal theories under which a plaintiff may prove a case of unlawful employment discrimination: disparate treatment and disparate impact (see Figure 1–2). A *disparate treatment* claim exists where an employer treats some individuals less favorably than others because of their race, color, religion, sex, or national origin. Proof of the employer's discriminatory motive is critical in a disparate treatment case.

A *disparate impact* claim exists where an employer's facially neutral employment practices, such as hiring or promotion examinations, though neutrally applied and making no adverse reference to race, color, religion, sex, or national origin, have a significantly adverse or disparate impact on a protected group, *and* the employment practice in question is not shown to be job related and consistent with business necessity by the employer. Under the disparate impact theory it is not a defense for an employer to demonstrate that the employer did not intend to discriminate. Technical rules exist concerning the burdens of proof and production of these two types of Title VII cases. Treatment of these rules is deferred to the next chapter so that the intervening text and materials may provide a foundation for better understanding the basis and application of these rules.

---

[6] 103 S.Ct. 2393 (1983). See also *Zipes v. TWA*, 455 U.S. 385 (1982), where the Supreme Court held that the filing period is not a jurisdictional prerequisite and is subject to equitable waiver, estoppel, and tolling.
[7] 33 DLR E-1 (Feb. 19, 1997).

FIGURE 1-2   Unlawful Discrimination Under Title VII of the Civil Rights Act of 1964 as Amended by the Civil Rights Act of 1991

Discriminatory treatment in employment decisions on the basis of
Race
Color
Religion
Sex
National Origin

Disparate Treatment Theory	**Disparate Impact Theory**
Nonneutral practice or Nonneutral application	Facially neutral practice and Neutral application
Requires proof of discriminatory intent	Does not require proof of discriminatory intent Requires proof of adverse effect on protected group and Employer is unable to show that the challenged practice is job related for the position in question and is consistent with business necessity
Either party has the right to require a jury trial when seeking compensatory or punitive damages	No right to a jury trial
Remedy:	**Remedy:**

Reinstatement, hiring, or promotion
Back pay less interim earnings
Retroactive seniority
Attorneys' and expert witness fees
 	
plus
 	
Compensatory* and punitive damages. Damages capped for cases of sex and religious discrimination depending on size of employer:
 	
Number of employees   Cap
 	
  100 or fewer $ 50,000
  101 to 200   100,000
  201 to 500   200,000
  Over 500   300,000
No cap on damages for race cases.
	Reinstatement, hiring, or promotion
	Back pay less interim earnings
	Retroactive seniority
	Attorneys' and expert witness fees

*Compensatory damages include future pecuniary losses and nonpecuniary losses such as emotional pain and suffering.	

Damages and Jury Trials

The broad scope of possible court-ordered remedies for violations of Title VII is covered in the next two chapters. Victims of discrimination are entitled to be made whole, including back pay and benefits, less their interim earnings as well as front pay.[8] In addition to these remedies, under the Civil Rights Act of 1991, victims of *intentional* discrimination can now receive compensatory and punitive damages.

In disparate treatment—intentional discrimination—cases, where compensatory or punitive damages are sought, either party may demand a jury trial. Victims are entitled to attorneys' fees and expert witness fees.

Compensatory damages may include future pecuniary losses, emotional pain, suffering, inconvenience, loss of enjoyment of life, and other nonpecuniary losses. Punitive damages may be assessed where there is "malice" or "reckless indifference to federally protected rights." Punitive damages may not be assessed against a governmental agency. The punitive and compensatory damages are capped according to the schedule set forth in Figure 1-2 for intentional discrimination based on sex, religion, and nonracial national origin discrimination. There is no cap on intentional discrimination based on race or color.[9]

Congressional Changes of Supreme Court Decisions

Between 1989 and 1991 the U.S. Supreme Court clearly reoriented Title VII jurisprudence to favor employers. The Civil Rights Act of 1991 modifies or reverses these decisions, augments the types of damages available to plaintiffs, and provides for jury trials in cases of intentional discrimination. The court decisions and the congressional corrections are presented at appropriate points throughout the chapters on fair employment practices.

Extraterritorial Employment

In *EEOC v. Arabian American Oil Co.*,[10] Ali Boureslan, a naturalized United States citizen born in Lebanon and working in Saudi Arabia, was discharged by his employer, Arabian American Oil Company, a Delaware corporation. Boureslan claimed that he

---

[8] An example of front pay is an instance in which a manager testifies on behalf of an employee that the company indeed did discriminate against the employee and, as a result of testifying, that manager is subsequently removed from the position. Retaliation for testifying in a Title VII action is a violation of the law. The manager is entitled to back pay and benefits. The court may deem the manager's relationship with other managerial employees to be so poor that there is no longer a possibility that the manager can effectively function as such. The court would then order that the manager receive front pay—the pay he or she would have earned in the future had he or she been returned to work in a management position.

[9] Section 102(b)(4) of CRA of 1991. Technically, to obtain uncapped damages for discrimination based on race or color, one would file under 42 U.S.C. Section 1981. When the Civil Rights Act of 1866 was passed, which law is the basis for a Section 1981 lawsuit, the definition of *race* was broadly understood to prohibit discrimination based on ancestry or ethnic characteristics, protecting Arabs, Jews, Gypsies, Mexicans, Swedes, Germans, Greeks, Irish, etc. What might be deemed "national origin" discrimination today may be the subject matter of a Section 1981 "racial" lawsuit with uncapped damages.

[10] 111 S.Ct. 1227 (1991).

had been discriminated against because of his race, religion, and national origin. The U.S. Supreme Court held that Title VII does not apply extraterritorially to regulate employment practices of U.S. employers who employ U.S. citizens abroad.

The Civil Rights Act of 1991 contained the congressional response to this decision, amending both Title VII and the Americans with Disabilities Act to cover U.S. citizens employed in foreign countries by American-owned or -controlled companies.[11] The 1991 Act contains an exemption if compliance with Title VII or the ADA would cause the company to violate the law of the foreign country in which it is located.

SECTION 3—RACE AND COLOR

The legislative history of Title VII of the Civil Rights Act demonstrates that a primary purpose of the Act is to provide fair employment opportunities for black Americans. The terms *race* and *color* as used in the Act clearly apply to blacks, and thus the protections of the Act are applied to blacks based on race or color. However, the word *race* as used in the Act applies to all members of the four major racial groupings: white, black, Native American, and Asian-Pacific. Native Americans can file charges and receive the protection of the Act on the basis of national origin, race, or in some instances color. Individuals of Asian-Pacific origin may file discrimination charges based on race, color, or in some instances national origin. Although not a common situation, whites are also protected against discrimination because of race and color. For example, two white professors at a predominately black university were successful in discrimination suits against the university where it was held that the university discriminated against them based on race and color in tenure decisions.[12]

Employment Atmosphere

The EEOC has determined that an employer is responsible for maintaining a working environment free of racial intimidation. Under this determination, for example, the employer must not tolerate racial or ethnic jokes by employees.

Grooming Policy

The courts have upheld evenhanded employer grooming policies, even where it has been argued that the employer's policy infringed on black employees' cultural identification.[13] However, a case may be made for a black male employee who is unable to shave due to a severe dermatitis condition affecting only black males on a disparate

---

[11] Section 109 of the Civil Rights Act of 1991, Pub. L. 102-166, 105 Stat. 1071.

[12] *Turgeon v. Howard University*, 32 FEP 927 (D.C. DC 1983).

[13] In *Brown v. D.C. Transit*, 523 F.2d 725, 10 FEP (D.C. Cir. 1975), the U.S. Court of Appeals for the District of Columbia held that a grooming policy barring muttonchops and long sideburns did not deprive black bus drivers of their racial identity so as to constitute a Title VII violation.

impact theory, where the employer is unable to demonstrate a business necessity for its grooming policy.[14]

Arrest and Conviction Inquiries

In *Gregory v. Litton Systems Inc.*,[15] the Ninth Circuit Court of Appeals upheld a district court's order for damages and attorneys' fees awarded pursuant to Title VII of the Civil Rights Act. It was stipulated that Litton's decision not to hire Gregory as a sheet metal worker was predicated upon Gregory's statement in Litton's employment questionnaire that he had been arrested 14 times and not upon any consideration of convictions. The trial court held, and it was approved on appeal, that Litton's employment questionnaire, which required each applicant to reveal the applicant's arrest record, was discriminatory against black job seekers. It was held that Litton had not demonstrated that it had any reasonable business purpose for asking prospective employees about their arrest records.

The EEOC has taken the position that review of arrest records is irrelevant. The EEOC has also maintained that convictions cannot always be regarded as relevant to the ability of an individual to perform a job. The burden of proof is on the employer to justify inquiries into an applicant's arrest-conviction record. The EEOC has ruled that an employee's false answer to an inquiry regarding an arrest conviction record did not justify discharge. The EEOC relied on statistics showing that in some areas racial minorities are arrested and convicted substantially more frequently than Caucasians and found that "the foreseeable impact of respondent's arrest-conviction inquiry is that a substantially disproportionate percentage of those persons rejected or discharged because of the inquiry either because they answered in the affirmative, not at all, or falsely, will be Negro. In these circumstances the arrest-conviction policy is unlawful, absent a showing of business necessity."

The EEOC in this particular decision found that "business necessity" was not involved since the charging party had performed satisfactorily during an 18-month period of employment prior to the discovery of the false statement in the job application. Business necessity would clearly allow an employer to reject an applicant for a security-sensitive position based on the applicant's criminal record for theft.

Residency Requirements

In the *U.S. v. Villages of Elmwood Park and Melrose Park* case presented in this section, the court struck down the villages' respective three- and five-year residency requirements for consideration for police and firefighting positions. These requirements were found to be artificial, arbitrary, and unnecessary barriers to employment that were unrelated to measuring job capabilities; thus they were prohibited by Title VII.

---

[14] In *Bradley v. Pizzaco of Nebraska, Inc.*, 939 F.2d 610 (8th Cir. 1991) the court held that the EEOC established a *prima facie* case of disparate impact on black males because of a no-beard policy since 25 percent of all black males cannot shave because of pseudofolliculitis barbae (PFB); but the court held that the plaintiff had a mild case of PFB and could shave. The matter was remanded for handling of the business necessity stage of the disparate impact case.
[15] 472 F2d 631 (9th Cir. 1972).

Specific Cases

In the landmark *Griggs v. Duke Power* decision, which is presented in this section, an employer was found to have discriminated against blacks as to transfers and hiring by the use of tests and its educational requirement of a high school diploma, both of which were not job related.

GRIGGS v. DUKE POWER COMPANY

Supreme Court of the United States, 401 U.S. 424 (1971).

BURGER, C. J.

We granted the writ in this case to resolve the question whether an employer is prohibited by the Civil Rights Act of 1964, Title VII, from requiring a high school education or passing of a standardized general intelligence test as a condition of employment in or transfer to jobs when (a) neither standard is shown to be significantly related to successful job performance, (b) both requirements operate to disqualify Negroes at a substantially higher rate than white applicants, and (c) the jobs in question formerly had been filled only by white employees as part of a long-standing practice of giving preference to whites.

Congress provided, in Title VII of the Civil Rights Act of 1964, for class actions for enforcement of provisions of the Act and this proceeding was brought by a group of incumbent Negro employees against Duke Power Company. All the petitioners are employed at the Company's Dan River Steam Station, a power generating facility located at Draper, North Carolina. At the time this action was instituted, the Company had 95 employees at the Dan River Station, 14 of whom were Negroes; 13 of these are petitioners here.

The District Court found that prior to July 2, 1965, the effective date of the Civil Rights Act of 1964, the Company openly discriminated on the basis of race in the hiring and assigning of employees at its Dan River plant. The plant was organized into five operating departments: (1) Labor, (2) Coal Handling, (3) Operations, (4) Maintenance, and (5) Laboratory and Test. Negroes were employed only in the Labor Department where the highest paying jobs paid less than the lowest paying jobs in the other four "operating" departments in which only whites were employed. Promotions were normally made within each department on the basis of job seniority. Transferees into a department usually began in the lowest position.

In 1955 the Company instituted a policy of requiring a high school education for initial assignment to any department except Labor, and for transfer from the Coal Handling to any "inside" department (Operations, Maintenance, or Laboratory). When the Company abandoned its policy of restricting Negroes to the Labor Department in 1965, completion of high school also was made a prerequisite to transfer from Labor to any other department. From the time the high school requirement was instituted to the time of trial, however, white employees hired before the time of the high school requirement continued to perform satisfactorily and achieve promotions in the "operating" departments. Findings on this score are not challenged.

The Company added a further requirement for new employees on July 2, 1965, the date on which Title VII became effective. To qualify for placement in any but the Labor Department it became necessary to register satisfactory scores on two professionally prepared aptitude tests, as well as to have a high school education. Completion of high school alone continued to render employees eligible for transfer to the four desirable departments from which Negroes had been excluded if the incumbent had been employed prior to the time of the new requirement. In September 1965 the Company began to permit incumbent employees who lacked a high school education to qualify for transfer from Labor or Coal Handling to an "inside" job by passing two tests—the Wonderlic Personnel Test, which purports to measure general intelligence, and the Bennett Mechanical Comprehension Test. Neither was directed or intended to measure the ability to learn to perform a particular job or category of jobs. The requisite scores used for both initial hiring and transfer approximated the national median for high school graduates.*

The District Court had found that while the Company previously followed a policy of overt racial discrimination in a period prior to the Act, such conduct had ceased. The District Court also concluded that Title VII was intended to be prospective only and, consequently, the impact of prior inequities was beyond the reach of corrective action authorized by the Act.

The Court of Appeals was confronted with a question of first impression, as are we, concerning the meaning of Title VII. After careful analysis a majority of that court concluded that a subjective test of the employer's intent should govern, particularly in a close case, and that in this case there was no showing of a discriminatory purpose in the adoption of a diploma and test requirements. On this basis, the Court of Appeals concluded there was no violation of the Act.

The Court of Appeals reversed the District Court in part, rejecting the holding that residual discrimination arising from prior employment practices was insulated from remedial action. The Court of Appeals noted, however, that the District Court was correct in its conclusion that there was no finding of a racial purpose or in-

vidious intent in the adoption of a high school diploma requirement or general intelligence test and that these standards had been applied fairly to whites and Negroes alike. It held that, in the absence of a discriminatory purpose, use of such requirements was permitted by the Act. In doing so, the Court of Appeals rejected the claim that because these two requirements operated to render ineligible a markedly disproportionate number of Negroes, they were unlawful under Title VII unless shown to be job-related. We granted the writ on these claims.

The objective of Congress in the enactment of Title VII is plain from the language of the statute. It was to achieve equality of employment opportunities and remove barriers that have operated in the past to favor an identifiable group of white employees over other employees. Under the Act, practices, procedures, or tests neutral on their face, and even neutral in terms of intent, cannot be maintained if they operate to "freeze" the status quo of prior discriminatory employment practices.

The Court of Appeals' opinion, and the partial dissent, agreed that, on the record in the present case, "whites register far better on the Company's alternative requirements" than Negroes.** This consequence would appear to be directly traceable to race. Basic intelligence must have the means of articulation to manifest itself fairly in a testing process. Because they are Negroes, petitioners have long received inferior education in segregated schools and this Court expressly recognizes the differences in *Gaston County v. United States*, 395 U.S. 285 (1969). There, because of the inferior education re-

---

* The test standards are thus more stringent than the high school requirement, since they would screen out approximately half of all high school graduates.

** In North Carolina, 1960 census statistics show that, while 34% of white males had completed high school, only 12% of Negro males had done so. U.S. Bureau of the Census of Population: 1960, Vol. 1, Characteristics of the Population, Part 35, Table 47.

Similarly, with respect to standardized tests, the EEOC in one case found that use of a battery of tests, including the Wonderlic and Bennett tests used by the Company in the instant case, resulted in 58% of whites passing the tests, as compared with only 6% of the blacks.

ceived by Negroes in North Carolina, this Court barred the institution of a literacy test for voter registration on the ground that the test would abridge the right to vote indirectly on account of race. Congress did not intend by Title VII, however, to guarantee a job to every person regardless of qualifications. In short, the Act does not command that any person be hired simply because he was formerly the subject of discrimination, or because he is a member of a minority group. Discriminatory preference for any group, minority or majority, is precisely and only what Congress has proscribed. What is required by Congress is the removal of artificial, arbitrary, and unnecessary barriers to employment when the barriers operate invidiously to discriminate on the basis of racial or other impermissible classification.

Congress has now provided that tests or criteria for employment or promotion may not provide equality of opportunity merely in the sense of the fabled offer of milk to the stork and the fox. On the contrary, Congress has now required that the posture and condition of the jobseeker be taken into account. It has—to resort again to the fable—provided that the vessel in which the milk is proffered be one all seekers can use. The Act proscribes not only overt discrimination but also practices that are fair in form, but discriminatory in operation. The touch-stone is business necessity. If an employment practice which operates to exclude Negroes cannot be shown to be related to job performance, the practice is prohibited.

On the record before us, neither the high school completion requirement nor the general intelligence test is shown to bear a demonstrable relationship to successful performance of the jobs for which it was used. Both were adopted, as the Court of Appeals noted, without meaningful study of their relationship to job-performance ability. Rather, a vice president of the Company testified, the requirements were instituted on the Company's judgment that they generally would improve the overall quality of the work force.

The evidence, however, shows that employees who have not completed high school or taken the tests have continued to perform satisfactorily and make progress in departments for which the high school and test criteria are now used. The promotion record of present employees who would not be able to meet the new criteria thus suggests the possibility that the requirements may not be needed even for the limited purpose of preserving the avowed policy of advancement within the Company. In the context of this case, it is unnecessary to reach the question whether testing requirements that take into account capability for the next succeeding position or related future promotion might be utilized upon a showing that such long-range requirements fulfill a genuine business need. In the present case the Company has made no such showing.

The Court of Appeals held that the Company had adopted the diploma and test requirements without any "intention to discriminate against Negro employees." We do not suggest that either the District Court or the Court of Appeals erred in examining the employer's intent; but good intent or absence of discriminatory intent does not redeem employment procedures or testing mechanisms that operate as "built-in headwinds" for minority groups and are unrelated to measuring job capability.

The Company's lack of discriminatory intent is suggested by special efforts to help the undereducated employees through Company financing of two-thirds the cost of tuition for high school training. But Congress directed the thrust of the Act to the *consequences* of employment practices, not simply the motivation. More than that, Congress has placed on the employer the burden of showing that any given requirement must have a manifest relationship to the employment in question.

The facts of this case demonstrate the inadequacy of broad and general testing devices as well as the infirmity of using diplomas or degrees as fixed measures of capability. History is filled with examples of men and women who rendered highly effective performance without the conventional badges of accomplishment in terms of certificates, diplomas, or degrees. Diplomas and tests are useful servants, but Congress has mandated the commonsense proposition that they are not to become masters of reality.

The Company contends that its general intelligence tests are specifically permitted by Section 703(h) of the Act. That section authorizes the use of "any professionally developed ability test" that is not "designed, intended *or used* to discriminate because of race. . . ." (Emphasis added.)

The Equal Employment Opportunity Commission, having enforcement responsibility, has issued guidelines interpreting Section 703(h) to permit only the use of job-related tests. The administrative interpretation of the Act by the enforcing agency is entitled to great deference. See *e.g., United States v. City of Chicago*, 400 U.S. 8 (1970). . . . Since the Act and its legislative history support the Commission's construction, this affords good reason to treat the guidelines as expressing the will of Congress. . . .

Nothing in the Act precludes the use of testing or measuring procedures, obviously they are useful. What Congress has forbidden is giving these devices and mechanisms controlling force unless they are demonstrably a reasonable measure of job performance. Congress has not commanded that the less qualified be preferred over the better qualified simply because of minority origins. Far from disparaging job qualifications as such, Congress has made such qualifications the controlling factor, so that race, religion, nationality, and sex become irrelevant. What Congress has commanded is that any tests used must measure the person for the job and not the person in the abstract.

The judgment of the Court of Appeals is, as to that portion of the judgment appealed from, reversed.

CASE QUESTIONS

1. What is the question before the Supreme Court?
2. What was the objective of Congress in the enactment of Title VII?
3. Would the Court order the case against the employer to be dismissed if it found that the employer had adopted the diploma and test requirements without any intention to discriminate against minority employees?
4. As a result of the *Griggs* decision, may employers insist that both minority and white job applicants meet the applicable job qualifications by the use of testing or measuring procedures?

U.S. v. VILLAGES OF ELMWOOD PARK AND MELROSE PARK

United States District Court, Illinois, 43 FEP 995 (1987).

[These actions were filed by the United States in December 1985 alleging a pattern or practice of unlawful discrimination in employment against black persons by the villages of Elmwood Park and Melrose Park in violation of Title VII of the Civil Rights Act of 1964. The United States moved for summary judgment on the issues of liability and prospective relief. The villages of Elmwood Park and Melrose Park are near the western boundary of the city of Chicago and are located within Cook County. According to the 1980 census, the labor force for Cook County is 20.7 percent black and for the Chicago standard metropolitan statistical area it is 16.2 percent black. No blacks live in Elmwood Park and 24 blacks live in Melrose Park. Both villages have a residency requirement of at least three years for police and firefighter applicants. The purposes of the requirement were said to be to "help its own" in granting employment opportunities and to maintain pride in the community through hiring individuals who live there. Most recruiting is done on a word-of-mouth basis.]

MARSHALL, D. J.

. . . In *Griggs v. Duke Power Co.*, 401 U.S. 424, 431 (1971) the Supreme Court ruled that Title VII of the Civil Rights Act of 1964, as amended, "proscribes not only overt discrimination, but also practices that are fair in form, but discriminatory in operation." Thus, employment practices that are shown to have a discriminatory impact on a group protected under Title VII, notwithstanding an absence of discriminatory intent, are prohibited unless shown to have a "manifest relationship to the employment in question." *Id.* at 432.

As the Court went on to say in *Griggs*, "Good intent or absence of discriminatory intent does not redeem employment practices . . . which operate as 'built-in headwinds' for minority groups and are unrelated to measuring job capability." . . .

In this case, the undisputed facts show that the practices of Elmwood Park and Melrose Park have had an overwhelmingly discriminatory impact. Elmwood Park has no black persons in its resident civilian labor force. Melrose Park has 24 out of 11,000 persons. Their durational residence requirements for police officer and firefighter applicants exclude all black persons residing in Cook County and the metropolitan statistical area from employment in those categories in Elmwood Park and Melrose Park. The "philosophy" of the defendants to favor resident applicants over non-resident applicants for all other positions similarly disfavors all black persons in [the] labor market from employment. These practices are precisely the kind of "artificial, arbitrary and unnecessary barriers" which are "unrelated to measuring job capability" that Congress prohibited in enacting Title VII. *Griggs v. Duke Power Co.*, supra, at 431, 432. The effect of these durational residency requirements and the "philosophy" of favoring resident applicants over non-resident applicants reduces the proportion of blacks in the relevant labor force from approximately 13% and 18% (the percentages of black persons employed privately in the communities) to zero. Thus, all black persons are effectively barred from consideration for employment by the defendants. Unless these practices are necessary to the efficient operation of the defendants, they are unlawful. None of the reasons advanced by the defendants validate the requirements. Both defendants seek to help "our own." But helping "our own" only exacerbates the situation when all of "our own" are white. *Local 53 Asbestos Workers v. Vogler*, 407 F.2d 1047 (5th Cir. 1969).

"Pride in the community" is advanced as a reason. Perhaps there is a modicum of justification which requires residency for incumbent employees, i.e., after employment is effected, but we are at a loss to comprehend community pride as a valid condition precedent to employment. We note that there is no claim that a resident could perform the job more efficiently.

In addition to their use of durational residence requirements for police and firefighter applicants and their preferences for residence for all other village jobs, the defendants use "word-of-mouth" as the sole method of recruiting applicants for municipal vacancies. This is an additional barrier to black employment. It appears that there are no blacks living in Elmwood Park and only a handful in Melrose Park. In these circumstances, local networking will not convey information of job opportunities to non-whites. A word-of-mouth recruitment system limits information about job openings to the friends and relatives of incumbent employees and given the all-white nature of the defendants' work forces, disproportionately deprives qualified black applicants of the information they need to apply for village jobs.

In short, the employment requirements and techniques used by the defendant Villages have had the effect of excluding all blacks from consideration for employment and actual employment in the two communities. The justifications advanced by defendants for these patently discriminatory employment practices are no justification at all. Indeed, if anything, they call into question the good faith of the defendants. The United States of America is entitled to summary judgment under the disparate impact analysis on the issues of liability and prospective relief. . . .

It is so ordered.

CASE QUESTIONS

1. Because of the residency requirements, what percentage of blacks were effectively barred from consideration for employment by the villages?

2. Assess the fairness of the villages' recruiting procedures.

3. Did the court agree that the villages had presented valid justification for their residency requirements?

SECTION 4—RELIGION

Under Section 701(j) employers have a duty to accommodate their employees' or prospective employees' religious practices. Under Section 702 religious organizations are exempt from Title VII prohibitions against discrimination on the basis of religion.

Employer's Duty to Accommodate

The 1972 amendments added to Title VII a definition of *religion* in Section 701(j), which provides:

> The term 'religion' includes all aspects of religious observance and practice, as well as belief, unless an employer demonstrates that he is unable to reasonably accommodate to an employee's or prospective employee's religious observance or practice without undue hardship on the conduct of the employer's business.

Most cases involving allegations of religious discrimination revolve around the determination of whether an employer has made reasonable efforts to accommodate its employees' religious beliefs. The 1972 definition includes all aspects of religious observance, practice, and belief, so as to require employers to make reasonable accommodations for employees whose religion may include observances, practices, and beliefs, such as Friday evening and Saturday religious observances, that differ from the employer's requirements regarding schedules or other business-related employment conditions. Failure to make accommodations is unlawful unless an employer can demonstrate that it cannot reasonably accommodate such beliefs, practices, or observances without undue hardship in the conduct of its business. The Supreme Court considered such an issue in *Trans World Airlines, Inc. v. Hardison.*[16] The Court of Appeals for the Eighth Circuit had ruled that TWA had not satisfied its duty to accommodate Hardison's religious views, which kept him from working Saturdays. Specifically, the court of appeals found that TWA could have permitted Hardison to work a four-day week despite the fact that this would have caused shop functions to suffer unless TWA had breached its seniority system or incurred overtime expense by keeping someone on the job. The Supreme Court reversed, holding that TWA made reasonable efforts to accommodate Hardison, and to force it to comply with the court of appeals ruling would

---

[16] 432 U.S. 63 (1977).

have created an undue hardship on TWA. Under *Hardison* the employer and union need not violate a seniority provision of a valid collective bargaining agreement, the employer has no obligation to impose undesirable shifts on nonreligious employees, and the employer has no obligation to call in substitute workers if such accommodation would require more than *de minimis* cost.

Where an employer is called upon to make reasonable accommodations for the religious practice of an employee, both the employer and the employee may make proposals to achieve this accommodation. In *Ansonia Board of Education v. Philbrick*,[17] Ronald Philbrick, a teacher, sued his school board because the school board's accommodation to his need to take six days off each school year for the holy days of his religion was to allow him to take three paid religious observance days granted him under the teachers' collective bargaining contract and three unpaid leaves. He had proposed as the appropriate accommodation that he take the three paid religious leave days plus three paid personal business leave days or that he pay the cost of a substitute teacher for the three days at $30 per day thus enabling him to receive his regular pay of $130 for each of these days. The Second Circuit agreed with Philbrick, holding that Title VII requires the employer to accept the employee's proposal unless it causes undue hardship to the employer's business. The Supreme Court held that the Second Circuit was in error and that the employer meets its obligation under Section 701(j) when it demonstrates that it has offered a reasonable accommodation to the employee which removes the conflict between the employment requirement and the religious practices of the individual. The extent of the undue hardship to the employer's business is only an issue when the employer claims it is unable to offer a reasonable accommodation without hardship.

The *Trans World Airlines, Inc. v. Hardison* and the *Philbrick* cases dealt with employees' refusal to work on certain days due to religious observance. In *Brown v. Polk County*, presented in this section, the U.S. Court of Appeals for the Eighth Circuit, sitting *en banc*, dealt with an employee's religious behavior at work. In a 6–5 decision, the court held that an employer must accommodate employees' religious activities on the job to the extent the activities do not create undue hardship to the public employer by disrupting the work environment and forcing the employer to sustain real, nonhypothetical costs.[18] The court concluded that the county defendant did not meet its burden under a mixed-motive test to demonstrate that Mr. Brown would have been fired anyway absent his religious activities.

Religious Organization Exemption

Section 702 of Title VII permits religious societies to grant hiring preferences in favor of members of their religion. The *Feldstein v. The Christian Science Monitor* decision, presented in this section, is an example of the application of Section 702. Section 702 provides in pertinent part that:

---

[17] 42 FEP 359 (1986).

[18] On August 14, 1997, President Clinton issued guidelines for federal workers and managers on the right of religious exercise and expression in the federal workplace. These guidelines may help employers and employees outside the federal workplace in how to treat religion at work. The guidelines are set forth in Appendix H.

This title shall not apply . . . to a religious corporation, association, educational institution, or society with respect to the employment of individuals of a particular religion to perform work connected with the carrying on by such corporation, association, educational institution, or society of its activities.

In *Mormon Church v. Amos,* presented in this section, the Supreme Court upheld the constitutionality of the Section 702 exemption, holding that Section 702 was not in violation of the Establishment Clause of the First Amendment. Thus the Mormon Church was allowed to terminate a building engineer, who had worked at its nonprofit gymnasium for 16 years, because he failed to maintain his qualifications for church membership. The decision to terminate was made on the basis of religion by the religious organization and was thus exempted from the Title VII prohibition against religious discrimination.

Section 703(e)(2) provides an exemption for educational institutions to hire employees of a particular religion if the institution is owned, controlled, or managed by a particular religious society. The exemption is a broad one and is not restricted to the religious activities of the institution.

FELDSTEIN v. THE CHRISTIAN SCIENCE MONITOR

United States District Court, 30 FEP 1842 (E.D. Mass, 1983).

[In January 1979 Mark Feldstein inquired at the *Christian Science Monitor* whether there would be job openings on its news reporting staff upon his graduation from college in June. At that time, Feldstein was a college student interested in pursuing a career in journalism. Upon making his inquiry, Feldstein was instructed to contact the personnel department of the church, where he was asked if he was a member of the Christian Science church. He indicated that he was not and was informed that he would stand little, if any, chance of becoming employed by the *Monitor* as a reporter, as only Christian Scientists were hired except in the rare circumstance that no qualified member of the church was available. Feldstein nevertheless requested and obtained an employment application for a reporter's position. The employment application, used for positions throughout the church, contained several questions relating to religious practice, including "Are you . . . a member of the Mother Church? A branch Church member? Class taught?"; "Are

you free from the use of liquor, tobacco, drugs, medicine?"; "Do you subscribe to the Christian Science periodicals?"; and "Are you a daily student of the lesson-sermon?" Inquiries were also directed to the applicant's present and past religious affiliation. References were sought from "two Christian Scientists who can comment on your character and your practice of Christian Science." The application closed with the following statement:

The First Church of Christ, Scientist, may by law apply the test of religious qualifications to its employment policies. Those who meet this requirement and are otherwise qualified will be hired, promoted, and transferred without regard to their race, national origin, sex, color, or age.

Feldstein filed his application with the church in March 1979, together with a copy of his curriculum vitae, letters of recommendation, and a portfolio of newspaper articles that he had written. In April he was notified by a church personnel representative that his application for employment as a reporter had been rejected.

Feldstein alleged that his application for employment was not given a full consideration because he was not a Christian Scientist.]

MAZZONE, D. J.

Title VII of the Civil Rights Act of 1964 was originally passed as an expression of Congress' laudable intention to eliminate all forms of unjustified discrimination in employment, whether such discrimination be based on race, color, religion, sex, or national origin. This posed a sharp question under the Establishment Clause of the First Amendment to the United States Constitution as to whether Congress could properly regulate the employment practices, and specifically the preference of co-religionists, of religious organizations in matters related to their religious activities. As a result, the original Title VII contained an exemption from the operation of Title VII's proscriptions with respect to the employment of co-religionists to perform work related to the employer's religious activity. Church-affiliated educational institutions were also permitted to hire on the basis of religion.

In 1972, a number of amendments to Title VII were proposed in an effort to alter and expand the existing exemption for religious organizations. . . .

. . . Title VII was amended to eliminate the qualification that only religious activities of religious organizations would be exempt from suit based on religious discrimination. Section 702 provides, as a result of the 1972 amendment:

This subchapter shall not apply . . . to a religious corporation, association, educational institution, or society with respect to the employment of individuals of a particular religion to perform work connected with the carrying on by such corporation, association, educational institution or society of its activities.

It is clear that the disposition of this matter turns on two key issues: first, whether the Monitor is a religious activity of a religious organization and therefore within the limited ex-

emption provided by Congress in the Civil Rights Act of 1964; and second, if it is not a religious activity of a religious organization, whether the 1972 amendment to Title VII excluding from the scope of Title VII *all* activities of whatever nature of a religious organization is constitutional in light of the requirements of the Free Exercise and Establishment Clauses of the First Amendment.

It is self-evident, as well as uncontested, that the First Church of Christ, Scientist is a religious organization. The status of the Christian Science Publishing Society and of the Monitor is less clear. The plaintiff has argued that the Monitor is a highly regarded and impartial newspaper carrying news stories, articles, features, columns, and editorials that are secular in nature and content. The defendants take exception to this characterization of the Monitor and make reference to a number of facts in support of their position that the newspaper is a religious activity of a religious organization and therefore exempt from regulation under Title VII. . . .

The deed of trust of the Publishing Society declares as its purpose "more effectually promoting and extending the religion of Christian Science." . . .

The plaintiff does not contest that the Christian Science Church is intimately involved with the management, the day-to-day operations, and the financial affairs of the Monitor. Paragraph 5 of his complaint states in part:

Defendant First Church of Christ, Scientist is a non-incorporated religious association. . . . Control of the Church is vested in a Board of Directors who serve in accordance with terms set out in the Church Manual. *Pursuant to the* Church Manual, *the Board has ultimate authority for and responsibility over the policy and operations of the Monitor. . . .*

. . . A religious activity of a religious organization does not lose that special status merely because it holds some interest for persons not members of the faith, or occupies a position of respect in the secular world at large. Though the "wall between church and state" is not absolute, I am nevertheless unwilling to involve the federal court in what is ultimately an internal administrative matter of a religious activity.

While fully crediting the plaintiff's statements that the Monitor holds itself out as an objective and unbiased reporter of world news and events, I cannot ignore the close and significant relationship existing between the Christian Science Church, the Publishing Society and the Monitor; or the declared purpose, both at the time of its founding and until the present, of the Monitor to promulgate and advance the tenets of Christian Science. I find the conclusion inescapable that the Monitor is itself a religious activity of a religious organization, albeit one with a recognized position and an established reputation in the secular community.

Having concluded that the Monitor is a religious activity of a religious organization, I find that the constitutionality of that part of Section 702 of Title VII, 42 U.S.C. § 2000e-1, that ex-

tends the exemption provided for religious organizations, to *all* their activities, secular and religious, is simply not here implicated.

Because I find that the Monitor is a religious activity of a religious organization, I find that it is permissible for the Monitor to apply a test of religious affiliation to candidates for employment. Therefore, I find as a matter of law that the defendants have not committed an unlawful employment practice under the Civil Rights Act of 1964. The defendants' motion for summary judgment is granted and the complaint is dismissed.

So ordered.

CASE QUESTIONS

1. Does the *Christian Science Monitor* violate Title VII by giving preference to Christian Scientists when hiring reporters for the newspaper?
2. Does Section 702 of Title VII allow religious societies to hire co-religionists for secular activities as opposed to religious activities?

BROWN v. POLK COUNTY, IOWA

United States Court of Appeals, 61 F.3d 650 (8th Cir. 1995).

[Isaiah Brown sued the county board of supervisors alleging discrimination based on race and religion in violation of Title VII, and in violation of his First Amendment right of freedom of association. From a judgment for the defendant county, Brown appealed. The Court of Appeals affirmed; and thereafter the appeal was heard *en banc*.]

ARNOLD, C. J. . . .
In mid-1986, Isaiah Brown, a black man who identifies himself as a born-again Christian, became the director of the information services (data processing) department for Polk County, Iowa. He reported directly to the county administrator and supervised approximately 50 employees.

In mid-1990, an internal investigation into religious activities conducted on government time by employees in Mr. Brown's department revealed that Mr. Brown had directed a secretary to type Bible study notes for him, that several employees had said prayers in Mr. Brown's office before the beginning of some workdays, that several employees had said prayers in Mr. Brown's office in department meetings held during the day, and that in addressing one meeting of employees, Mr. Brown had affirmed his Christianity and had referred to Bible passages related to slothfulness and "work ethics." Subsequently, the county administrator reprimanded Mr. Brown in writing for a "lack of judgment pertaining to his personal participation in and/or his knowledge of employees participating in activities that could be construed as the direct support of or the promotion of a religious organization or religious activities utilizing the resources of Polk County Government." The reprimand directed Mr. Brown "immediately [to] cease any activities that could be considered to be religious proselytizing, witnessing, or counseling and . . . further [to] cease to utilize County resources that in any way could be perceived as to be supporting a religious activity or religious organization." The reprimand also directed Mr. Brown to "insure a work environment that is free of the types of activities . . . described." Subsequently, on a separate occasion, the county administrator directed Mr. Brown to remove from his office all items with a religious connotation, including a Bible in his desk.

In late 1990, the county administrator again reprimanded Mr. Brown in writing, on that occasion for "lack of judgment" related to financial constraints in the county's budget. Two weeks later, after an internal investigation into personal use of county computers by employees in Mr. Brown's department, the county administrator asked Mr. Brown to resign; when he refused, the county administrator fired him. . . .

Federal and state laws forbid an employer to fire an employee because of that employee's race. The district court made the factual finding that racial animus played no part in the decision to fire Mr. Brown. . . .

. . . The district court's conclusion that Mr. Brown's race played no part in his discharge is not clearly erroneous. . . . We therefore affirm the district court judgment with respect to the statutory race discrimination claims and turn to the statutory religious discrimination claims.

Federal and state laws also forbid an employer to fire an employee because of that employee's religion . . . "Religion" includes "all aspects of religious observance and practice, as well as belief, unless an employer demonstrates that [it] is unable to reasonably accommodate to

an employee's . . . religious observance or practice without undue hardship on the conduct of the employer's business." . . .

The district court made the factual finding that religious animus played no part in the decision to fire Mr. Brown. . . . The district court found, instead, that the reason for Mr. Brown's discharge was inadequate performance, . . . specifically, the inability to supervise and administer his department. . . . Because we find that religious activities played a part in the decision to fire Mr. Brown, and that the proof was inadequate to show that Mr. Brown would have been fired if those activities had not been considered, we reverse the district court judgment with respect to the statutory religious discrimination claims.

In most of the cases alleging religious discrimination under Title VII, the employer is a private entity rather than a government, and the first amendment to the Constitution is therefore not applicable to the employment relationship. . . . In cases such as this one, however, where a government is the employer, we must consider both the first amendment and Title VII in determining the legitimacy of the county administrator's action. The first amendment is, of course, applicable to state-created government units by virtue of the fourteenth amendment. . . .

With specific reference to the free exercise clause, we hold that in the governmental employment context, the first amendment protects at least as much religious activity as Title VII does. . . .

The county administrator testified that he fired Mr. Brown "because of [a] culmination of incidents" that led him to conclude that Mr. Brown "had lost control of his department and was no longer in a position to manage effectively." The county administrator also testified, moreover, that the reprimand for "religious activities" was "a factor" in the decision to fire Mr. Brown. The labor relations manager for the county testified as well that, in asking for Mr. Brown's resignation and then firing him, the county administrator told Mr. Brown that the first reprimand was among the "concerns" prompting his discharge. Finally, Mr. Brown himself testified that the reasons given for his discharge by the county administrator were "the problems that [had] centered around [Mr. Brown's] department for [the] last two years, primarily religion." Unfortunately, none of the witnesses specified with any more particularity the exact actions to which the county administrator was alluding. We must, therefore, consider what activities were covered by the first reprimand and which, if any, of those activities were protected by Title VII. . . .

It is undisputed that the defendants made no attempt to accommodate any of Mr. Brown's religious activities. In those circumstances, the defendants may prevail only if they can show that allowing those activities "could not be accomplished without undue hardship." . . . Undue hardship is "not defined within the language of Title VII. Thus, the precise reach of the employer's obligation to its employee is unclear under the statute and must be determined on a case-by-case basis." . . .

"To require [an employer] to bear more than a *de minimis* cost . . . is an undue hardship." *Trans World Airlines, Inc. v. Hardison*, . . . "The cost of hiring an additional worker or the loss of production that results from not replacing a worker who is unavailable due to a religious conflict can amount to undue hardship." . . . *De minimis* cost, moreover, "entails not only monetary concerns, but also the employer's burden in conducting its business." *Beadle v. City of Tampa*, 42 F.3d 633, 636 (11th Cir. 1995). . . .

Any hardship asserted, furthermore, must be "real" rather than "speculative," . . . "merely conceivable," or "hypothetical," . . .

The first reprimand to Mr. Brown was precipitated by the internal investigation into religious activities conducted in mid-1990. The investigation revealed four actions attributed to him—directing a secretary to type his Bible study notes, allowing prayers in his office before the start of the workday, allowing prayers in his office during department meetings, and affirming his Christianity and referring to Bible passages about slothfulness and "work ethics" during one department meeting. We consider each of those activities in light of the commands of Title VII.

The defendants argue that allowing Mr. Brown to direct a county employee to type his Bible study notes would amount to an undue hardship on the conduct of county business, since the work that that employee would otherwise be doing would have to be postponed, done by another employee, or not done at all. We agree that such an activity creates more than a *de minimis* cost to the defendants. . . . We conclude, therefore, that the defendants may not be held liable under Title VII for their actions in relation to that activity.

With respect to Mr. Brown's allowing prayers in his office before the start of the workday, nothing in Title VII requires that an employer open its premises for use before the start of the workday. . . . We conclude, therefore, that Mr. Brown's allowing prayers in his office before the start of the workday was not an activity protected at all under the law in this case and, accordingly, that the defendants may not be held liable for their actions in relation to that activity.

Mr. Brown also allowed prayers in his office during several department meetings and affirmed his Christianity and referred to Bible passages related to slothfulness and "work ethics" during one department meeting. All of the testimony was that the prayers were entirely voluntary and "spontaneous," "did not occur regularly," and dealt with "matters related to Polk County business," and that Mr. Brown's affirmation of Christianity and reference to Bible passages on slothfulness and "work ethics" occurred during only one meeting. Given their context, all of those actions may well have been impolitic on Mr. Brown's part, but we think that they were inconsequential as a legal matter, especially since they were apparently spontaneous and infrequent.

The defendants argue that allowing spontaneous prayers, occasional affirmations of Christianity, and isolated references to Bible passages would amount to an undue hardship on the conduct of county business by virtue of eventual polarization between born-again Christian employees and other employees, and a concomitant perception that Mr. Brown "might favor those with similar beliefs" in making personnel decisions. . . .

No evidence whatsoever was presented from employees in Mr. Brown's department, however, or from anyone else, for that matter, to show that Mr. Brown's personnel decisions actually were affected by his religious beliefs or that employee concerns in that respect were either reasonable or legitimate. The investigation report, furthermore, stated only that Mr. Brown's religious activities had the *"potential effect"* (emphasis supplied) of "generating an impression of preference for those who share similar beliefs" and of "polarizing staff." The county administrator testified, moreover, that he never believed that Mr. Brown showed any "favoritism" or "actually did discriminate against anybody on the basis of their religion"; a former employee from Mr. Brown's department testified to the same effect. Finally, three other employees testified that although there was "a division in the office between Christians and those who were not Christians," "it really had no effect on the work," and that any morale problems in Mr. Brown's department stemmed from "disagreements about how [the work] should be done" and whether the department should be reorganized rather than about "religious issues."

In our view, the defendants' examples of the burden that they would have to bear by tolerating trifling instances such as those complained of are insufficiently "real," *Cook*, 981 F.2d at 339, and too "hypothetical," *Tooley*, 648 F.2d at 1243, to satisfy the standard required to show undue hardship. . . . On this record, we hold that the defendants failed to prove that accommodating such instances as they objected to would lead to undue hardship. . . . The defendants may be held liable, therefore, for firing Mr. Brown on account of those activities unless the defendants can prove that they would have fired

him regardless of those activities. *See, e.g., Price Waterhouse v. Hopkins*, 490 U.S. 228, 242, 244-46, 252-53, 258, . . . (1989) (plurality opinion).

The district court held that Mr. Brown had offered no direct evidence that he was fired on account of his religious activities. . . . We do not understand that conclusion, since, as we have already noted, the county administrator himself testified that the first reprimand, which was based on religious activities, was "a factor" in his decision to fire Mr. Brown. . . . We believe that Mr. Brown presented enough evidence to require the application of a "mixed-motives" analysis instead. *Price Waterhouse*, 490 U.S. at 252, . . . (plurality opinion).

In these circumstances, we could remand to the district court for findings on the question of whether the defendants proved that they would have fired Mr. Brown even if they had not considered his religious activities. . . . In this case, however, we hold that it would be futile to do so, since no reasonable person could conclude from the evidence presented that the defendants proved that they would have fired Mr. Brown anyway. Indeed, when asked specifically at the trial if Mr. Brown would have been fired absent the first reprimand, the county administrator responded, "I wouldn't want to speculate on that. . . . I just don't know." The defendants point to no evidence that would allow us to conclude that they met their burden under a mixed-motives test, and our independent examination of the record has revealed none. . . . We therefore reverse the judgment on the statutory religious discrimination claims and remand the case to the district court for consideration of the appropriate relief on those claims. . . .

We last consider constitutional claims that Mr. Brown did not link to his termination. We reverse the district court with respect to those claims and remand the case for consideration of the appropriate relief. . . .

Mr. Brown first asserts that his first amendment right to the free exercise of his religion was violated when the county administrator ordered him to "cease any activities that could be considered to be religious proselytizing, witnessing, or counseling" while he was on the job. . . .

We may concede for the sake of argument that Polk County has a legal right to ensure that its workplace is free from religious activity that harasses or intimidates. But any interference with religious activity that the exercise of that right entails must be reasonably related to the exercise of that right and must be narrowly tailored to its achievement. *See e.g., Thomas v. Review Board*, 450 U.S. 707, 718, . . . (1981). Here, there was not the least attempt to confine the prohibition to harassing or intimidating speech. Instead, Polk County baldly directed Mr. Brown to "cease any activities that *could be considered* to be religious proselytizing, witnessing, or counseling" (emphasis supplied). That order exhibited a hostility to religion that our Constitution simply prohibits. It would seem to require no argument that to forbid speech "that could be considered" religious is not narrowly tailored to the aim of prohibiting harassment, although it is certainly capable of doing that. If Mr. Brown asked someone to attend his church, for instance, we suppose that that "could be considered" proselytizing, but its prohibition runs afoul of the free exercise clause. Similarly, a statement to the effect that one's religion was important in one's life "could be considered" witnessing, yet for the government to forbid it would be unconstitutional. . . .

Mr. Brown also complains about the directive to remove from his office all items with a religious connotation, including a Bible that was in his desk. It is here, perhaps, that the zealotry of the county administrator is most clearly revealed. Mr. Brown had to remove a plaque containing the serenity prayer ("God, grant me the serenity to accept the things I cannot change, the courage to change the things I can, and the wisdom to know the difference"), another that said, "God be in my life and in my commitment," and a third containing the Lord's Prayer.

Most intrusive of all was the order to take down a poster that proclaimed some nonreligious inspirational commonplaces that were deemed inappropriate because their author, although he occupied no religious office, had "Cardinal" in his name. Mr. Brown testified that he was told that these items had to go because they might be considered "offensive to employees." . . .

. . . A phobia of religion, for instance, no matter how real subjectively, will not do. As Justice Brandeis has said, rather starkly, "Men feared witches and burnt women." *Whitney v. California*, 274 U.S. 357, 376, 47 S.Ct. 641, 648, 71 L.Ed. 1095 (1927) (Brandeis, J., concurring).

For the reasons indicated, we affirm the judgment of the district court in part, we reverse it in part, and we remand for further proceedings consistent with this opinion.

FAGG, Circuit Judge, dissenting, joined by LOKEN, HANSEN, and MURPHY, Circuit Judges.

The Court ignores a major defect in proof on Brown's free exercise claim and takes over the district court's fact-finding function on Brown's statutory claim of religious discrimination. I thus respectfully dissent. . . .

CASE QUESTIONS

1. Was it protected religious activity for Brown to have his secretary type Bible study notes? Was it protected religious activity for Brown to meet with interested employees before work in his office for prayer?
2. Was it an undue hardship on the public employer to tolerate a supervisor's occasional spontaneous prayer and isolated references to Christian belief?
3. Has the public employer demonstrated "undue hardship" which would excuse the employer's failure to accommodate a supervisory employee's religious activities if it can show that other employees were aware that there was a division in the office between Christians and non-Christians?

MORMON CHURCH v. AMOS

Supreme Court of the United States, 107 S.Ct. 2862 (1987).

[Mayson worked for sixteen years as a building engineer at the Mormon church's Deseret Gymnasium in Salt Lake City. He was discharged from this job because he failed to qualify for a "temple recommend," which is only issued to individuals observing the church's standards, such as regular church attendance; tithing; and abstinence from coffee, alcohol, and tobacco. A class action suit was brought on behalf of Mayson, Amos, and others claiming that Section 702 was in violation of the Establishment Clause of the First Amendment when construed to allow religious employers to discriminate on religious grounds in hiring and tenure for nonreligious jobs. The district court held that Section 702 was unconstitutional as applied to secular activities, and it reinstated Mayson with back pay.]

WHITE, J.

This Court has long recognized that the government may (and sometimes must) accommodate religious practices and that it may do so without violating the Establishment Clause. It is well established, too, that "[t]he limits of permissible state accommodation to religion are by no means co-extensive with the noninterference mandated by the Free Exercise Clause." There is ample room under the Establishment Clause for "benevolent neutrality which will permit religious exercise to exist without sponsorship and without interference." At some point, accommodation may devolve into "an unlawful fostering of religion," but this is not such a case, in our view. . . .

After a detailed examination of the legislative history of the 1972 amendment, the District Court concluded that Congress' purpose was to minimize governmental "interfer[ence] with the decision-making process in religions." We agree with the District Court that this purpose does not violate the Establishment Clause. . . .

Appellees argue that § 702 offends equal protection principles by giving less protection to the employees of religious employers than to the employees of secular employers. . . . To dispose of appellees' Equal Protection argument, it suffices to hold—as we now do—that as applied to the nonprofit activities of religious employers, § 702 is rationally related to the legitimate purpose of alleviating significant governmental interference with the ability of religious organizations to define and carry out their religious missions.

It cannot be seriously contended that § 702 impermissibly entangles church and state; the statute effectuates a more complete separation of the two and avoids the kind of intrusive inquiry into religious belief that the District Court engaged in in this case. . . .

The judgment of the District Court is reversed, and the case is remanded for further proceedings consistent with this opinion.

It is so ordered.

CASE QUESTIONS

1. Why was Mayson fired from his job?
2. Does Section 702 allow a religious organization to refuse to hire or to continue in employment individuals that are not members of the religious organization where the positions involved are nonreligious jobs?
3. Why did Congress enact Section 702?

SECTION 5—SEX

The amendment adding the word *sex* to Section 703 of Title VII of the Civil Rights Act was adopted one day before the House passed the Act. It was added without legislative hearings and with little debate.[19] As a result, the courts do not have the benefit of a fully developed legislative history to refer to in interpreting cases relating to sex discrimination. Courts therefore apply the plain and ordinary meaning of the word *sex*, and under such application employers who discriminate against female or male employees because of their sex are held to be in violation of Title VII.

Height, Weight, and Physical Ability Requirements

Under the *Griggs v. Duke Power* decision, an employer must be ready to demonstrate that criteria used to make an employment decision that has a disparate impact on women, such as minimum height and weight requirements, are in fact job related. All candidates for a position requiring physical strength must be given an opportunity to demonstrate their capability to perform the work. Women cannot be precluded from consideration just because they have not traditionally performed such work. In *Boyd v. Ozark Airlines*,[20] a woman contended that the airline's minimum height requirement for pilots discriminated against her on the basis of sex. The evidence established that the airline's 5-foot 7-inch minimum height requirement had a disparate impact on women. While the court agreed that minimum height requirements for the position of pilot are valid, it held that the airline's requirements were excessive and ordered the airline's height requirements lowered to 5 feet 5 inches.

Pregnancy-Related Benefits

Title VII arguments concerning the matters of disability due to pregnancy and loss of competitive seniority due to pregnancy have been considered by the United States Supreme Court. In the landmark case of *General Electric v. Gilbert*,[21] the Supreme Court held that a disability plan which did not cover pregnancy was not violative of Title VII absent any indication that the exclusion of pregnancy benefits was a pretext for discriminating against women. However, in *Nashville Gas v. Satty*[22] the Court held that a company policy which deprived female workers of their competitive seniority upon their return from maternity leave was violative of Title VII. In distinguishing *General Electric v. Gilbert*, the Court stated: "Here, by comparison, the [employer] has not merely refused to extend to women a benefit that men cannot and do not receive, but has imposed on women a substantial burden that men need not suffer."

---

[19] The amendment adding the word *sex* was offered by Congressman Howard Smith of Virginia, then chairman of the Rules Committee, who was an opponent of Title VII. The amendment was adopted by a majority, most of whom later voted against Title VII. Apparently it was thought that the amendment adding the word *sex* might kill the entire legislation.

[20] 419 F. Supp. 1061 (E.D. Mo. 1976).

[21] 423 U.S. 822 (1976).

[22] 434 U.S. 136 (1977).

In 1978 Title VII was amended by the Pregnancy Discrimination Act (PDA), which added to Section 701 a new subsection (k) clarification that the prohibitions against sex discrimination in the Act include discrimination in employment based on pregnancy, childbirth, or related medical conditions. The intent of the amendment was to reverse the *Gilbert* decision which held that disability plans that exclude pregnancy do not discriminate on the basis of sex in violation of the Act. The amendment prevents employers from treating pregnancy, childbirth, and related medical conditions in a manner different from the treatment of other disabilities. Thus women disabled due to pregnancy, childbirth, or other related medical conditions must be provided with the same benefits as other disabled workers. This includes temporary and long-term disability insurance, sick leave, and other forms of employee benefit programs. An employer who does not provide disability benefits or paid sick leave to other employees is not required to provide them for pregnant workers. Under the 1978 law, benefits do not have to be provided for abortion except where it is necessary to preserve the life of the mother or where medical complications have arisen from an abortion.[23]

In *Newport News Shipbuilding and Dry Dock Co. v. EEOC*,[24] the employer amended its health insurance plan after the Pregnancy Discrimination Act of 1978 to provide for benefits for pregnancy-related conditions for its female employees, with the plan providing for less extensive benefits for the wives of male employees. The Supreme Court held that such a plan discriminated against married male employees since their benefits package was less than that provided to married female employees, which was contrary to the Pregnancy Discrimination Act. The dissent argued that the Pregnancy Discrimination Act plainly speaks of female employees affected by pregnancy and says nothing about spouses of male employees.

Pension-Related Benefits

In the case of pension plans, employers have sometimes required their female employees to pay more into pension plan funds because, as a class, women outlive men and therefore receive benefits for a longer period of time. This practice was held to be in violation of Title VII by the Supreme Court in *City of Los Angeles v. Manhart*.[25] The Court reasoned that although the generalization that women live longer than men was true, it was an insufficient reason for burdening those women to whom the generalization did not apply. Since it could not be known to whom the generalization did apply while an employee was alive, it could not be used to justify requiring larger payments from any female employee.

In *Arizona Annuity Plans v. Norris*,[26] the Supreme Court followed its *Manhart* ruling in holding that the pension annuity plans administered for employees of the state of Arizona, which pay a woman lower monthly retirement benefits than a man who has

---

[23] The Pregnancy Discrimination Act of 1978, Pub. L. 95-555 (1978).
[24] 103 S.Ct. 2622 (1983).
[25] 435 U.S. 702 (1978).
[26] 103 S.Ct. 3492 (1983).

made the same contributions, were in violation of Title VII, constituting discrimination on the basis of sex.

Glass Ceiling

Because women and minorities continue to be underrepresented in management and decision-making positions in business, Congress, as part of Title II to the Civil Rights Act of 1991, set up a commission to identify the artificial barriers to the advancement of women and minorities in the workplace and to make recommendations for over-coming such barriers.[27] The Glass Ceiling Commission recommended that business and government take certain actions to break the glass ceiling.[28] It recommended that in business (1) all CEOs demonstrate commitment to workplace diversity; (2) all strate-gic business plans specify efforts to achieve diversity both at the senior management level and throughout the workforce; (3) all qualified individuals have an opportunity to compete based on ability and merit; (4) the organizations expand access to core areas of each business and establish formal mentoring programs to prepare minorities and women for senior positions; (5) the organizations provide formal training on company time; and (6) the organizations adopt policies that accommodate the balance between work and family responsibilities that impact career paths of all employees. The com-mission urged the government to (1) lead by example; (2) make certain that enforce-ment agencies have adequate resources to enforce laws; (3) improve data collection by government agencies; and (4) increase public exposure to diversity data.

Homosexuals and Transsexuals

The EEOC and the courts have uniformly held that Title VII does not prohibit em-ployment discrimination against homosexuals.[29] The EEOC and the courts have de-

---

[27] Section 202 of the Civil Rights Act of 1991. The term *glass ceiling* was initially used to describe the appar-ently invisible barrier that has kept women from obtaining top jobs in management; and relates to the con-tinuing current situation where just 1 percent of our nation's CEOs are women. The Department of Labor has concluded that glass ceiling is best defined today as those artificial barriers based on attitudinal or orga-nizational bias that prevent qualified individuals from advancing upward in their organization into manage-ment-level positions. The glass ceiling provision of the 1991 Act is developed in part from a Department of Labor, Office of Federal Contract Compliance Programs (OFCCP) study released on August 8, 1991, enti-tled "Report on the Glass Ceiling Initiative." Some summary findings on this very limited study (nine com-panies) are:

- If there is not a glass ceiling, there certainly is a point beyond which minorities and women have not advanced in some companies.
- Minorities have plateaued at lower levels of the workforce than women.
- Monitoring for equal access and opportunity, especially as managers move up the corporate ladder to senior management levels where important decisions are made, was almost never considered a corporate responsibility or part of the planning for developmental programs and policies.
- Appraisal and total compensation systems that determine salary, bonuses, incentives, and perquisites for employees were not monitored.
- There was a general lack of adequate records.

[28] The Glass Ceiling Commission Recommendations were released on Nov. 21, 1995; DLR No. 225 (Nov. 22, 1995).

[29] *Blum v. Gulf Oil Corp.*, 597 F.2d 936, 20 FEP 108 (5th Cir. 1979).

termined that the word *sex* as used in Title VII means a person's gender and not the person's sexual orientation.

The courts have also uniformly held that Title VII's ban on sex discrimination in employment practices does not encompass discrimination against transsexuals. This was the holding of the U.S. Court of Appeals for the Eighth Circuit in *Sommers v. Budget Marketing*. The *Sommers* decision, which contains a discussion of the meaning and application of the word *sex* as used in Title VII, is presented in this section.

State and local legislation, however, may provide specific protection against discrimination based on sexual orientation.[30] In *Dillon v. Frank*,[31] the U.S. Court of Appeals for the Sixth Circuit determined that a former postal employee who was taunted, ostracized, and physically beaten by co-workers because they believed he was a homosexual had no remedy under Title VII. The court pointed out that both criminal and tort law may provide individuals such as the former postal worker with protection against such harassment. The court further indicated that Title VII is not all inclusive, stating in part:

> We interpret Title VII to proscribe only specified discriminatory actions. What Title VII proscribes, although vitally important, is easily exceeded by what it does not. Employers or co-workers can still make the workplace unpleasant based on political belief ("damned Republican"), see Reichman v. Bureau of Affirmative Action, 536 F. Supp. 1149, 1176 (M.D. Pa. 1982) ("comments concerning the Arab-Israeli conflict and Menachem Begin were political opinions rather than disparagements of Judaism"); a co-worker's discussing sexual topics at work, see Fair, 742 F. Supp. at 155 ("petty, inappropriate remarks made by someone conducting himself in an improper and unprofessional manner" not sexual harassment); family antagonism ("damned Rockefeller"); college attended ("I'm a Harvardian, you Yalie"); eating practices ("how can you eat something that used to be alive"); or rooting for particular sports teams ("the Dodgers are bums"). . . .

---

[30] Some states and numerous cities have laws and ordinances protecting homosexuals from employment discrimination. For example, see *Borquez v. Ozer*, 923 P.2d 166 (Colo.App. 1995), involving an application of the city of Denver's ordinance protecting homosexuals from employment discrimination.
[31] 952 F.2d 403 (6th Cir. 1992).

AUDRA SOMMERS, a/k/a TIMOTHY K. CORNISH v. BUDGET MARKETING INC.

United States Court of Appeals, Eighth Circuit, 667 F.2d 748 (1982).

PER CURIAM:

Sommers claims to be "female with the anatomical body of a male."* Inasmuch as Sommers

---

* A medical affidavit submitted by Sommers stated that a psychological female with anatomical features of a male is one

type of transsexual but that transsexualism is not voluntarily assumed and is not a matter of sexual preference. A transsexual has been described as an individual who is mentally one sex but physically of the other. Annot., 63 A.L.R.3d 1199, n. 1 (1975), or as one born with the anatomical genitalia of one sex but whose self-identity is of the other sex. Annot., 78 A.L.R.3d 19, 54 (1977).

refers to herself in the feminine gender, this court will likewise do so. As Audra Sommers, appellant was hired by Budget on April 22, 1980, to perform clerical duties. On April 24, 1980, Sommers's employment was terminated. Budget alleged Sommers was dismissed because she misrepresented herself as an anatomical female when she applied for the job. It further alleged that the misrepresentation led to a disruption of the company's work routine in that a number of female employees indicated they would quit if Sommers were permitted to use the restroom facilities assigned to female personnel. After exhausting administrative remedies, Sommers brought action against Budget, alleging that she had been discharged on the basis of sex in violation of Title VII of the Civil Rights Act of 1964. . . .

. . . Sommers's amended complaint claimed she had been discriminated against because of her status as a female, that is, a female with the anatomical body of a male, and further stated that sexual conversion surgery had not been performed. Sommers nonetheless argued that the court should not be bound by the plain meaning of the term "sex" under Title VII as connoting either male or female gender, but should instead expand the coverage of the Act to protect individuals such as herself who are psychologically female, albeit biologically male. In response, Budget argued that Title VII provided no relief for a person like Sommers.

. . . The court entered summary judgment in favor of Budget. Sommers contends on this appeal that the district court erred in concluding that Title VII coverage did not extend to those discriminated against because of their transsexuality and therefore erred in awarding summary judgment to Budget. We disagree.

. . . Although this circuit has not previously considered the issue raised on this appeal, we are in agreement with the district court that for the purposes of Title VII the plain meaning

must be ascribed to the term "sex" in absence of clear congressional intent to do otherwise. Furthermore, the legislative history does not show any intention to include transsexualism in Title VII. The amendment adding the word "sex" to the Civil Rights Act was adopted one day before the House passed the Act without prior legislative hearing and little debate. It is, however, generally recognized that the major thrust of the "sex" amendment was towards providing equal opportunities for women.

Also, proposals to amend the Civil Rights Act to prohibit discrimination on the basis of "sexual preference" have been defeated. Three such bills were presented in the 94th Congress and seven were presented to the 95th Congress. Sommers's claim is not one dealing with discrimination on the basis of sexual preference. Nevertheless, the fact that the proposals were defeated indicates that the word "sex" in Title VII is to be given its traditional definition, rather than an expansive interpretation. Because Congress has not shown an intention to protect transsexuals, we hold that discrimination based on one's transsexualism does not fall within the protective purview of the Act.

We are not unmindful of the problem Sommers faces. On the other hand, Budget faces a problem in protecting the privacy interests of its female employees. According to affidavits submitted to the district court, even medical experts disagree as to whether Sommers is properly classified as male or female. The appropriate remedy is not immediately apparent to this court. Should Budget allow Sommers to use the female restroom, the male restroom, or one for Sommers's own use?

Perhaps some reasonable accommodation could be worked out between the parties. The issue before this court is not whether such an accommodation can be reached. Rather, the issue is whether Congress intended Title VII of the Civil Rights Act to protect transsexuals from discrimination. As explained above, we hold that such discrimination is not within the ambit of the Act.

The decision of the district court granting summary judgment in favor of the employer is affirmed.

CASE QUESTIONS

1. What did Sommers claim?
2. Does the Title VII ban on sex discrimination encompass discrimination based on transsexualism?

SECTION 6—EMPLOYER LIABILITY FOR SEXUAL HARASSMENT

In the mid-1970s the first sexual harassment cases appeared. The early cases generally held that actions taken by an employer against an employee were not based on the employee's sex but rather on whether the employee would acquiesce to sexual demands made by an employer and as such did not fall under the protection of Title VII.[32] Public awareness of the extensive problems relating to sexual harassment in the workplace became a major media issue in the late 1970s. The trend of the early court decisions was quickly reversed, and sexual harassment became generally recognized by the courts as a form of sex discrimination prohibited by Title VII.[33] On November 10, 1980, the EEOC issued *Sex Discrimination Guidelines* specifically dealing with the problem of sexual harassment. The guidelines define sexual harassment as follows:

> Unwelcome sexual advances, requests for sexual favors, and other verbal or physical conduct of a sexual nature constitute sexual harassment when (1) submission to such conduct is made either explicitly or implicitly a term or condition of an individual's employment, (2) submission to or rejection of such conduct by an individual is used as a basis for employment decisions affecting such individual, or (3) such conduct has the purpose or effect of unreasonably interfering with an individual's work performance or creating an intimidating, hostile, or offensive working environment.

The guidelines were immensely helpful in publicizing the problems relating to sexual harassment and in informing employers of their obligations. The guidelines are not administrative "regulations," and courts are not bound by the EEOC guidelines. However, the Supreme Court in *Griggs v. Duke Power Company* declared that EEOC guidelines should be shown "great deference" by the courts.[34] The courts then, and not the EEOC, have the final voice in settling the legal issues involving sexual harassment in the workplace.

Standing to File a Sexual Harassment Claim

Women and men are protected by Title VII from sexual harassment in the workplace and may bring a claim against a member of the opposite sex for sexual harassment.

---

[32] In *Tompkins v. Public Serv. Elec. & Gas Co.*, 422 F. Supp. 553 (D. N.J. 1976), the court held that sexual harassment did not constitute sexual discrimination under Title VII. So also, the same result was reached in *Corne v. Bausch and Lomb, Inc.*, 390 F. Supp. 161 (D. Ariz. 1975), when a male supervisor made sexual advances toward female employees.

[33] See, e.g., *Gerber v. Saxon Bus. Prod., Inc.*, 552 F.2d 1032 (4th Cir. 1977). See also *Barnes v. Costle*, 561 F.2d 983 (D.C. Cir. 1977).

[34] *Griggs v. Duke Power Company*, 401 U.S. 424, 433-434 (1971), and *Bushey v. N.Y. Civ. Serv. Comm'n.*, 733 F.2d 220 at 225 (2d Cir. 1984).

While men may be victims of sexual harassment, in most cases the perpetrators are men and the victims are women.[35] Federal courts across the country are split on the issue of whether Title VII applies to sexual harassment by males on males and females on females—referred to as "same-sex harassment." The dominant trend in the courts is that same-gender harassment is actionable under Title VII.[36]

Quid pro Quo Sexual Harassment by Supervisors

There are two broad classifications of sexual harassment involving supervisors: quid pro quo cases and hostile working environment cases. Quid pro quo harassment is discussed below.

Quid pro quo is a term commonly used in contract negotiations, whereby the parties negotiate "something for something." Quid pro quo cases of sexual harassment are those cases in which sexual favors are either explicitly or implicitly required as a condition of employment in return for tangible job benefits such as obtaining employment, continued employment, promotion, a raise, or a favorable job evaluation.

The leading case of quid pro quo harassment involved Paulette Barnes, who had her job terminated after she refused her supervisor's sexual advances. The Court of Appeals for the District of Columbia Circuit, in *Barnes v. Costle*,[37] heard the argument made by the employer that Barnes was pursuing an improper legal theory. The employer argued that the action based on sex discrimination was improper since Barnes's supervisor terminated her job because she had refused sexual advances, not because she was a woman. The court responded:

> But for her womanhood . . . [Barnes's] participation in sexual activity would never have been solicited. To say, then, that she was victimized in her employment simply because she declined the invitation is to ignore the asserted fact that she was invited only because she was a woman subordinate to the inviter in the hierarchy of agency personnel.[38]

The court concluded that sex discrimination within the meaning of Title VII is not confined to disparate treatment solely limited to gender. Also, the court held that the employer was chargeable with the Title VII violations of its supervisor under the facts before it.

It is now well settled that sexual harassment of an employee by a supervisor that affects tangible job benefits is sex discrimination in violation of Title VII, and such harassment gives rise to employer liability for the acts of the supervisor, regardless of whether the employer knew or should have known of the acts of the supervisor.[39]

---

[35] *David Huebshen v. Department of Health and Social Services*, 716 F.2d 1167 (7th Cir. 1983).

[36] *Sardinia v. Dellwood Foods Inc.*, 69 FEP 705 (S.D.N.Y. 1996); but see *Hopkins v. Baltimore Gas & Electric Co.*, 871 F.Supp. 822 (D.Md. 1994), for an opposing point of view.

[37] 561 F.2d 983 (D.C. Cir. 1977).

[38] *Id.* at 990.

[39] See *Horn v. Duke Homes, Inc., Div. of Windsor Mobile Homes*, 755 F.2d 599, 604-606 (7th Cir. 1985); *Craig v. Y&Y Snacks, Inc.*, 721 F. 2d 77, 80-81 (3d Cir. 1983); and *Katz v. Dole*, 709 F.2d 251, 255, n. 6 (4th Cir. 1983). See also *Karibian v. Columbia University*, 14 F.3d 773 (2d Cir. 1994).

The conduct of the supervisor in *Barnes* was repugnant, and in effect a form of extortion. Critical to proving a quid pro quo claim is establishing that the event occurred and that it was "unwelcome." Indeed, most courts give the benefit of the doubt to the victims on the issue of "unwelcomeness" in regard to supervisors' conduct, absent clear evidence to the contrary. Thus supervisors should be warned that dating employees with less authority than themselves is fraught with problems, where the supervisors must evaluate, assign, promote, transfer, and give raises and other job benefits in the context of personal relationships that are subject to change.

Hostile Working Environment Sexual Harassment

The Court of Appeals for the District of Columbia Circuit extended the scope of its *Barnes* decision, in *Bundy v. Jackson*,[40] holding that a plaintiff may establish a violation of Title VII by proving that discrimination based on sex has created a hostile or abusive work environment. Several leading cases including the *Bundy* decision have provided guidance in the development of this theory.

1. Developing Case Law

Unlike Paulette Barnes, Sandra Bundy was not terminated for refusing her supervisor's advances. Her claim in part stated that "conditions of employment" as set forth in Title VII include the psychological and emotional work environment. The sexually stereotyped insults and demeaning propositions to which she was subjected and which caused her anxiety illegally poisoned the work environment. The court of appeals set forth the following relevant fact pattern in its decision:

> The District Court's decision that sexual intimidation was a "normal condition of employment" in Bundy's agency finds ample support in the District Court's own chronology of Bundy's experiences there. Those experiences began in 1972 when Bundy, still a GS-5, received and rejected sexual propositions from Delbert Jackson, then a fellow employee at the agency but now its Director and the named defendant in this lawsuit in his official capacity. It was two years later, however, that the sexual intimidation Bundy suffered began to intertwine directly with her employment, when she received propositions from two of her supervisors, Arthur Burton and James Gainey.
>
> Burton became Bundy's supervisor when Bundy became an Employment Development Specialist in 1974. Shortly thereafter Gainey became her first-line supervisor and Burton her second-line supervisor, although Burton retained control of Bundy's employment status. Burton began sexually harassing Bundy in June 1974, continually calling her into his office to request that she spend the workday afternoon with him at his apartment and to question her about sexual proclivities. Shortly after becoming her first-line supervisor Gainey also began making sexual advances to Bundy, asking her to join him at a motel and on a trip to the Bahamas. Bundy complained about these advances to Lawrence Swain, who supervised both Burton and Gainey. Swain casually dismissed Bundy's complaints, telling her that "any man in his right mind would want

---

[40] 641 F.2d 934, 24 FEP 1155 (D.C. Cir. 1981).

to rape you," and then proceeding himself to request that she begin a sexual relationship with him in his apartment. Bundy rejected his request.[41]

The court held that Bundy had proved that she was a victim of sexual harassment in the context of a discriminatory work environment permitted by her employer. This sexual harassment, even if it did not result in a loss of tangible benefits, is illegal sex discrimination. The court stated that injunctive relief should be required. The court also ordered the agency's director to establish and publicize procedures whereby harassed employees could complain to the director immediately and confidentially. The director should promptly take all necessary steps to investigate and correct any harassment, including warnings and appropriate discipline directed at the offending party, and should generally develop other means of preventing harassment within the agency.

The court in *Bundy* provided injunctive relief and awarded attorney's fees to Bundy.

Where the complainant demonstrates that a hostile work environment affected a constructive termination of employment, a back pay remedy with compensatory and punitive damages under CRA 1991 may be in order.

In *Meritor Savings Bank v. Vinson*, the Supreme Court recognized that a cause of action can exist against an employer for a hostile environment created by a supervisor's sexual advances, even though there was no link to economic benefits in exchange for sexual favors. In *Harris v. Forklift Systems Inc.*, the Supreme Court dealt with the difficult question of how severe and pervasive the harassment must be to create a hostile working environment. The Court directed that whether or not an environment is hostile or abusive can be determined only by looking at all of the circumstances. In the *Yates v. Avco Corporation* decision, the egregious nature of the misconduct involved and the flaws in the company's sexual harassment procedures were exposed. All three cases are presented in this section.

2. *Prima Facie* Case of Sexual Harassment

To establish an actionable claim for hostile working environment sexual harassment, a plaintiff must demonstrate:

1. that she or he belongs to a protected class;
2. that she or he was subject to unwelcome sexual harassment;
3. that the harassment was based on sex;
4. that the harassment was so pervasive that it affected a "term, condition, or privilege of employment"; and
5. that the employer either knew or should have known of the harassment and failed to take remedial action.

Since both men and women are protected, the first element may be established by a stipulation that the victim is a man or woman. Concerning the second element, some types of conduct are so universally offensive in the workplace as to be clearly "unwelcome," including groping, pinching, or touching private parts of the body. Other less obvious

---

[41] 24 FEP at 1156, 1157.

types of harassment, like sexual jokes, gossip regarding one's sex life, or comments on an individual's body or sexual prowess, would require that the complainant take some steps to let it be known that the sexual advance or conduct was not welcome. The milder the conduct, the more responsibility the complainant has to express objection.

The "based on sex" element requires a showing that the harassment occurred because of the complainant's sex and did not occur to members of the opposite sex. Thus if a supervisor is equally abusive and demeaning to both men and women, there is no violation of Title VII even though a hostile work environment has been created.[42]

The "term, condition, or privilege of employment" (fourth) element requires a showing that the harassment complained of was so pervasive as to alter the conditions of employment and create an abusive working environment. Where to draw the line is a difficult task. In the *Ellison* case, presented in the next section, the court applied a reasonable woman standard in determining that the conduct of a co-employee created a hostile working environment. In the *DeAngelis* case, which is also presented in the following section, the court determined that while comments about a female police sergeant in a police union newsletter did engender offensive feelings in the complainant, they were not so severe or pervasive as to create an objectively hostile work environment.

The final element of a *prima facie* case of sexual harassment requires that the employer either knew or should have known of the action and failed to take prompt remedial action. In a quid pro quo case the employer is strictly liable for its supervisors' actions. However, if the employer takes preventive steps and prompt remedial action, it can avoid liability for hostile working environment cases.

3. Employer Preventive Steps

Based on EEOC *Sex Discrimination Guidelines* Section 1604.11(f) and the Supreme Court's analysis of Meritor Savings Bank's grievance procedure, as discussed in that case, an employer may avoid liability for hostile working environment sexual harassment by its supervisors where the employer affirmatively raises the subject, expresses strong disapproval, advises employees how to raise the issue according to the following outline, and takes prompt remedial action:

A. Develop and implement sexual harassment policy and communicate it to all employees. Set forth specific examples of conduct that will not be tolerated, such as:
- Unwelcome sexual advances whether they involve physical touching or not;
- Sexual epithets, jokes, written or oral references to sexual conduct, gossip regarding one's sex life; comments on an individual's body; comments about an individual's sexual activity, deficiencies, or prowess;
- Displaying of sexually suggestive objects, pictures, cartoons;
- Unwelcome leering, whistling, brushing against the body, sexual gestures, suggestive or insulting comments;
- Inquiries into one's sexual experiences; and
- Discussion of one's sexual activities.

---

[42] But see *Steiner v. Showboat Operating Co.*, 25 F.3d 1459 (9th Cir. 1994).

B. Establish ongoing educational programs, including role playing and films to demonstrate unacceptable behavior.

C. Designate a responsible senior official to whom complaints of sexual harassment can be made. Avoid any procedure that requires an employee to first complain to the employee's supervisor, since that individual may be the offending person. Make certain complainants know that there will be no retaliation for filing a complaint.

D. Investigate all complaints promptly and thoroughly.

E. Keep the complaint and investigation as confidential as possible and limit all information to only those that need to know.

F. If a complaint has merit, impose appropriate and consistent discipline.

MERITOR SAVINGS BANK v. VINSON

Supreme Court of the United States, 40 FEP 1822 (1986).

[Mechelle Vinson (respondent) brought this action against Sidney Taylor, a vice-president and branch manager of Meritor Savings Bank, and the bank (petitioners) claiming that during her four years at the bank she had been constantly subjected to sexual harassment by Taylor in violation of Title VII. She testified to over forty instances of sexual favors successfully sought by Taylor from 1974 to 1977 when these activities ceased after she started going with a steady boyfriend. Taylor denied allegations of sexual activity. He contended instead that respondent made her accusations in response to a business-related dispute. The bank also denied respondent's allegations and asserted that any sexual harassment by Taylor was unknown to the bank and engaged in without its consent or approval. The district court denied relief, finding in part that:

If (respondent) and Taylor did engage in an intimate or sexual relationship during the time of (respondent's) employment with [the bank], that relationship was a voluntary one having nothing to do with her continued employment at [the bank] or her advancement or promotions at that institution.

The court of appeals reversed the district court. The Supreme Court granted certiorari.]

REHNQUIST, J.

. . . [I]n 1980 the EEOC issued guidelines specifying that "sexual harassment" as there defined, is a form of sex discrimination prohibited by Title VII. . . .

Since the guidelines were issued, courts have uniformly held, and we agree, that a plaintiff may establish a violation of Title VII by proving that discrimination based on sex has created a hostile or abusive work environment. . . .

. . . [T]he District Court's conclusion that no actionable harassment occurred might have rested on its earlier "finding" that "[i]f [respondent] and Taylor did engage in an intimate or sexual relationship . . . that relationship was a voluntary one." But the fact that sex-related conduct was "voluntary," in the sense that the complainant was not forced to participate against her will, is not a defense to a sexual harassment suit brought under Title VII. The gravamen of any sexual harassment claim is that the alleged sexual advances were "unwelcome." While the question whether particular conduct was indeed unwelcome presents difficult problems of proof and turns largely on credibility determinations committed to the trier of fact, the District Court in this case erroneously focused on the "voluntariness" of respondent's participation in the claimed sexual episodes. The correct inquiry is whether respondent by her conduct indicated that the alleged sexual advances were unwelcome, not whether her actual participation in sexual intercourse was voluntary.

Petitioner contends that even if this case must be remanded to the District Court, the Court of Appeals erred in one of the terms of its remand. Specifically, the Court of Appeals stated that testimony about respondent's "dress and personal fantasies," which the District Court apparently admitted into evidence, "had no place in this litigation." The apparent ground for this conclusion was that respondent's voluntariness *vel non* in submitting to Taylor's advances was immaterial to her sexual harassment claim. While "voluntariness" in the sense of consent is not a defense to such a claim, it does not follow that a complainant's sexually provocative speech or dress is irrelevant as a matter of law in determining whether he or she found particular sexual advances unwelcome. To the contrary, such evidence is obviously relevant. The EEOC guidelines emphasize that the trier of fact must determine the existence of sexual harassment in light of "the record as a whole" and "the totality of circumstances, such as the nature of the sexual advances and the context in which the alleged incidents occurred." . . .

Although the District Court concluded that respondent had not proved a violation of Title VII, it nevertheless went on to consider the question of the bank's liability. Finding that "the bank was without notice" of Taylor's alleged conduct, and that notice to Taylor was not the equivalent of notice to the bank, the court concluded that the bank therefore could not be held liable for Taylor's alleged actions. The Court of Appeals took the opposite view, holding that an employer is strictly liable for a hostile environment created by a supervisor's sexual advances, even though the employer neither knew nor reasonably could have known of the alleged misconduct. The court held that a supervisor,

whether or not he possesses the authority to hire, fire, or promote, is necessarily an "agent" of his employer for all Title VII purposes, since "even the appearance" of such authority may enable him to impose himself on his subordinates. . . .

The EEOC suggests that when a sexual harassment claim rests exclusively on a "hostile environment" theory, however, the usual basis for a finding of agency will often disappear. In that case, the EEOC believes, agency principles led to

"a rule that asks whether a victim of sexual harassment had reasonably available an avenue of complaint regarding such harassment, and, if available and utilized, whether that procedure was reasonably responsive to the employee's complaint. If the employer has an expressed policy against sexual harassment and has implemented a procedure specifically designed to resolve sexual harassment claims, and if the victim does not take advantage of that procedure, the employer should be shielded from liability absent actual knowledge of the sexually hostile environment (obtained, e.g., by the filing of a charge with the EEOC or a comparable state agency). In all other cases, the employer will be liable if it has actual knowledge of the harassment or if, considering all the facts of the case, the victim in question had no reasonably available avenue for making his or her complaint known to appropriate management officials." Brief for United States and Equal Opportunity Employment Commission as Amici Curiae, 26. . . .

We therefore decline the parties' invitation to issue a definitive rule on employer liability, but we do agree with the EEOC that Congress wanted courts to look to agency principles for guidance in this area. While such common-law principles may not be transferable in all their particulars to Title VII, Congress' decision to define "employer" to include any "agent" of an employer, 42 U.S.C. § 2000e(b), surely evinces an intent to place some limits on the acts of employees for which employers under Title VII are to be held responsible. For this reason, we hold that the Court of Appeals erred in concluding that employers are always automatically liable for sexual harassment by their supervisors. For the same reason, absence of notice to an employer does not necessarily insulate that employer from liability.

Finally, we reject petitioner's view that the mere existence of a grievance procedure and a policy against discrimination, coupled with respondent's failure to invoke that procedure, must insulate petitioner from liability. While those facts are plainly relevant, the situation before us demonstrates why they are not necessarily dispositive. Petitioner's general nondiscrimination policy did not address sexual harassment in particular, and thus did not alert employees to their employer's interest in correcting that form of discrimination. Moreover, the bank's grievance procedure apparently required an employee to complain first to her supervisor, in this case Taylor. Since Taylor was the alleged perpetrator, it is not altogether surprising that respondent failed to invoke the procedure and report her grievance to him.

Petitioner's contention that respondent's failure should insulate it from liability might be substantially stronger if its procedures were better calculated to encourage victims of harassment to come forward. . . .

Accordingly, the judgment of the Court of Appeals reversing the judgment of the District Court is affirmed, and the case is remanded for further proceedings consistent with this opinion.

It is so ordered.

CASE QUESTIONS

1. Is the fact that the sex-related conduct by an employee and her supervisor was "voluntary" a defense to a sexual harassment charge?
2. Was it proper for a trial court to consider evidence of sexually provocative speech or dress on the part of the complainant in a sexual harassment suit?
3. Did Taylor in fact make unwelcome sexual advances to Vinson?
4. What was wrong with the bank's nondiscrimination policy and grievance procedure?

YATES v. AVCO CORPORATION

United States Court of Appeals, Sixth Circuit, 819 F.2d 630 (1987).

[Secretaries Charlotte Yates (Street) and Cheryl Mathis brought suit against their supervisor, Edwin Sanders, and Avco Corporation alleging sexual harassment under Title VII. Avco appealed the district court's finding that it was liable for the supervisor's actions.]

MARTIN, J. . . .

I.

. . . Cheryl Mathis's relationship with Mr. Sanders began on terms she described as good, but it later became clear that Sanders sought some kind of personal relationship with her. Whenever Mathis was in his office he wanted the door to outside offices closed, and he began

discussing very personal matters with her, such as the lack of a sexual relationship with his wife. He then began bombarding her with unwelcome invitations for drinks, lunch, dinner, breakfast, and asking himself to her house. Mathis made it clear that she was not interested in a personal relationship with her married boss. On a couple of occasions Sanders did in fact insist on coming to her apartment during the day and at those times Mathis asked a girlfriend from Avco to come with her.

Sanders also commented on Mathis's appearance, making lewd references to parts of her body. As Mathis rejected Sanders's advances, he would become belligerent. By the spring of 1983 Mathis began to suffer from severe bouts of trembling and crying which became progressively worse and eventually caused her to be hospitalized on two separate occasions, once for a week in June, 1983, and again in July for a few days. During this entire summer Mathis remained out on sick leave, not returning to work until September, 1983. She received her full pay until July 18, when her sick leave benefits expired. She was then compensated at the lesser "disability" rate of pay. When she returned from extended sick leave in September, 1983, Mathis held the same job, title, grade and compensation rate and remained under Sanders's supervision.

As soon as she returned to work, Sanders's harassment resumed. He talked of "putting her on his mistress list" and made lewd jokes and comments. When Mathis resisted his advances Sanders became hostile, giving her more work than she could handle during her part-time hours. Once again she began to experience trembling, crying and emotional distress, and once again she was forced to seek medical help and did not work.

The other employee in this litigation, Charlotte Street, had been transferred to Sanders's supervision in June, 1983 while Cheryl Mathis was on sick leave. Sanders's behavior toward Street was similar to his behavior with Mathis. He incessantly asked her to lunch, dinner and drinks, mentioned sleeping together on more than one occasion, tried to discuss his and her personal relationships and made frequent sexually suggestive comments. He would call Street into his office "because [he] wanted to watch [her] walk out" and then make groaning sounds.

The harassment not only tormented Street and Mathis, it created hostility between them and other members of the department who apparently resented the plaintiffs' familiarity with Sanders. When Street could stand no more of this, she complained to Joe Baron, Manager of Personnel. In October, 1983, while Mathis was out on sick leave, Avco became aware that Mathis's emotional problems were connected to the work situation at Avco and questioned her.

Avco then began an investigation of both complaints. During the initial part of the investigation Sanders continued in his job; however, he was later put on administrative leave pending a decision about his future with Avco. . . .

As a result of the Avco internal investigation Ed Sanders was found to have harassed employees, was drastically demoted, and received a substantial cut in salary. Though this meant Sanders would no longer be a supervisor, the plaintiffs were forced to endure unnecessary personal hardship to get to this state. Both of their personnel files contained references to extended sick leave rather than giving any indication of the true reason for their absences. Even after Sanders was penalized, Avco refused to correct their personnel records. Though the company arranged an administrative leave for Sanders while he was under investigation, this same arrangement was never made for Mathis or Street. These discrepancies help to demonstrate that Avco's sexual harassment policy was not functioning properly nor implemented equitably.

II.

Pursuant to 42 U.S.C. § 2000-e5(f)(5), the claims were referred to a magistrate on August 14, 1984, and a hearing was held in April 1985. The magistrate found that the plaintiffs had established a prima facie case against both defendants in that (1) as women they were members of a protected class; (2) they were subject to unwelcome sexual harassment, as it was not solicited and not desired; (3) the harassment was based on sex because there was no evidence that men were subjected to similar harassment; (4) because the harassment was sufficiently persistent and severe to affect the psychological well-being of the plaintiffs it affected a "term, condition, or privilege of employment;" and (5) a sufficient respondeat superior relationship existed to hold Avco liable for Sanders's actions. The magistrate found not only that Sanders had been given the authority to hire, fire and promote, but Avco had at least constructive knowledge of Sanders's behavior based on earlier allegations against him. Thus, he found both Sanders and Avco liable to Mathis and Street and ordered that they be awarded back pay for the time they were out on sick leave, plus prejudgment interest; . . . that Avco correct the misleading impressions in the personnel files, including placing a copy of his report in the files; and that Mathis and Street be awarded their expenses in bringing the action, including reasonable attorneys' fees. . . .

In this case Avco had a published procedure regarding sexual harassment. That procedure provided that the employee should report any conduct or circumstances which may constitute sexual harassment to the Employee Relations Department and to his immediate supervisor; that the Department would investigate complaints, determine corrective action, and notify the supervisor of steps to be taken; and that the supervisor would promptly implement the corrective action. Though the intent of this policy was commendable, the facts of the case demonstrate that not only was it vague on paper, it was vague and ad hoc in its administration and did not function effectively to eliminate harassment in the Avco Nashville plants.

First, the policy assumes that the supervisor is not the harasser, and gives the supervisor the responsibility for both reporting and correcting the harassment. Such a policy must necessarily discourage reporting and diminish an employee's faith in the system's ability to alleviate the problem when the supervisor is in fact the harasser.

Second, when Mathis and Street finally complained to Joe Baron about the harassment they were experiencing the matter was not dealt with effectively. Upon complaining, both Mathis and Street were told *not* to go to the EEOC, and that their complaints would be handled promptly within the company's harassment investigation framework. Taped testimony was taken and an investigation was begun, yet when Mathis and Street requested copies of their testimony their requests were denied. Street was told

that if she felt uncomfortable continuing to work under Sanders's supervision while he remained under investigation, an administrative leave could be arranged. However, when Street went to Joe Baron seeking such a leave, she was told repeatedly just to call in sick. When she complained to Baron about the practice, he told her to get a note from her doctor to make the sick leave legitimate. When Street attempted to do that, her doctor correctly refused, telling her that her leave should be handled by the company. The "confidential" procedures of the department meant that the plaintiffs' personnel files documented excessive absenteeism, and for all intents and purposes Charlotte Street believed she was endangering her position as an Avco employee. In addition, Street was not free to explain to Sanders why she was absent from work. This resulted in one visit by Sanders to her house during which she was terrified that he might realize she was in fact at home and try to come in. Avco's policy of not placing documentation of sexual harassment in personnel files seems to protect only Avco and the harasser, rather than the affected employee. An effective anti-harassment policy does not operate this way. . . .

Thus, we agree with the district court that the magistrate's finding that Avco at least reasonably should have known of Sanders's action was not clearly erroneous. We believe that because Sanders was both an agent and supervisor of Avco, it is easier to impute his own knowledge to the Avco management. We also find that although Avco took remedial action once the plaintiffs registered complaints, its duty to remedy the problem, or at a minimum, inquire, was created earlier when the initial allegations of harassment were reported. In addition, although its remedial action with regard to the plaintiffs' complaint was prompt, it was not adequate. . . .

IV.

As we noted above, we do not believe that the district court erred in awarding back pay to Mathis for the time she was on sick leave. The award of back pay is not the same as an award of damages for emotional distress which concededly is not recoverable under Title VII.

Because Mathis was forced to take extensive sick leave, she was compensated at a lower level than she would have been had she remained at work. We believe that she provided adequate proof that Sanders's behavior caused her absence from work and that the magistrate and district court properly ordered the company to compensate her.

V.

On the record before us we cannot recompute damages and we therefore remand to the district court for a recalculation of the damage award to both Mathis and Street in accordance with this opinion.

CASE QUESTIONS

1. Identify the harm caused by the supervisor's unlawful actions.
2. Evaluate the company's sexual harassment procedures.
3. Did the court of appeals find that Avco was not liable for the supervisor's misconduct?

HARRIS v. FORKLIFT SYSTEMS INC.

Supreme Court of the United States, 114 S. Ct. 367 (1993).

[Teresa Harris sued her former employer Forklift Systems Inc. under Title VII of the Civil Rights Act of 1964 claiming that the company's president, Charles Hardy, created "an abusive work environment" with a constant stream of sexually offensive jokes and remarks. When Hardy's conduct continued after Harris complained to him, she quit her job. A federal district court denied Harris' case because she had not shown severe psychological injury. The Sixth Circuit affirmed, and the case was appealed to the U.S. Supreme Court.]

O'CONNOR, J. . . .

Title VII of the Civil Rights Act of 1964 makes it "an unlawful employment practice for an employer . . . to discriminate against any individual with respect to his compensation, terms, conditions, or privileges of employment, because of such individual's race, color, religion, sex, or national origin." 42 U.S.C. § 2000e-2(a)(1). As we made clear in *Meritor Savings Bank v. Vinson*, 477 U.S. 57 (1986), this language "is not limited to 'economic' or 'tangible' discrimination." The phrase 'terms, conditions, or privileges of em-

ployment' evinces a congressional intent 'to strike at the entire spectrum of disparate treatment of men and women' in employment," which includes requiring people to work in a discriminatorily hostile or abusive environment. . . . When the workplace is permeated with "discriminatory intimidation, ridicule, and insult," . . . that is "sufficiently severe or pervasive to alter the conditions of the victim's employment and create an abusive working environment," . . . Title VII is violated.

This standard, which we reaffirm today, takes a middle path between making actionable any conduct that is merely offensive and requiring the conduct to cause a tangible psychological injury. As we pointed out in *Meritor*, "mere utterance of an . . . epithet which engenders offensive feelings in a employee," . . . does not sufficiently affect the conditions of employment to [violate] Title VII. Conduct that is not severe or pervasive enough to create an objectively hostile or abusive work environment—an environment that a reasonable person would find hostile or abusive—is beyond Title VII purview.

Likewise, if the victim does not subjectively perceive the environment to be abusive, the conduct has not actually altered the conditions of the victim's employment, and there is no Title VII violation.

But Title VII comes into play before the harassing conduct leads to a nervous breakdown. A discriminatorily abusive work environment, even one that does not seriously affect employees' psychological well-being, can and often will detract from employees' job performance, discourage employees from remaining on the job, or keep them from advancing in their careers. . . .

We . . . believe the District Court erred in relying on whether the conduct "seriously affect[ed] plaintiff's psychological well-being" or led her to "suffe[r] injury." Such an inquiry may needlessly focus the factfinder's attention on concrete psychological harm, an element Title VII does not require. Certainly Title VII bars conduct that would seriously affect a reasonable person's psychological well-being, but the statute is not limited to such control. So long as the environment would reasonably be perceived, and is perceived, as hostile or abusive, . . . there is no need for it also to be psychologically injurious.

This is not, and by its nature cannot be, a mathematically precise test. We need not answer today all the potential questions it raises. . . . But we can say that whether an environment is "hostile" or "abusive" can be determined only by looking at all the circumstances. These may include the frequency of the discriminatory conduct; its severity; whether it is physically threatening or humiliating, or a mere offensive utterance; and whether it unreasonably interferes with an employee's work performance. The effect on the employee's psychological well-being is, of course, relevant to determining whether the plaintiff actually found the environment abusive. But while psychological harm, like any other relevant factor, may be taken into account, no single factor is required.

[Judgment reversed and action remanded]

CASE QUESTIONS

1. Classify the form of sexual harassment claimed in this case.
2. Did the Court indicate that a reasonable woman standard should be applied in determining whether or not conduct was severe enough to create a hostile work environment?
3. List the factors that a fact finder may consider in determining whether or not a hostile work environment existed in a specific case.

SECTION 7—EMPLOYER LIABILITY FOR CO-WORKER AND NONEMPLOYEE SEXUAL HARASSMENT

Sexual harassment of employees by their co-workers is an issue faced by employers in today's workforce, as is the matter of employers' liability for the sexual harassment of their employees by nonemployees.

Employer Liability for Co-Worker Sexual Harassment

Most employers are aware of the problems of sexual harassment and now have procedures through which employees can rectify co-worker sexual harassment. Under the rules of conduct of many employers, the co-worker may be subject to discipline up to and including discharge for the sexual harassment of fellow workers in the form of sexual flirtations, propositions, or other sexually degrading conduct.[43] Employer liability

---

[43] See for example AT&T's affirmative action policy statement, which contains a section prohibiting sexual harassment. Under this section "sexually harassing conduct in the workplace, whether committed by super-

for co-worker sexual harassment is established under the theory of *respondeat superior*, whereby the employer can be held liable for the harassment perpetuated by its employees. However, the employer is liable only if it knew or should have known of the misconduct, and yet failed to take prompt and reasonable corrective action.[44] In *Kyriazi v. Western Electric Co.*,[45] where three male co-workers teased and tormented the complainant, Kyriazi, and made wagers concerning her virginity, the court found that Kyriazi's supervisors were aware of the harassment and made no attempt to discipline the co-workers involved. Not only did the court find the employer liable for violating Title VII for this and other employer-imputed conduct, the court, under state law claims made by Kyriazi, assessed $1,500 in punitive damages against each of the co-workers and explicitly prevented the employer from indemnifying these employees for their punitive damages.

In *Ellison v. Brady*, presented in this section, the court applied the reasonable woman standard in determining that the complainant was the victim of sexual harassment; and it faulted the employer for its ineffective corrective actions, including the fact that the victim ended up being transferred as a result of the harassment.

The EEOC's 1994 guidelines adopted the "reasonable person in the same or similar circumstances as the victim" test.[46] Thus, employers in evaluating a sexual harassment claim may be well advised to view the reported behavior in question from the point of view of a reasonable person of the same gender as the complainant test, until such time as the Supreme Court deals directly with this issue.

The *DeAngelis* case, presented in this section, sets forth and analyzes a fact pattern where the conduct was not sufficiently severe or pervasive to create an "objectively" hostile work environment.

Employer Liability for Sexual Harassment by Nonemployees

An employer may be held to have violated Title VII of the Civil Rights Act of 1964 if it permits its employees to be subjected to sexual harassment by nonemployees. In such a case the burden of proof would be on the complainant to show that the harassment in question created a hostile or abusive work atmosphere and that the employer knew or should have known of the harassment and failed to take reasonable measures to prevent it.

---

visors or non-supervisory personnel, is also prohibited. This includes: repeated, offensive sexual flirtations, advances, propositions, continual or repeated verbal abuse of a sexual nature; graphic verbal commentaries about an individual's body; sexually degrading words used to describe an individual; and the display in the workplace of sexually suggestive objects or pictures." In the AT&T and IBEW arbitration decision AAA 327-3, Arbitrator Robins upheld a five-day suspension concerning an offensive action in violation of the company's sexual harassment policy that the perpetrator believed to be a joke which would be seen as amusing by the individual who was the object of the action. See also Greyhound Lines, Inc. and IAM, AAA 325, p. 1, upholding discipline for "boisterous, profane or vulgar language."

[44] E.g., *Katz v. Dole*, 709 F.2d 251 at 256 (4th Cir. 1983), and *Henson v. City of Dundee*, 682 F.2d 897 at 905 (11th Cir. 1982).

[45] 461 F. Supp. 894 (D.N.J. 1978) enforced by 465 F. Supp. 1141 (D.N.J. 1979), modifying and enforcing, 476 F. Supp. 335 (D.N.J. 1979).

[46] EEOC Notice 915.002 Mar. 8, 1994.

Presently, sexual harassment by nonemployee cases relate to employers requiring employees to wear sexually provocative uniforms where the employers should reasonably know that wearing the uniforms would subject the employees to sexual harassment by nonemployees. In *EEOC v. Sage Realty Corp.*,[47] where a female lobby attendant was required to wear a uniform that resulted in her being subjected to sexual propositions and lewd comments by passersby, the court found that the employer, Sage, had violated Title VII of the Act. The court accepted the principle that an employer may impose "reasonable" dress requirements but held that the employer did not have the unfettered discretion to force employees to wear sexually provocative uniforms.

There is much discussion presently about sexual harassment issues relating to waitresses who accept jobs at "sex appeal" restaurants where they know they are required to wear "provocative" uniforms. Have the waitresses assumed the risk of harassment, or "welcomed" it by taking such jobs? Can the employer protect itself from liability by having a published policy and practice of immediately removing offensive patrons from the premises? In the next section the "BFOQ" defense will be discussed. Can an employer hire only waitresses with sex appeal for a sex appeal motif restaurant? End-of-chapter case problem 12 deals with these issues.

ELLISON v. BRADY

United States Court of Appeals, Ninth Circuit, 924 F.2d 872 (1991).

[Kerry Ellison, an IRS employee, brought a sexual harassment claim against her employer. The U.S. District Court granted summary judgment for her governmental employer, and she appealed.]

BEEZER, C.J.

. . . This appeal presents two important issues: (1) what test should be applied to determine whether conduct is sufficiently severe or pervasive to alter the conditions of employment and create a hostile working environment, and (2) what remedial actions can shield employers from liability for sexual harassment by coworkers. . . .

I.

Kerry Ellison worked as a revenue agent for the Internal Revenue Service in San Mateo, California. During her initial training in 1984 she met Sterling Gray, another trainee, who was also assigned to the San Mateo office. The two co-workers never became friends, and they did not work closely together.

Gray's desk was twenty feet from Ellison's desk, two rows behind and one row over. Revenue agents in the San Mateo office often went to lunch in groups. In June of 1986 when no one else was in the office, Gray asked Ellison to lunch. She accepted. Gray had to pick up his son's forgotten lunch, so they stopped by Gray's house. He gave Ellison a tour of his house.

Ellison alleges that after the June lunch Gray started to pester her with unnecessary questions and hang around her desk. On October 9, 1986, Gray asked Ellison out for a drink after work. She declined, but she suggested that they have lunch the following week. She did not want to have lunch alone with him, and she tried to stay away from the office during lunch

---

[47] *EEOC v. Sage Realty Corp.*, 25 E.P.D. ¶ 31,529 (SDNY 1981).

time. One day during the following week, Gray uncharacteristically dressed in a three-piece suit and asked Ellison out for lunch. Again, she did not accept.

On October 22, 1986 Gray handed Ellison a note he wrote on a telephone message slip which read:

I cried over you last night and I'm totally drained today. I have never been in such constant term oil (sic). Thank you for talking with me. I could not stand to feel your hatred for another day.

When Ellison realized that Gray wrote the note, she became shocked and frightened and left the room. Gray followed her into the hallway and demanded that she talk to him, but she left the building.

Ellison later showed the note to Bonnie Miller, who supervised both Ellison and Gray. Miller said "this is sexual harassment." Ellison asked Miller not to do anything about it. She wanted to try to handle it herself. Ellison asked a male co-worker to talk to Gray, to tell him that she was not interested in him and to leave her alone. The next day, Thursday, Gray called in sick.

Ellison did not work on Friday, and on the following Monday, she started four weeks of training in St. Louis, Missouri. Gray mailed her a card and a typed, single-spaced, three-page letter. She describes this letter as "twenty times, a hundred times weirder" than the prior note. Gray wrote, in part:

I know that you are worth knowing with or without sex. . . . Leaving aside the hassles and disasters of recent weeks. I have enjoyed you so much over these past few months. Watching you. Experiencing you from O so far away. Admiring your style and elan. . . . Don't you think it odd that two people who have never even talked together, alone, are striking off such intense sparks. . . . I will [write] another letter in the near future.

Explaining her reaction, Ellison stated: "I just thought he was crazy. I thought he was nuts. I didn't know what he would do next. I was frightened."

She immediately telephoned Miller. Ellison told her supervisor that she was frightened and really upset. She requested that Miller transfer either her or Gray because she would not be comfortable working in the same office with him. Miller asked Ellison to send a copy of the card and letter to San Mateo.

Miller then telephoned her supervisor, Joe Benton, and discussed the problem. That same day she had a counseling session with Gray. She informed him that he was entitled to union representation. During this meeting, she told Gray to leave Ellison alone.

At Benton's request, Miller apprised the labor relations department of the situation. She also reminded Gray many times over the next few weeks he must not contact Ellison in any way. Gray subsequently transferred to the San Francisco office on November 24, 1986. Ellison returned from St. Louis in late November and did not discuss the matter further with Miller.

After three weeks in San Francisco, Gray filed union grievances requesting a return to the San Mateo office. The IRS and the union settled the grievances in Gray's favor, agreeing to allow him to transfer back to the San Mateo office provided that he spend four months in San Francisco and promise not to bother Ellison. On January 28, 1987, Ellison first learned of Gray's request in a letter from Miller explaining that Gray would return to the San Mateo office. The letter indicated that management decided to resolve Ellison's problem with a six-month separation, and that it would take additional action if the problem recurred.

After receiving the letter, Ellison was "frantic." She filed a formal complaint alleging sexual harassment on January 30, 1987 with the IRS. She also obtained permission to transfer to San Francisco temporarily when Gray returned.

Gray sought joint counseling. He wrote Ellison another letter which still sought to maintain the idea that he and Ellison had some type of relationship.

The IRS employee investigating the allegation agreed with Ellison's supervisor that Gray's conduct constituted sexual harassment. In its final decision, however, the Treasury Department rejected Ellison's complaint because it believed that the complaint did not describe a pattern or practice of sexual harassment covered by the EEOC regulations. After an appeal, the EEOC affirmed the Treasury Department's decision on a different ground. It concluded that the agency took adequate action to prevent the repetition of Gray's conduct.

Ellison filed a complaint in September of 1987 in federal district court. The court granted the government's motion for summary judgment on the ground that Ellison had failed to state a prima facie case of sexual harassment due to a hostile working environment. Ellison appeals. . . .

II.

The parties ask us to determine if Gray's conduct, as alleged by Ellison, was sufficiently severe or pervasive to alter the conditions of Ellison's employment and create an abusive working environment. The district court, with little Ninth Circuit case law to look to for guidance, held that Ellison did not state a prima facie case of sexual harassment due to a hostile working environment. It believed that Gray's conduct was "isolated and genuinely trivial." We disagree. . . .

. . . To state a claim under Title VII, sexual harassment "must be sufficiently severe or pervasive to alter the conditions of the victim's employment and create an abusive working environment." . . .

We do not agree with the standards set forth in *Scott*. . . .

We have closely examined *Meritor* and our previous cases, and we believe that Gray's conduct was sufficiently severe and pervasive to alter the conditions of Ellison's employment and create an abusive working environment. We first note that the required showing of severity or seriousness of the harassing conduct varies inversely with the pervasiveness or frequency of the conduct. *See King v. Board of Regents of University of Wisconsin System*, 898 F.2d 533, 537 (7th Cir. 1990) ("[a]lthough a single act can be enough, . . . generally, repeated incidents create a stronger claim of hostile environment, with the strength of the claim depending on the number of incidents and the intensity of each incident.") . . .

Next, we believe that in evaluating the severity and pervasiveness of sexual harassment, we should focus on the perspective of the victim. . . . (courts "should consider the victim's perspective and not stereotyped notions of acceptable behavior.") If we only examined whether a reasonable person would engage in allegedly harassing conduct, we would run the risk of reinforcing the prevailing level of discrimination. Harassers could continue to harass merely because a particular discriminatory practice was common, and victims of harassment would have no remedy.

We therefore prefer to analyze harassment from the victim's perspective. A complete understanding of the victim's view requires, among other things, an analysis of the different perspectives of men and women. Conduct that many men consider unobjectionable may offend many women. . . . ("A male supervisor might believe, for example, that it is legitimate for him to tell a female subordinate that she has a 'great figure' or 'nice legs.' The female subordinate, however, may find such comments offensive"); *Yates*, 819 F.2d at 637, n. 2 ("men and women are vulnerable in different ways and offended by different behavior"). *See also* Ehrenreich, *Pluralist Myths and Powerless Men: The Ideology of Reasonableness in Sexual Harassment Law*, 99 Yale L.J. 1177, 1207–1208 (1990) (men tend to view some forms of sexual harassment as "harmless social interactions to which only overly-sensitive women would object"); Abrams, *Gender Discrimination and the Transformation of Workplace Norms*, 42 Vand.L.Rev.

1183, 1203 (1989) (the characteristically male view depicts sexual harassment as comparatively harmless amusement). . . .

In order to shield employers from having to accommodate the idiosyncratic concerns of the rare hyper-sensitive employee, we hold that a female plaintiff states a prima facie case of hostile environment sexual harassment when she alleges conduct which a reasonable woman* would consider sufficiently severe or pervasive to alter the conditions of employment and create an abusive working environment. *Andrews*, 895 F.2d at 1482 (sexual harassment must detrimentally affect a reasonable person of the same sex as the victim); *Yates*, 819 F.2d at 637 (adopting "reasonable woman" standard set out in *Rabidue*, 805 F.2d 611, 626 (Keith, J., dissenting)) . . .

We adopt the perspective of a reasonable woman primarily because we believe that a sex-blind reasonable person standard tends to be male-biased and tends to systematically ignore the experiences of women. The reasonable woman standard does not establish a higher level of protection for women than men. Instead, a gender-conscious examination of sexual harassment enables women to participate in the workplace on an equal footing with men. By acknowledging and not trivializing the effects of sexual harassment on reasonable women, courts can work towards ensuring that neither men nor women will have to "run a gauntlet of sexual abuse in return for the privilege of being allowed to work and make a living." *Henson v. Dundee*, 682 F.2d 897, 902 (11th Cir. 1982).

We note that the reasonable victim standard we adopt today classifies conduct as unlawful sexual harassment even when harassers do not realize that their conduct creates a hostile working environment. Well-intentioned compliments by co-workers or supervisors can form the basis of a sexual harassment cause of action if a reasonable victim of the same sex as the plaintiff would consider the comments sufficiently severe or pervasive to alter a condition of employment and create an abusive working environment. . . . To avoid liability under Title VII, employers may have to educate and sensitize their workforce to eliminate conduct which a reasonable victim would consider unlawful sexual harassment. *See* 29 C.F.R. § 1604.11(f) ("Prevention is the best tool for the elimination of sexual harassment.")

The facts of this case illustrate the importance of considering the victim's perspective. Analyzing the facts from the alleged harasser's viewpoint, Gray could be portrayed as a modern-day Cyrano de Bergerac wishing no more than to woo Ellison with his words. There is no evidence that Gray harbored ill will toward Ellison. He even offered in his "love letter" to leave her alone if she wished. Examined in this light, it is not difficult to see why the district court characterized Gray's conduct as isolated and trivial.

Ellison, however, did not consider the acts to be trivial. Gray's first note shocked and frightened her. After receiving the three-page letter, she became really upset and frightened again. . . .

Sexual harassment is a major problem in the workplace. Adopting the victim's perspective ensures that courts will not "sustain ingrained notions of reasonable behavior fashioned by the offenders." . . . Congress did not enact Title VII to codify prevailing sexist prejudices. To the contrary, "Congress designed Title VII to prevent the perpetuation of stereotypes and a sense of degradation which serve to close or discourage employment opportunities for women." *Andrews*, 895 F.2d at 1483. We hope that over time both men and women will learn what conduct offends reasonable members of the other sex. When employers and employees internalize the standard of workplace conduct we establish today, the current gap in perception between the sexes will be bridged.

---

* Of course, where male employees allege that co-workers engage in conduct which creates a hostile environment, the appropriate victim's perspective would be that of a reasonable man.

III.

We next must determine what remedial actions by employers shield them from liability under Title VII for sexual harassment by co-workers. The Supreme Court in *Meritor* did not address employer liability for sexual harassment by co-workers. In that case, the Court discussed employer liability for a hostile environment created by a supervisor. . . .

Here, Ellison's employer argues that it complied with its statutory obligation to provide a workplace free from sexual harassment. It promptly investigated Ellison's allegation. When Ellison returned to San Mateo from her training in St. Louis, Gray was no longer working in San Mateo. When Gray returned to San Mateo, the government granted Ellison's request to transfer temporarily to San Francisco.

We decline to accept the government's argument that its decision to return Gray to San Mateo did not create a hostile environment for Ellison because the government granted Ellison's request for a temporary transfer to San Francisco. Ellison preferred to work in San Mateo over San Francisco. We strongly believe that the victim of sexual harassment should not be punished for the conduct of the harasser. We wholeheartedly agree with the EEOC that a victim of sexual harassment should not have to work in a less desirable location as a result of an employer's remedy for sexual harassment. EEOC Compliance Manual (CCH) § 615.4(a)(9)(iii), ¶ 3103, at 3213 (1988). . . .

Ellison further maintains that her employer's decision to allow Gray to transfer back to the San Mateo office after a six-month cooling-off period rendered the government's remedy insufficient. She argues that Gray's *mere presence* would create a hostile working environment.

We believe that in some cases the mere presence of an employee who has engaged in particularly severe or pervasive harassment can create a hostile working environment. *See Paroline v. Unisys Corp.*, 879 F.2d 100, 106–07 (4th Cir. 1989). To avoid liability under Title VII for failing to remedy a hostile environment, employers may even have to remove employees from the workplace if their mere presence would render the working environment hostile. . . .

IV.

We reverse the district court's decision that Ellison did not allege a prima facie case of sexual harassment due to a hostile working environment, and we remand for further proceedings consistent with this opinion. We, of course, reserve for the district court the resolution of all factual issues.

Reversed and Remanded

STEPHENS, District Judge, dissenting: . . .

. . . A man's response to circumstances faced by women and their effect upon women can be and in given circumstances may be expected to be understood by men.

It takes no stretch of the imagination to envision two complaints emanating from the same workplace regarding the same conditions, one brought by a woman and the other by a man. Application of the "new standard" presents a puzzlement which is born of the assumption that men's eyes do not see what a woman sees through her eyes. I find it surprising that the majority finds no need for evidence on any of these subjects. . . .

It is my opinion that the case should be reversed with instructions to proceed to trial. . . .

The creation of the proposed "new standard" which applies only to women will not necessarily come to the aid of all potential victims of the type of misconduct that is at issue in this case. I believe that a gender neutral standard would greatly contribute to the clarity of this and future cases in the same area. . . .

CASE QUESTIONS

1. What test does the court apply to determine whether conduct is sufficiently severe or perva-

sive to alter the conditions of employment of the complainant and create a hostile working environment?
2. Express your opinion as to whether men and women have different views on what conduct constitutes sexual harassment.

3. Why did the court adopt the reasonable woman test versus a reasonable person standard?
4. What remedial actions can shield an employer from liability for co-worker sexual harassment?

DEANGELIS v. EL PASO MUNICIPAL POLICE OFFICERS ASSOCIATION

United States Court of Appeals, 51 F.3d 390 (5th Cir. 1995).

[Sergeant Sylvia DeAngelis brought a Title VII hostile work environment sexual harassment action and a retaliation action against a police officers' union. She was awarded $10,000 in compensatory damages and $50,000 in punitive damages, and the union appealed.]

JONES, EDITH H., CJ. . . .

The principal issue in this case is whether a jury verdict for the plaintiff in a Title VII sexual harassment case may be supported by evidence of a few written jibes, at women police officers generally and the plaintiff in particular, published in the police association newsletter. We hold that such evidence, rife as it is with first amendment overtones, will not suffice and so reverse the judgment.

BACKGROUND

After six years on duty with the El Paso Police Department as a patrol officer and detective, Sylvia DeAngelis became the first female sergeant in October, 1987. Within a few months of promotion, she was satirized by an anonymous writer in *The Silver Badge*, a newsletter of the El Paso Municipal Police Officers Association (the Association), an organization similar to a police officers union. The author's *nom de plume* was R. U. Withmi. He wrote as a patrol officer with nearly 20 years' experience "combatin' crime." His monthly column criticized, in an irreverent and colloquial manner, groups

including superior officers, "rear echelon" officers ("REMF's"), bureaucrats, and "weenie boys." R. U. Withmi lashed out at changing times in the police department while longing for the good old days. The incursion of females into the department, a quintessential element of modernization, did not escape his sharp pen.

This lawsuit arises from several of his columns, published between November 1987 and February 1990, that derogatorily referred to policewomen. About a thousand copies of *The Silver Badge* were printed monthly and distributed at a minimum to 700 police officer members of the Association.

Publication of the columns angered more than two dozen female police officers, who asked the police chief and officers of the Association to stifle R. U. Withmi. The police chief, despite his discomfiture, had no direct authority over the Association, and the Association, after a vote of the membership in early 1990, rejected their leaders' advice to require that R. U. Withmi unmask himself.

Peculiarly, although specifically offered the opportunity, none of the policewomen ever chose to write a response to R. U. Withmi for *The Silver Badge*.* The record mentions no

---

* Except perhaps a brief anonymous editorial from "I.N. Wifya" which expressed disgust and disagreement with R. U. Withmi on a variety of issues including remarks about the attractiveness of the new female recruits.

boycott of the Association or its newsletter, no challenge to the officers' election. Sergeant DeAngelis' Title VII claims are before this court.

DeAngelis secured jury findings that (1) R. U. Withmi's articles subjected her to harassment, creating a hostile and sexually abusive working environment, and (2) a reference in one of the columns to her "E-I-E-I-O" [EEOC] complaint amounted to retaliation for exercise of her Title VII rights. The jury awarded Sergeant DeAngelis $10,000 in compensatory damages and $50,000 punitive damages.

The Association has appealed on several grounds, the most compelling of which are sufficiency of evidence of liability and the assertion that, if this verdict is upheld, the First Amendment free speech rights of R. U. Withmi have been abridged. These issues must be discussed together. . . .

To establish an actionable claim of sexual harassment in the workplace, a plaintiff must demonstrate:

(1) That she belongs to protected class; (2) that she was subject to unwelcome sexual harassment; (3) that the harassment was based on sex; (4) that the harassment affected a "term, condition or privilege of employment"; and (5) that the employer either knew or should have known of the harassment and failed to take prompt remedial action.

. . . The Supreme Court recently affirmed that sexually discriminatory verbal intimidation, ridicule and insults may be sufficiently severe or pervasive to alter the conditions of the victim's employment and create an abusive working environment that violates Title VII. *Harris v. Forklift Systems, Inc.,* 114 S.Ct. 367, 370–71. *Nash v. Electrospace Systems, Inc.,* 9 F.3d 401, 403 (5th Cir. 1993).

A claim for a sexually hostile working environment is not a trivial matter. Its purpose is to level the playing field for women who work by preventing others from impairing their ability to compete on an equal basis with men. One must always bear this ultimate goal in mind. A hostile environment claim embodies a series of criteria that express extremely insensitive conduct against women, conduct so egregious as to alter the conditions of employment and destroy their equal opportunity in the workplace. Any lesser standard of liability, couched in terms of conduct that sporadically wounds or offends but does not hinder a female employee's performance, would not serve the goal of equality. In fact, a less onerous standard of liability would attempt to insulate women from everyday insults as if they remained models of Victorian reticence. A lesser standard of liability would mandate not equality but preference for women: it would create incentives for employers to bend over backwards in women's favor for fear of lawsuits. Now that most American women are working outside the home, in a broad range of occupations and with ever-increasing responsibility, it seems perverse to claim that they need the protection of a preferential standard. The careful, heightened phrasing of a hostile environment claim, enforceable where working conditions have palpably deteriorated because of sexually hostile conduct, aims to enforce equality, not preference. . . .

Lacking any other evidence of sexual discrimination or harassment, DeAngelis stakes her case on R. U. Withmi's columns and their effects. We will summarize each column that was offered at trial as critical of Sergeant DeAngelis or women police officers in general. Each column bore this disclaimer:

R.U. Withmi is a senior level patrol officer whose article appears monthly. It does not represent the official position of the EPMPOA [the Association] but presents a humorous satirical view by the author. Written comments to the editor are welcome.

One must infer that because the R. U. Withmi column appeared monthly in *The Silver Badge,* and the challenged articles appeared over a course of 30 months, none of the twenty articles not offered in evidence at the trial court was hostile to women.

1. *December 1987*—Well-low and BE-hold!!, the Holiday Season is here! It seems like just the other day we got a new Chief and them 87 low bid police cars had just arrived. As the new year fast approaches these here parts and we all git just a little older, I has begun to get a lil' nostalgic in my old age a remeberin' when things was a little different. It is my opinion that we here are in a new age of patrolmen, patrolwoman, defectowoman, sergeant dingy woman and now thanks to the appeal process, patrol other! I just think a people are changing and we are getting a new generation of patrolmen in as few as five years! I remember the good ol' days when finding the criminal was more important to the patrolmen then keeping your hair in place! I wonder how far back you remember? I remember these things, let's see if you do . . . Remember when? . . . Do you remember when there were no women workin' the streets? (Ah yes, those were the good days! . . . Sorry gals, truth hurts!) . . .

2. *February 1988*—I never thought I would make the newspaper El Paso Rag, an E-I-E-I-O complaint or be blasted out of my socks by our Presidente himself!

3. *March 1988*— . . . only REAL MEN wear them ole wool pants! You don't see any of the "jefes" with a bottle of hair spray on their Sam Browns! . . . And I don't EVEN want to start up against the "girls" so my Commandate Presidente don't get "scared" again with his poison pen!

4. *August 1988*—I was surprised to think they were also training some good lookin' K-9s up there but I was told those were the female recruits! I swear!, complete with collars! Oh well, my mistake!

5. *October 1988*—I understand I done rustled the feathers of a few Female Recruit Officers and their "Daddys" up there on the "HILL." Well, ole' RU's a so sorry because I sometimes get carried away with tellin' things they way it is. Don't worry, I think I was wrong because the public will treat you with all the "respect" you deserve IF you get out there, and they will never call you names other than "officer." And wherever you answer the call, you will always get the cooperation you deserve. And no one will call you names to your face. So, life will be a bowl of cherries on the streets and everythin' you've been told is the truth . . .

6. *January 1989*— . . . now the patrol stations have to pull out a FULL DUTY policeMAN from the field to do the desk work! . . . I just want a car that works, and a supervisor with some sense . . . and a female officer that places her ability before her gender and IA out of my way!

7. *February 1989*— . . . with just one whack of the pluma we had musical supervisors all over the City. . . . Chances are purty darn good that we all probably know who the real problem was. But no names these days because of them EEOC Fed boys!

8. *July 1989*—Anyway, fly that flag, be glad yore American, have a job, are male, and workin' patrol.

9. *February 1990*—We had a hell-uva BS session at shift meeting (a place REMF's know nuthin' about!) regarding women in combat. . . . Physically, the police broads just don't got it! Difference standards or not, on the real streets the crooks don't fight women different than men! Why shoot, a guy weighing 140 pounds is just a lil' bird to me, but a fit to fight police broad of 140 pounds ain't just around that often! Someone tell me I'm wrong!**

10. *April 1990*—My academy Joe weenie partner dun informed me that this here bits o truth I writes each months just plain gots alotta folks supportin' it!

Sergeant DeAngelis acknowledged that only the first column directly referred to her—as Sergeant "dingy woman," evidently a shorthand expression for "dingbat." She asserts that the column concerning her "E-I-E-I-O complaint" ridiculed her as well as EEOC. Another column singled her out as one of the few officers to carry a flashlight on her belt in the daytime. And she believes that the reference to musical supervisors in the February 1989 column implied that her troubles caused a shift around the police department. All of the other columns, DeAngelis conceded, refer to women in general, as was brought home to the police department and the Association by the uproar of many female police officers at their appearance.

Whether the four columns that refer to DeAngelis, taken alone or in conjunction with

---

** This column spawned the class action lawsuit in state court by 22 women police.

the other six columns appearing at irregular intervals in two and a half years, amounted to severe or pervasive sexually discriminatory intimidation, ridicule or insults depends in part upon their context. The R. U. Withmi column did not represent a boss's demeaning harangue, or a sexually charged invitation, or a campaign of vulgarity perpetrated by co-workers: the column attempted clumsy, earthy humor. R. U. Withmi intended to be a curmudgeon, the police department's Archie Bunker or Homer Simpson, who eyed with suspicion all authority figures, academy-trained officers, police dispatchers, newfangled procedures and gear—whatever had changed from the old days. Misogyny naturally came with R. U.'s territory, although, against the backdrop of his other barbs, it can hardly be called an obsession. In any event, much of his humor lacked volatility: his reference to a police officer as a "police-MAN" or his exhortation to "be glad you're male . . . ", for instance, hardly rank in the firmament of sexist vilification.

On occasion, the column was forced to acknowledge criticism and apologize in its way to its victims such as the dispatchers, female recruits, and the " 'Daddys' up there on the Hill." The column's severest attack on women—which compared police work to R. U.'s combat experiences in Viet Nam—may be read to include self-criticism: it notes that a hush fell over the room when this subject was discussed. That column did not refer to DeAngelis. R. U. Withmi columns ceased being published sometime during 1990.

We conclude that these columns are the equivalent of the "mere utterance of an . . . epithet which engenders offensive feelings in an employee." *Meritor Savings*, 477 U.S. at 67, 106 S.Ct. at 2405. Consequently, they were not severe or pervasive enough to create an objectively hostile or abusive work environment. *Harris*, 114 S.Ct. at 370. Four printed derogatory references to Sergeant DeAngelis at irregular intervals in two and a half years do not evince sufficient hostility toward her as a matter of law. . . .

Because we have concluded that insufficient evidence supports DeAngelis' claim of a sexually harassing work environment, we do not reach the difficult question whether Title VII may be violated by expressions of opinion published in the R. U. Withmi columns in the Association's newsletter. Where pure expression is involved, Title VII steers into the territory of the First Amendment. It is no use to deny or minimize this problem because, when Title VII is applied to sexual harassment claims founded solely on verbal insults, pictorial or literary matter, the statute imposes content-based, viewpoint-discriminatory restrictions on speech. . . .

Matching the infirmity of appellee's hostile sexual environment verdict is the retaliation finding, supported only by R. U. Withmi's reference to an "E-I-E-I-O" complaint and a report on her EEOC complaint among the Association minutes routinely published in *The Silver Badge*. DeAngelis also asserts as proof of "retaliation" an article in *The Silver Badge* that reported the Association's intention to sue her for damages if her lawsuit against the Union proved groundless. A retaliation claim requires, in addition to proof of the plaintiff's protected activity, an adverse employment action, and a causal connection between the adverse action and the protected activity. *EEOC v. J.M. Huber Corp.*, 927 F.2d 1322 (5th Cir. 1991). No matter how vehemently DeAngelis denounces these articles, they did not amount to an "adverse employment action" under any reasonable meaning of that term. The jury verdict lacks foundation.

CONCLUSION

Title VII cannot remedy every tasteless joke or groundless rumor that confronts women in the workplace. For DeAngelis, the price of success as the police department's first woman sergeant included transitory ribbing by R. U. Withmi. The newsletter columns, however, were not so frequent, pervasive or pointedly insulting to DeAngelis as to create an objectively hostile working environment. The totality of circumstance do not prove that her working conditions were disadvantaged because she was mentioned in four R. U. Withmi columns. Likewise, three printed references to her EEOC complaint do not constitute retaliation under Title VII.

The judgment of the district court is therefore REVERSED and RENDERED for the Association.

CASE QUESTIONS

1. What is the purpose of sexually hostile working environment cases according to Judge Edith Jones?

2. Did the court of appeals determine that Sergeant DeAngelis was a victim of retaliation for filing a Title VII claim?

3. In *Robinson v. Jacksonville Shipyards*, a U.S. district court sustained a Title VII sexually harassing work environment claim of a female welder whose workplace contained nude posters of women and who was subjected to continuing derogatory and suggestive sexual innuendo and insult. The court rejected the defendant's argument that this conduct was protected by the First Amendment. Where an employee's exercise of freedom of speech is so abusive that it undermines the morale of the workforce, may a public-sector employer take disciplinary action against the perpetrator? Did R. U. Withmi's columns undermine the morale of the workplace in this case and lose its First Amendment protections?

SECTION 8—NATIONAL ORIGIN, INCLUDING HISPANIC ORIGIN

National origin discrimination extends Title VII protection to members of all nationalities. As examples, national origin discrimination claims under Title VII have been brought on behalf of Spanish-surnamed persons; a person of Cajun descent; and persons of Hungarian, German, and Polish ancestry.[48]

The judicial principles that have emerged from cases involving other forms of employment discrimination are generally applicable to cases involving allegations of national origin discrimination. Thus physical standards such as minimum height requirements, which tend to exclude persons of a particular national origin because of the physical stature of the group, have been deemed unlawful where these standards cannot be justified by business necessity.[49]

Adverse employment decisions based on an individual's lack of English language skills have been considered violative of Title VII in those situations where the language requirement bears no demonstratable relationship to the successful performance of the job to which it is applied.

In *Fragante v. City and County of Honolulu*, presented in this section, the U.S. Court of Appeals for the Ninth Circuit cautioned that it is an easy refuge for an employer to unlawfully discriminate against an individual because of national origin by falsely claiming that the individual lacked the necessary communication skills demanded by the job in question. The court found no national origin discrimination however, because it determined that an honest assessment of Fragante's communication skills was made; and that he was passed over not because of his accent, but because of the deleterious effect of his accent on his ability to communicate orally.

---

[48] *Roach v. Dresser Industries*, 494 F. Supp. 215, FEP 1073 (W.D. La. 1980).
[49] *Davis v. County of Los Angeles*, 13 FEP 1217 (9th Cir. 1976), and *League of United Latin American Citizens v. City of Santa Ana*, 410 F. Supp. 873 (C.D. Calif. 1976).

An employer may forbid bilingual sales employees to speak anything but English in sales areas while on the job according to the *Garcia v. Gloor*[50] decision. An expert witness testified that the Spanish language is the most important aspect of ethnic identification for Mexican-Americans. However, the court held that Garcia was discharged not because he was the victim of discrimination based on national origin but rather because he had the ability to comply with the employer's "English-only" rule, but did not do so. English-only policies are legal in all but a few circumstances, such as when the employee speaks no English or when English-only rules foster a hostile working environment for persons based on their national origin.

Title VII does not prohibit discrimination on the basis of citizenship where an employer has a rule against employment of aliens and the application of the rule is not a pretext for excluding persons of a particular national origin.[51]

In *Fortino v. Quasar Co.*[52] the United States Court of Appeals for the Seventh Circuit reversed a $2,500,000 Title VII national origin discrimination judgment in favor of three former managers of Quasar Co., a subsidiary of Matsushita Electric Co. Ltd. of Japan. In a reduction in force, the company had terminated 66 of 89 managers working in the United States, while not one of the 10 Japanese executives was terminated. Under the Treaty of Friendship, Commerce and Navigation between the United States and Japan the companies of either the United States or Japan are free "to engage, within the territories of the other party . . . executive personnel of their choice." The Court of Appeals determined that action permitted by the treaty—discrimination in favor of citizens of the foreign country operating a subsidiary abroad—is not prohibited by Title VII, which proscribes discrimination based on "national origin," but not preferences based on citizenship.

FRAGANTE v. CITY AND COUNTY OF HONOLULU

United States Court of Appeals, Ninth Circuit, 888 F.2d 591 (1989).

[Manuel Fragante applied for a clerk's job with the City and County of Honolulu. Although he placed high enough on a civil service eligibility list to be chosen for the position, he was not selected because of a perceived deficiency in relevant oral communication skills caused by his "heavy Filipino accent." Fragante brought suit, alleging that the defendants discriminated against him on the basis of his national origin, in violation of Title VII of the Civil Rights Act. At the conclusion of the trial, the district court found that the oral ability to communicate effectively and clearly was a legitimate occupational qualification for the job in question. And, finding no proof of a discriminatory intent or motive by the defendant, the court dismissed Fragante's complaint. Fragante appealed.]

TROTT, C.J. . . . .

I.

The Statute and Its Purpose

Preliminarily, we do well to remember that this country was founded and has been built in large measure by people from other lands, many

---

[50] 618 F.2d 264, 22 FEP 1403 (5th Cir. 1980).
[51] *Espinoza v. Farah Manufacturing Co.*, 414 U.S. 86, 6 FEP 933 (1973).
[52] 950 F.2d 389 (7th Cir. 1991).

of whom came here—especially after our early beginnings—with a limited knowledge of English. This flow of immigrants has continued and has been encouraged over the years. From its inception, the United States of America has been a dream to many around the world. We hold out promises of freedom, equality, and economic opportunity to many who only know these words as concepts. It would be more than ironic if we followed up our invitation to people such as Manuel Fragante with a closed economic door based on national origin discrimination. It is no surprise that Title VII speaks to this issue and clearly articulates the policy of our nation: unlawful discrimination based on national origin shall not be permitted to exist in the workplace. But, it is also true that there is another important aspect of Title VII: the "preservation of an employer's remaining freedom of choice." . . .

Accent and national origin are obviously inextricably intertwined in many cases. It would therefore be an easy refuge in this context for an employer unlawfully discriminating against someone based on national origin to state falsely that it was not the person's national origin that caused the employment or promotion problem, but the candidate's inability to measure up to the communications skills demanded by the job. We encourage a very searching look by the district courts at such a claim.

An adverse employment decision may be predicated upon an individual's accent when—but only when—it interferes materially with job performance. There is nothing improper about an employer making an *honest* assessment of the oral communications skills of a candidate for a job when such skills are reasonably related to job performance. EEOC Compliance Manual (CCH) ¶ 4035 at 3877–78 (1986); *see also Mejia v. New York Sheraton Hotel*, 459 F. Supp. 375, 377 (S.D.N.Y. 1978) (Dominican chambermaid properly denied promotion to front desk because of her "inability to articulate clearly or coherently and to make herself adequately understood in . . . English"); *Carino v. University*

of Oklahoma Board of Regents, 750 F.2d 815, 819 (10th Cir. 1984) (plaintiff with a "noticeable" Filipino accent was improperly denied a position as supervisor of a dental laboratory where his accent did not interfere with his ability to perform supervisory tasks); *Berke*, 628 F.2d at 981 (employee with "pronounced" Polish accent whose command of English was "well above that of the average adult American" was improperly denied two positions because of her accent). . . .

. . . In a letter, dated June 28, 1982, the reasons why he was not selected were articulated as follows:

As to the reason for your non-selection we felt the two selected applicants were both superior in their verbal communication ability. As we indicated in your interview, our clerks are constantly dealing with the public and the ability to speak clearly is one of the most important skills required for the position. Therefore, while we were impressed with your educational and employment history, we felt the applicants selected would be better able to work in our office because of their communication skills.

The interviewers' record discloses Fragante's third place ranking was based on his "pronounced accent which is difficult to understand." Indeed, Fragante can point to no facts which indicate that his ranking was based on factors other than his inability to communicate effectively with the public. This view was shared by the district court. . . .

Fragante argues the district court erred in considering "listener prejudice" as a legitimate, nondiscriminatory reason for failure to hire. We find, however, that the district court did not determine defendants refused to hire Fragante on the basis that some listeners would "turn off" a Filipino accent. The district court after trial noted that: "Fragante, in fact, has a difficult manner of pronunciation and the Court further finds as a fact from his general testimony that he would often not respond directly to the questions as propounded. . . .

In sum, the record conclusively shows that Fragante was passed over because of the deleterious *effect* of his Filipino accent on his ability to communicate orally, not merely because he had such an accent.

The district court is
Affirmed.

CASE QUESTIONS

1. Why do courts take a very careful look at non-selection decisions based on foreign accents?
2. Why was Fragante not selected for the clerk's position when he had higher tests scores than the two successful candidates?

SECTION 9—TITLE VII: SECTION 703 EXCEPTIONS

Section 703 of the Act defines what employment activities are unlawful. This same section, however, also exempts several key practices from the scope of Title VII enforcement. The most important are the bona fide occupational qualification exception, the testing and educational requirement exception, and the seniority system exception.

Bona Fide Occupational Qualification Exception

Section 703(e) stipulates that it shall not be unlawful employment practice for an employer to hire employees on the basis of the religion, sex, or national origin in those certain instances where religion, sex, or national origin is a bona fide occupational qualification (BFOQ) reasonably necessary to the normal operation of a particular enterprise. The so-called BFOQ clause is construed narrowly by the courts, and the burden of proving the business necessity for any such restrictive occupational qualifications is on the employer.

In *Dothard v. Rawlinson,*[53] the Supreme Court, while recognizing that the BFOQ exception was meant to be an extremely narrow one, upheld as a BFOQ a male-only requirement for correctional counselor (guards) positions in male maximum security correctional institutions in Alabama. The Court referred to the substantial amount of testimony that the use of women as guards in "contact" positions under the existing conditions in Alabama maximum security male penitentiaries (which included 20 percent of the male prisoners being sex offenders housed throughout the facilities) would pose a substantial security problem directly linked to the sex of the prison guards.

In *UAW v. Johnson Controls, Inc.,* presented in this section, the Supreme Court dealt with the difficult issues relating to employer fetal protection policies under Title VII. The Court found that the employer's fetal protection policy which barred all fertile women from jobs involving lead exposure exceeding OSHA standards was discriminatory, since only women employees were affected by the policy. And the Court rejected the employer's BFOQ defense. Moreover, it determined that the Pregnancy Discrimination Act contained its own BFOQ standard, which requires employers to treat potentially pregnant employees the same as other employees if their ability to do the work is the same. The Court held that Title VII mandates that decisions about the welfare of future children be left to the parents who conceive, bear, support, and raise them, rather than to employers who hire those parents or to the courts.

---

[53] 433 U.S. 321, 15 FEP 10 (1977).

UAW v. JOHNSON CONTROLS, INC.

Supreme Court of the United States, 111 S.Ct. 1197 (1991).

[Johnson Controls, Inc. (JCI) manufactures batteries. A primary ingredient in the battery manufacturing process is lead. Occupational exposure to lead entails health risks, including the risk of harm to any fetus carried by a female employee. After eight of its employees became pregnant while maintaining blood lead levels exceeding levels set by the Centers for Disease Control (CDC) as critical for a worker planning to have a family, respondent announced a policy barring all women, except those whose infertility was medically documented, from jobs involving actual or potential lead exposure exceeding the OSHA standard. Petitioners filed a class action in the District Court, claiming that the policy constituted sex discrimination violative of Title VII of the Civil Rights Act of 1964, as amended. Among the individual plaintiffs were Mary Craig, who had chosen to be sterilized in order to avoid losing her job, Elsie Nason, a 50-year-old divorcee, who had suffered a loss in compensation when she was transferred out of a job where she was exposed to lead, and Donald Penney, who had been denied a request for a leave of absence for the purpose of lowering his lead level because he intended to become a father. The court granted summary judgment for respondent, and the Court of Appeals affirmed. The Supreme Court granted certiorari.]

BLACKMUN, J. . . .

I.

The bias in Johnson Controls' policy is obvious. Fertile men, but not fertile women, are given a choice as to whether they wish to risk their reproductive health for a particular job. Section 703(a) of the Civil Rights Act of 1964, 78 Stat. 255, as amended, 42 U.S.C. § 2000e-2(a), prohibits sex-biased classifications in terms and conditions of employment, in hiring and discharging decisions, and in other employment decisions that adversely affect an employee's status. Respondent's fetal-protection policy explicitly discriminates against women on the basis of their sex. The policy excludes women with childbearing capacity from lead-exposed jobs and so creates a facial classification based on gender. . . .

First, Johnson Controls' policy classifies on the basis of gender and childbearing capacity, rather than fertility alone. Respondent does not seek to protect the unconceived children of all its employees. Despite evidence in the record about the debilitating effect of lead exposure on the male reproductive system, Johnson Controls is concerned only with the harms that may befall the unborn offspring of its female employees. . . .

"The Pregnancy Discrimination Act has now made clear that, for all Title VII purposes, discrimination based on a woman's pregnancy is, on its face, discrimination because of her sex." *Newport News Shipbuilding & Dry Dock Co. v. EEOC*, 462 U.S. 669, 684 (1983). In its use of the words "capable of bearing children" in the 1982 policy statement as the criterion for exclusion, Johnson Controls explicitly classifies on the basis of potential for pregnancy. Under the PDA, such a classification must be regarded, for Title VII purposes, in the same light as explicit sex discrimination. Respondent has chosen to treat all its female employees as potentially pregnant; that choice evinces discrimination on the basis of sex.

We concluded above that Johnson Controls' policy is not neutral because it does not apply to the reproductive capacity of the company's male employees in the same way as it applies to that of the females. Moreover, the absence of a malevolent motive does not convert a facially discriminatory policy into a neutral policy with a discriminatory effect. . . .

. . . We hold that Johnson Controls' fetal-protection policy is sex discrimination forbidden under Title VII unless respondent can establish that sex is a "bona fide occupational qualification."

II.

Under § 703(e)(1) of Title VII, an employer may discriminate on the basis of "religion, sex, or national origin in those certain instances where religion, sex, or national origin is a bona fide occupational qualification reasonably necessary to the normal operation of that particular business or enterprise." We therefore turn to the question whether Johnson Controls' fetal-protection policy is one of those "certain instances" that come within the BFOQ exception.

The BFOQ defense is written narrowly, and this Court has read it narrowly. We have read the BFOQ language of § 4(f) of the Age Discrimination in Employment Act of 1967 (ADEA), 81 Stat. 603, as amended, 29 U.S.C. § 623(f)(1), which tracks the BFOQ provision in Title VII, just as narrowly. Our emphasis on the restrictive scope of the BFOQ defense is grounded on both the language and the legislative history of § 703.

The wording of the BFOQ defense contains several terms of restriction that indicate that the exception reaches only special situations. The statute thus limits the situations in which discrimination is permissible to "certain instances" where sex discrimination is "reasonably necessary" to the "normal operation" of the "particular" business. Each one of these terms—certain, normal, particular—prevents the use of general subjective standards and favors an objective, verifiable requirement. But the most telling term is "occupational"; this indicates that these objective, verifiable requirements must concern job-related skills and aptitudes.

Johnson Controls argues that its fetal-protection policy falls within the so-called safety exception to the BFOQ. Our cases have stressed that discrimination on the basis of sex because of safety concerns is allowed only in narrow circumstances. In *Dothard v. Rawlinson,* this Court indicated that danger to a woman herself does not justify discrimination. 433 U.S., at 335, 97 S. Ct. at 2729–2730. We there allowed the employer to hire only male guards in contact areas of maximum-security male penitentiaries only because more was at stake than the "individual woman's decision to weigh and accept the risks of employment." *Ibid.* We found sex to be a BFOQ inasmuch as the employment of a female guard would create real risks of safety to others if violence broke out because the guard was a woman. Sex discrimination was tolerated because sex related to the guard's ability to do the job—maintaining prison security. We also required in *Dothard* a high correlation between sex and ability to perform job functions and refused to allow employers to use sex as a proxy for strength although it might be a fairly accurate one. . . .

Our case law, therefore, makes clear that the safety exception is limited to instances in which sex or pregnancy actually interferes with the employee's ability to perform the job. This approach is consistent with the language of the BFOQ provision itself, for it suggests that permissible distinctions based on sex must relate to ability to perform the duties of the job. Johnson Controls suggests, however, that we expand the exception to allow fetal-protection policies that mandate particular standards for pregnant or fertile women. We decline to do so. Such an expansion contradicts not only the language of the BFOQ and the narrowness of its exception but the plain language and history of the Pregnancy Discrimination Act.

The PDA's amendment to Title VII contains a BFOQ standard of its own: unless pregnant employees differ from others "in their ability or inability to work," they must be "treated the same" as other employees "for all employment-related purposes." 42 U.S.C. § 2000e(k). This language clearly sets forth Congress' remedy for discrimination on the basis of pregnancy and potential pregnancy. Women who are either pregnant or potentially pregnant, must be treated like others "similar in their ability . . . to work." *Ibid.* In other words, women as capable of doing their jobs as their male counterparts may not be forced to choose between having a child and having a job. . . .

The legislative history confirms what the language of the Pregnancy Discrimination Act compels. Both the House and the Senate Reports accompanying the legislation indicate that this statutory standard was chosen to protect female workers from being treated differently from other employees simply because of their capacity to bear children. . . .

We conclude that the language of both the BFOQ provision and the PDA which amended it, as well as the legislative history and the case law, prohibit an employer from discriminating against a woman because of her capacity to become pregnant unless her reproductive potential prevents her from performing the duties of her job. We reiterate our holdings . . . that an employer must direct its concerns about a woman's ability to perform her job safely and efficiently to those aspects of the woman's job-related activities that fall within the "essence" of the particular business.

III.

We have no difficulty concluding that Johnson Controls cannot establish a BFOQ. Fertile women, as far as appears in the record, participate in the manufacture of batteries as efficiently as anyone else. Johnson Controls' professed moral and ethical concerns about the welfare of the next generation do not suffice to establish a BFOQ of female sterility. Decisions about the welfare of future children must be left to the parents who conceive, bear, support, and raise them rather than to the employers who hire those parents. Congress has mandated this choice through Title VII, as amended by the Pregnancy Discrimination Act. Johnson Controls has attempted to exclude women because of their reproductive capacity. Title VII and the

PDA simply do not allow a woman's dismissal because of her failure to submit to sterilization.

Nor can concerns about the welfare of the next generation be considered a part of the "essence" of Johnson Controls' business. Judge Easterbrook in this case pertinently observed: "It is word play to say that 'the job' at Johnson [Controls] is to make batteries without risk to fetuses in the same way 'the job' at Western Air Lines is to fly planes without crashing." 886 F.2d, at 913.

Johnson Controls argues that it must exclude all fertile women because it is impossible to tell which women will become pregnant while working with lead. . . . Johnson Controls' fear of prenatal injury, no matter how sincere, does not begin to show that substantially all of its fertile women employees are incapable of doing their jobs.

IV.

A word about tort liability and the increased cost of fertile women in the workplace is perhaps necessary. One of the dissenting judges in this case expressed concern about an employer's tort liability and concluded that liability for a potential injury to a fetus is a social cost that Title VII does not require a company to ignore. 886 F.2d, at 904–905. It is correct to say that Title VII does not prevent the employer from having a conscience. The statute, however, does prevent sex-specific fetal-protection policies. These two aspects of the Title VII do not conflict.

More than 40 States currently recognize a right to recover for a prenatal injury based either on negligence or on wrongful death. According to Johnson Controls, however, the company complies with the lead standard developed by OSHA and warns its female employees about the damaging effects of lead. It is worth noting that OSHA gave the problem of lead lengthy consideration and concluded that "there is no basis whatsoever for the claim that women of childbearing age should be excluded from the workplace in order to protect the fetus or the course of pregnancy." Instead, OSHA established a series of mandatory protections which, taken together, "should effectively minimize any risk to the fetus and newborn child." *Id.*, at 52966. Without negligence, it would be difficult for a court to find liability on the part of the employer. If, under general tort principles, Title VII bans sex-specific fetal-protection policies, the employer fully informs the woman of the risk, and the employer has not acted negligently, the basis for holding an employer liable seems remote at best. . . .

V.

Our holding today that Title VII, as so amended, forbids sex-specific fetal-protection policies is neither remarkable nor unprecedented. Concern for a woman's existing or potential offspring historically has been the excuse for denying women equal employment opportunities. See, *e.g., Muller v. Oregon,* 208 U.S. 412, 28 S. Ct. 324, 52 L.Ed. 551 (1908). Congress in the PDA prohibited discrimination on the basis of a woman's ability to become pregnant. We do no more than hold that the Pregnancy Discrimination Act means what it says.

It is no more appropriate for the courts than it is for individual employers to decide whether a woman's reproductive role is more important to herself and her family than her economic role. Congress has left this choice to the woman as hers to make.

The judgment of the Court of Appeals is reversed and the case is remanded for further proceedings consistent with this opinion.

It is so ordered.

Justice WHITE, with whom THE CHIEF JUSTICE and Justice KENNEDY join, concurring in part and concurring in the judgment.

The Court properly holds that Johnson Controls' fetal-protection policy overtly discriminates against women, and thus is prohibited by Title VII unless it falls within the bona fide occupational qualification (BFOQ) exception, set forth at 42 U.S.C. § 2000e-2(e). The Court erroneously holds, however, that the BFOQ defense is so narrow that it could never justify a sex-specific fetal-protection policy. I nevertheless concur in the judgment of reversal because on the record before us summary judgment in favor of Johnson Controls was improperly entered by the District Court and affirmed by the Court of Appeals. . . .

[Justice Scalia concurred in the judgment of the Court.]

CASE QUESTIONS

1. Did Johnson Controls' "fetal-protection policy" discriminate against women?
2. JCI's fetal-protection policy was implemented only after eight employees became pregnant, while maintaining blood lead levels exceeding the level set by the CDC as critical. Considering JCI's moral and ethical obligations to the unborn fetuses and its possible extensive liability in future lawsuits, should not the BFOQ defense be available to it?
3. Was JCI's policy within the so-called safety exception to the BFOQ?
4. Does the PDA contain a BFOQ standard of its own?

Testing and Educational Requirement Exception

Section 703(h) of the Act authorizes the use of "any professionally developed ability test [that is not] designed, intended, or used to discriminate." The Supreme Court held in *Griggs v. Duke Power Company* that employment testing and educational requirements must be "job related"; that is, the employers must prove that the tests and educational requirements bear a demonstrable relationship to job performance. The Court ruled that the employer's lack of intention to discriminate against blacks was irrelevant when the effect was to discriminate. As stated by the Supreme Court in *Griggs*, "What Congress has commanded is that any tests used must measure the person for the job and not the person in the abstract."

The EEOC has issued *Uniform Guidelines of Employee Selection Procedures* to assist employers in their compliance with EEOC laws. The *Uniform Guidelines* establish a "four-fifths" rule of thumb for determining when an adverse impact exists in employee selection. If the selection rate for a protected class of employees is less than four-fifths of the selection rate for the rest of the workforce or the qualified applicant pool, the test or requirement has an adverse impact. While some courts use the "four-fifths" rule as a guideline, it has not been universally adopted.

The *Albemarle Paper Co. v. Moody* decision, presented in the next chapter, demonstrates the requirement that where tests used by an employer have an adverse impact on a protected class under the Act, the validation studies of these tests must be able to withstand strict scrutiny that they are job related. Validation studies demonstrate the job relatedness or lack thereof in the selection procedure in question.[54]

The two most common methods of test validation are *content validation* and *criterion-related validation.*

Content validation is the measure of how well a test correlates to the specific job tasks that make up the job. In order for the test to withstand the strict scrutiny that it may be subject to in court, a detailed *job analysis* must be conducted by the employer, thoroughly analyzing the component functions of the job in question and identifying the tasks that make up the important elements of the job. Tests must then be designed to measure performance in these important functions. An example of a selection procedure based on content validity is the administration of typing and shorthand tests for a candidate for a secretarial position. An example of a content-validated job-related physical agility test for male and female state trooper candidates, agreed to in a consent decree between the state of Maine and the U.S. Justice Department, requires the following. Each applicant must be able to:

1. Push a standard size vehicle a distance of 12 feet on a level surface,
2. Rescue an injured child from a school bus,
3. Carry one end of a stretcher with a 175-pound mannequin a distance of 200 feet,
4. Climb a flatbed truck, and
5. Run 1.5 miles in a designated time period.[55]

Criterion-related validation is established by demonstrating that there is a significant positive correlation between success on the test (predictor) in question and comparative success on some measures of job performance (criteria). A *predictive* criterion validation study involves a test during the hiring process administered to a sample group, with members of the sample group being selected without reference to their test scores. Later the actual job performance of the sample group is evaluated and compared with the test scores to see if the test accurately predicted performance. The *concurrent*

---

[54] The *Uniform Guidelines of Employee Selection Procedures* represents a summary statement of legal and validation standards for determining the proper use of tests and other selection procedures in order to assist employers and others to comply with federal law prohibiting discriminatory employment practices. 29 CFR § 1607.

[55] *United States v. State of Maine,* CA-83-0195P, May 26, 1983.

criterion validation study involves the administration of a test to current employees, with their actual job performance being compared with their test scores to see if the test has validity. An example of a criterion-related validation study would be either a predictive or concurrent study to determine whether salespersons scoring higher on an intelligence test also tended to be among the better sales performers and whether this relationship was statistically significant.

Because of the fear of court rejection of employment tests in hiring practices and because of the expense involved in conducting job analyses, designing tests, and conducting validation studies, many employers abandoned the use of written tests. This is unfortunate since a properly designed test can be one of the least discriminatory ways of selecting employees.

Courts will accept prior court-approved validation studies developed for a different employer in a different state or region so long as it is demonstrated that the job for which the test was initially validated is essentially the same job function for which the test is currently being used. Thus a firefighters test that had been validated in a study in California was accepted as valid when later used in Richmond, Virginia. Such application is called *validity generalization.* Based on the use of validity generalization, employers seeking to use employment tests may be able to rely on validation studies for like job classifications prepared by other employers in the same industry or by professional test developers.

The Civil Rights Act of 1991 makes it an unlawful employment practice for an employer to adjust scores or use different cutoff scores or otherwise alter the results of employment tests on the basis of race, color, religion, sex, or national origin. This provision addresses the so-called race norming issue, whereby the results of hiring and promotion tests are adjusted to assure that a minimum number of minorities are included in application pools. The federal government's method of grading its General Aptitude Test Battery (GATB) based on percentiles within racial grouping was made unlawful by the 1991 law.

Seniority System Exception

Of the three major exceptions to Section 703, the one most important to workers is the seniority system exception found in Section 703(h). It provides that differences in employment conditions that result from a bona fide seniority system are sanctioned as long as the differences do not stem from an intention to discriminate. The term *seniority system* is generally understood to mean a set of rules that ensures that workers with longer years of continuous service for an employer will have a priority claim to a job over others with fewer years of service. Because such rules provide workers with considerable job security, organized labor has continually and successfully fought to secure seniority provisions in collective bargaining agreements.

In the *Teamsters v. United States*[56] decision, the court held that by virtue of Section 703(h), a bona fide seniority system does not become unlawful simply because it may perpetuate pre-Title VII discrimination. In *American Tobacco Company v. Patterson,*[57] the Supreme Court held that Section 703(h) is applicable as well to bona fide seniority

---

[56] 431 U.S. 324 (1977).
[57] 456 U.S. 63, 28 FEP (1982).

systems created after the passage of Title VII. As a result of the *American Tobacco* decision, even though a seniority system has disparate or adverse impact on a protected class of persons under the Act, such alone is insufficient to invalidate the seniority system. To invalidate a seniority system it has to be shown that the system is not bona fide because the *actual motive* of the parties in adopting the seniority system was to discriminate. In *Pullman-Standard v. Swint,*[58] the Supreme Court recognized that adverse impact on minorities is part of the evidence to be considered by the trial court in reaching a finding of fact on whether there was a discriminatory intent.

In *Firefighters Local 1784 v. Stotts,*[59] the city of Memphis planned to lay off employees due to budget cuts and had agreed with the city's unions that "seniority . . . shall govern layoffs and recalls." Minority firefighters sought a court injunction preventing the layoffs based on seniority in order to protect the employment gains of minority firefighters under court-approved consent decrees in 1974 and 1980. The district court approved and the court of appeals upheld a modified layoff plan that resulted in nonminority employees with more seniority than minority employees being laid off or reduced in rank. The Supreme Court reversed the lower courts, citing *Teamsters* as a precedent for its position that Section 703(h) permits, as in this case, the routine application of a seniority system absent proof of an intention to discriminate. The Supreme Court pointed out that there was no finding that any black protected from the layoffs had been an actual victim of discrimination and had received an award of competitive seniority.

In 1979 the IBEW and AT&T Technologies executed a new collective bargaining agreement making seniority in "tester" jobs dependent upon the time spent in a tester position, rather than the previous rule of plantwide seniority. Three years later, when a group of women were bumped from tester positions under the 1979 seniority language, they challenged the seniority provision in court, contending that the purpose of the 1979 change was to protect incumbent testers, who were mostly men, from female employees, who had greater plantwide seniority. In *Lorance v. AT&T Technologies, Inc.,*[60] the Supreme Court ruled that the lawsuit must be dismissed as time-barred since the women did not file their claim with the EEOC within the 180-day or 300-day requirements of Title VII. The Civil Rights Act of 1991 overturned the *Lorance* decision with respect to a seniority system which has been adopted for "intentionally discriminatory purposes." And the 1991 Act provides that a seniority system that *intentionally* discriminates, regardless of whether such discrimination is apparent, may be challenged when the system is adopted, when an individual becomes subject to it, or when a person is actually injured by it.[61]

SECTION 10—SELECTED CONSTITUTIONAL THEORIES ON DISCRIMINATION

Many employment discrimination problems have been approached on constitutional rather than statutory grounds, especially when public employees are involved. When

---

[58] 456 U.S. 273, 28 FEP 1073 (1982).
[59] 467 U.S. 561 (1984).
[60] 109 S.Ct. 2261 (1989).
[61] Section 112, Civil Rights Act of 1991.

statutory solutions, such as those provided by Title VII, are either inapplicable, inadequate, or too time-consuming, the constitutional guarantees of equal protection and due process found in the Fifth and Fourteenth Amendments have been argued in an attempt to remedy the allegedly discriminatory employment practices.

Race Discrimination

Since the passage of Title VII, cases involving alleged racially discriminatory employment practices have generally been argued in the courts on statutory, rather than constitutional grounds. This was not the case, however, in *Washington v. Davis*.[62] Here, the Supreme Court was faced with the question of whether a written personnel test used by the District of Columbia's police department to measure verbal skill, and failed by a higher percentage of blacks than whites, was violative of the equal protection component of the Due Process Clause of the Fifth Amendment. The district court ruled that the test was a reliable indication of job performance and was not designed to, and did not, discriminate against otherwise qualified blacks. The court of appeals reversed, basing its decision on the standards enunciated in *Griggs v. Duke Power Co*. The court of appeals held that the lack of discriminatory intent was irrelevant, that four times as many blacks as whites failed the test, and that such disproportionate impact sufficed to establish a constitutional violation. The Supreme Court reversed the court of appeals' decision and reinstated the order of the district court upholding the use of the test. The Supreme Court held that although disproportionate impact is not irrelevant, where a law or official conduct such as the administering of a personnel test is not designed to discriminate and serves legitimate governmental interests, it will not be struck down simply because it burdens blacks more than whites.

Sex Discrimination

The *Cleveland Board of Education v. LaFleur*[63] decision was initially successful in the court of appeals utilizing Equal Protection Clause arguments against mandatory maternity leave rules for pregnant teachers. However, the Supreme Court sustained the court of appeals on the basis of the Due Process Clause, finding the challenged maternity leave rules to be violative of due process since they created a conclusive presumption that every teacher who is four or five months pregnant is physically incapable of continuing her duties, whereas any such teacher's inability to continue past a fixed pregnancy period is an individual matter.

Freedom of the press contentions relating to employment opportunities advertising were considered by the U.S. Supreme Court. In *Pittsburgh Press Company v. Pittsburgh Commission on Human Relations*[64] the Supreme Court upheld an order of the Pittsburgh Commission on Human Relations that forbade placing help-wanted advertisements under the heading "Jobs–Male Interest" and "Jobs–Female Interest." The

---

[62] 426 U.S. 229 (1976).
[63] 414 U.S. 632 (1974).
[64] 413 U.S. 376 (1973).

majority of the Court took the position that the order came under the "commercial speech" exception to the First Amendment, while the four dissenters viewed it as a prior restraint on the press. The commission had ordered the *Pittsburgh Press* to stop using the headings in its help-wanted columns after the National Organization for Women, Inc., complained.

Speaking for the Supreme Court, Mr. Justice Powell held that the case came under the commercial speech doctrine of *Valentine v. Chrestensen*,[65] which sustained a city ordinance that banned the distribution of a handbill soliciting customers for a tour of a submarine. The Court distinguished the commercial speech cases from the holding of *New York Times v. Sullivan*,[66] a libel suit in which the Court held that paid political advertising was entitled to First Amendment protection. The help-wanted advertisements in *Pittsburgh Press*, the Court held, do not express a position on "whether as a matter of social policy, certain positions ought to be filled by members of one or the other sex. . . . Each is no more than a proposal of possible employment. The advertisements are thus classic examples of commercial speech." The Court added that nothing in its holding prevented the *Pittsburgh Press* from publishing advertisements commenting on the ordinance and the commission, or its enforcement practices, or the propriety of sex preferences in employment.

In his dissent Chief Justice Burger called the decision "a disturbing enlargement of the 'commercial speech' doctrine." Mr. Justice Douglas argued that the newspaper could print whatever it pleased without censorship or restraint by government. The want ads express the preference of the employer for the kind of help the employer wants, Justice Douglas said, and the commission might issue an order against the employer if discrimination in employment was shown. Mr. Justice Stewart, whose dissent Justice Douglas joined, declared that the issue was whether government "can tell a newspaper in advance what it can print and what it cannot." Mr. Justice Blackmun also dissented, substantially for the reasons stated by Mr. Justice Stewart.

In *University of Pennsylvania v. EEOC*,[67] Rosalie Tung filed a charge with the EEOC alleging discrimination on the basis of race, sex, and national origin, after she was denied tenure at the Wharton School. The university resisted an EEOC subpoena which sought Tung's tenure review file on the basis that it contained "confidential peer review information." The university argued that disclosure of peer evaluations would be a significant infringement on the university's First Amendment right of academic freedom, because the disclosure would have a "chilling effect" on candid evaluations by peers of tenure candidates. The Supreme Court rejected the university's position. It pointed out that Congress expressly extended Title VII's coverage to educational institutions without restriction on the right of access to evidence. The Court also stated that the claimed injury to academic freedom is speculative, since confidentiality is not the norm in all peer review systems; and the Court could not assume that most peer evaluators would become less candid if the possibility of disclosure increased.

---

[65] 316 U.S. 52 (1942).
[66] 376 U.S. 254 (1964).
[67] 110 S.Ct. 577 (1990).

Chapter Questions and Problems

1. List the major statutes dealing with the regulation of equal rights in employment.
2. Young, an African-American woman, sued the United Method Church under Title VII of the Civil Rights Act claiming the church discriminated against her based on race and color in refusing to promote her from the status of probationary minister to that of "elder" in the church. Will a court be allowed to determine if Young was qualified for this promotion but was turned down because of her race and color? [*Young v. Northern Illinois Conference of United Methodist Church*, 21 F.3d 184 (7th Cir.)]
3. Mercy Prado worked for L. Luria & Son Inc., a Florida-based general merchandise retail chain. She worked as the customer service manager at Luria's Coral Gables store. The store had a policy for workers of never speaking Spanish on the job unless a customer spoke it first. Her boss prohibited all employees from speaking Spanish before the store opened and even on breaks. Ms. Prado contends that she was so humiliated by her boss's chants of "English, English, English" that she quit. Luria's defends that the store manager in question did not speak any Spanish. And the store contends that Ms. Prado quit because she did not like the long hours and the pressure. Ms. Prado does not deny that job-related stress existed. She stated that her boss stood outside the bathroom listening for Spanish, and warned her to switch to English when she came out. Before quitting she told her co-workers, "This is a nightmare!" Did the enforcement of the employer's English-only rule effect a constructive discharge of Ms. Prado? [See A. Davis, "English-Only Rules Spur Workers to Speak Legalese," *Wall Street Journal*, Jan. 23, 1997, p. B-1.]
4. Continental Photo, Inc., is a portrait photography company. Alex Riley, a black man, applied for a position as a photographer with Continental. Riley submitted an application and was interviewed. In response to a question on a written application, Riley indicated that he had been convicted for forgery, a felony, six years prior to the interview and had received a suspended sentence. He also noted that he would discuss the matter with his interviewer if necessary. The subject of the forgery conviction was subsequently not mentioned by Continental's personnel director in his interview with Riley. Riley's application for employment was eventually rejected. Riley inquired as to the reason for his rejection by Continental. The personnel director, Geuther, explained to him that the prior felony conviction disclosed on his application and an unsatisfactory test score were the reasons for his rejection.

    Riley contended that the refusal to hire him because of his conviction record was actually discrimination against him because of his race in violation of Title VII. Riley felt that his successful completion of a five-year probation without incident and his steady work over the years qualified him for the job.

    Continental maintained that since its photographers handle approximately $10,000 in cash per year, its policy of not hiring applicants whose honesty was questionable was justified. Continental's policy excluded all applicants with felony convictions.

    What factors must be weighed in this case? Has Continental violated Title VII? Decide. Would the result be different if Riley had been a convicted murderer? [*Continental Photo, Inc.*, 26 FEP 1799 (EEOC)]
5. Sambo's Restaurants maintained a uniform grooming policy concerning each of its over one thousand establishments nationwide. The policy forbade restaurant

managers and other restaurant personnel to wear facial hair, with an exception for a neatly trimmed mustache. Sambo's has consistently enforced this grooming policy since the restaurant chain's inception in 1957. Grooming standards similar to Sambo's standards were common in the restaurant industry. Sambo's felt that the grooming policy reflected the restaurant's public image as a family-oriented business where food was served under sanitary conditions.

Mohen S. Tucker was a member of the Sikh religion. The practice of Sikhism forbids the cutting or shaving of facial hair and also requires the wearing of a turban that covers the head. In accordance with the dictates of his religion, Tucker wore a long beard. Tucker applied for a position as a Sambo's restaurant manager. While filling out the application, he was informed of Sambo's grooming policy, which would require that he shave his beard or be denied the position. Tucker informed Sambo's that it was against his religion to shave his beard. Sambo's responded that no exceptions were allowed under the grooming policy for religious reasons and denied his application.

Tucker brought a court action through the EEOC, claiming that Sambo's had violated Title VII by refusing to accommodate his religious practice. Sambo's denied any religious discrimination.

What standard of review should be employed to decide this case? What factors will be relevant? Decide the case. [*EEOC v. Sambo's of Georgia, Inc.*, 27 FEP 1210 (D.C. N.D. Ga.)]

6. Mercy Health Center in Oklahoma City, Oklahoma, was a hospital that provided extensive medical services including obstetrical and gynecological care. The labor and delivery area of the hospital hosted an average of 148 deliveries a month. Forty to fifty percent of those births were life threatening to the mother or infant and were therefore classified as high risk. Staff nurses in the labor and delivery area were involved in extensive contact with the expectant mother. Their duties included assessment and examination of the mother, which consisted of frequent contact with the mother's body. In order to minimize the tension, fear, and stress that accompanies the labor and delivery experience, Mercy did not hire males for the position of staff nurse in the labor and delivery area. The hospital cited its paramount concern for the privacy and comfort of the mother as a basis for its policy. Mercy also conducted a survey of parents involved in prenatal classes and found that 60 to 70 percent of the mothers and a larger percentage of the fathers objected to the use of male nurses in the labor and delivery area.

Andre Fontain applied for a job as a staff nurse in the labor and delivery area at Mercy. Because of the policy, he was denied employment.

Through the EEOC, Fontain alleged that Mercy discriminated against him on the basis of sex in violation of Title VII. The hospital denied the charge of discrimination.

Has Mercy violated Title VII? If so, what defense, if any, is available to the hospital? Decide the case. [*EEOC v. Mercy Health Center*, 29 FEP 159 (D.C. W.D. Okla.)]

7. DiMillo's Floating Restaurant on Long Wharf, Portland, Maine, ran a help-wanted ad in the *Portland Press Herald*, which read in part:

Bartenders/Cocktail Service, Experienced Only. Applicants must be able to wear uniforms sizes 8 to 12.

Complaints were made to the Maine Human Rights Commission. Antonio DiMillo defended the ad in a newspaper interview, expressing the view that all over the country the restaurant industry routinely hires waitresses based on their size. DiMillo was quoted as saying: "Do you go out to eat and drink? Do you like to see a fat big broad coming at you?"

Against whom, if anyone, does the ad discriminate? What responsibility, if any does the newspaper have in publishing employment advertisements that are found to discriminate? [See page 13 of the *Portland Press Herald*, Vol. 121, No. 127, Thursday, Nov. 18, 1982.]

8. Sylvia Hayes worked as a staff technician in the radiology department of Shelby Memorial Hospital, a county hospital located in Birmingham, Alabama. In early October Hayes was told by her physician that she was pregnant. When Hayes informed the doctor of her occupation as an X-ray technician, the doctor advised Hayes that she could continue working until the end of April as long as she followed standard safety precautions. On October 8 Hayes told Gail Nell, the director of radiology at Shelby, that she had discovered she was two months pregnant. On October 14 Hayes was discharged by the hospital. The hospital's reason for terminating Hayes was its concern for the safety of her fetus given the X-ray exposure that occurs during employment as an X-ray technician.

Hayes brought an action under Title VII claiming that her discharge was unlawfully based on her condition of pregnancy. She cited scientific evidence and the practice of other hospitals where pregnant women were allowed to remain in their jobs as X-ray technicians.

The hospital claimed that Hayes's discharge was based on business necessity. Specifically, the hospital claimed that the potential for future liability existed if an employee's fetus was damaged by radiation encountered at the workplace.

Has the hospital violated Title VII by discharging Hayes? What remedy, if any is appropriate in this case? Decide the case. [*Hayes v. Shelby Memorial Hospital*, 29 FEP 1173 (D.C. N.D. Ala.)]

9. Glenwood H. MacDougal, chairman of the Office Occupations Department at Northern Maine Vocational Technical Institute in Presque Isle, claimed that between September 1985 and September 1986 he received in the mail sexually suggestive items. Poems, letters, and cards were all signed "Love, Charlene." MacDougal's attorney stated that MacDougal became emotionally upset because of this, was forced to seek psychological counseling, and had been out of work for over six weeks due to these emotional problems. MacDougal brought suit against three female teachers at the institute, charging them with sexual harassment. MacDougal sought $1.6 million in damages.

The three teachers contended that there had been a history of good-humored practical jokes played by the faculty members at the school, that MacDougal himself participated, and that all they were doing was playing a practical joke on MacDougal. They claimed that they had no intention of harassing him.

Does the EEOC guidelines definition of sexual harassment apply to men? Assuming, for the sake of discussion, that men are protected from sexual harassment under the guidelines, was there a violation of the guidelines? What is the measure of damages in a case such as this? [*MacDougal v. Gregg, et al.*, the *Boston Herald*, Feb.26, 1987, p. 23]

10. A teenage female high school student named Salazar was employed parttime at Church's Fried Chicken restaurant. Salazar was hired and supervised by Simon Garza, the assistant manager of the restaurant. Garza had complete supervisory powers when the restaurant's manager, Garza's roommate, was absent. Salazar alleged that while she worked at the restaurant, Garza would refer to her and all other females by a Spanish term that she found objectionable. According to Salazar, Garza once purportedly made a lecherous comment about Salazar's body and repeatedly asked her about her personal life. On another occasion, Garza allegedly physically removed eyeshadow from Salazar's face because he felt that it looked ugly. Salazar also claimed that one night she was restrained in a back room of the restaurant while Garza and another employee fondled her. Later that night, when Salazar told a customer about what had happened, she was fired. Salazar believed that she was fired because she disclosed this incident.

Salazar filed an action under Title VII against Garza and Church's Fried Chicken, Inc., alleging sexual harassment. The defendants moved for summary judgment. Garza, who has since stopped working at Church's, contended that even if Salazar's allegations were true, she had not established sexual harassment under Title VII. Church's, the corporate defendant, maintained that it should not be held liable under Title VII for Garza's harassment. Church's grounded its argument on the existence of a published "fair treatment policy" and a grievance procedure that was not invoked by Salazar.

If Salazar's allegations are true, has she stated an actionable case under Title VII? May Church's be held liable for Garza's actions? If the case proceeds to trial, what remedies may Salazar seek? [*Salazar v. Church's Fried Chicken, Inc.*, 44 FEP 472 (S.D. Tex.)]

11. Sandra Shope had worked as chief of county housing services in Loudoun County, Virginia, for some six years when Timothy Krawczel was made her boss. Shope testified that Krawczel pounded his fists on her desk and called her a "stupid woman" in front of co-workers and berated her as "weak like a woman." Krawczel told Shope "I'm the boss at home and I will be the boss here." Shope testified that Krawczel never touched her or sought sexual favors. Krawczel was not abusive to men in the office; but the evidence suggested that other women in the office were subjected to "insults." The county defended that Krawczel was strict with Shope because she was not doing her job well. Shope responded that she worked more than 50 hours per week, and was a respected housing official. Shope sought relief from the all-male County Board of Supervisors, but her complaints were ignored. She became physically ill as a result of the treatment by Krawczel, and ultimately resigned.

Shope contends that the county and Krawczel constructively discharged her in violation of Title VII. She seeks back pay, compensatory damages for the pain and suffering involved, and punitive damages from Krawczel.

Can the county and Krawczel be guilty of sexual harassment where no sexual favors are sought and no sexual conduct is involved? Is the fact that Krawczel was not abusive to any male employees of any legal significance? Could the county be required to pay punitive damages? Decide. [*Shope v. Loudoun County, The Washington Post*, col. 3, p. 1, June 20, 1992]

12. Hooters Inc. is an Atlanta-based restaurant chain with over 170 locations. The company hires only female waitresses. Hooters states that "a lot of places serve good

burgers. The Hooters Girls, with their charm and all-American sex appeal, are what customers come for." The waitresses wear bright orange hot pants and tight, white T-shirts or tank tops. Several waitresses brought suit against the restaurant for sexual harassment, alleging that it established a work environment in which its customers felt free to make sexual comments and advances to waitresses. Some argue that the provocative uniforms and the name of the restaurant itself should lead to liability for Hooters Inc. Others argue that waitresses should not be able to recover for conduct they clearly should have anticipated at the time they chose to work for Hooters. What effect should the *Vinson* decision's pronouncement on speech and dress have on such a case? What effect should management policy to immediately remove offensive patrons have on a court case? Decide.

Four Chicago men sued Hooters for its policy of only hiring female waitresses. They contend that such a policy is sex discrimination. In the sex appeal restaurant business does Hooters Inc. have a BFOQ defense? Hooters Inc. has taken out full-page newspaper advertisements featuring a burly man with a blond wig wearing a Hooters uniform, holding a plate of chicken wings in protest of an EEOC recommendation that the restaurant hire male waiters. See *Wilson v. Southwest Airlines Co.*, 517 F. Supp 292 (N.D. Tex. 1981), where the BFOQ defense was narrowly applied against the airline's female-only flight attendants policy under a marketing scheme based on sex appeal. Southwest is in the business of transporting passengers. What if a primary aspect of Hooters Inc. is not just serving food and drink but sex appeal? Should the BFOQ defense succeed? Decide the case involving the four male applicants for the wait staff positions.

2
Procedures and Remedies

SECTION 11—BURDEN OF PROOF

As stated previously, there are two legal theories for a plaintiff to use in proving a case of unlawful discrimination: disparate treatment and disparate impact.

Disparate treatment is intentional employment discrimination where, for example, women are treated less favorably than men, or blacks are treated less favorably than whites. The burden of proof for disparate treatment cases is developed in this section.

Disparate impact is a theory of employment discrimination that focuses on the consequences of an employer's selection procedures for hiring and promotions. The theory was developed in the *Griggs v. Duke Power Company* decision. The practice occurs where an employer's facially neutral employment practices have a significant adverse or disparate impact on a protected group, and the employer is unable to show that the practice is job related. Proof of a discriminatory motive is not required. The burden of proof for disparate impact cases is also developed in this section.

Proof in Disparate Treatment Cases

In *McDonnell Douglas Corp v. Green*[1] the Supreme Court discussed how a *prima facie* showing of discrimination in the context of a disparate treatment case may be established. The plaintiff must show (1) that he or she belongs to a group protected from discrimination under Title VII on the basis of characteristics such as race, color, national origin, sex, or religion; (2) that he or she applied and was qualified for a job for which the employer was seeking applicants; (3) that, despite being qualified, he or she was rejected; and (4) that, after he or she was rejected, the position remained open and the employer continued to seek applicants whose qualifications were similar to those of the plaintiff. Once such a *prima facie* case is established, the burden shifts to the employer to articulate some legitimate, nondiscriminatory reason for its action. If such a reason is forthcoming, then the plaintiff is afforded an opportunity to demonstrate by a preponderance of the evidence that the supposedly valid reasons for the employer's actions were in fact a cover-up or pretext for a discriminatory decision.

Confusion existed in the federal trial courts and appeals courts as to the precise nature of the shifts of burdens of proof and persuasion after the plaintiff made out a *prima facie* case under the *McDonnell Douglas* model. The *Burdine* decision, presented in this section, confirms that the employer rebuts a *prima facie* case by producing admissible evidence of a legitimate reason for its decision to reject the plaintiff. Legitimate, nondiscriminatory reasons offered by an employer could be lesser comparative qualifications, inability to work in harmony with others, or violations of employer rules. Once a *prima facie* case is rebutted by the employer, the plaintiff can prevail by showing that the employer was motivated by a discriminatory reason or that the employer's reason is not believable. Under *Burdine*, then, the employer has an intermediate burden of production, but the ultimate burden of proving that the defendant-employer intentionally discriminated against the plaintiff remains with the plaintiff at all times.

The Supreme Court made an additional attempt to clarify its numerous decisions on proof in disparate treatment cases in *Postal Service v. Aikens*,[2] focusing in detail on its *McDonnell Douglas* and *Burdine* precedents. Under the *McDonnell Douglas-Burdine* model, as applied in *Aikens*, a three-stage process is followed. Stage 1 focuses on the plaintiff's burden to present sufficient evidence of discrimination to establish a *prima facie* case according to the elements set forth in *McDonnell Douglas*. At the end of the plaintiff's presentation of evidence, the district court may sustain the defendant-employer's motion to dismiss the case for lack of a *prima facie* case, and the case would be terminated. Stage 2 is reached if the court determines that the plaintiff has made out a *prima facie* case. At this stage the defendant must respond with evidence of a nondiscriminatory reason for the plaintiff's rejection. Stage 3 is sometimes referred to as the "pretext" stage in reference to *Burdine*. As set forth in *Burdine*, the plaintiff has the right to offer additional evidence rebutting the employer's asserted reason for the rejection. Alternatively, the plaintiff may simply rely on the evidence of a discriminatory motive introduced as part of its *prima facie* case. The Civil Rights Act of 1991 allows either party

---

[1] 411 U.S. 792 (1972).
[2] 460 U.S. 711 (1983).

to obtain a jury trial in these disparate treatment (intentional discrimination) cases where compensatory or punitive damages are sought. It is at this third stage that the jury must reach the ultimate question of fact by deciding which party's explanation of the employer's motivation in rejecting the plaintiff for employment is to be believed. The jury will weigh all the evidence of record in reaching its decision, with the ultimate burden of proof on the plaintiff.

In *St. Mary's Honor Center v. Hicks*,[3] decided in 1993 after passage of the Civil Rights Act of 1991, the Supreme Court reaffirmed the *McDonnell Douglas-Burdine* model. The *Hicks* Court concluded:

> We reaffirm today what we said in *Aikens*:
>
> [The] question facing triers of fact in discrimination cases is both sensitive and difficult. The prohibitions against discrimination contained in the Civil Rights Act of 1964 reflect an important national policy. There will seldom be 'eyewitness' testimony as to the employer's mental processes. But none of this means that trial courts or reviewing courts should treat discrimination differently from other ultimate questions of fact. Nor should they make their inquiry even more difficult by applying legal rules which were devised to govern the 'basic allocation of burdens and order of presentation of proof,' in deciding this ultimate question.[4]

As will be seen in later chapters, the *McDonnell Douglas* model is also applied to age and disability discrimination cases.

Mixed-Motive Cases

In *Price Waterhouse v. Hopkins*,[5] the Supreme Court held that even after a plaintiff proved that gender discrimination was a motivating factor in an employment decision, an employer could avoid liability for intentional discrimination in so-called mixed-motive cases if the employer could demonstrate by a preponderance of the evidence that the same adverse employment decision would have been taken based on other business considerations containing no discriminatory motives. Ann Hopkins was not made a partner at the Price Waterhouse accounting firm. Some evidence indicated that she was abrasive with staff members, a legitimate reason not to promote a person to partner. Other evidence indicated that the selection process was influenced by gender stereotyping, including one partner who advised her to improve her chances for partnership by stating, "walk more femininely, talk more femininely, dress more femininely, wear

---

[3] 113 S.Ct. 2742 (1993). In *Hicks*, Melvin Hicks alleged he was demoted and discharged because he is black, in violation of Title VII. A federal appeals court ruled that once Hicks proved that all of his employer's reasons for demoting and discharging him were not believable, he was entitled to judgment as a matter of law. In a 5–4 split the Supreme Court reversed, and held that once a plaintiff in a Title VII case shows that an employer's actual reasons for taking adverse job actions were not believable, a ruling in favor of the plaintiff is not required, but a jury can draw an inference that the employer intentionally discriminated against the plaintiff and no additional proof of discrimination is required by the plaintiff.

[4] *Id.* at 2756. See also *Kobrin v. University of Minn.*, 34 F.3d 698 (8th Cir. 1994) (plaintiff retains burden of persuading trier of fact of discrimination).

[5] 109 S.Ct. 1775 (1989).

makeup, have your hair styled, and wear jewelry."[6] On remand from the Supreme Court Ms. Hopkins was awarded the partnership, back pay, and attorneys' fees.

The Civil Rights Act of 1991 overturned the *Price Waterhouse v. Hopkins* decision in certain respects. The 1991 Act provides that if the plaintiff shows that a statutorily prohibited factor, such as race, sex, or religion, motivated an employment action, an unlawful employment practice is established at that point, even if other lawful factors also motivated the action. If the employer is able to demonstrate that the same adverse employment decision would have been made in the absence of the unlawful motive, a court is limited to awarding declaratory relief and attorneys' fees and costs to the plaintiff. It may not award the plaintiff "admission, reinstatement, hiring, promotion, or payment" of back pay or damages. Of course, if the employer is not able to meet this shifting burden of proof, the plaintiff is entitled to full remedies.

Disparate Impact Cases: *Wards Cove* and the 1991 Act

In *Wards Cove Packing Co. v. Atonio,*[7] the Supreme Court changed the burden of proof in Title VII disparate impact cases. Under *Wards Cove* a plaintiff was required to (1) prove a relevant statistical disparity in the workplace and (2) demonstrate that a specific or particular employment practice created the disparate impact under attack. The burden then shifted to the employer to produce evidence that the identified practice was justified. This "business justification" test lessened the burden on the employer that had existed since *Griggs v. Duke Power*, which placed a "business necessity" affirmative defense on the employer. Moreover, under *Wards Cove* the employer's burden was not to persuade but only to produce evidence in support of its position. The ultimate burden of proving the lack of business justification for the practice remains with the plaintiff. The Supreme Court recognized in *Wards Cove* that a plaintiff may establish unlawful disparate impact if it is shown that a less discriminatory "alternative practice" is available but the employer refuses to adopt it. However, consideration of cost and the burdens on the employer are relevant considerations.

The Civil Rights Act of 1991 (CRA 91) specifically responded to the *Wards Cove* decision. Section 2(2) of the 1991 Act set forth the finding that:

(2) the decision of the Supreme Court in *Wards Cove Packing Co. v. Atonio*, 490 U.S. 642 (1989) has weakened the scope and effectiveness of Federal civil rights protections. . . .

And Section 3(2) of the 1991 Act set forth as one of its purposes:

(2) to codify the concepts of 'business necessity' and 'job-related' enunciated by the Supreme Court in *Griggs v. Duke Power Co.*, 401 U.S. 424 (1971), and in the other Supreme Court decisions prior to *Wards Cove Packing Co. v. Atonio*. . . .

The 1991 law reaffirmed segments of *Wards Cove*, however. The case's discussion of the statistical comparisons needed to form a proper basis for initial inquiry still

---

[6] *Id.* at 1782.
[7] 109 S.Ct. 2115 (1989).

applies. Plaintiffs must still demonstrate that each particular challenged employment practice causes a disparate impact. An exception exists to this causation requirement where the plaintiff can demonstrate that the elements of the employer's decision-making process are not capable of separation for such a causation analysis. In such a situation the process may be analyzed as one employment practice. The 1991 Act allows a plaintiff to prove a case of disparate impact by demonstrating that less discriminatory alternative employment practices could be utilized but the employer refuses to adopt such practices. The extent of the proof requirements and considerations of costs and employer needs were purposely left unresolved by Congress, to be settled according to the law "as it existed" on the day before the *Wards Cove* decision.

Disparate impact analysis is not limited to "objective" employment practices such as testing or educational requirements. It is also applicable to subjective employment practices such as personal interviews and performance appraisals.[8] Disparate impact is not properly measured in terms of "bottom line" results of a hiring process, but rather at any point in the selection process where individuals are disproportionately excluded from equal employment opportunities.[9]

Proof in Disparate Impact Cases

Section 105 of the 1991 Act specifically overruled the *Wards Cove* burden of proof analysis; the Act codified the concepts of "business necessity" and "job related" enunciated in *Griggs*. The new shifting burdens of proof scheme that resulted is as follows:

1. The plaintiff must "demonstrate" through relevant statistical comparisons that a particular employment practice used in selecting or promoting employees "causes" a "disparate impact." A more complete discussion on statistical cases is presented in Section 102.
2. The defending employer may then proceed to "demonstrate" that a specific employment practice does not cause the disparate impact, *or*
3. The defending employer must demonstrate (with the burden of persuasion, not just production of evidence) that the challenged practice is "job related" for the position in question and consistent with "business necessity."

TEXAS DEPARTMENT OF COMMUNITY AFFAIRS v. BURDINE

Supreme Court of the United States, 450 U.S. 248 (1981).

[Petitioner, the Texas Department of Community Affairs (TDCA), hired the respondent, Burdine, in January 1972 for the position of accounting clerk in the Public Service Careers Division (PSC). PSC provided training and employment opportunities in the public sector for unskilled workers. When hired, Burdine possessed several years' experience in employment training. She was promoted

---

[8] *Watson v. Fort Worth Bank and Trust Co.*, 47 FEP 102 (Sup. Ct. 1988).
[9] *Connecticut v. Teal*, 457 U.S. 440 (1982).

to Field Services Coordinator in July 1972. Her supervisor resigned in November of that year, and she was assigned additional duties. Although she applied for the supervisor's position of Project Director, the position remained vacant for six months.

PSC was funded completely by the United States Department of Labor. The Department was seriously concerned about inefficiencies at PSC. In February 1973 the Department notified the Executive Director of TDCA, B. R. Fuller, that it would terminate PSC the following month. TDCA officials, assisted by Burdine, persuaded the Department to continue funding the program, conditioned upon PSC reforming its operations. Among the agreed conditions were the appointment of a permanent Project Director and a complete reorganization of the PSC staff. After consulting with personnel within TDCA, Fuller hired a male from another division of the agency as Project Director. In reducing the PSC staff, he terminated Burdine along with two other employees, and retained another male, Walz, as the only professional employee in the division. It is undisputed that respondent had maintained her application for the position of Project Director and had requested to remain with TDCA. Burdine soon was rehired by TDCA and assigned to another division of the agency.

Burdine filed this suit in the United States district court alleging that the failure to promote and the subsequent decision to terminate her had been predicated on gender discrimination in violation of Title VII. After a bench trial, the district court held that neither decision was based on gender discrimination. The court relied on the testimony of Fuller that the employment decisions necessitated by the commands of the Department of Labor were based on consultation among trusted advisors and nondiscriminatory evaluation of the relative qualifications of the individuals involved. He testified that the three individuals terminated did not work well together and that TDCA thought that eliminating this problem would improve PSC's efficiency. The court ac-

cepted this explanation as rational and, in effect, found no evidence that the decisions not to promote and to terminate respondent were prompted by gender discrimination. The Court of Appeals for the Fifth Circuit reversed in part the holding of the district court that Fuller's testimony sufficiently had rebutted Burdine's prima facie case of gender discrimination in the decision to terminate her employment at PSC. The court of appeals reaffirmed its previously announced views that the defendant in a Title VII case bears the burden of proving by a preponderance of the evidence the existence of legitimate nondiscriminatory reasons for the employment action and that the defendant also must prove by objective evidence that those hired or promoted were better qualified than the plaintiff. The Supreme Court granted certiorari.]

POWELL, J.

The burden of establishing a prima facie case of disparate treatment is not onerous. The plaintiff must prove by a preponderance of the evidence that she applied for an available position, for which she was qualified, but was rejected under circumstances which give rise to an inference of unlawful discrimination. The prima facie case serves an important function in the litigation: it eliminates the most common nondiscriminatory reasons for the plaintiff's rejection. As the Court explained in *Furnco Construction Co. v. Waters*, 438 U.S. 567, 577 (1978), the prima facie case "raises an inference of discrimination only because we presume these acts, if otherwise unexplained, are more likely than not based on the consideration of impermissible factors." Establishment of the prima facie case in effect creates a presumption that the employer unlawfully discriminated against the employee. If the trier of fact believes the plaintiff's evidence, and if the employer is silent in the face of the presumption, the court must enter judgment for the plaintiff because no issue of fact remains in the case.

The burden that shifts to the defendant, therefore, is to rebut the presumption of discrimination by producing evidence that the plaintiff was rejected, or someone else was preferred, for a legitimate, nondiscriminatory reason. The defendant need not persuade the court that it was actually motivated by the proffered reasons. It is sufficient if the defendant's evidence raises a genuine issue of fact as to whether it discriminated against the plaintiff. To accomplish this, the defendant must clearly set forth, through the introduction of admissible evidence, the reasons for the plaintiff's rejection. The explanation provided must be legally sufficient to justify a judgment for the defendant. If the defendant carries this burden of production, the presumption raised by the prima facie case is rebutted, and the factual inquiry proceeds to a new level of specificity. Placing this burden of production on the defendant thus serves simultaneously to meet the plaintiff's prima facie case by presenting a legitimate reason for the action and to frame the factual issue with sufficient clarity so that the plaintiff will have a full and fair opportunity to demonstrate pretext. The sufficiency of the defendant's evidence should be evaluated by the extent to which it fulfills these functions.

The plaintiff retains the burden of persuasion. She now must have the opportunity to demonstrate that the proffered reason was not the true reason for the employment decision. This burden now merges with the ultimate burden of persuading the court that she has been the victim of intentional discrimination. She may succeed in this either directly by persuading the court that a discriminatory reason more likely motivated the employer or indirectly by showing that the employer's proffered explanation is unworthy of credence.

In reversing the judgment of the District Court that the discharge of respondent from PSC was unrelated to her sex, the Court of Appeals adhered to two rules it had developed to elaborate the defendant's burden of proof. First, the defendant must prove by a preponderance of the evidence that legitimate, nondiscriminatory reasons for the discharge existed. Second, to satisfy this burden, the defendant "must prove that those he hired . . . were somehow *better* qualified than was plaintiff; in other words, comparative evidence is needed."

The Court of Appeals has misconstrued the nature of the burden that *McDonnell Douglas* and its progeny place on the defendant. We stated in *Sweeney* that "the employer's burden is satisfied if he simply 'explains what he has done' or 'produc[es] evidence of legitimate nondiscriminatory reasons.' " It is plain that the Court of Appeals required much more: it placed on the defendant the burden of persuading the court that it had convincing, objective reasons for preferring the chosen applicant above the plaintiff.*

The court placed the burden of persuasion on the defendant apparently because it feared that "[i]f an employer need only *articulate*— not prove—a legitimate, nondiscriminatory reason for his action, he may compose fictitious, but legitimate, reasons for his actions." We do not believe, however, that limiting the defendant's evidentiary obligation to a burden of production will unduly hinder the plaintiff. First, as noted above, the defendant's explanation of its legitimate reasons must be clear and

---

* The court reviewed the defendant's evidence and explained its deficiency:
   "Defendant failed to introduce comparative factual data concerning Burdine and Walz. Fuller merely testified that he discharged and retained personnel in the spring shakeup at TDCA primarily on the recommendations of subordinates and that he considered Walz qualified for the position he was retained to do. Fuller failed to specify any objective criteria on which he based the decision to discharge Burdine and retain Walz. He stated only that the action was in the best interest of the program and that there had been some friction within the department that might be alleviated by Burdine's discharge. Nothing in the record indicates whether he examined Walz' ability to work well with others. This court in East found such unsubstantiated assertions of 'qualification' and 'prior work record' insufficient absent data that will allow a true *comparison* of the individuals hired and rejected." 608 F.2d at 568, 21 FEP Cases at 979.

reasonably specific. This obligation arises both from the necessity of rebutting the inference of discrimination arising from the prima facie case and from the requirement that the plaintiff be afforded "a full and fair opportunity" to demonstrate pretext. Second, although the defendant does not bear a formal burden of persuasion, the defendant nevertheless retains an incentive to persuade the trier of fact that the employment decision was lawful. Thus, the defendant normally will attempt to prove the factual basis for its explanation. . . . Given these factors, we are unpersuaded that the plaintiff will find it particularly difficult to prove that a proffered explanation lacking a factual basis is a pretext. We remain confident that the *McDonnell Douglas* framework permits the plaintiff meriting relief to demonstrate intentional discrimination.

The Court of Appeals also erred in requiring the defendant to prove by objective evidence that the person hired or promoted was more qualified than the plaintiff. *McDonnell Douglas* teaches that it is the plaintiff's task to demonstrate that similarly situated employees were not treated equally. The Court of Appeals' rule would require the employer to show that the plaintiff's objective qualifications were inferior to those of the person selected. If it cannot, a court would, in effect, conclude that it has discriminated.

The court's procedural rule harbors a substantive error. Title VII prohibits all discrimination in employment based upon race, sex and national origin. "The broad, overriding interest, shared by employer, employee, and consumer, is efficient and trustworthy workmanship assured through fair and . . . neutral employment and personnel decisions." Title VII, however, does not demand that an employer give preferential treatment to minorities or women. 42 U.S.C. § 2000e–2(j). The statute was not intended to "diminish traditional management prerogatives." It does not require the employer to restructure his employment prac-

tices to maximize the number of minorities and women hired.

The views of the Court of Appeals can be read, we think, as requiring the employer to hire the minority or female applicant whenever that person's objective qualifications were equal to those of a white male applicant. But Title VII does not obligate an employer to accord this preference. Rather, the employer has discretion to choose among equally qualified candidates, provided the decision is not based upon unlawful criteria. The fact that a court may think that the employer misjudged the qualifications of the applicant does not in itself expose him to Title VII liability, although this may be probative of whether the employer's reasons are pretexts for discrimination.

In summary, the Court of Appeals erred by requiring the defendant to prove by a preponderance of the evidence the existence of nondiscriminatory reasons for terminating the respondent and that the person retained in her stead had superior objective qualifications for the position. When the plaintiff has proved a prima facie case of discrimination, the defendant bears only the burden of explaining clearly the nondiscriminatory reasons for its actions. The judgment of the Court of Appeals is vacated and the case is remanded for further proceedings consistent with this opinion.

It is so ordered.

CASE QUESTIONS

1. State the facts of this case.
2. After a *prima facie* case has been made out, what is the defendant's "burden"?
3. Under the *Burdine* rule is the employer required to prove by a preponderance of the evidence that the person who was hired, promoted, or retained was better qualified than the person who was rejected?
4. Under *Burdine* is an employer required to hire, promote, or retain a minority or female employee whenever this individual's objective qualifications are equal to those of white male applicants?

SECTION 12—STATISTICAL CASES

In *Hazelwood School District v. United States*[10] the Supreme Court dealt with the matter of statistical proof in Title VII cases. The Hazelwood School District was formed by 13 rural school districts outside of St. Louis, Missouri. Of the more than 19,000 teachers employed in the St. Louis area, 15.4 percent were black. This figure included the St. Louis City School District, which had a policy of attempting to maintain a 50 percent black teaching staff. Apart from the city district, 5.7 percent of the teachers in the county were black according to the 1970 census. In the 1972–73 school year Hazelwood employed 16 black teachers on its staff of 1,107 (1.4 percent), and by the 1973–74 school year 22 of 1,231 (1.8 percent) of the teachers were black. The attorney general of the United States brought a "pattern or practice" of discrimination suit against the school district. This suit was unsuccessful in the U.S. District Court but successful in the U.S. Court of Appeals. The Supreme Court granted certiorari. In its decision the Court set forth certain principles for statistical cases and remanded the case for further proceedings.

Qualified Labor Market

A "population-workforce" comparison makes a statistical comparison of the percentage of blacks, Hispanics, or women in the population of a specific geographic area to the number of blacks, Hispanics, or women employed by a defendant employer. In *Hazelwood* the Supreme Court cautioned that the statistical data for such comparisons should be based on the "qualified" labor market. The Court stated:

> When special qualifications are required to fill particular jobs, comparisons to the general population (rather than to the smaller group of individuals who possess the necessary qualifications) may have little probative value.[11]

Relevant Geographic Area

The *Hazelwood* decision emphasized the importance of determining the relevant geographic area for statistical comparison purposes. The objective is to define the area from which applicants are likely to come, absent discrimination. Thus commuting patterns, availability of public transportation, and the geographic scope of the employer's recruiting practices are all relevant considerations. For example, if the employer recruits for executives on a nationwide basis, the relevant geographic area would be the entire country, and nationwide statistics would be applicable.

Relevant Time Frame

Hazelwood recognized the concept of "relevant time frame" statistics, which focuses on the employment decisions made during the relevant time period of the litigation rather

---

[10] 433 U.S. 299, 15 FEP 1 (1977).
[11] 433 U.S. 229, 308 n. 13, 15 FEP 1, 5 (1977).

than looking at "static" statistics. The relevant time period is after the effective date of Title VII. However, under the Supreme Court's *United Air Lines v. Evans*[12] decision, the Court considers discriminatory acts occurring before the charge-filing period to be the legal equivalent of acts occurring before the effective date of Title VII. Thus the relevant time frame for a Title VII case is the period starting 300 days prior to the filing of a charge with the EEOC. For example, if an employer had few blacks in its work-force but in the two years prior to the filing of a charge had hired blacks at a rate equal to or above the percentage of blacks in the workforce of the area, the relevant time frame analysis would lead to a finding that Title VII was not violated even though a "static analysis"—which is simply the actual percentage of blacks employed in the employer's total workforce on a given date regardless of hiring dates—would show a gross disparity. The *Evans* Court would consider the statistical significance of the static analysis, which would indicate the existence of past discrimination as "merely an unfortunate event in history which has no present legal consequences."

Sufficiency of Statistical Disparity

Ultimately in a statistical case a court is called upon to make determinations based on the statistical evidence before it. The Court in *Hazelwood* made it clear that the statistical disparity must be a "gross" disparity in order for there to be a finding of discrimination based on the statistical evidence. The *Hazelwood* Court set forth a "standard deviations" analysis that has been followed by numerous lower courts. The Supreme Court did not resolve the discrimination issue before it in *Hazelwood* and remanded the case to the district court for further proceedings on the geographic scope of the relevant labor market utilizing the statistical methodology explained in *Castaneda v. Partida*.[13] Footnote 17 of the *Hazelwood* decision states:

> Indeed, under the statistical methodology explained in *Castaneda* . . . involving the calculation of the standard deviation as a measure of predicted fluctuations, the difference between using 15.4% and 5.7% as the areawide figure would be significant. If the 15.4% figure is taken as the basis for comparison, the expected number of Negro teachers hired by Hazelwood in 1972–1973 would be 43 (rather than the actual figure of 10) of a total of 282, a difference of more than five standard deviations; the expected number in 1973–1974 would be 19 (rather than the actual figure 5) of a total of 123, a difference of more than three standard deviations. For the two years combined, the difference between the observed number of 15 Negro teachers hired (of a total of 405) would vary from the expected number of 62 by more than six standard deviations. Because a fluctuation of more than two or three standard deviations would undercut the hypothesis that decisions were being made randomly with respect to race, each of these statistical comparisons would reinforce rather than rebut the Government's other proof. If, however, the 5.7% areawide figure is used, the expected number of Negro teachers hired in 1972–1973 would be roughly 16, less than two standard deviations from the observed number of 10; for 1973–1974, the expected value would be roughly seven, less than one standard deviation from the observed value of 5; and for the two years com-

---

[12] 431 U.S. 553, 14 FEP 1510 (1977).
[13] 430 U.S. 482 (1977).

bined, the expected value of 23 would be less than two standard deviations from the observed total of 15. . . .

These observations are not intended to suggest that precise calculations of statistical significance are necessary in employing statistical proof, but merely to highlight the importance of the choice of the relevant labor market area.

Please note in footnote 17 that the Supreme Court has adopted a rule of thumb for the number of standard deviations that would undercut the hypothesis that the decisions were being made randomly with respect to race, etc., and that it is a greater than "two or three standard deviations" rule.

The binomial test used by the Supreme Court in *Castaneda* may be summarized in terms of a set of equations using the following symbols to represent the variables.[14] Thus,

n = number of binomial trials in a particular experiment
p = probability of a success on each trial
e = expected number of successes
o = observed number of successes
SD = standard deviation
Z = Z statistic or Z score, which is the number of standard deviations by which the number of successes actually observed differs from the number expected

1. In *Castaneda* the statistical analysis sought to assess if the shortage in the number of Mexican-Americans called to serve on grand juries in Hidalgo County, Texas, could have occurred by chance. The total number of persons selected for grand jury was 870; thus "n" = 870. Mexican-Americans made up 79.1% of the population from which grand jurors were drawn; thus "p" = .791. The actual number of Mexican-Americans selected for grand jury duty was 339; thus "o" = 339. To find the expected number of successes, multiply "n" times "p" (e = n × p):

$$e = 870 \times .791 = 688$$

2. To calculate the standard deviation (SD), take the square root of the product of the number of trials, the probability of a success, and the probability of a failure [SD = $\sqrt{n \times p \times (1 - p)}$]:

$$SD = \sqrt{870 \times .791 \times .209} = \sqrt{143.83} = 11.99$$

3. To calculate the Z statistics or score, which is the number of standard deviations by which the number of successes actually observed differs from the number of successes expected, the numerator consists of the expected number minus the observed number, or

$$Z = \frac{e - o}{SD} : Z = \frac{688 - 399}{11.99} = 29.1$$

A fluctuation of more than two or three standard deviations—that is, a Z score of greater than 2 or 3—would undercut the hypothesis that the selection process was

---

[14] See Sugrue and Fairley, *A Case of Unexamined Assumptions: The Use and Misuse of the Statistical Analysis of* Castaneda/Hazelwood *in Discrimination Litigation*, 24 B.C. Law Rev. 925 (1983).

being made randomly with respect to national origin. In *Castaneda* the fluctuation was so great that the Court concluded that the statistical disparities established a *prima facie* case of discrimination against Mexican-Americans in the selection process.

In *EEOC v. Sears*,[15] the Equal Employment Opportunity Commission brought a discrimination case against Sears that was based almost entirely on statistics. The case was the culmination of 12 years of work and expense on both sides. The trial lasted some ten months, and $3 million was paid in expert witness fees alone. The court decided the case against the EEOC, finding that the EEOC did not prove even one instance of discrimination by Sears. On appeal the EEOC contended that its statistical analysis showed that only sex discrimination could explain the predominance of males in the most lucrative sales jobs, while mostly females worked the lower-paying noncommission sales jobs. The court of appeals, however, determined that the EEOC's statistical evidence was flawed in that it inflated the percentage of qualified female applicants.[16] Moreover, the court of appeals held that the district court had properly credited Sears's defense that during the period of time in question, 1973 through 1980, women were historically not interested in the irregular hours, the compensation risks, and the products involved in commission sales.

As will be seen later in this chapter, a voluntary affirmative action plan under the so-called *Weber* standards requires that an employer self-analysis be made as part of the plan to determine if and where conspicuous racial or gender imbalances exist. An affirmative action plan may then seek to remedy such imbalances. It is very important that the self-analysis be conducted in accordance with the *Hazelwood* standards. In evaluating its workforce to see if conspicuous racial or gender imbalances exist and in setting goals to remedy imbalances, the employer should take into account the number of women and minorities qualified for the individual positions in the relevant geographic area.[17]

SECTION 13—TITLE VII COURT-ORDERED REMEDIES

The remedial powers of federal courts deciding Title VII actions include injunctions against unlawful practices, affirmative orders requiring the reinstatement or the hiring of employees, and the awarding of back pay, front pay, and seniority rights. Back pay orders are limited to a period of two years prior to the filing of the charge.[18] The Civil Rights Act of 1991 provides for increased damages, including compensatory and punitive damages, as summarized in Figure 1–2.

Make-Whole Remedies for Victims

In the *Albemarle Paper Company* decision, reported in this section, the Supreme Court held that back pay should only be denied in limited situations and for reasons which

---

[15] 39 FEP 1652 (1986).

[16] 45 FEP 1257 (7th Cir. 1988).

[17] Please see Justice O'Connor's concurring opinion in *Johnson v. Transportation Agency*, 107 S.Ct. 1442, 1463 (1987).

[18] 42 USC Section 706(g).

would not frustrate the purposes of Title VII. The *Bowman* decision is an example of a remedy fashioned from legislative intent. There the Supreme Court held that the awarding of seniority rights was necessary to eradicate the effects of post-Title VII discrimination against black employees.

Court-Ordered Affirmative Action for Nonvictims

In *Sheet Metal Workers' Local 28 v. EEOC*,[19] the Supreme Court held that district courts were not limited to awarding preferential relief only to the actual victims of unlawful discrimination. The courts may order preferential relief, such as requiring the employer to meet goals and timetables for the hiring of minorities, where an employer or labor union has engaged in persistent and egregious discrimination or where it is necessary to dissipate the lingering effects of pervasive discrimination. The Court stated, however, that in the majority of Title VII cases where Title VII has been found to have been violated, the district court will need only to order the employer or union to cease the unlawful practices and award make-whole relief to the individuals victimized by those practices.

Award of Attorneys' Fees

Section 706(k) of Title VII provides that the court in its discretion may allow the prevailing party, other than the EEOC and the United States, a reasonable attorney's fee. In *New York Gaslight Club Inc. v. Carey*,[20] the Supreme Court held that a federal court may allow the prevailing party attorneys' fees before a state administrative proceeding that Title VII requires federal claimants to invoke. The 1991 Act provides that the court may also award as part of the attorneys' fees a fee for expert witnesses.

The Supreme Court in *Christiansburg Garment Co. v. EEOC*[21] set forth a standard that allows district courts the discretion to award attorneys' fees to a prevailing defendant where the plaintiff's case is "frivolous, unreasonable, or without foundation." In *Arnold v. Burger King Corporation*,[22] the Fourth Circuit Court of Appeals affirmed an award of $10,744 in attorneys' fees against an unsuccessful plaintiff in a race discrimination case. The plaintiff, Arnold, a black male, was employed as a manager of a Burger King when several female employees formally complained to management that Arnold had sexually harassed them. The complaints accused Arnold of various incidents of misconduct including propositions and acts of deliberate and suggestive physical conduct. Following the complaints, Arnold was discharged. He then filed a race discrimination charge with the EEOC. After the EEOC issued a right-to-sue letter, Arnold took his former employer to court, where his only evidence was testimony from several co-workers and friends attesting to his good character. Burger King cited evidence that the workforce was half white and half black, that the number of blacks in

---

[19] 106 S.Ct. 3019 (1986).
[20] 477 U.S. 54, 22 FEP 1642 (1980).
[21] 434 U.S. 412 (1978).
[22] 32 FEP 1769 (4th Cir. 1983).

management had risen, and that a white employee involved in a less severe sexual harassment incident was fired before Arnold. The district court ruled that Arnold's case was frivolous and groundless from the outset and dismissed the case. The district court also awarded the $10,744 in attorneys' fees to be paid by Arnold, which fees were upheld by the court of appeals.

ALBEMARLE PAPER COMPANY v. MOODY

Supreme Court of the United States, 422 U.S. 405 (1975).

[Respondents, a certified class of present and former Negro employees, brought this action against petitioners, their employer, Albemarle Paper Co., and the employees' union, seeking injunctive relief against "any policy, practice, custom or usage" at the plant violative of Title VII of the Civil Rights Act of 1964, as amended by the Equal Employment Opportunity Act of 1972, and after several years of discovery moved to add a class back pay demand. At this trial, the major issues were the plant's seniority system, its program of employment testing, and back pay. The district court found that, following a reorganization under a new collective bargaining agreement, the Negro employees had been "locked" in the lower paying job classification, and ordered petitioners to implement a system of plantwide seniority. The court refused, however, to order back pay for losses sustained by the plaintiff class under the discriminatory system, on the grounds that (1) Albemarle's breach of Title VII was found not to have been in "bad faith" and (2) respondents had initially disclaimed interest in back pay and delayed making their back pay claim until five years after the complaint was filed, thereby prejudicing petitioners. The court also refused to enjoin or limit Albemarle's testing program, which respondents had contended had a disproportionate adverse impact on blacks and was not shown to be related to job performance. The court concluded that "personnel tests administered at the plant have undergone validation studies and have been proven to be job-related." Respondents appealed on the back pay and preemployment test issues. The court of appeals reversed the district court's judgment.]

STEWART, J.

The District Court's decision must therefore be measured against the purposes which inform Title VII. As the Court observed in *Griggs v. Duke Power Co.*, the primary objective was a prophylactic one:

It was to achieve equality of employment opportunities and remove barriers that have operated in the past to favor an identifiable group of white employees over other employees.

Back pay has an obvious connection with this purpose. If employers faced only the prospect of an injunctive order, they would have little incentive to shun practices of dubious legality. It is the reasonably certain prospect of a back pay award that "provide[s] the spur or catalyst which causes employers and unions to self-examine and to self-evaluate their employment practices and to endeavor to eliminate, so far as possible, the last vestiges of an unfortunate and ignominious page in this country's history."

It is also the purpose of Title VII to make persons whole for injuries suffered on account of unlawful employment discrimination. This is shown by the very fact that Congress took care to arm the courts with full equitable powers. . . .

It follows that, given a finding of unlawful discrimination, back pay should be denied only for reasons which, if applied generally, would not frustrate the central statutory purposes of eradicating discrimination throughout the economy and making persons whole for injuries suffered through past discrimination. The courts of appeals must maintain a consistent and principled application of the back pay provision, consonant with the twin statutory objectives, while at the same time recognizing that the trial court will often have the keener appreciation of those facts and circumstances peculiar to particular cases.

The District Court's stated grounds for denying back pay in this case must be tested against these standards. The first ground was that Albemarle's breach of Title VII had not been in "bad faith." This is not a sufficient reason for denying back pay. Where an employer *has* shown bad faith — by maintaining a practice which he knew to be illegal or of highly questionable legality — he can make no claims whatsoever on the Chancellor's conscience. But, under Title VII, the mere absence of bad faith simply opens the door to equity; it does not depress the scales in the employer's favor. If back pay were awardable only upon a showing of bad faith, the remedy would become a punishment for moral turpitude, rather than a compensation for workers' injuries. This would read the "make whole" purpose right out of Title VII, for a worker's injury is no less real simply because his employer did not inflict it in "bad faith." Title VII is not concerned with the employer's "good intent or absence of discriminatory intent" for "Congress directed the thrust of the Act to the *consequences* of employment practices, not simply the motivation." To condition the awarding of back pay on a showing of "bad faith" would be to open an enormous chasm between injunctive and back pay relief under Title VII. There is nothing on the face of the statute or in its legislative history that justifies that creation of drastic and categorical distinctions between those two remedies. . . .

[A synopsis of the remainder of the Court's opinion is as follows:

As is clear from *Griggs, supra*, and the Equal Employment Opportunity Commission's guidelines for employers seeking to determine through professional validation studies whether employment tests are job-related, such tests are impermissible unless shown, by professionally acceptable methods, to be "predictive of or significantly correlated with important elements of work behavior which comprise or are relevant to the job or jobs for which candidates are being evaluated." Measured against the standard, Albemarle's validation study is materially defective in that (1) it would not, because of the odd patchwork of results from its application, have "validated" the two general ability tests used by Albemarle for all the skilled lines of progression for which the two tests are, apparently, now required; (2) it compared test scores with subjective supervisorial rankings, affording no means of knowing what job performance criteria the supervisors were considering; (3) it focused mostly on job groups near the top of various lines of progression, but the fact that the best of those employees working near the top of the lines of progression score well on a test does not necessarily mean that the test permissibly measures the qualifications of new workers entering lower level jobs; and (4) it dealt only with job-experienced white workers, but the tests themselves are given to new job applicants who are younger, largely inexperienced, and in many instances nonwhite.]

Accordingly, the judgment is vacated, and these cases are remanded to the district court for proceedings consistent with this opinion.

It is so ordered.

FRANKS v. BOWMAN TRANSPORTATION CO., INC.

Supreme Court of the United States, 424 U.S. 747 (1976).

A trucking company had discriminated against blacks after the passage of Title VII by denying

them employment as over-the-road drivers. In holding that a remedy which included seniority rights was necessary, the Court reviewed the legislative intent behind Section 706(g) of the Act.

Last term's *Albemarle Paper Company v. Moody*, 422 U.S. 405, 418 (1975), consistent with the congressional plan, held that one of the central purposes of Title VII is "to make persons whole for injuries suffered on account of unlawful employment discrimination." To effectuate this make-whole objective, Congress in Section 706(g) vested broad equitable discretion in the federal courts to order such affirmative action as may be appropriate, which may include, but is not limited to, reinstatement or hiring of employees, with or without back pay . . . , or any other equitable relief as the court deems appropriate. The legislative history supporting the 1972 Amendments of Section 706(g) of Title VII affirms the breadth of this discretion. The provisions of [Section 706(g)] are intended to give the courts wide discretion exercising their equitable powers to fashion the most complete relief possible. . . . [T]he Act is intended to make the victims of unlawful employment discrimination whole, and . . . the attainment of this objective . . . requires that persons aggrieved by the consequences and effects of the unlawful employment practice be so far as possible, restored to a position where they would have been were it not for the unlawful discrimination. Sec-

tion-by-Section Analysis of H. R. 1746, accompanying the Equal Employment Opportunity Act of 1972—Conference Report, 118 Cong. Rec. 7166, 7168 (1972). This is emphatic confirmation that federal courts are empowered to fashion such relief as the particular circumstances of a case may require to effect restitution, making whole insofar as possible the victims of racial discrimination in hiring. Adequate relief may well be denied in the absence of a seniority remedy slotting the victim in that position in the seniority system that would have been his had he been hired at the time of his application. It can hardly be questioned that ordinarily such relief will be necessary to achieve the make-whole purposes of the Act.

CASE QUESTIONS

1. In *Albemarle* did a showing that the employer had not acted in bad faith relieve the employer from a back pay obligation?
2. Why did the district court in *Albemarle* refuse to order a back pay remedy?
3. Does the Supreme Court agree with the district court's ruling in *Albemarle* that it has unfettered discretion in fashioning a remedy?
4. According to the House Report quoted in the *Bowman* decision, what is the primary intention of Title VII?

SECTION 14—CONSENT DECREES AND VOLUNTARY AFFIRMATIVE ACTION PLANS

Employers have an interest in affirmative action because it is fundamentally fair to have a diverse and representative workforce. Moreover, affirmative action is an effective means of avoiding litigation costs associated with discrimination cases while at the same time preserving management prerogatives and preserving rights to government contracts. Employers, under affirmative action plans (AAPs), may undertake special recruiting and other efforts to hire and train minorities and women and help them advance within the company. However, the plan may also provide job preferences for minorities and women. Such aspects of affirmative action plans have resulted in numerous lawsuits contending that Title VII of the Civil Rights Act of 1964, the Fourteenth Amendment, or collective bargaining contracts have been violated. The Supreme Court has not been able to settle the many difficult issues before it with a clear and consistent majority. The Court has decided cases narrowly, with individual justices often feeling compelled to speak in concurring or dissenting opinions.

Private-Sector AAPs

The Supreme Court, in the landmark *Griggs v. Duke Power Co.* decision, made a statement on discriminatory preferences and Title VII:

> The Act does not command that any person be hired simply because he was formerly the subject of discrimination, or because he is a member of a minority group. Discriminatory preference for any group, minority or majority, is precisely and only what Congress has proscribed. What is required by Congress is the removal of artificial, arbitrary, and unnecessary barriers to employment when the barriers operate invidiously to discriminate on the basis of racial or other impermissible classification.

In *McDonald v. Santa Fe Trail Transportation Co.*,[23] the Supreme Court held that discrimination against whites was prohibited by Title VII. In *Regents of the University of California v. Bakke*,[24] the Supreme Court held that Allan Bakke, an applicant for admission to the University of California Medical School at Davis, was denied admission to the school solely on racial grounds and that the Constitution forbids such.

It was in the above context that the Supreme Court considered the question of whether Title VII allows an employer and union in the private sector to implement an affirmative action plan that granted a racial preference to blacks where there was no finding of proven discrimination by a court but where there was a conspicuous racial imbalance in the employer's skilled craft workforce. The Court decided this question in *Steelworkers v. Weber*, presented in this section. The Court held that the employer could implement such a plan under Title VII. It thus rejected the contentions of the white male plaintiff that the selection of junior black employees over more senior white male employees discriminated against the white males because of their color and was "reverse discrimination" contrary to Title VII. The Court majority chose not to define in detail a line of demarcation between permissible and impermissible affirmative action plans, but certain principles may be extracted from the majority opinion as to what is permissible:

1. The affirmative action must be in connection with a "plan."
2. There must be a showing that affirmative action is justified as a remedial measure. The plan then must be remedial to open opportunities in occupations closed to protected classes under Title VII or designed to break down old patterns of racial segregation and hierarchy. In order to make a determination that affirmative action is justified, the parties must make a self-analysis to determine if and where conspicious racial imbalances exist.
3. The plan must be voluntary.
4. The plan must not unnecessarily trammel the interests of whites.
5. The plan must be temporary.

---

[23] 427 U.S. 273, 12 FEP 1577 (1976).
[24] 438 U.S. 265, 17 FEP 1000 (1978).

The *Weber* decision is the cornerstone on which many subsequent Supreme Court decisions on affirmative action issues are structured.

Public-Sector AAPs

In *Wygant v. Jackson Board of Education,*[25] where five judges wrote opinions on the issues before the Court, a sufficient number of justices supported various aspects of the concept of a public-sector employer's right to implement a race-conscious affirmative action plan. However, the Court struck down a layoff preference for blacks as violative of the Fourteenth Amendment. Under *Wygant* a majority of the Supreme Court justices recognized affirmative action in the public sector as permissible where (1) there is convincing evidence of prior discrimination by the governmental unit involved (the affirmative action is justified as a remedial measure) and (2) the means chosen to accomplish the remedial purpose is "sufficiently narrowly tailored" to achieve its remedial purpose. A majority of justices concluded, however, that the layoffs were not sufficiently narrowly tailored to survive the Fourteenth Amendment challenge.

The plurality opinion rejected the theory that providing minority role models for minority students to alleviate societal discrimination justified the layoff preference provision for black teachers, saying that such is insufficient to justify racial classifications.

Most of the justices agreed that the public employer does not have to wait for a court finding that it has been guilty of past discrimination before it takes action. However, compelling evidence of past discrimination must be shown before affirmative action preferences may be implemented.

In *Johnson v. Santa Clara County Transportation,*[26] involving public-sector affirmative action, the Supreme Court applied the *Weber* principles and upheld the public employer's decision under a voluntary AAP to promote a qualified woman over a more qualified man. It is thus evident that voluntary affirmative action is permissible in both the public and private sectors.

The Supreme Court has dealt with three types of specific issues involving public-sector AAPs and has reached narrow determinations on these issues as follows:

1. *Consideration of sex in AAPs:* In the *Johnson v. Santa Clara County Transportation* decision, referred to above and presented in this section, the Supreme Court decided that the public employer did not violate Title VII by promoting a female employee to the position of dispatcher over a more qualified male employee under the terms of its voluntary affirmative action plan.
2. *Promotion quotas:* In *United States v. Paradise,*[27] a sharply divided Court approved a promotion quota for the Alabama State Police requiring that one black state trooper be promoted for each white state trooper. The plurality opinion found the quota "narrowly tailored" to serve its purpose. Justice Stevens, who cast the deciding vote, believed the relief to be proper because of the state agency's egregious past violations of the Equal Protection Clause.

---

[25] 476 U.S. 267 (1986).
[26] 480 U.S. 616 (1987).
[27] 480 U.S. 149 (1987).

3. *Layoff preferences:* In *Wygant v. Jackson Board of Education,*[28] the Supreme Court struck down a layoff provision in a collective bargaining agreement that gave preferences to blacks. This provision was held to violate the Equal Protection Clause of the Fourteenth Amendment. The plurality opinion stated in part:

> While hiring goals impose a diffuse burden, often foreclosing only one of several opportunities, layoffs impose the entire burden of achieving racial equality on particular individuals, often resulting in serious disruption of their lives. That burden is too intrusive. We therefore hold that, as a means of accomplishing purposes that otherwise may be legitimate, the Board's layoff plan is not sufficiently narrowly tailored. Other, less intrusive means of accomplishing similar purposes—such as the adoption of hiring goals—are available.[29]

In reading Justice O'Connor's concurring opinion in *Wygant* in conjunction with the plurality decision, it is apparent that racially based layoff procedures are of dubious legality.

Consent Decrees

Citing *Steelworkers v. Weber,* the Supreme Court stated in *Firefighters Local 93 v. City of Cleveland*[30] that voluntary action available to employers and unions seeking to eradicate racial discrimination may include reasonable race-conscious relief that benefits individuals who are not actual victims of discrimination. In *Weber* the voluntary action was the private contractual agreement between the employer and the union. In *Firefighters Local 93* a federal district court approved a consent decree between the city of Cleveland and an organization of black and Hispanic firefighters who brought suit against the city charging racial discrimination in promotions and assignments. The terms of a consent decree are arrived at through agreement of the parties to a lawsuit; the court reviews and approves it, and the decree is enforceable by the court. In the *Firefighters Local 93* case, while not a party to the lawsuit, Local 93 was recognized as an intervenor. Local 93 did not approve of the consent decree, which set forth a quota system for the promotion of minorities over a four-year period. Local 93 had contended before the district court that "promotions based upon a criterion other than competence, such as a racial quota system, would deny those most capable from their promotions and deny . . . the City . . . the best possible firefighting force.[31]

The Supreme Court rejected the union's argument that Section 706(g) of Title VII precludes the courts from approving consent decrees benefiting individuals who were not the actual victims of discrimination.

The importance of the *Local 93* decision is that while Section 706(g) restricts the district court's powers to order relief, such as hiring or promotion orders for individuals who have not actually suffered discrimination, a consent decree is not an "order of the

---

[28] 476 U.S. 267 (1986).
[29] *Id.* at 283.
[30] 478 U.S. 501 (1986).
[31] *Id.* at 507.

court" according to the Supreme Court majority. Thus it may go beyond what a court could have ordered if the case had been litigated to its conclusion.

Union or Individual Challenges to Consent Decrees

In *Martin v. Wilks*,[32] black individuals brought suit against the city of Birmingham, Alabama, alleging that the city had engaged in racially discriminatory hiring and promotion practices in violation of Title VII. Consent decrees were eventually entered that included goals for hiring and promoting blacks as firefighters. Thereafter, white firefighters who had not intervened in the earlier litigation, which resulted in the consent decrees, challenged the employment decisions taken pursuant to the decrees. The Supreme Court allowed this challenge to the consent decrees.

The Civil Rights Act of 1991 altered the *Martin v. Wilks* decision. The 1991 law bars challenges to consent decrees by persons who had actual notice of the proposed order and a reasonable opportunity to present objections, and those whose interests were adequately represented by another person who challenged the decree on the same legal grounds and similar facts, unless there has been an intervening change in the law or facts.[33]

STEELWORKERS v. WEBER
Supreme Court of the United States, 443 U.S. 193 (1979).

[In 1974 petitioners United Steelworkers of America (USWA) and Kaiser Aluminum & Chemical Corp. (Kaiser) entered into a master collective bargaining agreement covering terms and conditions of employment at fifteen Kaiser plants. The agreement included an affirmative action plan designed to eliminate racial imbalances in Kaiser's craft workforces by reserving for black employees 50 percent of the openings in in-plant craft training programs until the percentage of black craft workers in a plant was commensurate with the percentage of blacks in the local labor force. This litigation arose from the operation of the affirmative action plan at Kaiser's Gramercy, Louisiana, plant where, prior to 1974, 1.83 percent of the skilled craft workers were black and the local workforce was approximately 39 percent black.

Pursuant to the national agreement, Kaiser, rather than continuing its practice of hiring trained outsiders, established a training program to train its production workers to fill craft openings. Kaiser selected trainees on the basis of seniority and race so that at least 50 percent of the trainees were black until the percentage of black skilled craft workers in the plant approximated the percentage of blacks in the local labor force. During the plan's first year of operation, seven black and six white craft trainees were selected from the plant's production workforce, with the most senior black trainee having less seniority than several white production workers whose bids for admission to the training program were rejected. Thereafter, respondent Brian Weber, one of those white production workers, instituted a class action in federal

---

[32] 490 U.S. 755 (1989).
[33] Section 108 of the Civil Rights Act of 1991.

district court, alleging that because the affirmative action program had resulted in junior black employees receiving training in preference to senior white employees, respondent and other similarly situated white employees had been discriminated against in violation of the provisions of Section 703(a) and (d) of Title VII, which makes it unlawful to "discriminate . . . because of . . . race" in hiring and in the selection of apprentices for training programs. The district court held that the affirmative action plan violated Title VII, entered judgment in favor of the plaintiff class, and granted injunctive relief. The court of appeals affirmed, holding that all employment preferences based upon race, including those preferences incidental to bona fide affirmative action plans, violated Title VII's prohibition against racial discrimination in employment. The Supreme Court granted certiorari.]

BRENNAN, J.

We emphasize at the outset the narrowness of our inquiry. Since the Kaiser-USWA plan does not involve state action, this case does not present an alleged violation of the Equal Protection Clause of the Fourteenth Amendment. Further, since the Kaiser-USWA plan was adopted voluntarily, we are not concerned with what Title VII requires or with what a court might order to remedy a past proved violation of the Act. The only question before us is the narrow statutory issue of whether Title VII forbids private employers and unions from voluntarily agreeing upon bona fide affirmative action plans that accord racial preferences in the manner and for the purpose provided in the Kaiser-USWA plan. That question was expressly left open in *McDonald v. Santa Fe Trail Transp. Co.*, 427 U.S. 273 (1976), which held, in a case not involving affirmative action, that Title VII protects whites as well as blacks from certain forms of racial discrimination.

Respondent argues that Congress intended in Title VII to prohibit all race-conscious affirmative action plans. Respondent's argument rests upon a literal interpretation of §§ 703(a) and (d) of the Act. Those sections make it un-

lawful to "discriminate . . . because of . . . race" in hiring and in the selection of apprentices for training programs. Since, the argument runs, *McDonald v. Santa Fe Trail Transp. Co.*, *supra*, settled that Title VII *forbids* discrimination against whites as well as blacks, and since the Kaiser-USWA affirmative action plan operates to discriminate against white employees solely because they are white, it follows that the Kaiser-USWA plan violates Title VII.

Respondent's argument is not without force. But it overlooks the significance of the fact that the Kaiser-USWA plan is an affirmative action plan voluntarily adopted by private parties to eliminate traditional patterns of racial segregation. In this context respondent's reliance upon a literal construction of §§ 703(a) and (d) and upon *McDonald* is misplaced. It is a "familiar rule, that a thing may be within the letter of the statute and yet not within the statute, because not within its spirit, nor within the intention of its makers." The prohibition against racial discrimination in §§ 703(a) and (d) of Title VII must therefore be read against the background of the legislative history of Title VII and the historical context from which the Act arose. Examination of those sources makes clear that an interpretation of the sections that forbade all race-conscious affirmative action would "bring about an end completely at variance with the purpose of the statute" and must be rejected.

Congress' primary concern in enacting the prohibition against racial discrimination in the Title VII of the Civil Rights Act of 1964 was with "the plight of the Negro in our economy." As Senator Clark told the Senate:

The rate of Negro unemployment has gone up consistently as compared with white unemployment for the past 15 years. This is a social malaise and a social situation which we should not tolerate. That is one of the principal reasons why the bill should pass.

. . . Accordingly, it was clear to Congress that "[t]he crux of the problem [was] to open employment opportunities for Negroes in occupations which have been traditionally closed to them," and it was to this problem that Title VII's prohibition against racial discrimination in employment was primarily addressed. . . .

Given this legislative history, we cannot agree with respondent that Congress intended to prohibit the private sector from taking effective steps to accomplish the goal that Congress designed Title VII to achieve. The very statutory words intended as a spur or catalyst to cause "employers and unions to self-examine and to self-evaluate their employment practices and to endeavor to eliminate, so far as possible, the last vestiges of an unfortunate and ignominious page in this country's history," Albemarle Paper Co. v. Moody, 422 U.S. 405 (1975), cannot be interpreted as an absolute prohibition against all private, voluntary, race-conscious affirmative action efforts to hasten the elimination of such vestiges. . . .

Our conclusion is further reinforced by examination of the language and legislative history of § 703(j) of Title VII. . . .

. . . The section provides that nothing contained in Title VII "shall be interpreted to *require* any employer . . . to grant preferential treatment . . . to any group because of the race . . . of such . . . group on account of" a de facto racial imbalance in the employer's work force. The section does *not* state that "nothing in Title VII shall be interpreted to *permit*" voluntary affirmative efforts to correct racial imbalances. The natural inference is that Congress chose not to forbid all voluntary race-conscious affirmative action. . . .

. . . In view of [the] legislative history and in view of Congress' desire to avoid undue federal regulation of private businesses, use of the word "require" rather than the phrase "require or permit" in § 703(j) fortifies the conclusion that Congress did not intend to limit traditional business freedom to such a degree as to prohibit all voluntary race-conscious affirmative action.

We therefore hold that Title VII's prohibition in §§ 703(a) and (d) against racial discrimination does not condemn all private, voluntary, race-conscious affirmative action plans.

We need not today define in detail the line of demarcation between permissible and impermissible affirmative action plans. It suffices to hold that the challenged Kaiser-USWA affirmative action plan falls on the permissible side of the line. The purposes of the plan mirror those of the statute. Both were designed to break down old patterns of racial segregation and hierarchy. Both were structured to "open employment opportunities for Negroes in occupations which have been traditionally closed to them."

At the same time, the plan does not unnecessarily trammel the interests of the white employees. The plan does not require the discharge of white workers and their replacement with new black hirees. Nor does the plan create an absolute bar to the advancement of white employees; half of those trained in the program will be white. Moreover the plan is a temporary measure. . . .

We conclude, therefore, that the adoption of the Kaiser-USWA plan for the Gramercy plant falls within the area of discretion left by Title VII to the private sector voluntarily to adopt affirmative action plans designed to eliminate conspicuous racial imbalance in traditionally segregated job categories. Accordingly, the judgment of the Court of Appeals for the Fifth Circuit is reversed.

So ordered.

[BRENNAN, J., *delivered the opinion of the Court, in which STEWART, WHITE, MARSHAL, and BLACKMUN joined. BLACKMUN, J., filed a concurring opinion. BURGER, C. J., filed a dissenting opinion. REHNQUIST, J., filed a dissenting opinion, in which BURGER, C. J., joined. POWELL and STEVENS, J. J., took no part in the consideration or decision of the cases.]*

Dissenting Opinions

BURGER, C. J.

The court reaches a result I would be inclined to vote for were I a Member of Congress considering a proposed amendment of Title VII. I cannot join the Court's judgment, however, because it is contrary to the explicit language of the statute and arrived at by means wholly incompatible with long-established principles of separation of powers. Under the guise of statutory "construction," the Court effectively rewrites Title VII to achieve what it regards as a desirable result. It "amends" the statute to do precisely what both its sponsors and its opponents agreed the statute was not intended to do.

When Congress enacted Title VII after long study and searching debate, it produced a statute of extraordinary clarity, which speaks directly to the issue we consider in this case. In § 703(d) Congress provided:

It shall be an unlawful employment practice for any employer, labor organization, or joint labor-management committee controlling apprenticeship or other training or retraining, including on-the-job training programs to discriminate against any individual because of his race, color, religion, sex, or national origin in admission to, or employment in, any program established to provide apprenticeship or other training.

Often we have difficulty interpreting statutes either because of imprecise drafting or because legislative compromises have produced genuine ambiguities. But here there is no lack of clarity, no ambiguity. The quota embodied in the collective-bargaining agreement between Kaiser and the Steelworkers unquestionably discriminates on the basis of race against individual employees seeking admission to on-the-job training programs. And, under the plain language of § 703(d), that is "an unlawful employment practice." . . .

REHNQUIST, J.

Contrary to the Court's analysis, the language of § 703(j) is precisely tailored to the objection voiced time and again by Title VII's opponents. Not once during the 83 days of debate in the Senate did a speaker, proponent, or opponent, suggest that the bill would allow employers *voluntarily* to prefer racial minorities over white persons. In light of Title VII's flat prohibition on discrimination "against any individual . . . because of such individual's race," § 703(a), 42 U.S.C. § 2000e–2(a) [42 U.S.C.S. § 2000e–2(a)], such a contention would have been, in any event, too preposterous to warrant response. . . .

In light of the background and purpose of § 703(j), the irony of invoking the section to justify the result in this case is obvious. The Court's frequent references to the "voluntary" nature of Kaiser's racially discriminatory admission quota bear no relationship to the facts of this case. Kaiser and the Steelworkers acted under pressure from an agency of the Federal Government, the Office of Federal Contract Compliance, which found that minorities were being "underutilized" at Kaiser's plants. That is, Kaiser's workforce was racially imbalanced. Bowing to that pressure, Kaiser instituted an admissions quota preferring blacks over whites, thus confirming that the fears of Title VII's opponents were well founded. Today, § 703(j), adopted to allay those fears, is invoked by the Court to uphold imposition of a racial quota under the very circumstances that the section was intended to prevent. . . .

CASE QUESTIONS

1. State the facts that led Kaiser to contract with the union concerning the affirmative action training program.
2. What did the Court state was the question before it?
3. Do you believe that the Supreme Court applied Section 703(d) as written by Congress in this case?
4. Does the Court set guidelines for what are permissible and impermissible affirmative action plans?

JOHNSON v. SANTA CLARA COUNTY TRANSPORTATION AGENCY
Supreme Court of the United States, 480 U.S. 616 (1987).

[In 1978 an affirmative action plan (Plan) for hiring and promoting minorities and women was voluntarily adopted by the Santa Clara County Transportation Agency (Agency). The Plan provided *inter alia* that in making promotions to positions within a traditionally segregated job classification in which women have been significantly underrepresented, the Agency was authorized to consider, as one factor, the sex of a qualified applicant. The Plan was intended to achieve a statistically measurable yearly improvement in hiring and promoting minorities and women in job classifications where they were underrepresented. The long-term goal was to attain a workforce whose composition reflected the proportion of minorities and women in the area labor force. The Plan set aside no specific number of positions for minorities or women but required that short-range goals be established and annually adjusted to serve as the most realistic guide for actual employment decisions. When the Agency announced a vacancy for the position of road dispatcher, none of the 238 positions in the skilled craft worker job classification, which included the dispatcher position, was held by a woman. The qualified applicants for the position were interviewed. The Agency, pursuant to the Plan, ultimately passed over petitioner, Paul Johnson, and promoted a female, Diane Joyce. After receiving a right-to-sue letter from the EEOC, Johnson filed suit in federal court. The court held that the Agency had violated Title VII of the Civil Rights Act of 1964. The court found that Joyce's sex was the determining factor in her selection and that the Agency's Plan was invalid under the criterion announced in *Steelworkers v. Weber*, 443 U.S. 193, that the Plan be temporary. The court of appeals reversed.]

BRENNAN, J.
The assessment of the legality of the Agency Plan must be guided by our decision in *Weber*. . . .

The first issue is therefore whether consideration of the sex of applicants for skilled craft jobs was justified by the existence of a "manifest imbalance" that reflected underrepresentation of women in "traditionally segregated job categories." In determining whether an imbalance exists that would justify taking sex or race into account, a comparison of the percentage of minorities or women in the employer's workforce with the percentage in the area labor market or general population is appropriate in analyzing jobs that require no special expertise, see *Teamsters v. United States*, 431 U.S. 324 (1977) (comparison between percentage of blacks in employer's workforce and in general population proper in determining extent of imbalance in truck driving positions), or training programs designed to provide expertise, see *Weber, supra* (comparison between proportion of blacks working at plant and proportion of blacks in area labor force appropriate in calculating imbalance for purpose of establishing preferential admission to craft training program). Where a job requires special training, however, the comparison should be with those in the labor force who possess the relevant qualifications. See *Hazelwood School District v. United States*, 433 U.S. 299 (1977) (must compare percentage of blacks in employer's work ranks with percentage of qualified black teachers in area labor force in determining underrepresentation in teaching positions). The requirement that the "manifest imbalance" relate to a "traditionally segregated job category" provides assurance both that sex or race will be taken into account in a manner consistent with Title VII's purpose of eliminating the effects of employment discrimination, and that the interests of those employees not benefitting from the plan will not be unduly infringed. . . .

It is clear that the decision to hire Joyce was made pursuant to an Agency plan that directed that sex or race to taken into account for the purpose of remedying underrepresentation. The Agency Plan acknowledged the "limited opportunities that have existed in the past," for women to find employment in certain job classifications "where women have not been traditionally employed in significant numbers." As a result, observed the Plan, women were concentrated in traditionally female jobs in the Agency, and represented a lower percentage in other job classifications than would be expected if such traditional segregation had not occurred. Specifically, 9 of the 10 Para-Professionals and 110 of the 145 Office and Clerical Workers were women. By contrast, women were only 2 of the 28 Officials and Administrators, 5 of the 58 Professionals, 12 of the 124 Technicians, none of the Skilled Craft Workers, and 1 — who was Joyce — of the 110 Road Maintenance Workers. The Plan sought to remedy these imbalances through "hiring, training and promotion of . . . women throughout the Agency in all major job classifications where they are underrepresented."

As an initial matter, the Agency adopted as a benchmark for measuring progress in eliminating underrepresentation the long-term goal of a workforce that mirrored in its major job classifications the percentage of women in the area labor market. Even as it did so, however, the Agency acknowledged that such a figure could not by itself necessarily justify taking into account the sex of applicants for positions in all job categories. For positions requiring specialized training and experience, the Plan observed that the number of minorities and women "who possess the qualifications required for entry into such job classifications is limited." The Plan therefore directed that annual short-term goals be formulated that would provide a more realistic indication of the degree to which sex should be taken into account in filling particular positions. The Plan stressed that such goals "should not be construed as 'quotas' that must be met," but as reasonable aspirations in correcting the imbalance in the Agency's workforce. . . .

As the Agency Plan recognized, women were most egregiously underrepresented in the Skilled Craft job category, since *none* of the 238 positions was occupied by a woman. In mid-1980, when Joyce was selected for the road dispatcher position, the Agency was still in the process of refining its short-term goals for Skilled Craft Workers in accordance with the directive of the Plan. This process did not reach fruition until 1982, when the Agency established a short-term goal for that year of three women for the 55 expected openings in that job category — a modest goal of about 6% for that category. . . .

The Agency's Plan emphatically did *not* authorize . . . blind hiring. It expressly directed that numerous factors be taken into account in making hiring decisions, including specifically the qualifications of female applicants for particular jobs. Thus, despite the fact that no precise short-term goal was yet in place for the Skilled Craft category in mid-1980, the Agency's management nevertheless had been clearly instructed that they were not to hire solely by reference to statistics. The fact that only the long-term goal had been established for this category posed no danger that personnel decisions would be made by reflexive adherence to a numerical standard.

Furthermore, in considering the candidates for the road dispatcher position in 1980, the Agency hardly needed to rely on a refined short-term goal to realize that it had a significant problem of underrepresentation that required attention. Given the obvious imbalance in the Skilled Craft category, and given the Agency's commitment to eliminating such imbalances, it was plainly not unreasonable for the Agency to determine that it was appropriate to consider as one factor the sex of Ms. Joyce in making its decision. The promotion of Joyce thus satisfies the first requirement enunciated in *Weber*, since it was undertaken to further an affirmative action plan designed to eliminate Agency workforce imbalances in traditionally segregated job categories.

We next consider whether the Agency Plan unnecessarily trammeled the rights of male employees or created an abolute bar to their advancement. In contrast to the plan in *Weber*, which provided that 50% of the positions in the craft training program were exclusively for blacks, and to the consent decree upheld last term in *Firefighters v. Cleveland*, 478 U.S. 501 (1986), which required the promotion of specific numbers of minorities, the Plan sets aside no positions for women. The Plan expressly states that "[t]he 'goals' established for each Division should not be construed as 'quotas' that must be met." Rather, the Plan merely authorizes that consideration be given to affirmative action concerns when evaluating qualified applicants. As the Agency Director testified, the sex of Joyce was but one of numerous factors he took into account in arriving at his decision. The Plan thus resembles the "Harvard Plan" approvingly noted by JUSTICE POWELL, in University of California Regents v. Bakke, 438 U.S. 265, 316–319 (1978), which considers race along with other criteria in determining admission to the college. As JUSTICE POWELL observed, "In such an admissions program, race or ethnic background may be deemed a 'plus' in a particular applicant's file, yet it does not insulate the individual from comparison with all other candidates for the available seats." *Id.*, at 317. Similarly, the Agency Plan requires women to compete with all other qualified applicants. No persons are automatically excluded from consideration; *all* are able to have their qualifications weighed against those of other applicants.

In addition, petitioner had no absolute entitlement to the road dispatcher position. Seven of the applicants were classified as qualified and eligible, and the Agency Director was authorized to promote any of the seven. Thus, denial of the promotion unsettled no legitimate firmly rooted expectation on the part of the petitioner. Furthermore, while the petitioner in this case was denied a promotion, he retained his employment with the Agency, at the same salary and with the same seniority, and remained eligible for other promotions. . . .

. . . In this case . . . substantial evidence shows that the Agency has sought to take a moderate, gradual approach to eliminating the imbalance in its workforce, one which establishes realistic guidance for employment decisions, and which visits minimal intrusion on the legitimate expectations of other employees. Given this fact, as well as the Agency's express commitment to "attain" a balanced workforce, there is ample assurance that the Agency does not seek to use its Plan to maintain a permanent racial and sexual balance. . . .

Affirmed.

Dissenting Opinion

JUSTICE SCALIA, with whom THE CHIEF JUSTICE joins, and with whom JUSTICE WHITE joins [in part], dissenting.

With a clarity which, had it not proven so unavailing, one might well recommend as a model of statutory draftsmanship, Title VII of the Civil Rights Act of 1964 declares:

"It shall be an unlawful employment practice for an employer—

"(1) to fail or refuse to hire or to discharge any individual, or otherwise to discriminate against any individual with respect to his compensation, terms, conditions, or privileges of employment, because of such individual's race, color, religion, sex, or national origin; or

"(2) to limit, segregate, or classify his employees or applicants for employment in any way which would deprive or tend to deprive any individual of employment opportunities or otherwise adversely affect his status as an employee, because of such individual's race, color, religion, sex, or national origin." 42 U.S.C. § 2000e–2(a).

The Court today completes the process of converting this from a guarantee that race or sex will *not* be the basis for employment determinations, to a guarantee that it often *will*. Ever so subtly, without even alluding to the last obstacles preserved by earlier opinions that we now push out of our path, we effectively replace the goal of a discrimination-free society with the quite incompatible goal of proportionate representation by race and by sex in the workplace. . . .

After a two-day trial, the District Court concluded that Diana Joyce's gender was *"the determining factor"* in her selection for the position. Specifically, it found that "[b]ased upon the examination results and the departmental interview, [Mr. Johnson] was more qualified for the position of Road Dispatcher than Diane Joyce"; that "[b]ut for [Mr. Johnson's] sex, male, he would have been promoted to the position of Road Dispatcher"; and that "[b]ut for Diane Joyce's sex, female, she would not have been appointed to the position. . . ." The Ninth Circuit did not reject these factual findings as clearly erroneous, nor could it have done so on the record before us. We are bound by those findings under Federal Rule of Civil Procedure 52(a).

The most significant proposition of law established by today's decision is that racial or sexual discrimination is permitted under Title VII when it is intended to overcome the effect, not of the employer's own discrimination, but of societal attitudes that have limited the entry of certain races, or of a particular sex, into certain jobs. . . .

CASE QUESTIONS

1. Assess the truth of the statement: "But for Diane Joyce's sex, female, she would not have been appointed to the position."
2. Did the agency's AAP authorize "blind hiring" practices requiring the hiring of a specified number of women regardless of the number of qualified applicants?
3. Did the Court follow the principles set forth in the *Weber* decision in assessing the legality of the agency's plan?
4. Did the agency's plan unnecessarily trammel male employees' rights?

SECTION 15—REVERSE DISCRIMINATION AND AFFIRMATIVE ACTION PLANS

When an employer's affirmative action plan is not shown to be justified or when it "unnecessarily trammels" the interests of nonminority employees in regards to promotions, training, or other employment expectations, it is said that the employer's action is unlawful "reverse discrimination." In the so-called reverse discrimination cases, the courts apply the *Weber* principles to test the validity of the employer action in question.

In *Jurgens v. Thomas,*[34] a reverse discrimination suit brought by white male employees of the Equal Employment Opportunity Commission, the court held that the EEOC itself had acted contrary to the *Weber* decision in its promotion and hiring procedures. The court determined that clear evidence of preferences for minorities and women was found in the EEOC's affirmative action plans, its Special Hiring Plan for Hispanics, and its District Directors Selection Program. After extensive discussion and an analysis of statistics on the affirmative action plans, the court held that the evidence showed that through the process of reorganization, white male district directors were reduced from ten to two. Also, the Special Hiring Plan for Hispanics was discussed by the court in the lengthy decision. Hispanics constituted 6.8 percent of the national population but 12.9 percent of the EEOC workforce, and the plan called for a 10 percent hiring goal even in field offices where the local population was less than 10 percent

---

[34] 29 FEP 1561 (1982).

Hispanic. The preferences of this plan were not temporary, according to the court, because of the follow-up procedure built into the plan whereby those offices that did not meet initial hiring goals "committed" one or more positions to future recruitment of Hispanics. The court held that the affirmative action plans were not remedial because the jobs were not traditionally closed to women and minorities; nor were they temporary, for the preferences appeared in slightly different form in each of the seven plans at issue. The court held that *Weber's* language should not be read to permit an employer with statistical parity in its own plant to use "status" as a basis for decisions as a means of compensating for unremedied societal discrimination elsewhere. The court held that the EEOC's affirmative action plans unnecessarily trammeled the interests of the plaintiffs and violated Title VII.

In the *San Francisco Police Officers' Association v. San Francisco* decision, the U.S. Court of Appeals applied the *Weber* standards and found that the city's decision to rescore promotional tests in order to achieve specific and identified racial and gender percentages for promotion purposes "unnecessarily trammeled" the interests of white male police officers.

Affirmative Action After *Adarand Constructors, Inc. v. Pena*

In its 1995 landmark *Adarand Constructors, Inc. v. Pena*[35] decision, the Supreme Court placed significant limits on the federal government's authority to implement programs favoring businesses owned by racial minorities over white-owned businesses. The decision reinstated a reverse discrimination challenge to a federal program designed to provide highway construction contracts to "disadvantaged" subcontractors where race-based presumptions were used to identify such individuals. The Court found the program to be violative of the equal protection component of the Fifth Amendment's Due Process Clause.

Following the Court's *Adarand* decision the EEOC issued a statement on affirmative action, stating in part:

> . . . Affirmative action is lawful only when it is designed to respond to a demonstrated and serious imbalance in the work force, is flexible, time-limited, applies only to qualified workers, and respects the rights of non-minorities and men.[36]

In *Eldredge v. Carpenters*, which was decided subsequent to the *Adarand* decision, the Ninth Circuit Court of Appeals imposed an AAP setting a goal of 20 percent female participation in a carpentry apprentice training program, after 21 years of litigation. The court determined that the remedy was needed to dissipate the lingering effect of pervasive discrimination. The *Eldredge* case is presented in this section.

---

[35] 115 S.Ct. 2097 (1995).
[36] BNA Daily Labor Report No. 147, S-47, Aug. 1, 1995.

SAN FRANCISCO POLICE OFFICERS' ASSOCIATION v. CITY AND COUNTY OF SAN FRANCISCO

United States Court of Appeals, Ninth Circuit, 812 F.2d 1125 (1987).

[The city and county of San Francisco (City) and the Civil Service Commission (Commission) entered into a consent decree that required the City to employ good faith efforts to achieve particular goals for employment of women and minorities. The Police Officers' Association (POA) intervened in those actions and agreed to the consent decree. The consent decree specifically prohibited the City from unlawfully discriminating in any manner on the basis of sex, race, or national origin. In 1983 the City administered selection procedures for the positions of assistant inspector and sergeant. The promotional examinations had three parts: a multiple-choice test, a written examination, and an oral examination. Part way through the examination, the Commission set the weights for all three components. When the examinations were scored, the results showed an adverse impact on minorities in both ranks and a slight adverse impact on women for the assistant inspector examination. This adverse impact led the Commission to revise the scoring procedures for the examinations. The Commission regarded the multiple-choice and written examination components on a pass-fail basis and used the oral examination as the sole criterion for ranking candidates who passed the multiple-choice and written examinations. The police union brought suit, objecting to the new grading procedures. The district court ruled in favor of the City, and the union appealed.]

WIGGINS, C. J.

The critical issue in this case is whether the Commission acted lawfully in reweighing the examination components. The district court viewed this question in terms of fairness and held a fairness hearing in order to determine if the Commission's decision to reweigh was a valid affirmative action plan under *United Steelworkers of America v. Weber,* 443 U.S. 193 (1979).

In *Weber,* the Supreme Court identified four criteria that make an affirmative action plan valid under Title VII: (1) it is designed to break down old patterns of racial segregation and hierarchy; (2) it does not create an absolute bar to the advancement of nonminority employees; (3) it is a temporary measure, "not intended to maintain racial balance, but simply to eliminate a manifest racial imbalance"; and (4) it does not unnecessarily trammel the interests of non-minority employees. *Weber,* 443 U.S. at 208. *Weber* did not hold that these criteria were absolute requirements, but did hold that these aspects of the plan in *Weber* placed it on the permissible side of the line between permissible and impermissible plans. Here, the district court found that reweighing fit all four *Weber* criteria and was therefore permissible. We reverse the district court because reweighing the examination unnecessarily trammeled the interests of the nonminority police officers.

In analyzing whether the interests of non-minorities were unnecessarily trammeled, the district court focused on what rights the candidates possessed and how those rights were affected by reweighing. It determined that the City did not overtly take into account race or sex in the decision to reweigh. . . .

We find that the district court clearly erred when it determined that the decision to reweigh was not a race and gender conscious act. . . .

Reweighing unlawfully displaced candidates on the basis of their race and gender. The information about the candidates' performance on the individual components led the Commission to choose the oral component as the sole ranking device. If the results of the examinations had been different, the written component or the multiple-choice component might have been the new ranking device. Without re-administering the test, the Commission examined the results from each component based on race and gender criteria and rescored the test to achieve specific and identified racial and gender percentages. This type of result-oriented scoring is offensive.

Candidates who participate in promotional examinations expect to have an equal opportunity to score well and to achieve promotion. This neutrality cannot exist if the City can rescore the examinations to achieve a particular race and gender balance after it analyzes the results. Permitting an employer to rescore examinations with knowledge of the ultimate results undermines the integrity of the examination process.

Moreover, candidates for promotion should be on notice of how their performance will be evaluated in order to prepare themselves effectively for an examination. . . .

. . . Here . . . the Commission's decision to reweigh unlawfully restricted the promotional opportunities of nonminority candidates because the tests were scored to achieve a particular racial result. It trammeled the interests of nonminorities, in that the candidates were led to believe that the promotions would be based on merit alone. This harm to nonminorities was unnecessary because a less burdensome alternative, such as administering a new selection procedure, would have better achieved the goals of the consent decree without violating Title VII.

The City was obligated under the consent decree to administer an examination that would not have an adverse effect on minorities and women. When it failed in its first attempt to achieve that goal, the City inappropriately attempted to take short-cuts to meet its obligations. It did so in order to save time. Although we are sympathetic to the City's time dilemma, using an unlawful procedure is not acceptable. The City was required either to validate its initial examination or, if it could not, to devise and administer an alternative selection procedure that did not have an adverse impact.

The City was additionally obligated under the consent decree not to practice racial or sexual discrimination—no more against white males than against others. The POA was a party to the consent decree. The POA has a right to insist that this unequivocal renunciation of all discrimination means what it says. The reweighing as practiced here violated the consent decree.

The judgment is reversed and remanded.

CASE QUESTIONS

1. Did the district court determine that the decision to rescore the components of the exam was not a race- and gender-conscious act?
2. How did the commission's decision to rescore the components of the exam unnecessarily trammel the interests of nonminorities?
3. Was the city's obligation under the consent decree not to practice racial or sexual discrimination applicable to white male police officers?

ELDREDGE v. CARPENTERS
United States Court of Appeals, 94 F.3d 1366 (9th Cir. 1996).

[Contractors and the Carpenters Union administer a 4-year Joint Apprenticeship and Training Committee (JATC) in Northern California which leads to journeyman status as a carpenter. Having a job working in the carpentry trade is vital dur-

ing the apprenticeship, for a jobless apprentice will obtain no on-the-job experience. Under a so-called "hunting license" system a contractor would ask for particular apprentices by name for employment with the contractor, and these individuals were usually male. As a result women have always made up less than 3% of any group of apprentices. After 21 years of ineffective efforts to open up carpentry training to women, when the matter came back to the Ninth Circuit for a fifth time (Eldredge V) the Court set a 20 percent females participation goal for the apprenticeship program.]

FLETCHER, C. J. . . .

The district court abused its discretion by declining to implement the affirmative action plan proposed by the plaintiff class. . . . Under this plan, at least one out of every five applicants dispatched under the referral list must be a woman. If the first four applicants on the list are men, the next dispatch must be the highest listed female applicant. If there is no female applicant listed, the JATC must undertake affirmative efforts to encourage women to apply. The plan terminates when 20% of the apprentices are women.

Court-ordered affirmative action "may be appropriate where an employer or a labor union has engaged in persistent or egregious discrimination, or where necessary to dissipate the lingering effects of pervasive discrimination." . . . As the Supreme Court recently explained in *Adarand Constructors, Inc. v. Pena*, 115 S.Ct. 2097 (1995), federal courts may order affirmative action to remedy an employer's " 'pervasive, systematic, and obstinate discriminatory conduct.' " In the words of Justice Scalia, "we have permitted federal courts to prescribe quite severe, race-conscious remedies when confronted with egregious and persistent unlawful discrimination." *City of Richmond v. J. A. Croson Co.*, 488 U.S. 469, 521 (1988) (Scalia, J., concurring in the judgment) (citing Paradise and Sheet Metal Workers). . . .

Affirmative action remedies are appropriate in this case. The JATC's reliance on the hunting license system has for decades kept women out of the carpentry trade. Fewer than 3% of the applicants admitted to the apprenticeship program are women. Female applicants are only half as likely as male applicants to obtain admission. The data for 1985–1990 were even more discouraging th[a]n the data for 1976–1984. It is no surprise that women constitute only 5% of the JATC's applicant pool.

In the face of the blatantly obvious effects of the hunting license system, the conduct of the JATC has been egregious and obstinate. Twenty-one years and three appeals after Linda Eldredge first filed her action, the JATC persists in exclusionary policies. Nine years after we remanded this case to determine the appropriate remedy for "Title VII liability based on the JATC's use of the 'hunting license' system," Eldredge IV, 833 F.2d at 1341, the JATC is still arguing for the retention of the hunting license system, albeit in mutilated form. Though we have twice rejected the JATC's claim that the real culprits are the employers, Eldredge II, 662 F.2d at 536 (holding that the employers are not necessary parties); Eldredge IV, 833 F.2d at 1337 (holding that the JATC is responsible for decisions it delegates to the employers), the JATC persists in claiming that we cannot render effective relief in the absence of the employers. After the district court took the parties' recommendations under submission, the JATC unilaterally implemented its own facially discriminatory proposals. The bottom line is that women historically have been systematically excluded from carpentry work and for more than two decades have sought relief through the courts while the JATC, the craft's gatekeeping organization, has waged a relentless battle to preserve the status quo.

When deciding whether an affirmative action remedy for an employer's past discrimination is appropriate, "we look to several factors, including the necessity for the relief and the efficacy of alternative remedies; the flexibility and duration of the relief, including the availability of waiver provisions; the relationship of the numerical goals to the relevant labor market; and the impact of the relief on the rights of third parties." . . . The proposal of the plaintiff class passes muster.

First, affirmative action is necessary in this case. Given the JATC's decades-long history of recalcitrance and foot-dragging, it is highly unlikely that the JATC will facilitate or even permit the entry of women into the apprenticeship program on equal footing with men without clear numerical goals. Moreover, as a direct result of the JATC's long-term use of the hunting license system, women have had far less than an equal opportunity to enter the carpentry trade. This discrimination is probably the leading reason why women make up only 5% of the JATC's current applicant pool. The extreme shortage of female applicants certainly cannot be explained by any sort of biological determinism. Until a critical mass of women has successfully entered the carpentry trade, it is unlikely that other women will believe that the arbitrary barriers to their admission have been lifted. Without a temporary and narrowly tailored affirmative action program, the necessary critical mass of female carpenters cannot be achieved.

Second, the proposal of the plaintiff class is flexible and temporary. It terminates under its own terms as soon as women comprise 20% of the apprentices. It does not set an arbitrary deadline. If the JATC cannot satisfy the one-in-five ratio with its existing applicant pool, it need take only reasonable steps to recruit more female applicants. Rather than seeking a one-for-one parity between the genders, it simply sets "a benchmark against which the court [can] gauge [the JATC]'s efforts to remedy past discrimination." Sheet Metal Workers, 478 U.S. at 478.

Third, there is a proper relationship between the proposal's numerical goals and the relevant labor market. Guidelines of the United States Department of Labor addressing affirmative action in apprenticeship programs recommend "a goal for women . . . at a rate which is not less than 50 percent of the proportion women are of the workforce in the program sponsor's labor market area . . . ." 29 C.F.R. S 30.5(f). Unrebutted evidence at trial indicates that the one-in-five goal recommended by the plaintiff class is a conservative estimate based on this equation. While the JATC need by no means adopt a one-in-two ratio, it is equally clear that some critical mass of female carpenters is necessary to get the ball rolling in the right direction; a one-in-five ratio is a reasonable and modest accommodation.

Finally, the proposal of the plaintiff class imposes no undue burden on male applicants, who will still obtain up to 80% of the apprentice positions. The plan does not require the termination of men already admitted to the program, but only may defer temporarily the admission of some male applicants. Female applicants must meet the same minimum requirements as male applicants, including a high school or equivalent education, so qualified men will not be pushed aside to make room for unqualified women.

Remanded with instructions per-opinion.

CASE QUESTIONS

1. Explain the "hunting license" system.
2. Explain the court's reference to the JATC as the craft's gatekeeping organization.
3. Is the court's AAP goal of 20 percent women for the apprenticeship program within the rule of *Adarand Constructors, Inc.?*

SECTION 16—EXECUTIVE ORDER 11246: AFFIRMATIVE ACTION PROGRAMS

The Civil Rights Act, federal funding laws, and federal licensing laws have provided statutory authority for requiring certain employers to take affirmative action to improve the job opportunities for women and minorities.[37] The Rehabilitation Act of 1973 requires affirmative action by federal departments and government contractors to improve job opportunities for the handicapped. The Vietnam Veterans Readjustment Act of 1974 requires certain federal contractors to develop written affirmative action plans to hire veterans of the Vietnam War. The major source of affirmative action requirements, however, is presidential Executive Order 11246.

The Office of Federal Contract Compliance Programs

Under Executive Order 11246 the Secretary of Labor is charged with supervising and coordinating the compliance activities of the federal contracting agencies. The Secretary of Labor has established the Office of Federal Contract Compliance Programs (OFCCP) to administer the order. The OFCCP, having the responsibility to implement equal opportunity in the federal procurement area, has set forth regulations that apply to service and supply contractors and subcontractors as well as construction contractors and subcontractors. The OFCCP has full responsibility for conducting service, supply, and construction compliance review for the Department of Defense, the General Services Administration, Housing and Urban Development, the Department of Transportation, the Department of Interior, the Environmental Protection Agency, the Treasury Department, the Department of Commerce, and the Small Business Administration.

Each contract that the federal government awards amounting to $10,000 or more must contain an equal employment clause that is binding on the contractor or subcontractor for the duration of the contract. The clause contains the following commitments by the contractor:

1. Not to discriminate against any employee or job applicant because of race, color, sex, religion, or national origin.
2. To state in all employment advertisements that applicants will be considered on the basis of their qualifications.
3. To advise all unions of the employer's commitments.
4. To include the same type of equal employment opportunity agreement in every subcontract or purchase order.

Whenever the director of the OFCCP has reason to believe that a contractor has violated the equal employment opportunity clause in the contract, the director may initiate administrative proceedings to seek correction of the violation. The contractor must be afforded a full hearing before an administrative law judge before a sanction

---

[37] Civil Rights Act of 1964, Title VII, as amended. Federal funding laws: Title VI of the 1964 Civil Rights Act prohibits employment discrimination in any program or activity receiving federal financial assistance when the primary objective of the program is employment; sex discrimination is prohibited in HEW's aid-to-education programs by the terms of the Education Amendments of 1972. Federal licensing laws: the Federal Communications Commission has taken the position that it has authority to require licensees to take affirmative action to improve job opportunities for women and minorities; the Securities and Exchange Commission has authority to require corporations registering securities to report on significant developments in their equal employment practices.

can be imposed. The OFCCP has the power to cancel or suspend contracts for failure to comply with a nondiscrimination clause. The OFCCP may also require contracting agencies to refrain from entering into new contracts with "debarred" or ineligible contractors.

Service and Supply Contracts

Service and supply contractors and subcontractors having 50 or more employees and a contract exceeding $50,000 must develop written affirmative action plans for the increased utilization of women and minorities. In assessing whether a contract exceeds $50,000, the OFCCP counts the total value of the various orders anticipated in certain blanket purchase agreements (BPAs) rather than counting each order as a single contract.

Some requirements for an acceptable affirmative action program are as follows:

1. An analysis of all major job categories at a facility must be conducted with explanations if minority group members are being underutilized in job categories.
2. Goals, timetables, and affirmative action commitments must be designed to correct any identifiable deficiencies. When deficiencies exist, the regulations require the contractor to create specific goals and a timetable as part of its written affirmative action program.[38]
3. Support data for the program and analysis should be compiled and maintained as part of the contractor's affirmative action program.
4. Contractors shall direct special attention in their analysis and goal setting to six categories identified by the government as most likely to show underutilization of minorities—officials and managers, professionals, technicians, sales workers, office and clerical workers, and skilled craft workers.

Construction Contracts

The primary difference between affirmative action approaches for construction contractors and service and supply contractors is that minority goals and timetables for construction contractors are set periodically for "covered geographic areas" by the director of the OFCCP using Standard Metropolitan Statistical Area (SMSA) data. The service and supply contractors generate their own goals and timetables on an individual basis. The director has used the SMSA data and will use census data to set the goals for minority utilization equal to the percentage of minorities in the civilian labor force in the relevant area. The director has set a 6.9 percent nationwide goal for the utilization of women by contractors working on federally assisted construction contracts by $100,000 or more. The goal is not on a trade by trade basis but applies in the aggregate.

---

[38] The "goals and timetables" approach to affirmative action programs, required of federal contractors by the OFCCP, has been approved by several circuit courts. See *Contractors Association of Eastern Pennsylvania v. Shultz*, 442 F.2d 159 (3d Cir. 1971); *Southern Illinois Builders Association v. Ogilvie*, 471 F.2d 680 (7th Cir. 1972); and *Associated General Contractors of Massachusetts, Inc. v. Altshuler*, 490 F.2d 9 (1st Cir. 1973). These cases predate the so-called reverse discrimination cases of *Regents of the University of California v. Bakke*, 438 U.S. 265 (1978); *Steelworkers v. Weber*, 443 U.S. 193 (1979); *Fullilove v. Klutznick*, 448 U.S. 448 (1980); and *Adarand Constructors, Inc. v. Pena*, 115 S.Ct. 2097 (1995).

The "80 Percent" Rule

The revised Labor Department regulations outlining the affirmative action obligations of federal contractors under Executive Order 11246 continue to include an "80 percent" or "four-fifths" rule for determining underutilization of minorities and women. Under this rule an adverse impact is presumed if the selection rate for minorities and women from the relevant applicant pool is less than four-fifths or 80 percent of the selection rate for whites or males. The 80 percent rule has been sharply criticized for failing to account for differences in sampling size and test results in the applicant population and has had mixed acceptance by the courts. This rule is subject to modification at any time. It is considered by the EEOC and the OFCCP as a practical device for reviewing company employee profiles to see if serious discrepancies exist in the hiring and promotion policies of a company.

Compliance Reviews

The Labor Department issued new compliance and record keeping regulations in August 1997 to verify that government contractors have developed and implemented affirmative actions plans.[39] OFCCP can conduct "off-site" reviews of records obtained from contractors as well as more "focused" on-site reviews of contractors' affirmative action obligations where necessary. OFCCP conducts pre-award reviews of contractors seeking contracts of $10 million or more. Contractors must keep affirmative action records for two years and must provide OFCCP with access to computerized affirmative action records.

Sanctions for Noncompliance

Where it has been determined that a contracting firm has not made adequate good faith efforts to hire minority workers or women for federal or federally assisted projects, the OFCCP, after notice and a hearing, is authorized to debar the firm from participating in such projects.

Construction firms may apply to the OFCCP for reinstatement; however, they must show that they have made good faith efforts to increase minority hiring and must agree to additional terms set by the OFCCP. For example, a construction firm that had been debarred because of its failure to make good faith efforts to hire minorities on a federally assisted hospital project in New Haven, Connecticut, applied for reinstatement with the OFCCP. After an investigation established that the firm had made renewed efforts to comply with Executive Order 11246, it was reinstated with certain conditions.

Under the terms of the reinstatement order by the OFCCP, the firm was required to pay back wages of $13,606 to three workers who were found to have been victims of past discrimination. In addition, the company agreed to submit to the Labor Department copies of its monthly payroll records for at least two years and to employ minority apprentices and trainees at the completion of their training if employment opportunities were available. Further, it agreed to establish and maintain a current list of minority

---

[39] 41 CFR Parts 60-1, 60-60 (Aug. 19, 1997).

recruitment sources and minority job applicants towards which it would direct recruitment efforts, and to encourage minority employees to recruit other minority persons, including students, for summer or part-time work.

Short of debarment, the OFCCP may negotiate settlements. Bluegrass Coca-Cola Bottling Co. is a federal contractor since it supplies Coca-Cola products to all military installations in the Louisville, Kentucky, area. OFCCP conducted a compliance review in July 1995 and discovered that in the year of March 1994 through February 1995, Bluegrass had discriminated against qualified minorities and female job applicants. The company agreed to pay $475,000 in back wages and benefits to certain qualified individuals who were not hired, and it agreed to review its selection procedures every year to ensure that future hiring decisions are free from discrimination.[40] A most egregious case of discrimination was discovered and remedied by OFCCP at First Alabama Bank, where the personnel officer's interview notes indicated that a black candidate not selected for a job had "very large lips and hips . . . appearance is not good enough to meet public," while the white candidate selected for the job was described as "attractive . . . blond hair, blue eyes, teller-type appearance."[41]

SECTION 17—OTHER REMEDY OPTIONS

Because of an EEOC case backlog or the desire to avoid EEOC procedures, grievants have sometimes chosen to circumvent Title VII procedures. There are three principal avenues other than the Title VII approach to remedy discriminatory employment practices: (1) district court action under the Civil Rights Act of 1866, (2) private grievance and arbitration proceedings, and (3) NLRA unfair labor practice proceedings.

The Civil Rights Act of 1866

Following the Civil War, Congress enacted the Civil Rights Act of 1866 pursuant to the congressional power to eradicate slavery provided by the Thirteenth Amendment, which had been ratified in 1865. To remove any doubt as to its constitutionality, the statute was reenacted in 1870 following ratification of the Fourteenth Amendment in 1868 and was codified as 42 U.S.C. Sections 1981 and 1982. Lawsuits under the Civil Rights Act of 1866 are commonly referred to as Section 1981 and Section 1982 lawsuits.

In *Johnson v. Railway Agency*,[42] the Supreme Court held that Section 1 of the Civil Rights Act of 1866, and therefore its derivative 42 U.S.C. Section 1981, provides an independent remedy for discrimination in employment. The Court noted that filing a Section 1981 claim does not foreclose the use of EEOC procedures.

In *General Building Contractors Association v. Pennsylvania*,[43] the Supreme Court considered whether discrimination under Section 1981 could be proved by establishing that the defendant's policies had a disparate impact without proving intentional dis-

---

[40] DLR No. 163, A-3 (Aug. 22, 1997).
[41] DLR No. 225, A-1 (Nov. 21, 1997).
[42] 421 U.S. 454 (1975).
[43] 458 U.S. 375, 29 FEP 139 (1982).

crimination. The Court decided that Section 1981 can be violated only by purposeful discrimination.

In *Patterson v. McLean Credit Union*,[44] the Supreme Court read the language of Section 1981—"all persons . . . shall have the same right . . . to make and enforce contracts . . . as enjoyed by white citizens"—as prohibiting racial discrimination in the making and enforcement of private contracts, that is, in hiring decisions or the right to enforce contracts. The Court held that Section 1981 did not provide a remedy for racial harassment on the job. This decision limiting the application of Section 1981 was overturned by Congress in the Civil Rights Act of 1991, which specifies that Section 1981 covers all forms of racial discrimination in employment.[45]

In Chapter 1 of this text the time limitation for filing charges concerning alleged violations of Title VII is set forth. Where an individual misses the relatively short filing deadlines under Title VII, the individual may be able to bring a race discrimination case under the longer time limits allowed under Section 1981 (formerly six years, presently two years).

Section 1981 covers only claims of intentional discrimination based on race. Jury trials, with "uncapped" punitive and compensatory damages, may be obtained.

In *Saint Francis College v. Al-Khazraji*, presented in this section, the plaintiff's Title VII claims had been dismissed as untimely, but the Supreme Court upheld his right to sue under Section 1981 alleging racial discrimination based on his Arabian ancestry. In a related case, *Shaare Tefila Congregation v. Cobb*, also presented in this section, the Supreme Court determined that Jews can, under Section 1982 of the Civil Rights Act of 1866, sue those who allegedly desecrated a synagogue, since Jews were among the peoples considered to be distinct races at the time the 1866 Act was passed.

The Civil Rights Act of 1871, codified as 42 U.S.C. Section 1983, may be the basis of an action against state or local governments in an employment context when citizens are deprived of rights, privileges, and immunities secured by the U.S. Constitution or federal statutes.[46]

SAINT FRANCIS COLLEGE v. AL-KHAZRAJI

Supreme Court of the United States, 481 U.S. 604 (1987).

[Respondent, a U.S. citizen born in Iraq, was an associate professor of behavioral science at St. Francis College in Pennsylvania. He filed suit in federal district court against the college and its tenure committee alleging that by denying him tenure nearly three years before, they had discriminated against him on the basis of his Arabian race in violation of 42 U.S.C. Section 1981. His Title VII claims of discrimination based on national origin, religion, and race were dismissed as untimely. The district

---

[44] 109 S.Ct. 2363 (1989).
[45] Section 101 of the Civil Rights Act of 1991.
[46] In *Brown v. Polk County, Iowa*, 61 F.3d 650 (8th Cir. 1995) Isaiah Brown, a black man who identifies himself as a born-again Christian, was successful in part in a Section 1983 action against a county employer which required him to remove from his office all items with a religious connotation. See page 20 of this text for the decision.

court granted a summary judgment for the college, finding that Section 1981 does not cover claims based on Arabian ancestry. The court of appeals reversed, holding that the respondent had properly alleged racial discrimination in that, although Arabs are Caucasians under current racial classifications, Congress, when it passed what is now Section 1981, did not limit its protections to those who today would be considered members of a race different than the defendant's. The Supreme Court granted certiorari.]

WHITE, J.

Section 1981 provides:

All persons within the jurisdiction of the United States shall have the same right in every State and Territory to make and enforce contracts, to sue, be parties, give evidence, and to the full and equal benefit of all laws and proceedings for the security for persons and property as is enjoyed by white citizens, and shall be subject to like punishment, pains, penalties, taxes, licenses, and exactions of every kind, and to no other.

Although § 1981 does not itself use the word "race," the Court has construed the section to forbid all "racial" discrimination in the making of private as well as public contracts. *Runyon v. McCrary*, 427 U.S. 160, 168, 174–175 (1976). The petitioner college, although a private institution, was therefore subject to this statutory command. There is no disagreement among the parties on these propositions. The issue is whether respondent has alleged *racial* discrimination within the meaning of § 1981.

Petitioners contend that respondent is a Caucasian and cannot allege the kind of discrimination § 1981 forbids. Concededly, *McDonald v. Santa Fe Trail Transportation Co.*, 427 U.S. 273 (1976), held that white persons could maintain a § 1981 suit; but that suit involved alleged discrimination against a white person in favor of a black, and petitioner submits that the section does not encompass claims of discrimination by one Caucasian against another. We are quite sure that the Court of Appeals properly rejected this position.

Petitioner's submission rests on the assumption that all those who might be deemed Caucasians today were thought to be of the same race when § 1981 became law in the 19th century; and it may be that a variety of ethnic groups, including Arabs, are now considered to be within the Caucasian race. The understanding of "race" in the 19th century, however, was different. Plainly, all those who might be deemed Caucasian today were not thought to be of the same race at the time § 1981 became law. . . .

Encyclopedias of the 19th century . . . described race in terms of ethnic groups, which is a narrower concept of race than petitioners urged. Encyclopedia Americana in 1858, for example, referred in 1854 to various races such as Finns, Gypsies, Basques, and Hebrews. The 1863 version of the New American Cyclopaedia divided the Arabs into a number of subsidiary races, represented the Hebrews as of the Semitic race, and identified numerous other groups as constituting races, including Swedes, Norwegians, Germans, Greeks, Finns, Italians, Spanish, Mongolians, Russians, and the like. The Ninth edition of the Encyclopedia Britannica also referred to Arabs, Jews, and other ethnic groups such as Germans, Hungarians, and Greeks, as separate races.

These dictionary and encyclopedic sources are somewhat diverse, but it is clear that they do not support the claim that for the purposes of § 1981, Arabs, Englishmen, Germans and certain other ethnic groups are to be considered a single race. We would expect the legislative history of § 1981, which the Court held in *Runyon v. McCrary* had its source in the Civil Rights Act of 1866, as well as the Voting Rights Act of 1870, to reflect this common understanding, which it surely does. The debates are replete with references to the Scandinavian races, Cong. Globe, 39th Cong., 1st Sess, 499 (1866) (remarks of Sen. Cowan), as well as the Chinese (remarks of Sen. Davis), Latin (remarks of Rep. Kasson during debate of home rule for the District of Columbia), Spanish (remarks of Sen. Davis during debate of District of Columbia suffrage) and Anglo-Saxon races (remarks of Rep. Dawson). Jews, Mexicans (remarks of Rep. Dawson), blacks, and Mongolians (remarks of Sen. Cowan), were similarly categorized. Gypsies were referred to as a race (remarks of Sen. Cowan). . . .

Based on the history of § 1981, we have little trouble in concluding that Congress intended to protect from discrimination identifiable classes of persons who are subjected to intentional discrimination solely because of their ancestry or ethnic characteristics. Such discrimination is racial discrimination that Congress intended § 1981 to forbid, whether or not it would be classified as racial in terms of modern scientific theory. The Court of Appeals was thus quite right in holding that § 1981, "at a minimum," reaches discrimination against an individual "because he or she is genetically part of an ethnically and physiognomically distinctive subgrouping of *homo sapiens.*" It is clear from our holding, however, that a distinctive physiognomy is not essential to qualify for § 1981 protection. If respondent on remand can prove that he was subjected to intentional discrimination based on the fact that he was born an Arab, rather than solely on the place or nation of his origin, or his religion, he will have made out a case under § 1981.

The judgment of the Court of Appeals is accordingly

Affirmed

CASE QUESTIONS

1. Why did the plaintiff bring a Section 1981 claim rather than rely on a Title VII claim?
2. Can a Section 1981 claim encompass a charge of discrimination by one Caucasian against another?
3. Did the plaintiff prove that St. Francis College had discriminated against him because of his Arabian ancestry?

SHAARE TEFILA CONGREGATION v. COBB

Supreme Court of the United States, 481 U.S. 615 (1987).

[After their synagogue was painted with anti-Semitic slogans, phrases, and symbols, petitioners brought suit in federal district court alleging that the desecration by respondents violated 42 U.S.C. Section 1982. The district court dismissed petitioners' claims, and the court of appeals affirmed, holding that discrimination against Jews was not racial discrimination under Section 1982. The Supreme Court granted certiorari.]

WHITE, J.

We agree with the Court of Appeals that a charge of racial discrimination within the meaning of § 1982 cannot be made out by alleging only that the defendants were motivated by racial animus; it is necessary as well to allege that defendants' animus was directed towards the kind of group that Congress intended to protect when it passed the statute. To hold otherwise would unacceptably extend the reach of the statute.

We agree with petitioners, however, that the Court of Appeals erred in holding that Jews cannot state a § 1982 claim against other white defendants. That view rested on the notion that because Jews today are not thought to be members of a separate race, they cannot make out a claim of racial discrimination within the meaning of § 1982. That construction of the section we have today rejected in *Saint Francis College v. Al-Khazraji.* Our opinion in that case observed that definitions of race when § 1982 was passed were not the same as they are today and concluded that the section was "intended to protect from discrimination identifiable classes of persons who are subject to intentional discrimination solely because of their ancestry or ethnic characteristics." As *St. Francis* makes clear, the question before us is not whether Jews are considered to be a separate race by today's standards, but whether, at the time § 1982 was adopted, Jews constituted a group of people that Congress intended to protect. It is evident from the legislative history of the section reviewed in *Saint Francis College*, a review that we need not repeat here, that Jews and Arabs were among the peoples then considered to be distinct races and hence within the protection of the statute. Jews are not foreclosed from stating a cause of action

against other members of what today is considered to be part of the Caucasian race.

The judgment of the Court of Appeals is therefore reversed and the case is remanded for further proceedings consistent with this opinion.

CASE QUESTIONS

1. Why did the district court dismiss the congregation's Section 1982 claim?
2. Can Jews state a Section 1982 claim against other white defendants?

Grievance and Arbitration

An employee may seek a remedy against discriminatory employment practices through the grievance and arbitration procedures in an existing collective bargaining agreement. The advantage to the grievance and arbitration process is that it can be implemented with far less delay than the Title VII procedures, a suit under the Civil Rights Act of 1866, or NLRB proceedings. A difficulty with arbitration in employment discrimination cases is that the individual grievant is often left without adequate representation in the arbitration proceedings. The Supreme Court recognized in *Vaca v. Sipes* that because the remedies of grievance arbitration are devised and controlled by the union and the employer, "they may very well prove unsatisfactory or unworkable for the individual grievant.[47] Indeed a union may often have an interest in perpetuating a discriminatory practice. A further difficulty with arbitration is that labor arbitrators are not as experienced in dealing with racial, religious, or sex discrimination grievances as the EEOC or federal judges. Indeed an arbitrator may feel bound by the collective bargaining contract and thus may never reach the substantive legal questions inherent in racial, religious, or sex discrimination charges.

In *Alexander v. Gardner-Denver Company*,[48] the United States Supreme Court considered the question of whether an individual grievant's election to invoke grievance and arbitration machinery that resulted in an adverse arbitration award precludes the individual from filing a subsequent Title VII claim. The Court found that it did not. The Court held that Title VII was designed by Congress to supplement existing laws and institutions relating to employment discrimination and that the doctrine of election of remedies was inapplicable in the present context, which involved statutory rights distinctly separate from the employee's contractual rights, regardless of the fact that violation of both rights may have resulted from the same factual occurrence. The Court held, however, that the arbitral decision may be admitted as evidence at the Title VII trial in a federal court and set forth in its much-discussed footnote 21 the weight to be accorded the arbitral decision. Footnote 21 states:

---

[47] 386 U.S. 171, 185 (1967).
[48] 415 U.S. 147 (1974).

We adopt no standards as to the weight to be accorded an arbitral decision, since this must be determined in the court's discretion with regard to the facts and circumstances of each case. Relevant factors include the existence of provisions in the collective-bargaining agreement that conform substantially with Title VII, the degree of procedural fairness in the arbitral forum, adequacy of the record with respect to the issue of discrimination, and the special competence of particular arbitrators. Where an arbitral determination gives full consideration to an employee's Title VII rights, a court may properly accord it great weight. This is especially true where the issue is solely one of fact, specifically addressed by the parties and decided by the arbitrator on the basis of an adequate record. But courts should ever be mindful that Congress, in enacting Title VII, thought it necessary to provide a judicial forum for the ultimate resolution of discriminatory employment claims. It is the duty of courts to assure the full availability of this forum.

NLRA Remedies

An employer's racial discrimination is an unfair labor practice in violation of Section 8(a)(1) of the NLRA if it is found that this discrimination interferes with the affected employees' Section 7 rights to act concertedly for their own protection.[49] In *Jubilee Manufacturing Co.*,[50] the Board pointed out that it was "by no means inevitable" that an employer's racial or sex discrimination would set one group of employees against the other. The Board stated that a finding of a violation of the NLRA would depend upon a showing of "the necessary direct relationship" between the alleged race or sex discrimination and interference with employee rights under Section 7.

In *King Soopers, Inc.*,[51] the Board found an employer to be in violation of Section 8(a)(1) of the NLRA for suspending a Spanish-American employee for filing charges with the EEOC alleging promotional discrimination. The Board also found the union to be in violation of Section 8(b)(1)(A) for refusing to represent and process the grievances of the charging party. The Board's order held the company and the union jointly and severally liable for back pay damages. It should be pointed out that the NLRA does not protect picketing, handbilling, or other concerted activity by a group of minority employees seeking to bargain directly with an employer concerning alleged racial discrimination by the employer when the minority employees circumvented their elected bargaining representative and refused to participate in the contract grievance procedure.

In *Frank Briscoe v. NLRB*,[52] 12 ironworkers were laid off in February 1979. Four of the laid-off ironworkers were black, and they filed Title VII charges of discrimination based on race. When the weather improved, the company began rehiring but refused to hire any of the 12 laid-off workers. The company stated that to rehire those who did not file charges would be evidence of discrimination. Some of the ironworkers obtained other work, and eight of the workers laid off in February, including three of the black workers who filed Title VII charges, brought unfair labor charges before the NLRB. The

---

[49] *Tipler v. E. I. du Pont de Nemours & Co.*, 443 F.2d 125 (6th Cir. 1971).
[50] 202 NLRB 2 (1973).
[51] 222 NLRB 80 (1976).
[52] 637 F.2d 946, 106 LRRM 2155 (3d Cir. 1981).

U.S. Court of Appeals held that the filing of a complaint with the Equal Employment Opportunity Commission by the black employees under Title VII could constitute "concerted activity" protected by Section 7 of the NLRA. The court determined that retaliation by the employer against those employees and the others affected thereby was an unfair practice giving rise to the remedial measures of the NLRA. The court held that the availability of a remedy from the EEOC under Title VII does not preclude a plaintiff from seeking and obtaining relief under the NLRA. Indeed a remedy under the NLRA may provide a faster resolution to a problem than under Title VII procedures.

Employers are also protected from racial and religious prejudice in relation to Board election activities. In *M & M Supermarkets, Inc. v. NLRB*,[53] the Eleventh Circuit Court of Appeals let it be clearly known that appeals to racial and religious prejudice have no place in our system of justice or in an NLRB-conducted election. During the course of an election campaign, the company's personnel director, Ms. Patrick, made a presentation to a small group of employees at which a union supporter began to berate the company's owners as follows:

> The damn Jews who run this Company are all alike. They pay us pennies out here in the warehouse, and take all their money to the bank. The Jews ought to remember their roots. Norton Malaver ought to remember his roots. Us blacks were out in the cotton field while they, the damned Jews, took their money from the poor hardworking people.
>
> As Patrick attempted to defend the reputation of Norton Malaver and his family as liberal and community-minded people, Charles Wade angrily interrupted her and continued loudly. . . . [54]

The union, which did not condone the remarks, won the election, and the Board issued a bargaining order. The court of appeals refused to enforce the order, stating that the remarks were "so inflammatory and derogatory that they inflamed racial and religious tensions against the . . . owners of the company and destroyed the laboratory conditions necessary for a free and open election.[55]

Chapter Questions and Problems

1. What remedies are available to individuals charging discriminatory employment practices?
2. What guidelines did the *Weber* Court set forth for permissible affirmative action plans?
3. On what authority do federal agencies require bidders on government contracts to formulate and carry out affirmative action plans?
4. If the program referred to in *Adarand Constructors, Inc. v. Pena* reserved a percentage of highway work for "disadvantaged subcontractors" and, instead of using "race-based" presumptions to identify who were disadvantaged subcontractors, used an economic standard to identify the disadvantaged subcontractors eligible for the program, would the Court's decision have been the same?

---

[53] 125 LRRM 2918 (11th Cir. 1987).
[54] *Id.* at 2919.
[55] *Id.* at 2922.

5. Manual Lerma, a Mexican-American, responded to an advertisement announcing the availability of a custodial position at the Harlingen, Texas, post office. The applications were independently rated. Lerma placed third on the hiring list with a score of 95 points out of 110. Immediately behind Lerma was a white male named Ricky Schwab with a rating of 94. Schwab had worked at the Harlingen post office on a temporary basis in the past. After interviewing the four top candidates, the postmaster appointed Schwab to the vacant custodial position. The postmaster cited the favorable recommendation of a supervisor who had observed Schwab during his temporary work at the post office as a persuasive factor in his decision to choose Schwab over the other candidates.

    Lerma brought a Title VII action against the Postal Service alleging that the failure to hire him was discrimination based on his race and national origin.

    The Postal Service contended that no discrimination took place, that Lerma failed to establish a *prima facie* case under Title VII, and that legitimate reasons existed for selecting Schwab over Lerma.

    On the basis of the facts given, did Lerma establish a *prima facie* case under Title VII? If so, what must the defendant do to avoid liability? Decide. [*Lerma v. Balger*, 29 FEP 1829 (5th Cir.)]

6. The New Bedford Police Department required all police officers, both male and female, to satisfy a 5-foot 6-inch minimum height requirement. Maria Costa wished to become a police officer. She had passed the city's physical examination and had scored 93 percent on the state civil service examination. Costa's successful completion of these requirements gained her a ranking as the number one candidate on the eligibility list for female officers. When two vacancies for a female police officer occurred, Costa was interviewed for the position but was rejected due to her failure to satisfy the minimum height requirement. The second ranked female applicant was also rejected under the height requirement. The city hired the third and fourth ranked women, who did meet the minimum height.

    Costa brought an action under Title VII, producing undisputed evidence that less than 20 percent of women attain the height of 5 feet 6 inches. Therefore, Costa claimed that the police department's minimum height policy had a disparate impact upon women in violation of Title VII.

    The city denied this allegation by claiming that its policy did not result in a disparate impact upon women since it hired women for the vacancies.

    Does the city policy violate Title VII? Decide the case. [*Costa v. Markey*, 706 F.2d 1 (1st Cir.)]

7. In 1985 a U.S. district court approved an affirmative action plan for the Washington, D.C. (D.C.), fire department that required that 60 percent of new hires be black. D.C. itself was predominantly black, with 65 percent of the workforce and up to 75 percent of the applicants from D.C. being black. Twenty-nine percent of the entire metropolitan Washington, D.C., area, from which D.C. recruited firefighters, was black. In 1983, 80 percent of the new hires were black. In 1982, 67.5 percent of the new hires were black. Over a four-year period an average of 75 percent of those hired were black. Between 1980 and 1984 virtually every candidate who showed up to take the test for firefighter passed it because the cutoff score was set so low that even random answering of questions would lead to a passing mark. D.C.'s goal in its affirmative action plan was to achieve racial parity in its firefighting force.

The plaintiffs contended that the evidence was clear that the fire department was not engaging in hiring practices that discriminated against blacks and that no dismantling of the structures of past discrimination remained for the courts. They contended that the plan and its goal were illegal.

D.C. stated that the fire department was just 38 percent black, while the working age population of D.C. was 70 percent black. D.C. contended that "plantation politics" were practiced in D.C. for over a century. It stated that the plaintiffs urged D.C. to forget the bad old days of discrimination and concentrate on the parity of current practices; however, it argued that racial parity would be lost without the 60 percent hiring goal.

What standard must a court apply in reviewing whether a city's race-conscious affirmative action quotas are permissible? On the limited evidence before you, were D.C.'s hiring practices discriminatory considering the qualified and relevant labor market? Is D.C.'s goal of achieving racial parity constitutionally valid? [*Hammond v. Barry*, 42 EPD ¶ 36,804 (D.C. Cir.)]

8. The First Alabama Bank of Montgomery was a party to various contracts with the United States in which it agreed to be bound by the terms of Executive Order 11246. The bank formulated an affirmative action plan. The Office of Federal Contract Compliance Programs notified First Alabama that it wished to review the compliance with Executive Order 11246, Section 503 of the Rehabilitation Act of 1973, and Section 402 of the Vietnam Veterans Readjustment Assistance Act of 1974. Accordingly, the OFCCP asked the bank to submit a copy of its affirmative action plan and other supporting documentation.

   The bank refused to supply the requested information or to allow an OFCCP compliance officer to conduct an on-site review. The bank stated that it had undergone three compliance reviews under Executive Order 11246 in the last ten years and had been found to be in compliance each time. Furthermore, the bank stated that it had been a defendant in a ten-year race discrimination action under Title VII during which it had filed quarterly reports with the court. The litigation had ended with a finding by the court that the bank did not discriminate against blacks in its hiring practices.

   Given the bank's refusal to comply, the Department of Labor issued a complaint against the bank asking that First Alabama be debarred from receiving government contracts until it convinced the Secretary of Labor that it was in compliance with the affirmative action obligations of Executive Order 11246. After notice and hearing, the secretary's complaint was sustained and First Alabama was debarred.

   Citing its compliance history and the favorable decision in the Title VII case, First Alabama sought judicial review of the debarment in district court.

   Should the debarment decision be upheld as proper? If so, what must First Alabama do to renew its eligibility as a government contractor? [*First Alabama Bank of Montgomery, N.A. v. Donovan*, 30 FEP 4448 (11th Cir.)]

9. Clara Watson, who is black, was hired by the Fort Worth Bank and Trust Co. in August in 1973 and was promoted to teller in 1976. Between 1980 and 1981 Watson applied for four supervisory jobs, but white employees were selected for these positions. The bank, which had some 80 employees, had not developed formal criteria for evaluating candidates but relied on the subjective judgment of supervisors who were acquainted with the candidates and the nature of the jobs to be filled.

In a Title VII lawsuit against the bank, the trial court, following a disparate treatment model, concluded that Watson had established a *prima facie* case; the bank had rebutted it by presenting legitimate, nondiscriminatory reasons for each challenged promotion decision; and Watson had failed to show that the reasons were pretexts. Watson presented evidence that showed that the bank had only one black supervisor from 1975 to 1983, and a statistician testified on her behalf that a white applicant had a four times better chance of being hired than a black applicant. Watson claimed that a disparate impact model analysis of the employer's subjective promotion policy standards indicated that she was discriminated against in violation of Title VII. The court refused to apply a disparate impact analysis to subjective promotion procedures such as job interviews and performance evaluations, saying that disparate impact analysis was meant to evaluate objective criteria such as testing or diploma requirements.

Watson contended that if an employer's undisciplined system of subjective decision making had precisely the same effect as a system pervaded by impermissible intentional discrimination, it was difficult to see why Title VII was not violated. She contended, moreover, that the *Griggs* decision would be nullified if disparate impact analysis were applied only to objective selection practices.

The bank contended that employers would have to abandon subjective methods of evaluating candidates for promotion, such as interviews or performance evaluations, if it were forced to defend disparate impact cases, and its only alternative would be to adopt a quota system in order to ensure that no plaintiff could establish a *prima facie* case. It stated that quota systems were clearly contrary to Title VII. Further, the bank stated that Watson had full opportunity to prove that the bank did not promote her because of her race, and she failed to prove her case.

Did the trial court err in failing to apply disparate impact analysis to Watson's claims of discrimination in promotion? [*Watson v. Fort Worth Bank and Trust Co.*, 47 FEP 102 (U.S. S.Ct.)]

10. Connie Cunico, a white woman, was employed by the Pueblo, Colorado, School District as a social worker. She and other social workers were laid off in seniority order due to the district's poor financial situation. However, the school board thereafter decided to retain Mr. Wayne Hunter, a black social worker with less seniority than Ms. Cunico, because he was the only black on the administrative staff. No racial imbalance existed in the relevant workforce; and black persons constituted 2 percent of the workforce. Ms. Cunico, who was rehired over two years later, claimed that she was the victim of reverse discrimination. She stated that she lost $110,361 in back wages, plus $76,000 in attorneys' fees and costs. The school district responded that it was correct in protecting with special consideration the only black administrator in the district under the general principles it set forth in its AAP.

Refer to the text discussion of *Wygant v. Jackson Board of Education.* Did the school board grant a layoff preference based on race in this case?

Using standards developed in *Weber* and *Johnson*, did the employer show that its affirmative action in retaining Mr. Hunter was justified as a remedial measure? Decide. [*Cunico v. Pueblo School District No. 6*, 917 F.2d 431 (10th Cir.)]

3
Pay Equity; Age Discrimination

SECTION 18—EQUAL PAY FOR EQUAL WORK

The principle of equal pay for equal work regardless of sex is set forth in the Equal Pay Act of 1963, which was enacted as Section 6(d) of the Fair Labor Standards Act (FLSA). The Equal Pay Act prohibits employers from discriminating against employees covered by the minimum wage provisions of the FLSA by paying lower wages to employees of one sex than to employees of the opposite sex for equal work in the same establishment on jobs that require equal skill, effort, and responsibility and are performed under similar working conditions.[1] The Equal Pay Act was intended as a broad charter of women's rights in the business world. The Act seeks to eliminate the depressing effects on living standards caused by reduced wages for female workers. The Act does not prohibit any variation in wage rates paid men and women but only those variations based solely on

---

[1] 29 U.S.C. Section 206(d)(1).

sex. The Act sets forth four exceptions, allowing variances in wages to be based on (1) a seniority system, (2) a merit system, (3) a system that measures earnings by quantity or quality of production, or (4) a differential based on any factor other than sex.[2]

The 1974 amendments to the FLSA make the Act applicable to employees of the federal, state, and local governments and their agencies.[3] Enforcement of the Act is the responsibility of the Equal Employment Opportunity Commission.

Congress, in prescribing equal pay for equal work, did not require that the jobs in question be identical but only that the jobs be "substantially equal."[4] In applying this "substantially equal" test, the courts have had no difficulty finding that it is the job content, not the job description, that is controlling.[5]

The courts have uniformly found that the enforcing federal agency bears the initial burden of proving that the employer pays employees of one sex less than employees of the other sex for performing equal work. Once the enforcing agency sustains its initial burden of proof, the burden shifts to the employer to show that the differential is justified by one of the four allowable exceptions.

In *Shultz v. Wheaton Glass Co.*,[6] the Third Circuit Court of Appeals found that a manufacturing plant's 10 percent pay differential for male selector-packers over the pay for female selector-packers, where the male selector-packers spent a relatively small portion of their time doing the additional tasks of "snap-up boys," a lower paying classification requiring lifting and other unskilled tasks, was a violation of the Equal Pay Act. The court did not require the skill, effort, and responsibility of the female selector-packers' work to be precisely equal to the male selector-packers' work but rather that the work be substantially equal.

The *Corning Glass Works* decision, presented in this section, discusses several important aspects of the Equal Pay Act. This case was brought at a time when enforcement of the Act was the responsibility of the Department of Labor's Employment Standards Administration and court actions were brought in the name of the Secretary of Labor. The Equal Pay Act is now administered by the EEOC.

CORNING GLASS WORKS v. BRENNAN

Supreme Court of the United States, 415 U.S. 972 (1974).

MARSHALL, J.

These cases arise under the Equal Pay Act of 1963, 29 U.S.C. Section 206(d)(1), which added to the Fair Labor Standards Act the principle of equal pay for equal work regardless of sex. The principal question posed is whether Corning Glass Works violated the Act by paying a higher base wage to male night shift inspectors than it paid to female inspectors performing the same tasks on the day shift, where the higher wage was

---

[2] *Id.*
[3] See Section 3(d) of the FLSA as amended in 1974, P.L. 93-259.
[4] *Shultz v. Wheaton Glass Co.*, 421 F.2d 259 (3d Cir. 1970).
[5] *Brennan v. Victoria Bank & Trust Co.*, 493 F.2d 896 (5th Cir. 1974).
[6] 421 F.2d 259 (3d Cir. 1970).

paid in addition to a separate night shift differential paid to all employees for night work. In No. 73–29, the Court of Appeals for the Second Circuit, in a case involving several Corning plants in Corning, New York, held that this practice violated the Act 474, F.2d 226 (1973). In No. 73–695, the Court of Appeals for the Third Circuit, in a case involving a Corning plant in Wellsboro, Pennsylvania, reached the opposite conclusion. 480 F.2d 1254 (1973). We granted certiorari and consolidated the cases to resolve this unusually direct conflict between two circuits. Finding ourselves in substantial agreement with the analysis of the Second Circuit, we affirm in No. 73–29 and reverse in No. 73–695.

I.

Prior to 1925, Corning operated its plants in Wellsboro and Corning only during the day, and all inspection work was performed by women. Between 1925 and 1930, the company began to introduce automatic production equipment which made it desirable to institute a night shift. During this period, however, both New York and Pennsylvania law prohibited women from working at night. As a result, in order to fill inspector positions on the new night shift, the company had to recruit male employees from among its male day workers. The male employees so transferred demanded and received wages substantially higher than those paid to women inspectors engaged on the two day shifts. During this same period, however, no plant-wide shift differential existed and male employees working at night, other than inspectors, received the same wages as their day shift counterparts. Thus a situation developed where the night inspectors were all male, the day inspectors all female, and the male inspectors received significantly higher wages.

In 1944, Corning plants at both locations were organized by a labor union and a collective bargaining agreement was negotiated for all production and maintenance employees. This agreement for the first time established a plantwide shift differential, but this change did not eliminate the higher base wage paid to male night inspectors. Rather, the shift differential was superimposed on the existing differences in base wages between male night inspectors and female day inspectors.

Prior to the June 11, 1964, effective date of the Equal Pay Act, the law in both Pennsylvania and New York was amended to permit women to work at night. It was not until some time after the effective date of the Act, however, that Corning initiated efforts to eliminate the differential rates for male and female inspectors. Beginning in June 1966, Corning started to open up jobs on the night shift to women. Previously separate male and female seniority lists were consolidated and women became eligible to exercise their seniority, on the same basis as men, to bid for the higher paid night inspection jobs as vacancies occurred.

On January 20, 1969, a new collective bargaining agreement went into effect, establishing a new "job evaluation" system for setting wage rates. The new agreement abolished for the future the separate base wages for day and night shift inspectors and imposed a uniform base wage for inspectors exceeding the wage rate for the night shift previously in effect. All inspectors hired after January 20, 1969, were to receive the same base wage, whatever their sex or shift. The collective bargaining agreement further provided, however, for a higher "red circle" rate for employees hired prior to January 20, 1969, when working as inspectors on the night shift. This "red circle" rate served essentially to perpetuate the differential in base wages between day and night inspectors.

The Secretary of Labor brought these cases to enjoin Corning from violating the Equal Pay Act and to collect back wages allegedly due female employees because of past violations. Three distinct questions are presented: (1) Did Corning ever violate the Equal Pay Act by paying male night shift inspectors more than female day shift inspectors? (2) If so, did Corning cure its violation of the Act in 1966 by permitting women to work as night shift inspectors? (3) Finally, if the violation was not remedied in 1966, did Corning cure its violation in 1969 by equalizing day and night inspector wage rates but establishing higher "red circle" rates for existing employees working on the night shift?

II.

Congress' purpose in enacting the Equal Pay Act was to remedy what was perceived to be a serious and endemic problem of employment discrimination in private industry—the fact that the wage structure of "many segments of American industry has been based on an ancient but outmoded belief that a man, because of his role in society, should be paid more than a woman, even though his duties are the same." S. Rept. No. 176, 88th Cong., 1st Sess. (1963), at 1. The solution adopted was quite simple in principle: to require that "equal work be rewarded by equal wages." *Ibid.*

The Act's basic structure and operation are similarly straightforward. In order to make out a case under the Act, the Secretary must show that an employer pays different wages to employees of opposite sexes "for equal work on jobs the performance of which requires equal skill, effort, and responsibility, and which are performed under similar working conditions." Although the Act is silent on this point, its legislative history makes plain that the Secretary has the burden of proof on this issue, as both of the courts below recognized.

The Act also establishes four exceptions— three specific and one a general catchall provision—where different payment to employees of opposite sexes "is made pursuant to (i) a seniority system; (ii) a merit system; (iii) a system which measures earnings by quantity or quality of production; or (iv) a differential based on any other factor other than sex." Again, while the Act is silent on this question, its structure and history also suggest that once the Secretary has carried his burden of showing that the em-

ployer pays workers of one sex more than workers of the opposite sex for equal work, the burden shifts to the employer to show that the differential is justified under one of the Act's four exceptions. All of the many lower courts that have considered this question have so held, and this view is consistent with the general rule that the application of an exemption under the Fair Labor Standards Act is a matter of affirmative defense on which the employer has the burden of proof.

The contentions of the parties in this case reflect the Act's underlying framework. Corning argues that the Secretary has failed to prove that Corning ever violated the Act because day shift work is not "performed under similar working conditions" as night shift work. The Secretary maintains that day shift and night shift work are performed under "similar working conditions" within the meaning of the Act. . . .

Congress' intent, as manifested in [the Act's] history, was to use these terms to incorporate into the new federal act the well-defined and well-accepted principles of job evaluation so as to ensure that wage differentials based upon bona fide job evaluation plans would be outside the purview of the Act. . . .

While a layman might well assume that time of day worked reflects one aspect of a job's "working conditions," the term has a different and much more specific meaning in the language of industrial relations. As Corning's own representative testified at the hearings, the element of working conditions encompasses two subfactors: "surroundings" and "hazards." "Surroundings" measure the elements, such as toxic chemicals or fumes, regularly encountered by a worker, their intensity, and their frequency. "Hazards" take into account the physical hazards regularly encountered, their frequency, and the severity of injury they can cause. This definition of "working conditions" is not only manifested in Corning's own job evaluation plans but is also well accepted across a wide range of American industry.

Nowhere in any of these definitions is time of day worked mentioned as a relevant criterion. The fact of the matter is that the concept of "working conditions," as used in the specialized language of job evaluation systems, simply does not encompass shift differentials. Indeed, while Corning now argues that night inspection work is not equal to day inspection work, all of its own job evaluation plans, including the one now in effect, have consistently treated them as equal in all respects, including working conditions. And Corning's Manager of Job Evaluation testified in No. 73–29 that time of day worked was not considered to be a "working condition." . . .

The question remains, however, whether Corning carried its burden of proving that the higher rate paid for night inspection work, until 1966 performed solely by men, was in fact intended to serve as compensation for night work, or rather constituted an added payment based upon sex. We agree that the record amply supported the District Court's conclusion that Corning had not sustained its burden of proof. As its history revealed, "the higher night rate was in large part the product of the generally higher wage level of male workers and the need to compensate them for performing what were regarded as demeaning tasks." 474 F.2d, at 233.

The differential in base wages originated at a time when no other night employees received higher pay than corresponding day workers and it was maintained long after the company instituted a separate plant-wide differential which was thought to compensate adequately for the additional burdens of night work. The differential arose simply because men would not work at the low rates paid women inspectors, and it reflected a job market in which Corning could pay women less than men for the same work. That the company took advantage of such a situation may be understandable as a matter of economics, but its differential nevertheless became illegal once Congress enacted into law the principle of equal pay for equal work. . . .

The judgment in No. 73–29 is affirmed. The judgment in No. 73–695 is reversed and the case remanded to the Court of Appeals for further proceedings consistent with this opinion.

It is so ordered.

CASE QUESTIONS

1. Summarize the facts of the case.
2. Who brought the two court actions against Corning Glass Works?
3. Does the statutory term *working conditions* encompass the time of day worked?

SECTION 19—THE *GUNTHER* DECISION AND COMPARABLE WORTH

In spite of the passage of the Equal Pay Act of 1963 and Title VII of the Civil Rights Act of 1964, a substantial earnings gap exists between the average earnings of women working full time and the average earnings of men working full time. The disparity has closed from 62 percent in 1979 to 75 percent in 1996.[7] It is generally accepted that the reason the overall statistics show that women earn substantially less than men is that a large proportion of working women are employed in certain predominantly female occupations, such as nursing, secretarial work, social work, clerical work, school teaching, food service, and domestic service, that have significantly lower pay scales relative to other occupations where men are dominant. The Equal Pay Act has been very successful in remedying pay disparity between men and women performing the same work for their

[7] Bureau of Labor Statistics Annual Report (U.S. Government Printing Office, 1997). As of December 1996, the average weekly income for men was $557, while the average weekly income for women was $418.

employer. Thus female full-time college professors earn about the same as male full-time college professors of similar qualifications; female autoworkers earn the same as male autoworkers doing the same work.

Advocates of the concept of *comparable worth* believe that female employees whose jobs are separate and distinct from jobs performed by male employees but are of comparable worth or value to the employer are entitled to wages comparable to those of male employees. Advocates of comparable worth believe that if comparable wages are not paid, female employees should be entitled to relief under Title VII of the Civil Rights Act of 1964. This theory has not been accepted in the courts.

Sex-Based Discrimination in Job Compensation

In *County of Washington v. Gunther,* presented in this section, the Supreme Court considered the claims of four women employed as matrons at the Washington County, Oregon, jail. These women claimed that the pay differential between them and male corrections officers was attributable to intentional sex discrimination even though the matron's job was not substantially the same job as that of the corrections officers. The Supreme Court set forth the narrow holding that the plaintiffs' claim of low pay because of discrimination based on sex was not barred by Section 703(h) of Title VII, the Bennett Amendment, merely because the plaintiffs did not perform work "equal" to that of the male corrections officers. The significance of the decision is that women may now bring a sex discrimination suit on the basis of low compensation even if they cannot prove that male co-workers are being paid higher wages for substantially the same job. The Court majority emphasized that its narrow holding did not require it to take a position on the issue of comparable worth.

Comparable Worth

The *Gunther* decision was widely acclaimed by advocates of comparable worth as a first step in the direction of court acceptance of that doctrine. In *AFSCME v. State of Washington* (AFSCME I),[8] a U.S. district court judge held that the state violated Title VII by its failure to pay men and women the same wages for work of comparable, but not equal, worth. The judge found that the state's practice of taking prevailing market rates into account in setting employee wages had an adverse impact on women, who have historically received lower wages than men in the labor market. The judge ordered implementation of a salary schedule based on comparable worth and ordered back pay of up to $800 million.

In *AFSCME v. State of Washington* (AFSCME II),[9] the Ninth Circuit Court of Appeals reversed the trial court's decision. The court of appeals rejected the doctrine of comparable worth, holding that reliance on market forces to set wages did not violate Title VII. The appeals court stated that the value of a job depends on factors other than

---

[8] 578 F. Supp. 846 (W.D. Wash. 1983).
[9] 770 F.2d 1401 (9th Cir. 1985).

just the actions performed on the job, factors such as the availability of workers and the effectiveness of unions in negotiating wages. Moreover, the court stated that the legislative history of Title VII did not indicate that Congress intended "to abrogate fundamental economic principles such as the laws of supply and demand."[10]

AFSCME and the state of Washington reached a pay equity agreement in resolution of the comparable worth dispute. This agreement calls for the state to spend some $482.4 million over six years to raise salaries of certain underpaid workers.

In *American Nurses Ass'n v. State of Illinois*,[11] a sex discrimination case brought by nurses against the state of Illinois, the Seventh Circuit Court of Appeals stated in part:

> An employer (private or public) that simply pays the going wage in each of the different types of jobs in its establishment, and makes no effort to discourage women from applying for particular jobs, would justifiably be surprised to discover that it may be violating federal law because each wage rate and therefore the ratio between them have been found to be determined by cultural or psychological factors attributable to the history of male domination of society; that it has to hire a consultant to find out how it must, regardless of market conditions, change the wages it pays, in order to achieve equity between traditionally male and traditionally female jobs; and that it must pay back pay to boot.[12]

In cases dealing with comparable worth issues, employers have a valid defense if they relied on market forces to set wages. The *Gunther* decision may be shown to be consistent with cases such as *AFSCME II* in that the compensation system in *Gunther* tied wages to market rates, but the violation of Title VII occurred when it did not pay the same percentage of the market rate to women as it did to men. The decision not to pay the women the full rate was attributable to intentional sex discrimination.

COUNTY OF WASHINGTON v. GUNTHER

Supreme Court of the United States, 452 U.S. 161 (1981).

[The plaintiffs were four women employed as matrons at the Washington County, Oregon, jail. The county also employed male corrections officers and deputy sheriffs. The matrons under Oregon law guarded female inmates, while the corrections officers and deputy sheriffs guarded male inmates. Effective February 1, 1973, the matrons were paid monthly salaries of between $525 and $668, while the salaries for the male guards ranged from $701 to $904. The plaintiffs filed suit under Title VII, alleging that they were paid unequal wages for work substantially equal to that performed by their male counterparts and, in the alternative, that part of the pay differential was attributable to intentional sex discrimination. The district court found that the male corrections officers supervised up to ten times as many prisoners per guard as did the matrons and that the females devoted much of their time to less valuable clerical duties such as processing fingerprint cards and mug shots, filing reports, keeping medical records, recording deputy sheriffs'

---

[10] *Id.* at 1407.
[11] 783 F.2d 716 (7th Cir. 1986).
[12] *Id.* at 720.

activities, and censoring mail. The district court held that the plaintiffs' jobs were not substantially equal to those of the male guards, and the plaintiffs were thus not entitled to equal pay. The district court also dismissed the claim based on intentional sex discrimination, holding as a matter of law that sex-based wage discrimination cannot be brought under Title VII unless it would satisfy the "equal work" standard of the Equal Pay Act. The court of appeals reversed the district court on this point, and the Supreme Court granted certiorari.]

BRENNAN, J.

The question presented is whether § 703(h) of Title VII of the Civil Rights Act of 1964, restricts Title VII's prohibition of sex-based wage discrimination to claims of equal pay for equal work.

I.

We emphasize at the outset the narrowness of the question before us in this case. Respondents' claim is not based on the controversial concept of "comparable worth," under which plaintiffs might claim increased compensation on the basis of a comparison of the intrinsic worth or difficulty of their job with that of other jobs in the same organization or community. Rather, respondents seek to prove, by direct evidence, that their wages were depressed because of intentional sex discrimination, consisting of setting the wage scale for female guards, but not for male guards, at a level lower than its own survey of outside markets and the worth of the jobs warranted. The narrow question in this case is whether such a claim is precluded by the last sentence of § 703(h) of Title VII, called the "Bennett Amendment."

II.

Title VII makes it an unlawful employment practice for an employer "to discriminate against any individual with respect to his compensation, terms, conditions, or privileges of employment, because of such individual's . . .

sex. . . ." The Bennett Amendment to Title VII, however, provides:

"It shall not be an unlawful employment practice under this subchapter for any employer to differentiate upon the basis of sex in determining the amount of the wages or compensation paid or to be paid to employees of such employer if such differentiation is authorized by the provisions in Section 206(d) of Title 29." Section 703(h).

To discover what practices are exempted from Title VII's prohibitions by the Bennett Amendment, we must turn to § 206(d) of Title 29—the Equal Pay Act—which provides the relevant part:

"No employer having employees subject to any provisions of this section shall discriminate, within any establishment in which such employees are employed, between employees on the basis of sex by paying wages to employees in such establishment at a rate less than the rate at which he pays wages to employees of the opposite sex in such establishment for equal work on jobs the performance of which requires equal skill, effort, and responsibility, and which are performed under similar working conditions, except where such payment is made pursuant to (i) a seniority system; (ii) a merit system; (iii) a system which measures earnings by quantity or quality of production; or (iv) a differential based on any other factor other than sex." 29 U.S.C. § 206(d)(1).

On its face, the Equal Pay Act contains three restrictions pertinent to this case. First, its coverage is limited to those employers subject to the Fair Labor Standards Act. Thus, the Act does not apply, for example, to certain businesses engaged in retail sales, fishing, agriculture, and newspaper publishing. Second, the Act is restricted to cases involving "equal work on jobs the performance of which requires equal skill, effort, and responsibility, and which are performed under similar working conditions." Third, the Act's four affirmative defenses exempt any wage differentials attributable to seniority, merit, quantity or quality of production, or "any other factor other than sex."

Petitioner argues that the purpose of the Bennett Amendment was to restrict Title VII sex-based wage discrimination claims to those that could also be brought under the Equal Pay Act, and thus that claims not arising from "equal work" are precluded. Respondents, in contrast, argue that the Bennett Amendment was designed merely to incorporate the four affirmative defenses of the Equal Pay Act into Title VII for sex-based wage discrimination claims. Respondents thus contend that claims for sex-based wage discrimination can be brought under Title VII even though no member of the opposite sex holds an equal but higher-paying job, provided that the challenged wage rate is not based on seniority, merit, quantity or quality of production, or "any other factor other than sex." The Court of Appeals found respondents' interpretation the "more persuasive." 623 F.2d at 1311, 20 FEP Cases, at 797. While recognizing that the language and legislative history of the provision are not unambiguous, we conclude that the Court of Appeals was correct. . . .

The legislative background of the Bennett Amendment is fully consistent with this interpretation. . . .

"Mr. BENNETT. Mr. President, after many years of yearning by members of the fair sex in this country, and after very careful study by the appropriate committees of Congress, last year Congress passed the so-called Equal Pay Act, which became effective only yesterday.

"By this time, programs have been established for the effective administration of this act. Now, when the civil rights bill is under consideration, in which the word 'sex' has been inserted in many places, I do not believe sufficient attention may have been paid to possible conflicts between the wholesale insertion of the word 'sex' in the bill and in the Equal Pay Act.

"The purpose of my amendment is to provide that in the event of conflicts, the provisions of the Equal Pay Act shall not be nullified.

"I understand that the leadership in charge of the bill have agreed to the amendment as a proper technical correction of the bill. If they will confirm that understand [sic], I shall ask that the amendment be voted on without asking for yeas and nays.

"Mr. HUMPHREY. The amendment of the Senator from Utah is helpful. I believe it is needed. I thank him for his thoughtfulness. The amendment is fully acceptable.

"Mr. DIRKSEN. Mr. President, I yield myself 1 minute.

"We were aware of the conflict that might develop, because the Equal Pay Act was an amendment to the Fair Labor Standards Act. The Fair Labor Standards Act carries out certain exceptions.

"All that the pending amendment does is recognize those exceptions, that are carried in the basic act.

"Therefore, this amendment is necessary, in the interest of clarification." 110 Cong. Rec. 13647 (1964).

As this discussion shows, Senator Bennett proposed the Amendment because of a general concern that insufficient attention had been paid to the relation between the Equal Pay Act and Title VII, rather than because of a *specific* potential conflict between the statutes. His explanation that the Amendment assured that the provisions of the Equal Pay Act "shall not be nullified" in the event of conflict with Title VII may be read as referring to the affirmative defenses of the Act. Indeed, his emphasis on the "technical" nature of the Amendment and his concern for not disrupting the "effective administration" of the Equal Pay Act are more compatible with an interpretation of the Amendment as incorporating the Act's affirmative defenses, as administratively interpreted, than as engrafting all the restrictive features of the Equal Pay Act onto Title VII. . . .

Thus, although the few references by Members of Congress to the Bennett Amendment do not explicitly confirm that its purpose was to incorporate into Title VII the four affirmative defenses of the Equal Pay Act in sex-based wage discrimination cases, they are broadly consistent with such a reading, and do not support an alternative reading.

Our interpretation of the Bennett Amendment draws additional support from the remedial purposes of Title VII and the Equal Pay Act. . . .

Under petitioner's reading of the Bennett Amendment, only those sex-based wage discrimination claims that satisfy the "equal work" standard of the Equal Pay Act could be brought under Title VII. In practical terms, this means that a woman who is discriminatorily underpaid could obtain no relief—no matter how egregious the discrimination might be—unless her employer also employed a man in an equal job in the same establishment, at a higher rate of pay. Thus, if an employer hired a woman for a unique position in the company and then admitted that her salary would have been higher had she been male, the woman would be unable to obtain legal redress under petitioner's interpretation. Similarly, if an employer used a transparently sex-biased system for wage determination, women holding jobs not equal to those held by men would be denied the right to prove that the system is a pretext for discrimination.

III.

Petitioner argues strenuously that the approach of the Court of Appeals places "the pay structure of virtually every employer and the entire economy . . . at risk and subject to scrutiny by the federal courts." It raises the spectre that "Title VII plaintiffs could draw any type of comparison imaginable concerning job duties and pay between any job predominantly performed by women and any job predominantly performed by men." But whatever the merit of petitioner's arguments in other contexts, they are inapplicable here, for claims based on the type of job comparisons petitioner describes are manifestly different from respondents' claim. Respondents contend that the County of Washington evaluated the worth of their jobs; that the county determined that they should be paid approximately 95 percent as much as the male correctional officers; that it paid them only about 70 percent as much, while paying the male officers

the full evaluated worth of their jobs; and that the failure of the county to pay respondents the full evaluated worth of their jobs can be proven to be attributable to intentional sex discrimination. Thus, respondents' suit does not require a court to make its own subjective assessment of the value of the male and female guard jobs, or to attempt by statistical technique or other method to quantify the effect of sex discrimination on the wage rates.

We do not decide in this case the precise contours of lawsuits challenging sex discrimination in compensation under Title VII. It is sufficient to note that respondents' claims of discriminatory undercompensation are not barred by § 703(h) of Title VII merely because respondents do not perform work equal to that of male jail guards. The judgment of the Court of Appeals is therefore

Affirmed.

Dissenting Opinion

REHNQUIST, J., joined by BURGER, C. J., and STEWART and POWELL, J. J.

The Court today holds a plaintiff may state a claim of sex-based wage discrimination under Title VII without even establishing that she has performed "equal or substantially equal work" to that of males as defined in the Equal Pay Act. Because I believe that the legislative history of both the Equal Pay Act and Title VII clearly establish that there can be no Title VII claim of sex-based wage discrimination without proof of "equal work," I dissent. . . .

CASE QUESTIONS

1. What does the Bennett Amendment provide?
2. What did the employer argue was the purpose of the Bennett Amendment?
3. State the Supreme Court's decision.
4. If the equal work standard were to apply, could situations exist where a discriminatorily underpaid woman would be unable to obtain a remedy?

SECTION 20—AGE DISCRIMINATION

The Age Discrimination in Employment Act of 1967 (ADEA) as amended forbids discrimination against men and women over 40 years of age by employers, unions, employment agencies, state and local governments, and the federal government.[13] Employees of the U.S. Senate, the U.S. House of Representatives, and the executive branch are also protected from age discrimination under special procedures set forth in the Government Employees Rights Act of 1991.[14]

Enforcement of the ADEA is the responsibility of the EEOC. Procedures and time limitations for filing and processing ADEA charges are the same as those under Title VII. After receiving a right-to-sue letter from the EEOC, the aggrieved person has 90 days to initiate a court lawsuit in a federal court.[15]

Most ADEA suits are brought on a disparate treatment theory of intentional discrimination because of age. Procedures are similar in many respects to those previously set forth in the text on Title VII. The burden of proof framework of the *McDonnell Douglas prima facie case* is commonly applied to ADEA disparate treatment cases. However, the *prima facie* showing of age discrimination does not require that the plaintiff's replacement (if any) be a person younger than the protected age group—that is, younger than 40 years old. In *O'Connor v. Consolidated Coin Caterers Corp.*,[16] the Supreme Court held that replacement by someone under 40 was not a necessary element of an ADEA *prima facie* case. The *McDonnell Douglas* model is not the exclusive method of assessing an ADEA disparate treatment case. For example, where there is direct evidence of discrimination, a determination may be made on that basis alone.

In the *Crawford v. Medina General Hospital* case, presented in this section, the U.S. Court of Appeals for the Sixth Circuit determined that a hostile working environment claim can be brought under the ADEA. However, the court held that the plaintiff did not meet her burden of proof in making out a *prima facie* case.

An individual whose claim of age discrimination before a state administrative agency is rejected may nevertheless bring an action in a U.S. district court under the ADEA. In *Astoria Federal Savings and Loan v. Solimino*,[17] the Supreme Court held that a state court finding of no probable cause of termination on account of age under state law does not preclude federal litigation of an ADEA claim.

In *McKennon v. Nashville Banner Publishing Co.*,[18] the Supreme Court held that an employee who is discharged in violation of the ADEA is not completely barred from relief when the employer subsequently discovers evidence of the employee's misconduct that would have been just cause for terminating the employee. Christine McKennon was terminated from her job as a confidential secretary by the Nashville Banner Publishing Co., publisher of the *Nashville Banner* newspaper, after 39 years of service due to "a reduction in force." She was then 62 years old. However, two days prior to her

---

[13] 29 U.S.C. Section 623.
[14] PL 102-166, Nov. 21, 1991.
[15] Section 115, Civil Rights Act of 1991; 29 USC 626(e).
[16] 116 S.Ct. 1307 (1996).
[17] 111 S.Ct. 2166 (1991).
[18] 115 S.Ct. 879 (1995).

termination the Banner hired a 26-year-old secretary. McKennon sued the Banner for age discrimination. In a deposition taken by the Banner in preparation for the ADEA lawsuit, the employer discovered that McKennon had copied certain confidential documents at work and showed them to her husband. The Banner then sent her notification that such a breach of her responsibilities was a dismissal offense. The district court granted the Banner's motion for a summary judgment, determining that such a breach of confidentiality was a just cause for dismissal. Under the Supreme Court's decision, the plaintiff would receive back pay for an ADEA violation from the time of her discharge in violation of the Act until the employer discovered the after-acquired evidence that would justify her termination. The remedies of additional back pay, reinstatement, and front pay will generally be precluded when the after-acquired evidence justifies termination. The *McKennon* rule should also apply in Title VII, EPA, and ADA cases according to the EEOC.[19]

CRAWFORD v. MEDINA GENERAL HOSPITAL
United States Court of Appeals, 69 EPD § 44,276 (6th Cir. 1996).

[Mary Ann Crawford filed suit against her employer, Medina General Hospital, as well as her supervisor, Darla Kermendy, alleging that they discriminated against her in violation of the Age Discrimination in Employment Act of 1967 by creating a hostile working environment. The U.S. district court disposed of the ADEA claim on summary judgment, reasoning that Crawford had failed to prove her *prima facie* case].

RYAN, C. J. . . .
The billing department at Medina General Hospital appears to have deep morale problems. To get the flavor of the situation, as well as to appreciate our resolution of the issue, requires that we burden our opinion with a rather detailed recitation of the evidence. The plaintiff, Mary Ann Crawford, began working at Medina in September 1964, when she was 28 years old. The defendant, Darla Kermendy, whose age is not apparent from the record, became Crawford's supervisor in June 1991. It is unclear what the atmosphere in the Medina billing depart-

ment was like prior to Kermendy's tenure, but once she came aboard, at least Crawford became unhappy. Crawford complains that beginning with Kermendy's hire, "there were racial remarks flying, old age remarks flying, [and] the younger women would make remarks and insulting remarks." There were also "sexual remarks, filthy remarks, and [Kermendy] had a habit of putting her hands" on Crawford, apparently in an aggressive manner.

Crawford points to several "old age remarks" in support of her hostile environment claim. Crawford alleges that "Kermendy made a comment, 'I don't think women over 55 should be working.'" Crawford did not hear that remark, since she was at home ill at the time the alleged remark was made, but two coworkers told her that Kermendy "had made that remark in their presence." They told Crawford that Kermendy was talking to them about Crawford when she made the comment. Kermendy filed an affidavit countering that her comment was simply that *she* would like to retire by the age of 55, and that

---

"[t]he comment was not directed to anyone other than [her]," as she "do[es] not care at what age anyone else may desire to retire." Her affidavit purported to explain that she wanted to retire at 55 because various family members had gotten sick shortly after attaining that age.

Next, Crawford complains that Kermendy said, within Crawford's hearing, that "[o]ld people should be seen and not heard." Crawford was "embarrassed" and "humiliated" by the comment. She does not know to whom the comment was made, because she could not actually see Kermendy at the time; she could only hear her voice, which was "[r]ude and unpleasant." Crawford, however, assumed the comment "was meant to include [her]." Crawford therefore "leaned around the file cabinet and . . . said, 'I heard that, Darla.' And she didn't respond." Crawford feels that Kermendy meant to suggest that "old people were somehow less than young people."

Crawford also generally alleges that "there were about five different girls" in the billing department "who would just constantly make . . . miserable" the lives of "the older ladies"; those five would "every once in a while" make negative comments, and "equate old with being stupid, useless, dumb." For instance, Crawford was once passing the door of a room where a group of people were having a pizza party, and one of the five looked out and saw her pass, and said, "It's just my luck in an office with an old dumb side to have to sit on that side." Crawford claims that Kermendy was in the room at the time, and "laughed and pointed and looked at [the woman making the comment]," and said "Oh, that's good." That comment apparently referred to the fact that a number of the older women sat on one particular side of the office. Crawford claims that the side was referred to as "the old side, the dumb side, worthless side." She also claims that Kermendy "refused to walk on that side of the office for a whole day once."

In sum, Crawford asserts that the office is "totally divided" on the basis of age. She con-

tends that in addition to verbal insults, the older women are "not included in anything," such as parties, as well as information about minor changes in office procedures. She further contends that Kermendy "calls the young people in[to Kermendy's office] and questions them about what the older people are doing, what they're saying, and then she encourages them to go out and confront those people." She claims that Kermendy "called attention" to Crawford's "extremely sensitive hearing" in a staff meeting once, and that Kermendy said that all another older worker, who had false teeth, "wanted for Christmas was her front teeth"; it is Crawford's belief that these comments are age-related.

That there was tension in the billing department is by now apparent. While it is Crawford's contention that the hostility directed at her was age-based, it is clear that Crawford treated others with hostility as well. For example, she refused to sign one coworker's birthday card, because, as Crawford explained, "I don't like her . . . because she's mean to me." She referred to one coworker as "the widow" because "she always wears black." She nicknamed one supervisor "Pat" because "at times [Crawford] feel[s] [the supervisor is] pathetic." Another coworker is nicknamed "Sluggo" because "she reminds [Crawford] of that cartoon character." Another is "Freak" because "she wears outlandish clothes and hairdos and that type of thing." She calls two coworkers "Miss Piggy," and another "fatso." Moreover, Crawford argued even with those other workers whom she considered her allies; for example, a note from one of Crawford's diaries, referring to a coworker that Crawford described as "older," reads as follows:

Ruth has gone over [to] the other side. Tell her nothing from now on.

According to Crawford, "the other side" denoted "the people who were against the older people."

Crawford herself says that, despite the incidents complained of, and despite being "unhappy" about the way Kermendy treated her, she "liked [her] job very well." She has continued to work at Medina throughout this course of events, and has suffered no demotion or reduction in pay. But in November 1993, she filed a complaint in federal district court, alleging that she was being subjected to a hostile working environment as a result of age discrimination. Her complaint also contained state-law claims for false imprisonment and for assault and battery, based on incidents not germane to her age discrimination claim.

The district court disposed of the plaintiff's ADEA claim on summary judgment, and dismissed the supplemental state-law claims. Although holding that a hostile work environment claim was cognizable under the ADEA, the district court concluded that the plaintiff had failed to produce evidence that the alleged harassment had the effect of unreasonably interfering with her performance and creating an intimidating, hostile, or offensive work environment that seriously affected her psychological well-being. The court noted, moreover, that most of the incidents complained of by Crawford "indicate[d] hostility between co-workers rather than an age-related hostile environment."

Crawford filed a timely notice of appeal as to defendants Medina, Kermendy, and Milligan only, thus abandoning her claims against defendant Slee. *See* Fed. R. App. P. 3(c). We note further that the notice of appeal named one Judy Reidell; because this is an individual not named in Crawford's complaint, it is clear that Reidell is not properly a party to this appeal.

The ADEA makes it unlawful for any employer to discharge any individual or otherwise discriminate against any individual with respect to his compensation, terms, conditions, or privileges of employment, because of such individual's age. . . .

While, as far as we can discern, no circuit has as yet applied the hostile-environment doctrine in an ADEA action. . . . we find it a relatively uncontroversial proposition that such a theory is viable under the ADEA. For at least these reasons, in light of the ADEA's employment of the "terms, conditions, or privileges of employment" language, we have no doubt that a hostile work environment claim may be stated. The broad application of the hostile-environment doctrine in the Title VII context; the general similarity of purpose shared by Title VII and the ADEA; and the fact that the Title VII rationale for the doctrine is of equal force in the ADEA context, all counsel this result. We thus hold that a plaintiff may advance a hostile-environment claim under the ADEA. These are the criteria for a *prima facie* claim:

1. The employee is 40 years old or older;
2. The employee was subjected to harassment, either through words or actions, based on age:
3. The harassment had the effect of unreasonably interfering with the employee's work performance and creating an objectively intimidating, hostile, or offensive work environment; and
4. The existence of some basis for liability on the part of the employer. . . .

The plaintiff's claim fails due to her lack of proof under both the second and third prongs of the *prima facie* case. First, the plaintiff has virtually no evidence that the "harassment" of which she complains was in any way based on her age. Instead, her theory appears wholly based on a false syllogism: A) My coworkers hate me; B) I am old; C) My coworkers hate me because I'm old. The plaintiff points to only two comments that are objectively indicative of age-based animus: Kermendy's comments that she does not "think women over 55 should be working," and that "[o]ld people should be seen and not heard." Other than those two remarks, however, there is virtually no evidence, apart from Crawford's self-serving conclusions, that the hostility in the Medina workplace was in any way related to age. Unquestionably, there was hostility and abusiveness in this working environment, but the evidence suggests that the atmosphere stemmed from a simple clash of personalities. In any event, there is an absence of evidence that it stemmed from a dislike of people over a particular age.

Indeed, many of the comments that Crawford asserts were age-based were, in reality, neutral. Thus, it is Crawford who insists on separating the Medina workforce into age categories; it is Crawford who consistently employs such terms as "older ladies"; and, importantly, it is Crawford who simply assumes, without objectively articulable support, that when she was insulted with age-neutral insults, it was *because of* her age.

Along those same lines, we think it is patent that we must entirely discount the plaintiff's complaints insofar as they focus on coworkers having parties without inviting her, or coworkers being surly or impolite. Even if coworkers failed to invite her to parties *because* she was over 55, it seems obvious that the ADEA was not intended to remedy minor social slights and the resulting hurt feelings. Pizza parties are simply not a term, condition, or privilege of employment of which Congress has taken cognizance.

In any event, even apart from the fact that only two comments were actually discernibly age-based, there is simply no question that the hostility at Medina, while not insubstantial, was not particularly severe or degrading. Crawford's complaints are of "mere offensive utterance[s]," as opposed to physically threatening or humiliating conduct. Saying "[o]ld people should be seen and not heard" is certainly rude, but it is not enough to create a hostile working environment within the meaning of *Harris* [*v. Forklift Sys. Inc.* 114 S.Ct. 1367 (1993)]. Similarly, while a supervisor's opinion that women should

retire at age 55 may be unenlightened and logically indefensible, and might be circumstantial evidence of age discrimination if the supervisor were later to have fired Crawford, it hardly rises even to the level of an "offensive utterance," as it is simply one person's opinion, susceptible to retort and dispute.

Finally, relatedly, Crawford has not produced any evidence tending to show that the harassment interfered with her work performance and/or created an objectively intimidating, hostile, or offensive work environment, within the meaning of *Harris*. We note there is absolutely no suggestion that the environment impeded Crawford's work performance; indeed, she herself claims to like her job, despite Kermendy's asserted abusiveness.

Because Crawford has not shown that she was subjected to harassment based on her age, or that the harassment unreasonably interfered with her work performance and created an objectively hostile environment, we AFFIRM.

CASE QUESTIONS

1. Did the court recognize the existence of a hostile working environment theory under the ADEA?
2. Do workers have a cause of action under federal discrimination laws when their working environment contains hostility and abusiveness due to deep morale problems and a clash of personalities?
3. Was the alleged harassment inflicted on Crawford sufficiently severe or pervasive so as to alter the conditions of employment and amount to an objectively hostile work environment?

SECTION 21—PROHIBITED PRACTICES AND DAMAGES

Section 4(a) of the ADEA sets forth the employment practices that are unlawful under the Act, including the failure to hire because of age and the discharge of employees because of age. Labor organizations are prohibited from discriminating because of age or attempting to cause employees to violate the ADEA under Section 4(b) of the Act.

Examples of what not to do are set forth in excerpts from the *EEOC v. Liggett & Meyers Inc.* decision, presented in this section. In this case the employer was ordered to pay back wages and benefits plus liquidated damages to more than 100 terminated employees. The *Rhodes v. Guiberson Oil Tools* case demonstrates the continuing problem of age discrimination in the workplace

Liability under the ADEA depends on whether the protected trait—age—actually motivated the employer's decision. In *Hazen Paper Co. v. Biggin*[20] the Supreme Court held that an employer did not violate the ADEA just by interfering with an older employee's pension benefits that would have vested by virtue of the employee's years of service. The employer's decision to fire an older employee solely because he had nine plus years of service and was close to having his pension vested upon completion of ten years of service was not discrimination based on "age." It was, however, a violation of Section 510 of ERISA to fire the employee in order to prevent the individual's pension from vesting. But it was not, without more evidence proving age as a motivating factor, a violation of the ADEA.

Damages

It should be noted that Section 7(b) of the ADEA allows for the doubling of damages in cases of "willful violations" of the Act. Consequently, an employer who willfully violates the ADEA is liable not only for back wages and benefits but also for "an additional amount as liquidated damages." Thus, individuals like the employee terminated in the *Hazen Paper Co.* case, referred to above, had an economic incentive to bring an ADEA lawsuit in an attempt to qualify for double changes under Section 7(b) of the ADEA.

In *Trans World Airline Inc. v. Thurston*,[21] the Supreme Court held that where an employer's officers acted nonrecklessly and in good faith in attempting to determine whether their prohibition against pilots exercising bumping rights to flight engineer positions upon mandatory retirement as pilots at age 60 would violate the ADEA, their conduct was not "willful." Although determined to be violative of the ADEA, the plaintiffs were not entitled to double damages. The plaintiffs were, however, entitled to back wages and benefits.

In the *Hazen Paper Co.* decision, the Supreme Court clarified the definition of "willful" as meaning that the employer either knew or showed reckless disregard for the matter of whether the conduct was prohibited by the ADEA. Once a "willful" violation has been shown, the employee need not demonstrate that the employer's conduct was outrageous in order to qualify for liquidated damages.

In *IRS Commissioner v. Schleier*,[22] the Supreme Court ruled that back pay and liquidated damages recovered under the ADEA are not excludable from gross income under the Internal Revenue Code. Schleier had received $72,800 in back pay and an equal amount in liquidated damages under a class action settlement against United Airlines resulting from its policy of forcing pilots to retire at age 60. The Court ruled that the damages were not based upon tort or tort-type rights, which would have qualified for exclusion from gross income.

---

[20] DLR No. 75, D-1 (Apr. 21, 1993).
[21] 469 U.S. 111 (1985).
[22] 67 FEP 1745 (Sup. Ct. 1996).

EEOC v. LIGGETT & MEYERS INC.

United States District Court for Eastern North Carolina, 29 FEP 1611 (1982).

MERHIGE, D. J.

Plaintiff's case rests upon its contention that pursuant to a plan or pattern, a large number of defendant's employees were discriminated against by the defendant company by reason of each being 40 years of age or older.

Defendant, on the other hand, denies any such plan or pattern and indeed that any employee has been discriminated against, by reason of age or any other reason, in either being terminated from his or her respective position or not being offered another position. . . .

The sad saga seems to have begun in February of 1971 when the Company appointed J. C. Gfeller, then 35 years of age, as its director of sales. Shortly thereafter he also became vice president in charge of the Sales Department. At the time the Company's sales had declined from a high 68.9 billion in 1952 to 33.5 billion in 1970. Cigarette sales continued to decline, as did the Company's percentage share of the market.

The sales quota for 1971 was established at 39 billion cigarettes, but it was reduced to 35 billion in September, and 32 billion was the actual amount sold in 1971.

The Hiring of New Top Management

The Company hired Ken McAllister as president of the cigarette and tobacco division, and Jack Southard as vice president of marketing. Both had consumer package goods backgrounds.

In February 1971 the Company hired John Gfeller as vice president of sales. His business background was consumer package goods. Gfeller's charge was to help turn around the decline in the Company's cigarette sales. He was expected to show a dramatic improvement in sales within 18 months.

As senior sales officer it was Gfeller's responsibility to achieve and maintain the distribution of the product line—to make sure the

right amount of the product line was in the right place at the right time, properly priced and displayed. The sales responsibility ended at the retail shelf. Inducing the consumer to take the product off the shelf once the sales department got it there was the responsibility of marketing. . . .

Manpower Planning and Analysis—Age and Minority Reports

In late February 1971, Gfeller requested an analysis of field sales personnel showing ages and minority representation. He requested for each management level an age breakout in five-year groups and the average age for each level. For minority groups he asked for a breakout showing the numbers of each level and the percentage they represented.

In April 1971, Gfeller hired Tom McMorrow as Director of Sales Planning. His job was to maximize promotion effectiveness and coordinate all promotion activities. Also he reviewed all communications between field and headquarters and put a new Headquarters Communication Program into effect.

Gfeller requested and received two updates of the age report—one dated July 31, 1971, and another dated September 30, 1971. This information showed the average age of sales representatives to be 33 and that of first-line managers to be 42. . . .

McMorrow was appointed National Field Sales Manager on June 21, 1971, and was instructed by Gfeller to find out what the problems were in the field that were causing the continuing sales decline. McMorrow went into the field and worked with all levels of the sales force and called on customers. . . .

. . . Based on his visits and investigation, McMorrow concluded that field sales had an inferior management team compared to those of companies he had formerly worked for.

Personnel Changes—Sales Department

Thus, the Company set out on an intensive program of personnel changes. Gfeller and McMorrow instructed top management personnel to move against certain older managers working under their supervision. If the top manager delayed or sought to justify keeping the older manager, he was informed that he was "not getting the message." The key phrase used was that certain individuals were "not able to adapt" to the new procedures to be used by the Company. Throughout this period, Gfeller and McMorrow emphasized that they wanted young and aggressive people, that older individuals were not able to conform or adapt to the new procedures. In specific reference to R. E. Moran, the defendant's top division manager for the year 1971, they made statements such as "he is over the hill" and "he is too old to learn." They also had a frequent saying when it was suggested that an employee had numerous years of experience: that it was not twenty years' experience, but rather one year's experience twenty times. Gfeller also commented in specific reference to L. D'Erasmo, who was 27 years of age in 1971, and who replaced R. E. Moran as area sales manager on September 1, 1972, that he was just the type of young man needed.

The terminations under Gfeller's plan to reorganize the sales force began with the region managers. They were all replaced with younger people. The first one terminated was W. F. Barrow, then 41 years of age, who had been employed in September 1954 and had been promoted to Central Region Manager in July 1970. He was terminated on September 10, 1971, when Gfeller and McMorrow told him he was no longer needed. The only reason they gave him was that he had a "human relations problem." He had no notice from defendant of any deficiency in his duties prior to his termination date. In fact, less than two months earlier Gfeller had notified him by letter dated July 15, 1971, in pertinent part, as follows:

My heartiest congratulations on your outstanding performance during the month of June in achieving and exceeding your assigned quota.

This month was particularly important to all of us in that it was the first month of our recently assigned new specific sales objectives, the first month of your new incentive compensation program and the first month, as I view it, that you were given specific directions, specific tools and you dramatically demonstrated your individual and personal ability to rise to the occasion.

Barrow, so the Court finds, had a history of outstanding performance. . . .

C. Schmidt was the second region manager to be terminated. He was then 46 years of age, had been employed for 21 years, and had in 1969 been promoted to Western Region Manager. Without prior notice, McMorrow came to his office on October 28, 1971, and read a letter to him from Gfeller stating that for the best interest of the Company he should be terminated. McMorrow told him that he (McMorrow) felt nervous about having Schmidt as his representative. The Court finds that McMorrow told Schmidt he felt him inadequate. Schmidt did not receive a copy of the Gfeller letter. At that time his region ranked first for the year to date of the four regions, having met 97.56% of the assigned quota. The only document in his personnel file relating to his dismissal is a termination form indicating his resignation was requested for inability to perform duties. The Court finds that shortly after Schmidt's discharge, McMorrow stated he "needed younger men," and further that Schmidt "was not competent." Age obviously was a factor. Effective November 1, 1971, Hal Grant was appointed Western Region Manager.

Shortly thereafter, Grant began terminations in California. On February 7, 1972, Grant went to the office of E. W. Gardiner (age 46), the San Francisco Department Manager, and terminated him as of that date. Gardiner had no prior knowledge that he was to be terminated.

Grant told him he was too old for the job and indicated that Gardiner did not fit the new youthful image the Company wanted to project. At the time, Gardiner's department had a 9% share of the market, which was substantially higher than the defendant's share of the national market. Grant never notified him of any charged deficiencies in his performance. Gardiner (age 46) was replaced by T. Jennings (age 32). Thereafter, on August 7, 1972, the date he received his final salary check, Gardiner wrote a letter to the president of Liggett & Meyers in which, among other things, he specified how Grant had informed him "I was too old for the job." He received no response to the letter. . . .

T. Jennings immediately began to complete the reorganization of the San Francisco Department. He terminated R. J. Asche (age 41) on March 7, 1972. Asche had been an employee for 17 years. There was no BDR [an evaluation of the employee, called a business development review or BDR] or evaluation prepared on Asche. The records in his personnel file reflect that he was a highly qualified employee. Jennings told him that he was to be replaced by a younger person. Jennings stated to him that many were to be replaced by younger, more qualified persons. Asche heard Jennings place an order with an employment agency for individuals under 35. Asche offered to take any other job, including sales representative, but Jennings told him that he would not fit in, he would not be happy, and they had no room for him. . . .

[Here the court sets forth the details of numerous terminations in the sales department.]

A similar pattern occurred in the terminations of older sales representatives. J. T. Owens (age 42) and V. H. Hall (age 42) were terminated as sales representatives in the Nashville division on September 15, 1972, by H. M. Clunan (age 26), who was hired as a supervisor in Nashville on July 3, 1972. Clunan and D. O. Johnson (age 25), who was hired as the assistant department manager for the Memphis district on May 29, 1972, had visited Nashville after

Clunan's appointment. At the first meeting in Nashville, Johnson commented to Clunan in the presence of Owens that some of the gentlemen were too old to be in the business. Later, Johnson asked Owens what a man his age was doing in this business. At this time, the Nashville division had five sales representatives: M. D. Garner (age 37), E. V. Holt (age 34), H. Vance Owens (age 33), and Hall. Clunan kept the youngest, H. Vance, and terminated the remaining four. Clunan replaced them with K. Ingram (age 23), hired September 1, 1972, B. Marshall (age 25), hired September 1, 1972, R. Puettman (age 23), employed September 1, 1972 (transferred from Alabama), and S. Roberts (age 23), hired October 9, 1972. Clunan also hired L. Winn (age 26) on September 18, 1972.

Clunan gave Owens no reason for termination. On the termination report, Clunan gave the reason that he felt Owens "could not adapt to new configuration." On the payroll notification form, the reason given was that Owens was "not adapted to our type of work." . . .

T. T. Clarke, Jr. (age 55), who was employed as a sales representative in the Manchester, New Hampshire division, was forced to take early retirement on September 1, 1972. At the time, he was the oldest sales representative in that division. He had suffered a slight heart attack in 1966 but had returned to work. In 1972, he missed only two days of work up until his termination, and the Court rejects the Company's contention that health was the major factor in Clarke's forced retirement.

By letter dated May 8, 1972, the Connecticut division manager requested J. P. Duffy (age 47) to submit his resignation as a sales representative in Hartford, Connecticut effective May 12, 1972. The reason given in the letter was that "[d]uring the past months you have not met the standards of performance which indicates your inability to adapt to the change." The letter further stated that it was "this inability to change that prompts this request." In the last appraisal in his file dated February 5, 1971, he was ranked first out of six representatives; he was the second oldest. In the evaluation, the interviewer stated that he discussed with Duffy "the high level of efficiency maintained by him over the 20 years he has been in our employ." On June 26, 1972, E. Chapman (age 23) and J. Radeno (age 24), were hired in Connecticut as sales representatives. . . .

The vast majority of sales representatives hired from 1971 through 1973 were in their twenties. In 1971 the defendant hired 194 sales representatives, of whom 142 were in their twenties, 47 were in their thirties, and five were in their forties (oldest 43). In 1972, the year the major first line management changes were made, the defendant hired 180 sales representatives, of whom 162 were in their twenties, 16 in their thirties, and two in their forties (oldest 42). Even more significantly, the two over 40, one hired November 16, 1973, and the other November 19, 1973, and 12 of the other individuals over 30 were all hired after September 7, 1973, when the compliance officer began his investigation and the defendant had notice of possible age discrimination. Thus, from January 1, 1973, through September 7, 1973, the defendant had hired no sales representatives age 40 or above, and only nine in their thirties. . . .

Personnel Changes—Leaf Department
In April 1973, the Leaf Department, which was responsible for purchasing tobacco, was notified that for economic reasons there would have to be cost reductions which would require the termination of personnel. Initially, J. C. Burton, vice president of the Leaf Department, attempted to place selected employees in the domestic sales department. . . . [Burton was not successful, and as a result he was required to terminate 33 individuals on July 31, 1973.]

In the various employee classifications, Burton made the following selections. In supervisors, he terminated the oldest of nine. In head buyers, he terminated the oldest eight of nineteen. In buyers, he terminated 13 of 73. The 13

terminations included the seven oldest, three more in the age group 49 to 57, and three age 48. He retained everyone under the age of 48, a group of 26 employees. . . .

While the Company's explanation that it was undergoing a reduction in force for valid business reasons must be accepted, the Court is of the view that the plaintiff has borne the ultimate burden of establishing that age was a determining factor in the Company's choice of discharging or forcing retirement on the discriminatees listed in Appendix "I." The assigned reasons were pretextual. . . .

The bottom line is probably best exemplified by Burton's response to how B. P. Franklin, age 63, H. C. Chinn, age 60, and J. C. Payne, age 61, were selected for termination. Burton said,

We selected them because of their nearness to mandatory retirement. If we kept them, we would not have been able to reduce people, because we would have to pick or take people and train them to take their place in a couple of years or so.

In short, but for their age, they would not have been terminated.

Personnel Changes—Legal Department
In 1974, it was determined to move the Legal Department from New York to Durham, North Carolina. Charles B. Morganthaler, the second-ranking attorney in the department, was notified by the general counsel in January 1974 that he was being asked to relocate and that he would be entitled to three house-hunting trips to Durham. Morganthaler notified the general counsel in January that he intended to relocate. On April 4, 1974, the general counsel, F. P. Haas, informed Morganthaler that he, Morganthaler, would be retiring soon and that he was too old to make the move. Morganthaler was then forced to take early retirement effective January 1, 1975, at age 62. A contract was executed relating to his payment, but it contained no provision in regard to the age discrimination claim. Even if there had been a release, it would have been

void as against public policy. . . . [The facts set forth above demonstrate that the company was in violation of the Age Discrimination in Employment Act. The court held that the company's disavowal of any discriminatory attitude on age was overcome by overwhelming evidence. It finds that although there may have been factors other than age considered, in each instance age was one of the determining factors, and that this is impermissible under the law. The court determined that the violations of the company were willful, thereby triggering liquidated damages in addition to the lost wages and benefits.]

So ordered.

CASE QUESTIONS

1. What options did the employer have at its disposal to improve the performance of the sales department other than the massive terminations of its older employees?
2. Speculate as to why Gfeller and McMorrow favored younger employees over older employees.
3. Did the employer have a valid business reason for the RIF in the legal department? Is a company immune from damages if it proves a valid business reason for a RIF?
4. If a person, wrongfully forced to take early retirement, signs a release not to sue the company for violation of the ADEA, is that release a defense in a subsequent ADEA lawsuit?

RHODES v. GUIBERSON OIL TOOLS

United States Court of Appeals, 75 F.3d 989 (5th Cir. 1996).

[Calvin Rhodes began his employment with Dresser Industries in 1955 as a salesman to the oil industry. In the throes of a severe economic downturn, Rhodes took a job selling oil field equipment at another Dresser company which became Guiberson Oil. After seven months he was discharged, being told that it was a reduction in force and that he would be eligible for rehiring. At that time he was fifty-six years of age. Within two months Guiberson Oil hired a forty-two-year-old salesperson to do the same job. Rhodes sued Guiberson Oil for violating the ADEA. A jury found for the plaintiff, but a divided panel of the Court of Appeals rendered judgment for the employer. The matter was reheard *en banc* before the Court of Appeals.]

DAVIS, C. J. . . .

Lee Snyder terminated Rhodes on October 31, 1986. Mr. Snyder told Rhodes he was part of a reduction in force (RIF) because of adverse economic conditions that persisted in the oilfield. Snyder told Rhodes, however that Guiberson would consider him for reemployment. Rhodes' personnel file reflected this same reason for the discharge. It was uncontradicted that Rhodes' position remained unfilled for only 6 weeks and that Guiberson knew at the time of termination or soon after that Rhodes would be replaced. . . .

Lee Snyder, Rhodes' supervisor, testified via deposition that more than one salesman was clearly needed for the territory. Jack Givens, who had been Snyder's supervisor, testified that he told Snyder to replace Rhodes. Givens also testified that the business required more than one salesman, and that Rick Attaway, had been hired to replace Rhodes. James Sewell, Snyder's other supervisor, testified that Rhodes was told that his position was being eliminated and that this statement was not true. The evidence supports a finding that Guiberson did not tell Rhodes the truth about why it was discharging him.

Guiberson Oil's defense at trial was not that Rhodes was RIF'd, but that he was discharged because of his poor work performance. Here too, Rhodes presented evidence to counter Guiberson's assertion. . . .

Guiberson officials' testimony . . . provided support for Rhodes' contention that Guiberson's "productivity" justification of his termination was a pretext for age discrimination. Lee Snyder testified that the memo placed in Rhodes' file explaining that Rhodes lacked technical expertise in downhole operations was substantially true but noted that it was also a "CYA . . . (cover your _ss)" letter. Snyder testified that Rhodes was a good salesman with strong customer contacts and noted that Jack Givens—Snyder's boss who instructed Snyder to fire Rhodes—once said that he could hire two young salesmen for what some of the older salesmen were costing. Snyder quickly backed away from this statement and said that Givens had said he could hire two *new* salesman for what some of the *others* were costing him. Givens said he was not aware of telling Snyder this. He also admitted that he had never talked to any of Rhodes' customers about Rhodes' performance as a salesman.

James Sewell, Snyder's other supervisor, testified that he had been very impressed with Rhodes' sales plans and that technical ability was not necessary to sell the product. He also testified that Rhodes had a poor customer base, but admitted that he did not know who Rhodes' customers were, had not talked to any of Rhodes' customers, and had no documentation to support his testimony about Rhodes' poor performance.

Lloyd Allen, the other salesman in the New Orleans office with whom Rhodes was compared, at first testified that his sales were much higher than Rhodes' but clarified on cross-examination that Rhodes' sales during the period in question nearly matched his own. Allen also admitted that the records sup-porting his testimony may have been incomplete, that Rhodes may have made another sale for which Allen had not credited him, and that another salesman may have been responsible for one of the sales Allen credited to himself. . . .

Based on this evidence, the jury was entitled to find that the reasons given for Rhodes' discharge were pretexts for age discrimination. The jury was entitled to find that Guiberson's state[d] reason for discharging Rhodes—RIF—was false. Additionally, the reason for discharge that Guiberson Oil proffered in court to meet Rhodes' prima facie case was countered with evidence from which the jury could have found that Rhodes was an excellent salesman who met Guiberson Oil's legitimate productivity expectations. Viewing this evidence in the light most favorable to Rhodes, a reasonable jury could have found that Guiberson Oil discriminated against Rhodes on the basis of his age.

CONCLUSION

After considering all of the evidence in the record under the standard set forth in *Boeing Co. v. Shipman*, we are convinced that the district court properly accepted the jury's verdict on liability and willfulness. Guiberson Oil's motion for JNOV was properly denied. . . .

[Judgment affirmed.]

CASE QUESTIONS

1. Why did the employer tell Rhodes that he was being terminated because of a RIF, and why did Supervisor Snyder place a memo in Rhodes's file about lacking expertise in downhole operations?
2. Evaluate the statement attributed to Jack Givens, the person who directed that Rhodes be fired, that "I could hire two young salesmen for what some of the older salesmen are costing."
3. Was the jury entitled to find the reasons given by the employer for Rhodes's discharge were pretexts for age discrimination?

SECTION 22—ARBITRATION OF ADEA CLAIMS

An individual may not have a judicial remedy where the individual is bound by a broad arbitration clause to arbitrate the dispute with an employer. In *Gilmer v. Interstate/ Johnson Lane,* presented in this section, the U.S. Supreme Court held that Robert Gilmer's age discrimination lawsuit against his former employer could be stayed under Section 3 of the Federal Arbitration Act (FAA) and that he could be compelled to arbitrate his claim under Section 4 of the FAA. Gilmer's registration form with the New York Stock Exchange had a broad arbitration clause requiring arbitration of "any controversy" between registered representatives and member organizations. While the Court left for another day the question of whether the language in Section 1 of the FAA—". . . nothing herein contained shall apply to contracts of employment of seamen, railroad employees, or any other class of worker engaged in foreign or interstate commerce . . ."—excludes all contracts of employment from enforcement under the FAA, the Court's decision furthers the judicial trend towards a liberal federal policy favoring arbitration. Indeed, Section 118 of the Civil Rights Act of 1991 sets forth a policy statement favoring alternative means of dispute resolution. The significance of the *Gilmer* decision is that, if broadly applied, a substantial amount of ADEA litigation could be diverted to arbitration tribunals.

However, in *Prudential Insurance Co. of America v. Lai,*[23] the Ninth Circuit Court of Appeals determined that Congress intended to encourage arbitration only when the parties have knowingly and voluntarily waived their statutory remedies and agreed to arbitrate the dispute; and the court held that the appellants in that case were not bound to arbitrate their Title VII discrimination claims. It may well be that the arbitration clause may need to explicitly describe all disputes the parties agree to arbitrate if the *Gilmer* rule is to apply.

GILMER v. INTERSTATE/JOHNSON LANE

Supreme Court of the United States, 111 S.Ct. 1647 (1991).

[Petitioner Robert Gilmer was required by his employer to register as a securities representative with the New York Stock Exchange (NYSE). His registration application contained an agreement to arbitrate any controversy arising out of a registered representative's employment or termination of employment. The employer terminated Gilmer at age 62. Thereafter, he filed a charge with the Equal Employment Opportunity Commission (EEOC) and brought suit in the district court, alleging that he had been discharged in vio-

lation of the Age Discrimination in Employment Act of 1967 (ADEA). The employer moved to compel arbitration. The court denied the motion, based on *Alexander v. Gardner-Denver Co.* The court of appeals reversed, and the Supreme Court granted certiorari.]

WHITE, J. . . .
We . . . are unpersuaded by the argument that arbitration will undermine the role of the EEOC in enforcing the ADEA. An individual

---

[23] 42 F.3d 1299 (9th Cir. 1994).

ADEA claimant subject to an arbitration agreement will still be free to file a charge with the EEOC, even though the claimant is not able to institute a private judicial action. Indeed, Gilmer filed a charge with the EEOC in this case. In any event, the EEOC's role in combating age discrimination is not dependent on the filing of a charge; the agency may receive information concerning alleged violations of the ADEA "from any source," and it has independent authority to investigate age discrimination. See 29 CFR §§ 1626.4, 1626.13 (1990). Moreover, nothing in the ADEA indicates that Congress intended that the EEOC be involved in all employment disputes. . . .

Gilmer also argues that compulsory arbitration is improper because it deprives claimants of the judicial forum provided for by the ADEA. Congress, however, did not explicitly preclude arbitration or other nonjudicial resolution of claims, even in its recent amendments to the ADEA. "[I]f Congress intended the substantive protection afforded [by the ADEA] to include protection against waiver of the right to a judicial forum, that intention will be deducible from text or legislative history." Mitsubishi, 473 U.S., at 628, 105 S.Ct. at 3354. . . .

I.

In addition to the arguments discussed above, Gilmer vigorously asserts that our decision in Alexander v. Gardner-Denver Co., 415 U.S. 36, . . . precludes arbitration of employment discrimination claims. Gilmer's reliance on the case, however, is misplaced. . . .
There are several important distinctions between the *Gardner-Denver* line of cases and the case before us. First, those cases did not involve the issue of the enforceability of an agreement to arbitrate statutory claims. Rather, they involved the quite different issue whether arbitration of contract-based claims precluded subsequent judicial resolution of statutory claims. Since the employees there had not agreed to arbitrate their statutory claims, and the labor arbitrators were not authorized to resolve such claims, the arbitration in those cases understandably was held not to preclude subsequent statutory actions. Second, because the arbitration in those cases occurred in the context of a collective bargaining agreement, the claimants there were represented by their unions in the arbitration proceedings. An important concern therefore was the tension between collective representation and individual statutory rights, a concern not applicable to the present case. Finally, those cases were not decided under the FAA, which, as discussed above, reflects a "liberal federal policy favoring arbitration agreements." Mitsubishi, 473 U.S., at 625. Therefore, those cases provide no basis for refusing to enforce Gilmer's agreement to arbitrate his ADEA claim.

II.

We conclude that Gilmer has not met his burden of showing that Congress, in enacting the ADEA, intended to preclude arbitration of claims under the Act. Accordingly, the judgment of the Court of Appeals is
Affirmed.

Justice STEVENS, *with whom Justice* MARSHALL *joins, dissenting.*

Section 1 of the Federal Arbitration Act (FAA) states:

"[N]othing herein contained shall apply to contracts of employment of seamen, railroad employees, or any other class of workers engaged in foreign or interstate commerce." 9 U.S.C. § 1.

The Court today, in holding that the FAA compels enforcement of arbitration clauses even when claims of age discrimination are at issue, skirts the antecedent question of whether the coverage of the Act even extends to arbitration clauses contained in employment contracts, regardless of the subject matter of the claim at issue. In my opinion, arbitration clauses contained in employment agreements are specifically exempt from coverage of the FAA, and for that reason respondent Interstate/Johnson Lane Corporation cannot, pursuant to the FAA, compel petitioner to submit his claims arising under the Age Discrimination in Employment Act of 1967 (ADEA), 29 U.S.C. § 621 *et seq.*, to binding arbitration. . . .

2. Did Congress intend to preserve an individual's right to a judicial forum in an ADEA case from waiver?

3. Did the Court hold that the *Alexander v. Gardner-Denver* decision precluded arbitration of employment discrimination claims?

CASE QUESTIONS

1. Is the EEOC's role in combating age discrimination dependent on filing an age discrimination charge?

SECTION 23 — THE OLDER WORKERS BENEFIT PROTECTION ACT; ADEA EXEMPTIONS AND DEFENSES

The Older Workers Benefit Protection Act (OWBPA) of 1990 amended the ADEA by prohibiting age discrimination in employee benefits and establishing minimum standards for determining the validity of waivers of age claims.[24] The OWBPA establishes that the ADEA prohibition of discrimination in "compensation, terms, conditions, or privileges of employment" encompasses all employee benefits, including those provided under a bona fide employee benefit plan. The 1990 Act amends the ADEA by adopting an "equal benefit or equal cost" standard which provides that older workers must be given benefits which are at least equal to those provided to younger workers unless the employer can prove that the cost of providing an equal benefit would be more for an older worker than for a younger one.

Early retirement incentive plans are exempted from the "equal benefit or equal cost" standard, so long as the plans are bona fide. Employers may make Social Security "bridge" payments to early retirees until the affected individuals reach eligibility age.

Exemptions and Defenses

Section 4(f) of the ADEA sets forth certain exemptions from the strictures of the Act for employers. Thus where an individual is terminated because of a bona fide seniority plan, the employer is not responsible for an ADEA violation. Also, if the employer discharges or disciplines an employee for "good cause," the employer is not in violation of the Act. Thus if a 60-year-old employee is discovered stealing from an employer, the employer may terminate that individual without being in violation of the Act.

State and local governments may make age-based hiring and retirement decisions for firefighters and law enforcement officers if the particular age limitation was in effect on March 3, 1983, and the action taken is pursuant to a bona fide hiring or retirement

---

[24] PL 101-422, Oct. 16, 1990. This law reverses the Supreme Court's 1989 ruling in *Public Employees Retirement System of Ohio v. Betts*, which had the effect of exempting employee benefit programs from the ADEA.

plan that is not a subterfuge to evade the purposes of the Act.[25] The ADEA permits the compulsory retirement of certain bona fide executives or high policymaking personnel at age 65.[26]

Section 4(f) provides employer defenses for "reasonable factors other than age" (RFOA) and "bona fide occupational qualifications reasonably necessary to the normal operation of a particular business" (BFOQ).

Generally the BFOQ defense is raised by employers in cases involving public safety. This was the defense in *Hodgson v. Greyhound Lines Inc.*[27] There the company had a policy of limiting new driver applicants to persons under the age of 35. The district court judge held that Greyhound failed to meet its "burden of demonstrating that its policy of age limitation is reasonably necessary to the normal and safe operation of its business." However, the judge's ruling was overturned by a three-member panel of the U.S. court of appeals, holding that Greyhound did not violate the Act because its hiring-age limitation had a rational basis in fact to believe that elimination of the policy would increase the likelihood or risk of harm to its passengers and others. The courts generally require the employer to prove that the BFOQ is reasonably necessary to the essence of its business and that the employer has a factual basis for believing that all or substantially all persons within the affected class would be unable to perform the duties involved safely and efficiently.

In recent years large-scale reductions in forces (RIFs) have taken place in many industries and in public-sector occupations such as schoolteachers, police, and fire personnel. Where the RIFs take place according to a bona fide seniority plan, no violation of the Act occurs. Where no collective bargaining agreement restricts an employer as to the manner of a RIF, the employer has the right to use reasonable factors other than age (RFOA) in implementing the reduction in force. For example, the employer may consider the relative performances of employees in each classification in deciding which employee to terminate. However, the risks are high that an employer may be found to be in violation of the ADEA because statistical and other evidence of discrimination may be developed, as cost-cutting workforce reduction decisions tend to encourage the termination of highly paid, experienced employees, who tend to be older employees.

Waivers

Faced with the need to reduce labor costs, the risks of ADEA lawsuits, and the desire to treat older workers "right," many employers have opted to provide early retirement incentive programs. Employers commonly require that employees electing to take early retirement waive all claims against the employer, including their rights or claims under the ADEA. Congress recognized the utility of these programs in the Older Workers Benefit Protection Act of 1990, but wanted to make sure that employees fully understood that they were making knowing and voluntary waivers of ADEA claims. Congress established specific statutory requirements which must be met before an employee can

---

[25] See age discrimination employment amendments of 1996, PL 104–208.
[26] Section 12(c)(1).
[27] 499 F.2d 859, 7 FEP 817 (7th Cir. 1974).

waive the right to litigate ADEA claims. The burden of proof for establishing such a waiver rests with the employer, who must establish that all of the requirements have been met. The requirements include that:

1. The waiver is part of a written agreement.
2. It makes specific reference to rights or claims under the ADEA and may refer to Title VII and all other claims.
3. It does not apply to rights or claims which may occur after the agreement had been signed.
4. It is exchanged for value that is in addition to what the employee would otherwise be entitled to receive.
5. The employee is given written advice from the employer to consult with an attorney.
6. The employee is given a 21-day waiting period to consider the agreement, and a 7-day period to revoke the agreement. For an agreement in connection with an early retirement program offered to a group of employees, the waiting period is 45 days rather than 21 and the employer must disclose all eligibility factors and the terms and inclusions of the program.

In the *Adams v. Philip Morris, Inc.*, case, John Adams signed a broad general release of his employment rights at Philip Morris Co. (PM) in exchange for a special severance pay, some eight months prior to the passage of the OWBPA in 1990. When the job he left again became available a year later, he applied for it; but the job was awarded to a young black candidate whom Adams claimed had no experience with the high-speed cigarette machines being used by the company. Adams brought ADEA and reverse discrimination lawsuits against PM. The court of appeals determined that the release was an effective waiver of any claims Adams had at the time of his original termination from the company. However, it remanded the case to the district court for further considerations and findings because an employer cannot purchase a license to discriminate by attempting to have an employee waive rights which may occur after the agreement has been signed.

ADAMS v. PHILIP MORRIS, INC.

United States Court of Appeals, 67 F.3d 580 (6th Cir. 1995).

[John O. Adams, a white male approximately fifty-five years of age, brought an Age Discrimination in Employment Act (ADEA) claim and a reverse discrimination claim based on race against Philip Morris, Inc., "PM," his former employer. He alleges that PM failed to consider adequately his application for reemployment after having entered into a termination agreement providing for special severance pay. The district court granted defendant's motion for summary judgment based on a broad, general, release signed by Adams at the time of his separation from employment, and Adams appealed.]

WELLFORD, J. . . .
Adams began work at PM's cigarette manufacturing plant in Louisville in 1980. During his nine-and-a-half year tenure with the company,

Adams worked as a mechanical supervisor responsible for the maintenance of the company's high speed cigarette manufacturing machines. Several letters of recommendation on behalf of Adams favorably describe his work for the company.

On January 29, 1990, PM announced a layoff of 52 employees, including Adams, at the Louisville plant. Adams, and the others affected, were offered severance packages that included salary continuation, health insurance coverage for an extended time, and certain other benefits. In addition, these workers were offered enhanced severance packages if they signed a general release of liability. Adams chose to accept the enhanced package and, as a result, received approximately twice the amount of salary continuation benefits for a period of approximately eighteen months instead of sixteen weeks, and certain employment assistance, including financial aid of up to $5,500. Adams signed the following release on January 29, 1990:

KNOW ALL PERSON BY THESE PRESENT, THAT I, John O. Adams, residing at 1212 Weible Road, Crestwood, Kentucky, 40014, for and in consideration of severance pay in the amount of $32,767.00 payable in form of salary continuation . . . and a lump-sum payment of 3,542.00 Dollars for accrued but unused vacation, . . . together with continued benefit coverage . . . [and] outplacement assistance, release, remise and forever discharge Philip Morris Companies, Inc. . . . of and from all and in all manner of presently existing actions, causes of action, suits, debts, claims and demands whatsoever in law or equity arising from my employment with the Company. . . .

The release also specifically acknowledged that Adams was "settling all claims which I have ever had *or may have with the Company.*" In addition, the release contained a provision that stated: "[I] do hereby forever waive any and all right to assert any claim or demand for *re-employment* or tenure with the Company or for any benefits, etc., not specifically enunciated herein." Before signing this release, Adams had five days to consider whether to sign

it and also had an opportunity to consult with an attorney.

A little more than a year later, on March 3, 1991, while still receiving extra benefits, Adams read a local newspaper notice advertising what appeared to be his former position. Adams contacted Hayes, a friend who was a production supervisor with PM, who told him that a position had become open after another employee, Frank Zanchi, had left the company. The production superintendent for the plant told Adams that he was eligible to apply for the open position, and that he would "have a leg up on anybody else that applies."

Adams then applied, but the job was awarded to a young, black candidate, who Adams claims, had "no experience with high speed cigarette machines." Adams then filed a complaint with the EEOC, alleging age discrimination and reverse discrimination based on race, but the EEOC issued a no-cause response after investigation. Adams subsequently filed an action in district court. . . .

Although Adams does not directly challenge whether the release was knowingly and voluntarily executed, he alludes to this issue by suggesting that he "was forced to sign the general release" out of "extreme economic distress" and that he "was given a mere five days to sign and return the release." . . .

We have recognized that under particular circumstances employers and employees may negotiate a valid release of ADEA and Title VII claims. . . . We have applied ordinary contract principles in determining whether such a waiver is valid, remaining alert to ensure that employers do not defeat the policies of the ADEA and Title VII by taking advantage of their superior bargaining position or by overreaching. . . . In evaluating whether a release has been knowingly and voluntarily executed, we look to (1) plaintiff's experience, background, and education; (2) the amount of time the plaintiff had to consider whether to sign the waiver, including whether the employee had an opportunity to consult with a lawyer; (3) the clarity of the waiver; (4) consideration for the waiver; as well as (5) the totality of the circumstances. *See, e.g., Bormann v. A.T.&T. Communications*, 875 F.2d 399 (2d Cir.), *cert. denied*, 493 U.S. 924 (1989). . . .

It is evident, from Adams' correspondence in the record and his supervisory experience, that he was generally knowledgeable and aware of his rights. The waiver is plain and unambiguous, and easily understandable by someone of Adams' abilities. Adams had five days in which to consider whether to sign the waiver, and was advised by PM to consult with an attorney before doing so. By signing the waiver, Adams received approximately twice as much in termination benefits than he would have been entitled to under the normal severance package plans. Although he certainly felt some economic pressure to accept the attractive severance package and settle any potential claims he might have against PM, this pressure does not rise to the level of economic duress. Accordingly, we hold that the release was knowingly and voluntarily executed by Adams and we AFFIRM summary judgment for PM in this respect.

The language of the "general" release in this case is concededly very broad. Adams does not contend on appeal that the release is ineffective to waive his employment claims arising from the reduction-in-force; rather, he contends that the release is ineffective to waive his prospective claims arising from his reapplication with PM. . . .

This is a case of contract construction. The scope of a release, like any contract, depends on ascertaining the intent of the parties at the time of signing the release. The dispositive inquiry is "what did the parties intend?" Intent is determined by reviewing the language of the entire instrument and all surrounding facts and circumstances under which the parties acted in light of the applicable law as to

employment discrimination at the time. It is necessary to examine all the circumstances surrounding the formation of the release. Whether it was the intent of the parties to bar Adams from its particular labor pool forever is a question of fact not answered on the record before us. Summary judgment is, therefore, inappropriate at this time on this record as to this contract issue. . . .

An employer cannot purchase a license to discriminate. *See United States v. Trucking Employers, Inc.*, 561 F.2d 313, 319 (D.C. Cir. 1977) ("An employer cannot purchase a license to avoid its duty to eliminate practices which perpetuate prior discriminatory acts any more than it can circumvent its responsibility for future acts of purposeful discrimination.") An employment agreement that attempts to settle prospective claims of discrimination for job applicants or current employees may violate public policy under *Gardner-Denver* and related cases unless there were continuing or future effects of past discrimination, or unless the parties contemplated an unequivocal, complete and final dissolution.

In summary, we hold that PM is entitled to summary judgment on the issue of the execution of the release and waiver, and the execution thereof, by Adams knowingly and voluntarily. We must, however, REVERSE and REMAND on the issue of the intent of the parties in executing the agreement of waiver and release in light of the then existing employment discrimination law.

CASE QUESTIONS

1. Compare the release signed by Adams with the content requirements of the OWBPA set forth in the text.
2. Assess the economic value of the severance package from Adams's point of view in exchange for giving up all rights to employment and reemployment with the company.
3. What did the court of appeals decide in this case?

Chapter Questions and Problems

1. In reviewing a claim under the Equal Pay Act, do the courts require that the jobs in question be identical?
2. As a result of the passage of the Equal Pay Act of 1963 and Title VII of the Civil Rights Act of 1964, have the overall earnings for women become roughly comparable to that of men?
3. Can an employer terminate older employees as a reduction in the employer's workforce without violating the ADEA?
4. Della Janich was employed as a matron at the Yellowstone County Jail in Montana. The duties of the position of matron resemble those of a parallel male position—jailer. Both employees have the responsibility for booking prisoners, showering and dressing them, and placing them in the appropriate section of the jail depending on the sex of the offender. Because 95 percent of the prisoners at the jail were men and 5 percent were women, the matron was assigned more bookkeeping duties than the jailer. At all times during Della's employment at the jail, her male counterparts received $125 more per month as jailers.

   Della brought an action under the Equal Pay Act alleging discrimination against her in her wages because of her sex. The county sheriff denied the charge.

   What factors must be considered by the court when deciding this case under the Equal Pay Act? Decide the case. [*Janich v. Sheriff*, 29 FEP 1195 (D.C. Mont.)]
5. The Federal Aviation Administration (FAA) has promulgated a federal regulation that prohibits airlines from employing pilots or copilots past age 60. The FAA's rule is recognized by the courts as a bona fide occupational qualification under the ADEA due to the administration's recognition that the possible onset of disease or debilitating condition would pose a flight safety risk.

   Western Airlines maintained a policy that all flight deck personnel must retire at age 60. Flight deck personnel include the pilot, copilot, and second officer (sometimes referred to as a flight engineer). The duties of a flight engineer are performed at a separate instrument panel, where various systems necessary for the operation of the aircraft, such as the electrical and hydraulic systems, are monitored and adjusted. The engineer does not manipulate the flight controls, and in the event of an emergency, all pilots and copilots having previously served as flight engineers are qualified to perform the necessary duties.

   Albert Ron worked as a flight engineer for Western Airlines for over 30 years. As his 60th birthday approached, he informed Western management that he wished to continue working past age 60. The airline told Ron that as a member of the flight deck, second officers were required to retire at 60 for the same reasons as pilots and copilots.

   Ron brought an action against Western under the Age Discrimination in Employment Act, claiming that Western's mandatory retirement policy was a form of age discrimination against flight engineers. Western denied the claim.

   What defenses, if any, are available to Western Airlines to support its retirement policy? Has Western engaged in age discrimination? Decide the case. [*Criswell v. Western Airlines*, 472 U.S. 400]
6. Carlyle Cline, age 42, was employed for ten years by Roadway Express Company, most recently as a loading dock supervisor at a Roadway terminal in North Carolina.

Cline had received periodic merit pay raises, and his personnel file contained an even amount of both complimentary and critical evaluations by supervisors. When R. W. Hass became vice-president for Roadway's southern division, he decided that the division needed to "upgrade" the quality of its personnel. Hass directed terminal managers to "look at" employees who had been with the company for five years without being promoted and decide whether they should be replaced with higher quality employees, preferably college graduates. Thus the ultimate decision regarding "promotability" was left to the terminal managers. They were not told that they were not to consider age when determining promotability. After the announcement of the new policy, Cline was discharged and classified "unpromotable." The terminal manager compiled a list of negative comments from Cline's file as evidence that Cline was discharged for "poor work performance." Roadway immediately replaced Cline with a man in his early thirties.

Cline brought an action against Roadway under the Age Discrimination in Employment Act, claiming he was discharged "because of his age in violation of the Act." Roadway maintained that Cline was discharged because of poor work performance.

Has Roadway violated the ADEA? Decide the case. [*Cline v. Roadway Express*, 29 FEP 1365 (4th Cir.)]

7. Harris-Stowe State College devised a reduction in force plan that selected both tenured and nontenured faculty members for termination. Leftwich, a 47-year-old tenured biology professor, sued the college for age discrimination under the ADEA. The college articulated its rationale for the termination plan based on tenure, stating that younger, nontenured faculty would have new ideas and that since tenured faculty were generally paid more than untenured faculty, a greater cost savings per person would be achieved by eliminating some tenured positions. The college states that its RIF plan never referred to age, and thus it clearly did not violate the ADEA. Leftwich disagrees. Decide. [*Leftwich v. Harris-Stowe State College*, 702 F.2d 686 (8th Cir.)]

8. Local 350 represents pipe fitters and plumbers in northern Nevada and parts of California. Together with industry employers, Local 350 operates a hiring hall. The hiring dispatcher keeps four "out-of-work lists," with different qualifications and priorities, from which members are hired. The dispatcher sends members out to jobs in the order in which they signed up. Donald Pilot, a member of Local 350, retired in 1983. After retirement, he paid retired members' dues. In 1984, he decided to return to work, and signed onto the out-of-work list. Local 350 removed his name from the list, stating he was not eligible. In a letter dated April 20, 1984, Local 350 informed Pilot that "as a retiree, having applied for and been granted pension, you are not presently eligible for dispatch through the UA Local 350 Hiring Hall." The EEOC claims that Local 350's policy violates 29 U.S.C. 623(c)(2) because it discriminates against older workers.

Section 623(c)(2) provides:

It shall be unlawful for a labor organization. . . . (2) to limit, segregate, or classify its membership, or fail or refuse to refer for employment any individual, in any way which would deprive or tend to deprive any individual of employment opportunities or otherwise adversely affect his status as an employee or as an applicant for employment, because of such individual's age.

"An employer discriminates 'because of' age whenever age is 'but for' cause of discrimination." Local 350 defends that its policy is not discriminatory because the "but for" cause of discrimination is not the retiree's age, but his voluntary decision to retire. Decide. [*EEOC v. Local 350, Plumbers and Pipefitters*, 982 F.2d 1305 (9th Cir.)]

4
Disability Discrimination Laws: Workers' Compensation

SECTION 24—DISCRIMINATION AGAINST DISABLED WORKERS

Some 43 million people have one or more physical or mental disabilities. Some impairments are obvious, such as paraplegia or blindness. Others may not be readily noticeable, such as heart disease, high blood pressure, and diabetes. In some cases, persons have recovered from their disabilities but have encountered job discrimination because of their past medical records. Cancer and mental or emotional disorders are examples of past medical conditions that may be associated with job discrimination.

The right of "handicapped persons" to enjoy equal employment opportunities was established on the federal level with the enactment of the Rehabilitation Act of 1973.[1] Although not designed specifically as an employment discrimination measure but rather as a comprehensive plan to meet many of the needs of the handicapped, the

---

[1] 29 U.S.C. §§ 701–794.

Rehabilitation Act does contain three sections that provide guarantees against discrimination in employment. As set forth below in detail, Section 501 of the Act is applicable to the federal government itself, Section 503 applies to federal contractors, and Section 504 applies to the recipients of federal funds.

Title I of the Americans with Disabilities Act of 1990 (ADA)[2] extends employment protection for disabled persons beyond the federal level to state and local governmental agencies and to all private employers with 15 or more employees. The ADA refers to *qualified individuals with disabilities* as opposed to the term *handicapped persons* used in the Rehabilitation Act. In drafting the ADA, Congress relied heavily on the language of the Rehabilitation Act and its regulations. It is anticipated that the body of case law developed under the Rehabilitation Act will provide guidance in the interpretation and application of the ADA.

The EEOC is responsible for enforcing the employment provisions of the ADA, under the same procedures as Title VII of the Civil Rights Act of 1964.[3]

Moreover, in cases of *intentional* disability discrimination, the Civil Rights Act of 1991 allows for reinstatement, hiring or promotion with back pay and attorneys' fees plus compensatory and punitive damages, subject to the same cap on damages as applied to sex and religious discrimination cases. Congress specified that the capped compensatory and punitive damages are only available in "intentional" cases.

In cases involving bias on the basis of an asserted lack of reasonable accommodation for a disability, damages may not be awarded against a covered entity that makes a good faith effort to reasonably accommodate a person with a disability that would provide that individual with an equally effective opportunity.

Under the Rehabilitation Act disabled individuals did not have the same private rights of action and remedies as are afforded disabled persons under the Civil Rights Act of 1991.

In legal actions against both public-sector employers and private-sector employers who receive federal funds, it is common for plaintiffs to allege violations of both the Rehabilitation Act and the ADA. Because of the similarity of the two acts, claims under both acts may be handled in the same fashion concerning elements of a cause of action, defenses, and burdens of proof.

Workers' compensation laws are also considered in this chapter. The Occupational Safety and Health Act of 1970 has had a significant impact on the improvement of workplace safety and health. Workers' compensation laws and the resulting insurance costs assessed to employers based on the quantity and monetary amounts of claims also provide a significant incentive for employers to provide a safe work environment. Inevitably there will be occupational injuries, and some conflicts may arise as to employers' obligations to employees with occupational injuries covered under state workers' compensation laws and their obligations to disabled employees protected under the ADA who are not occupationally injured. However, with the existence of these federal and state laws, and the general acceptance by the business and governmental communities of the

---

[2] PL 101–336, 42 U.S.C. §§ 12101–12117.
[3] ADA Section 107.

fundamental fairness of providing the basic dignity of a work life for disabled Americans, there have been expanded opportunities in our society for disabled persons. The *Quaker Oats Co. v. Ciha* case, presented later in this chapter, not only sets forth some basic principles of workers' compensation law, but also provides insight into the extensive accommodations made by an employer for a severely-disabled employee.

SECTION 25—THE REHABILITATION ACT OF 1973

Section 501

Section 501 of the Rehabilitation Act requires the federal government as an employer to develop and implement affirmative action plans on behalf of handicapped employees. Congress enacted Section 501 with the expectation that governmental policy regarding the employment of handicapped individuals would serve as a model for other employers. In *Mantolete v. Bolger*,[4] a person with epilepsy sued the U.S. Postal Service under Section 501 because she was denied a position as a letter-sorting machine operator because of her handicap. The court of appeals overturned the trial court's decision in favor of the Postal Service. The case was remanded for further consideration based on the requirement that the Postal Service demonstrate that the individual's handicap would result in a reasonable probability of substantial harm to Mantolete and/or her co-workers if she were to work the machine. The court made clear that employment decisions cannot be based on unsubstantiated generalizations and stereotypes but must instead be made on the basis of individual qualifications, taking into account the employee's handicap.

Section 503

Section 503 requires all contractors having federal contracts in excess of $2,500 to take affirmative action to employ the handicapped. Enforcement of Section 503 is carried out by the Department of Labor's Office of Federal Contract Compliance Programs (OFCCP). There is no private right of action under Section 503.[5] A handicapped individual must file a complaint with the OFCCP within 180 days of the occurrence of the alleged discriminating act in violation of Section 503. The complaint will then be investigated, and thereafter the matter may be heard at an administrative hearing. If a finding of discrimination is made and the employer disagrees with the finding, the OFCCP will initiate legal proceedings. The vast majority of Section 503 cases are resolved at or prior to the hearing before the administrative law judge.

Section 504

Section 504 of the Rehabilitation Act deals with discrimination in broader terms than the affirmative action requirements of Section 503. Section 504 prohibits federally

---

[4] 767 F.2d 1416, 38 FEP 1081 (9th Cir. 1985).
[5] See *Auffant v. Searle and Co.*, 25 FEP 1254 (D.P.R. 1981), and *Davis v. UAL, Inc.*, 622 F.2d 120, 26 FEP 1527 (2d Cir. 1981).

funded programs and government agencies from excluding from employment an "otherwise qualified handicapped individual . . . solely by reason of [his or her] handicap." Enforcement of Section 504 rests with each federal agency providing financial assistance. The attorney general of the United States has responsibility for the coordination of the enforcement efforts of the agencies. A private right of action for compensatory damages in cases of intentional discrimination exists under Section 504, so long as all administrative remedies have been exhausted.[6]

Under the Rehabilitation Act a *handicapped person* is defined as one who (1) has an impairment that affects a major life activity, (2) has a history of such an impairment, or (3) is considered as having one. The term *major life activity* includes such functions as caring for oneself, seeing, speaking, or walking.

To be entitled to the protection of the Rehabilitation Act with respect to employment, the individual must meet the requirements set forth in the definition of a handicapped person and must be an "otherwise qualified . . . individual" as set forth in Section 504. An *otherwise qualified individual* is one who can perform "the essential functions" of the job in question.

The *Cook v. State of Rhode Island Department of MHRH* decision, presented in this section, is an application of the Rehabilitation Act to the state's rejection of an extremely overweight individual for employment.

Contagious Diseases

In *School Board of Nassau County, Florida v. Arline*, presented in this section, the Supreme Court determined that a person afflicted with tuberculosis may be a handicapped person as defined in Section 504. The fact that such a person is also contagious does not remove that person from Section 504's coverage. Under *Arline* a district court must determine whether the handicapped person is "otherwise qualified" under Section 504. The district court must conduct an individualized inquiry and make appropriate findings of fact based on reasonable medical judgments, given the state of medical knowledge, about (1) the nature of the risk (e.g., how the disease is transmitted), (2) the duration of the risk (how long the carrier is infectious), (3) the severity of the risk (what the potential harm is to third parties), and (4) the probabilities that the disease will be transmitted and cause varying degrees of harm. In making these findings, courts normally should defer to the reasonable medical judgments of public health officials. Courts must then determine, in light of these findings, whether any "reasonable accommodation" can be made by the employer. Since the district court did not make the appropriate findings in *Arline*, the case was remanded.

In *Chalk v. U.S. District Court*,[7] the U.S. Court of Appeals for the Ninth Circuit relied on the *School Board of Nassau County, Florida v. Arline* decision in concluding that discrimination on the basis of AIDS violates the Rehabilitation Act. In the *Chalk* case the court of appeals ruled that the Orange County Department of Education

---

[6] See *Conrail v. Darrone*, 465 U.S. 624 (1984).
[7] 46 FEP 279 (9th Cir. 1988).

violated the Rehabilitation Act when it reassigned Vincent Chalk from his position as a teacher of hearing-impaired students to an administrative position after Chalk was diagnosed as having AIDS. The court ruled that Chalk, who was "handicapped" as a result of the disease, was "otherwise qualified" for classroom duty because the medical evidence indicated that the disease could not be transmitted through normal classroom contact.[8]

COOK v. STATE OF RHODE ISLAND DEPARTMENT OF MHRH

United States Court of Appeals, 10 F.3d 17 (1st Cir. 1993).

[Bonnie Cook applied for the position of institutional attendant at the Ladd Center, a state residential facility for retarded persons. She was 5'2" tall and weighed over 320 pounds. During a pre-hire physical examination administered by a nurse, no limitation was found that infringed on her ability to do the job. The Department of Mental Health, Retardation and Hospitals (MHRH) refused to hire her because her obesity was a health risk to herself, and she may put retarded residents at risk in emergency situations because of her limited mobility. The agency was also concerned over possible absenteeism and costs of workers' compensation injuries which could occur because of her obesity. Ms. Cook sued RI–MHRH under the Rehabilitation Act.]

SELYA, C.J. . . .
At the times material hereto, defendant-appellant Department of Mental Health, Retardation, and Hospitals (MHRH), a subdivision of the Rhode Island state government, operated the Ladd Center as a residential facility for retarded persons. Plaintiff-appellee Bonnie Cook worked at Ladd as an institutional attendant for the mentally retarded from 1978 to 1980, and again from 1981 to 1986. Both times she departed voluntarily, leaving behind a spotless work record. The defendant concedes that Cook's past performance met its legitimate expectations.

In 1988, when plaintiff reapplied for the identical position, she stood 5'2" tall and weighed over 320 pounds. During the routine pre-hire physical, a nurse employed by MHRH concluded that plaintiff was morbidly obese but found no limitations that impinged upon her ability to do the job. Notwithstanding that plaintiff passed the physical examination, MHRH balked. It claimed that Cook's morbid obesity compromised her ability to evacuate patients in case of an emergency and put her at greater risk of developing serious ailments (a "fact" that MHRH's hierarchs speculated would promote absenteeism and increase the likelihood of workers' compensation claims). Consequently, MHRH refused to hire plaintiff for a vacant IA-MR position.

Cook did not go quietly into this dark night. Invoking section 504, she sued MHRH in federal district court. . . .

In due season, the parties tried the case to a jury. At the close of the evidence, appellant moved for judgment as a matter of law. The court reserved decision, *see* Fed.R.Civ.P. 50(a), and submitted the case on special interrogatories (to which appellant interposed no objections). The jury answered the interrogatories favorably to plaintiff and, by means of the accompanying general verdict, awarded her $100,000 in compensatory damages. The district court denied appellant's motions for judgment as a matter of law and for a new trial, entered judgment on the verdict, and granted

---

[8] Also, HIV, the AIDS virus, is not considered as a pathogen transmitted by food contamination by infected persons who handle food, under the ADA.

equitable relief to the plaintiff. MHRH lost little time in filing a notice of appeal.

In handicap discrimination cases brought pursuant to federal law, the claimant bears the burden of proving each element of her [claim]. The elements derive from section 504 of the Rehabilitation Act, which provides in relevant part: "[n]o otherwise qualified individual . . . shall, solely by reason of her or his disability, . . . be subjected to discrimination under any program or activity receiving Federal financial assistance." . . . To invoke the statute in a failure-to-hire case, a claimant must prove four things: (1) that she applied for a post in a federally funded program or activity, (2) that, at the time, she suffered from a cognizable disability, (3) but was, nonetheless, qualified for the position, and (4) that she was not hired due solely to her disability. Here, MHRH concedes that it received substantial federal funding for the operation of the Ladd Center. . . .

The plaintiff proceeded below on a perceived disability theory, positing that she was fully able although MHRH regarded her as physically impaired. These allegations state a cause of action under the Rehabilitation Act, for the prophylaxis of section 504 embraces not only those persons who are in fact disabled, but also those persons who bear the brunt of discrimination because prospective employers view them as disabled. See 29 U.S.C. § 706(8)(B) (defining a disabled person, for Rehabilitation Act purposes, as any person who actually has, or who "is regarded" as having, a "physical or mental impairment which substantially limits one or more of such person['s] major life activities"). Up to this point in time, however, few "perceived disability" cases have been litigated and, consequently, decisional law involving the interplay of perceived disabilities and section 504 is hen's-teeth rare. Thus, this case calls upon us to explore new frontiers. . . .

On one hand, the jury could plausibly have found that plaintiff had a physical impairment; after all, she admittedly suffered from morbid obesity, and she presented expert testimony that morbid obesity is a physiological disorder involving a dysfunction of both the metabolic system and the neurological appetite-suppressing signal system, capable of causing adverse effects within the musculoskeletal, respiratory, and cardiovascular systems. On the second hand, the jury could have found that plaintiff, although not handicapped, was treated by MHRH as if she had a physical impairment. Indeed, MHRH's stated reasons for its refusal to hire—its concern that Cook's limited mobility impeded her ability to evacuate patients in case of an emergency, and its fears that her condition augured a heightened risk of heart disease, thereby increasing the likelihood of workers' compensation claims—show conclusively that MHRH treated plaintiff's obesity as if it actually affected her musculoskeletal and cardiovascular systems.

Appellant counterattacks on two fronts. Neither foray succeeds.

1. *Mutability.* MHRH baldly asserts that "mutable" conditions are not the sort of impairments that can find safe harbor in the lee of section 504. It exacuates this assertion by claiming that morbid obesity is a mutable condition and that, therefore, one who suffers from it is not handicapped within the meaning of the federal law because she can simply lose weight and rid herself of any concomitant disability. This suggestion is as insubstantial as a pitchman's promise. . . .

In deciding this issue, the jury had before it credible evidence that metabolic dysfunction, which leads to weight gain in the morbidly obese, lingers even after weight loss. Given this evidence, the jury reasonably could have found that, though people afflicted with morbid obesity can treat the manifestations of metabolic dysfunction by fasting or perennial undereating, the physical impairment itself—a dysfunctional metabolism—is permanent. *Cf. Gilbert v. Frank,* 949 F.2d 637, 641 (2d Cir. 1991) (finding that kidney disease controllable by weekly dialysis constitutes a handicap under § 504 of the Rehabilitation Act); *Reynolds v. Brock*; 815 F.2d 571, 573 (9th Cir. 1987) (holding that epilepsy controllable by medication qualifies as a handicap under § 504). Hence, the jury's resolution of the mutability question rested on a sufficiently sturdy evidentiary platform. . . .

Appellant's second assault regains no ground. MHRH asseverates that, because morbid obesity is caused, or at least exacerbated, by voluntary conduct, it cannot constitute an impairment falling within the ambit of section 504. But, this asseveration rests on a legally faulty premise. The Rehabilitation Act contains no language suggesting that its protection is linked to how an individual became impaired, or whether an individual contributed to his or her impairment. On the contrary, the Act indisputably applies to numerous conditions that may be caused or exacerbated by voluntary conduct, such as alcoholism, AIDS, diabetes, cancer resulting from cigarette smoking, heart disease resulting from excesses of various types, and the like. . . . Consequently, voluntariness, like mutability, is relevant only in determining whether a condition has a substantially limiting effect.

Appellant's premise fares no better as a matter of fact. The instructions (to which appellant did not object) specifically restricted disabilities to those conditions "that the person affected is powerless to control." Given the plethoric evidence introduced concerning the physiological roots of morbid obesity, the jury certainly could have concluded that the metabolic dysfunction and failed appetite-suppressing neural signals were beyond plaintiff's control and rendered her effectively powerless to manage her weight.

The regulations implementing section 504 define "major life activities" to include walking, breathing, working, and other manual tasks. *See id.* § 84.3(j)(2)(ii). In this case, Dr. O'Brien testified that he refused to hire plaintiff because he believed that her morbid obesity interfered with her ability to undertake physical activities, including walking, lifting, bending, stooping, and kneeling, to such an extent that she would be incapable of working as an IA-MR. On this basis alone, the jury plausibly could have found that MHRH viewed plaintiff's suspected impairment as interfering with major life activities.

Proceeding to the merits, we think that the degree of limitation fell squarely to the jury and that the evidence warrants its finding that appellant regarded plaintiff as substantially impaired. By his own admission, Dr. O'Brien believed plaintiff's limitations foreclosed a broad range of employment options in the health care industry, including positions such as community living aide, nursing home aide, hospital aide, and home health care aide. Detached jurors reasonably could have found that this pessimistic assessment of plaintiff's capabilities demonstrated that appellant regarded Cook's condition as substantially limiting a major life activity—being able to work. . . .

Here, the jury rationally could have concluded that MHRH's perception of what it thought to be plaintiff's impairment, as exhibited in its refusal to hire her for the IA-MR position, foreclosed a sufficiently wide range of jobs to serve as proof of a substantial limitation. Accordingly, the district court appropriately refused to direct a verdict for the employer.

The next stop on our odyssey requires us to consider whether there was sufficient evidence for the jury to conclude that plaintiff was "otherwise qualified" to work as an IA-MR. Once again, an affirmative answer emerges.

"An otherwise qualified person is one who is able to meet all of a program's requirements in spite of h[er] handicap." Although an employer is not required to be unfailingly correct in assessing a person's qualifications for a job, an employer cannot act solely on the basis of subjective beliefs. An unfounded assumption that an applicant is unqualified for a particular job, even if arrived at in good faith, is not sufficient to forestall liability under section 504. *See*

Pushkin v. Regents of Univ. of Colo., 658 F.2d 1372 (10th Cir. 1981) (rejecting good faith as a defense under § 504 because "[d]iscrimination on the basis of handicap usually . . . occurs under the guise of extending a helping hand or a mistaken, restrictive belief as to the limitations of handicapped persons"); *see also Carter v. Casa Central*, 849 F.2d 1048, 1056 (7th Cir. 1988) (explaining that "[a]n employer's concerns about the abilities of a handicapped employee . . . must be based on more than 'reflective' reactions about a handicapped individual's ability to do the job, no matter how well-intentioned"). The employer's belief must be objectively reasonable. It cannot rest on stereotypes and broad generalizations. After all, "mere possession of a handicap is not a permissible ground for assuming an inability to function in a particular context." *Davis*, 442 U.S. at 405, 99 S.Ct. at 2366 (footnote omitted).

Appellant's position, insofar as we can understand it, is that plaintiff's morbid obesity presented such a risk to herself and the Ladd Center's residents that she was not otherwise qualified, or, in the alternative, that it was reasonable for appellant to believe that she was not otherwise qualified. This protestation is undone by . . . independent considerations. . . .

We will not paint the lily. Several pieces of evidence loom large on this issue. Plaintiff received a satisfactory report following the physical examination conducted by appellant's own nurse; the IA-MR position for which she applied did not demand any elevated level of mobility, lifting ability, size, or stature; plaintiff had satisfactorily performed all her duties and responsibilities as an IA-MR during her previous five years of employment; and MHRH acknowledged that those duties and responsibilities have not changed. From this, and other, evidence, we believe that the jury lawfully could have found plaintiff, apart from any impairment, "otherwise qualified" to work as an IA-MR.

Our last port of call requires that we determine whether the evidence justified a finding that MHRH turned down plaintiff's request for employment due solely to her morbid obesity. This final piece of the puzzle is straightforward.

MHRH has not offered a hint of any non-weight-related reason for rejecting plaintiff's application. Rather, it has consistently conceded that it gave plaintiff the cold shoulder because Dr. O'Brien denied her medical clearance. The record is pellucid that Dr. O'Brien's refusal had three foci, each of which related directly to plaintiff's obesity. On this record, there was considerable room for a jury to find that appellant declined to hire Cook "due solely to" her perceived handicap.

CONCLUSION

We need go no further. In a society that all too often confuses "slim" with "beautiful" or "good," morbid obesity can present formidable barriers to employment. Where, as here, the barriers transgress federal law, those who erect and seek to preserve them must suffer the consequences. In this case, the evidence adduced at trial amply supports the jury's determination that MHRH violated section 504 of the Rehabilitation Act. And because MHRH refused to hire plaintiff due solely to her morbid obesity, there is no cause to disturb either the damage award or the equitable relief granted by the district court.

Affirmed.

CASE QUESTIONS

1. Are extremely overweight individuals protected under the Rehabilitation Act from discrimination based on their morbid obesity?
2. Can a person be considered as having a disability and thus be eligible for the protections of the Act when that individual can rid herself of the "disability" by simply losing weight?
3. Assess the judge's remarks in the first three sentences of the conclusion of the decision.

SCHOOL BOARD OF NASSAU COUNTY, FLORIDA v. ARLINE
Supreme Court of the United States, 480 U.S. 273 (1987).

[Respondent Gene Arline was hospitalized for tuberculosis in 1957. The disease went into remission for the next twenty years, during which time she began teaching elementary school in Florida. In 1977, March 1978, and November 1978 she had relapses. After the latter two relapses she was suspended with pay for the rest of the school year. At the end of the 1978–1979 school year, the school board discharged her after a hearing because of the continued recurrence of tuberculosis. After she was denied relief in state administrative proceedings, she brought suit in federal district court, alleging a violation of Section 504 of the Rehabilitation Act. The district court held that although Arline suffered a handicap, she was not a handicapped person under the statute since it was difficult "to conceive that Congress intended contagious diseases to be included within the definition of a handicapped person." The court of appeals reversed, and the Supreme Court granted certiorari.]

BRENNAN, J.

I.

In enacting and amending the Act, Congress enlisted all programs receiving federal funds in an effort "to share with handicapped Americans the opportunities for an education, transportation, housing, health care, and jobs that other Americans take for granted." 123 Cong. Rec. 13515 (1977) (statement of Sen. Humphrey). To that end, Congress not only increased federal support for vocational rehabilitation, but also addressed the broader problem of discrimination against the handicapped by including § 504, an antidiscrimination provision patterned after Title VII of the Civil Rights Act of 1964. Section 504 of the Rehabilitation Act reads in pertinent part:

"No otherwise qualified handicapped individual in the United States, as defined in section 706(7) of this title, shall, solely by reason of his handicap, be excluded from participation in, be denied the benefits of, or be subjected to discrimination under any program or activity receiving Federal financial assistance...." 29 U.S.C. § 794.

In 1974 Congress expanded the definition of "handicapped individual" for use in § 504 to read as follows:

"[A]ny person who (i) has a physical or mental impairment which substantially limits one or more of such person's major life activities, (ii) has a record of such an impairment, or (iii) is regarded as having such an impairment." 29 U.S.C. § 706(7)(B).

The amended definition reflected Congress' concern with protecting the handicapped against discrimination stemming not only from simple prejudice, but from "archaic attitudes and laws" and from "the fact that the American people are simply unfamiliar with and insensitive to the difficulties confront[ing] individuals with handicaps." To combat the effects of erroneous but nevertheless prevalent perceptions about the handicapped, Congress expanded the definition of "handicapped individual" so as to preclude discrimination against "[a] person who has a record of, or is regarded as having, an impairment [but who] may at present have no actual incapacity at all." *Southeastern Community College v. Davis,* 442 U.S. 397, 405–406, n. 6 (1979).

In determining whether a particular individual is handicapped as defined by the Act, the regulations promulgated by the Department of Health and Human Services are of significant assistance. . . . The regulations are particularly significant here because they define two critical terms used in the statutory definition of handicapped individual. "Physical impairment" is defined as follows:

"*[A]ny physiological disorder or condition, cosmetic disfigurement, or anatomical loss affecting one or more of the following body systems: neurological; musculoskeletal; special sense organs; respiratory, including speech organs; cardiovascular; reproductive, digestive, genitourinary; hemic and lymphatic; skin; and endocrine.*" *45 CFR § 84.3(j)(2)(i) (1985).*

In addition, the regulations define "major life activities" as:

"*functions such as caring for one's self, performing manual tasks, walking, seeing, hearing, speaking, breathing, learning, and working.*" *§ 84.3j(2)(ii).*

II.

Within this statutory and regulatory framework, then, we must consider whether Arline can be considered a handicapped individual. According to the testimony of Dr. McEuen, Arline suffered tuberculosis "in an acute form in such a degree that it affected her respiratory system," and was hospitalized for this condition. Arline thus had a physical impairment as that term is defined by the regulations, since she had a "physiological disorder or condition . . . affecting [her] . . . respiratory [system]." This impairment was serious enough to require hospitalization, a fact more than sufficient to establish that one or more of her major life activities were substantially limited by her impairment. Thus, Arline's hospitalization for tuberculosis in 1957 suffices to establish that she has a "record of . . . impairment" within the meaning of 29 U.S.C. § 706(7)(b)(ii), and is therefore a handicapped individual.

Petitioners concede that a contagious disease may constitute a handicapping condition to the extent that it leaves a person with "diminished physical or mental capabilities," and concede that Arline's hospitalization for tuberculosis in 1957 demonstrates that she has a record of a physical impairment. Petitioners maintain, however, Arline's record of impairment is irrelevant in this case, since the School Board dismissed Arline not because of her diminished physical capabilities, but because of the threat that her relapses of tuberculosis posed to the health of others.

We do not agree with petitioners that, in defining a handicapped individual under § 504, the contagious effects of a disease can be meaningfully distinguished from the disease's physical effects on a claimant in a case such as this. Arline's contagiousness and her physical impairment each resulted from the same underlying condition, tuberculosis. It would be unfair to allow an employer to seize upon the distinction between the effects of a disease on others and the effects of a disease on a patient and use that distinction to justify discriminatory treatment.*

Nothing in the legislative history of § 504 suggests that Congress intended such a result. . . .

. . . Few aspects of a handicap give rise to the same level of public fear and misapprehension as contagiousness. Even those who suffer or have recovered from such noninfectious diseases as epilepsy or cancer have faced discrimination based on the irrational fear that they might be contagious. The Act is carefully structured to replace such reflexive reactions to actual or perceived handicaps with actions based on reasoned and medically sound judgments: the definition of "handicapped individual" is broad, but only those individuals who are both handicapped *and* otherwise qualified are

---

* The United States argues that it is possible for a person to be simply a carrier of a disease, that is, to be capable of spreading a disease without having a "physical impairment" or suffering from any other symptoms associated with the disease. The United States contends that this is true in the case of some carriers of the Acquired Immune Deficiency Syndrome (AIDS) virus. From this premise the United States concludes that discrimination solely on the basis of contagiousness is never discrimination on the basis of a handicap. The argument is misplaced in this case, because the handicap here, tuberculosis, gave rise both to a physical impairment *and* to contagiousness. This case does not present, and we therefore do not reach, the questions whether a carrier of a contagious disease such as AIDS could be considered to have a physical impairment, or whether such a person could be considered, solely on the basis of contagiousness, a handicapped person as defined by the Act.

eligible for relief. The fact that *some* persons who have contagious diseases may pose a serious health threat to others under certain circumstances does not justify excluding from the coverage of the Act *all* persons with actual or perceived contagious diseases. Such exclusion would mean that those accused of being contagious would never have the opportunity to have their condition evaluated in light of medical evidence and a determination made as to whether they were "otherwise qualified." Rather, they would be vulnerable to discrimination on the basis of mythology—precisely the type of injury Congress sought to prevent. We conclude that the fact that a person with a record of a physical impairment is also contagious does not suffice to remove that person from coverage under § 504.

III.

The remaining question is whether Arline is otherwise qualified for the job of elementary school teacher. To answer this question in most cases, the District Court will need to conduct an individualized inquiry and make appropriate findings of fact. Such an inquiry is essential if § 504 is to achieve its goal of protecting handicapped individuals from deprivations based on prejudice, stereotypes, or unfounded fear, while giving appropriate weight to such legitimate concerns of grantees as avoiding exposing others to significant health and safety risks. The basic factors to be considered in conducting this inquiry are well established. In the context of the employment of a person handicapped with a contagious disease, we agree with *amicus* American Medical Association that this inquiry should include:

"[findings of] facts, based on reasonable medical judgments given the state of medical knowledge, about (a) the nature of the risk (how the disease is transmitted), (b) the duration of the risk (how long the carrier is infectious), (c) the severity of the risk (what the potential harm is to third parties) and (d) the probabilities the disease will be transmitted and will cause varying degrees of harm." Brief for American Medical Association as Amicus Curiae 19.*

In making these findings, courts normally should defer to the reasonable medical judgments of public health officials. The next step in the "otherwise-qualified" inquiry is for the court to evaluate, in light of these medical findings, whether the employer could reasonably accommodate the employee under the established standards for that inquiry.

Because of the paucity of factual findings by the District Court, we, like the Court of Appeals, are unable at this stage of the proceedings to resolve whether Arline is "otherwise qualified" for her job. The District Court made no findings as to the duration and severity of Arline's condition, nor as to the probability that she would transmit the disease. Nor did the court determine whether Arline was contagious at the time she was discharged, or whether the School Board could have reasonably accommodated her. Accordingly, the resolution of whether Arline was otherwise qualified requires further findings of fact.

IV.

We hold that a person suffering from the contagious disease of tuberculosis can be a handicapped person within the meaning of the § 504 of the Rehabilitation Act of 1973, and that respondent Arline is such a person. We remand the case to the District Court to determine whether Arline is otherwise qualified for her position. The judgment of the Court of Appeals is
  Affirmed.

CASE QUESTIONS

1. Why did the school board terminate Arline?
2. When a person with a record of physical impairment is also contagious, is that person removed from coverage under Section 504?
3. Did Congress seek to prevent discrimination against handicapped individuals based on the fear and mythology of contagiousness when it enacted Section 504?
4. Did the Court find that Arline was otherwise qualified?

SECTION 26—THE AMERICANS WITH DISABILITIES ACT

The Americans with Disabilities Act (ADA) defines *disability* in Section 3(2) as (1) any physical or mental[9] impairment that substantially limits a major life activity, (2) having a record of such an impairment, or (3) being regarded by others as having such an impairment.

The first part of the definition makes clear that the ADA applies to persons who have substantial, as distinct from minor, impairments, and that these must be impairments that limit major life activities such as seeing, hearing, speaking, walking, breathing, performing manual tasks, learning, caring for oneself, and working. An individual with paralysis, a substantial hearing or visual impairment, mental retardation, or a learning disability would be covered, but an individual with a minor, nonchronic condition of short duration, such as a sprain, infection, or broken limb, generally would not be covered.

The second part of the definition includes, for example, a person with a history of cancer that is currently in remission or a person with a history of mental illness.

The third part of the definition protects individuals who are regarded and treated as though they have a substantially limiting disability, even though they may not have such an impairment. For example, this provision would protect a severely disfigured qualified individual from being denied employment because an employer feared the "negative reactions" of others.

The ADA prohibits all private employers with 15 or more employees from discriminating against disabled individuals, who, with or without reasonable accommodations, are qualified to perform the essential functions of the job.

Under a new "user friendly" publication of the EEOC entitled *Guidance on Pre-employment Inquiries Under the ADA*, the employer may ask applicants whether they will need reasonable accommodation for the hiring process. And if the answer is yes, the employer may ask for reasonable documentation of the disability.[10] In general, the employer may not ask questions about whether an applicant will need reasonable accommodations to do the job. However, an employer may make preemployment inquiries into the ability of a job applicant to perform job-related functions.

Section 102(b)(5)(A) of the Act states that a covered entity commits discrimination by:

> [N]ot making reasonable accommodations to the known physical or mental limitations of an otherwise qualified individual with a disability who is an applicant or employee, unless such covered entity can demonstrate that the accommodation would impose an undue hardship on the operation of the business of such covered entity.

Section 101(9) defines "reasonable accommodation" to include:

(A) making existing facilities used by employees readily accessible to and usable by individuals with disabilities; and

(B) job restructuring, part-time or modified work schedules, reassignment to a vacant position, acquisition or modification of equipment or devices, appropriate

---

[9] On March 25, 1997, the EEOC issued enforcement guidance on the EEOC's position on the application of the ADA to individuals with psychiatric disabilities. Excerpts from this document are presented in Appendix F.
[10] *EEOC Guidance on Pre-employment Inquiries Under the ADA*, Oct. 10, 1995.

adjustment or modifications of examinations, training materials or policies, the provision of qualified readers or interpreters, and other similar accommodations for individuals with disabilities.

Exclusions from Coverage

The Act excludes from its coverage employees or applicants who are "currently engaging in the illegal use of drugs." The exclusion does not include an individual who has been successfully rehabilitated from such use or is participating in or has completed supervised drug rehabilitation, and is no longer engaging in the illegal use of drugs.[11]

In *Wallace v. Veterans Administration*,[12] Dorothy Wallace, a registered nurse, was a former drug abuser who had successfully undergone treatment for this condition and remained drug free during the period prior to applying for a position as an intensive care nurse at a VA hospital. She was refused employment because her own physician recommended that she not administer narcotics to patients. The hospital considered this restriction a basis to reject her application because she could not fully perform the functions of a registered nurse. Wallace challenged the decision in court. Utilizing a fact-based analysis, the court found that less than 2 percent of a nurse's time in the intensive care unit of the VA hospital was spent handling narcotics. Further, the court found that through the less burdensome process of job restructuring, Wallace could be accommodated by having another nurse, if necessary, dispense narcotics to her patients. In addition, another option was also available as an accommodation. She could be assigned primarily to heart and liver patients who received no narcotics.

Alcoholics are not excluded from the coverage of the ADA. The ADA thus may protect an individual from discrimination based on his or her status as an alcoholic. However, alcoholics are not protected from the consequences of their conduct. In *Larson v. Koch Refining Co.*,[13] Lloyd Larson, a supervisor at the refinery, was terminated after he was arrested for drunk driving and assault. Larson argued that his employer violated the ADA when it failed to provide him alcohol counseling and other reasonable accommodations. The court held that the employer did not know of Larson's disability prior to his discharge. And a pattern of absenteeism coupled with the drunk driving and assault arrest gave the employer a valid basis to terminate this supervisor. The court relied on the "alcoholics are not protected from the consequences of their conduct" principle.

Title V of the Act states that homosexuality and bisexuality, and behaviors such as transvestism, transsexualism, pedophilia, exhibitionism, compulsive gambling, kleptomania, pyromania, or psychoactive substance use disorders resulting from current illegal use of drugs are not—in and of themselves—considered disabilities.

---

[11] Section 124.
[12] 683 F. Supp 758 (D. Kan. 1988). See also *Chairi v. City of League City*, 920 F.2d 311 (5th Cir. 1991).
[13] 920 F.Supp. 1000 (D.C. MN. 1995).

Conflicts with Collective Bargaining Agreements

Potential conflicts may exist between an employer's obligations under a collective bargaining agreement and the employer's obligations under the ADA. The ADA provides that an employer cannot participate in a contractual arrangement that violates the ADA; while the NLRA prohibits midterm modification of contract terms without bargaining with the union. Under EEOC regulations interpreting the ADA, a "reasonable accommodation" for a disabled worker may require the employer to consider job assignments or job restructuring in a manner prohibited by the union contract. The parties may well be expected to bargain and reach an agreement on how to resolve all matters where their collective bargaining agreements are in conflict with the ADA.

Reasonable Accommodations

Section 101(9) of the ADA defines an employer's obligation to make "reasonable accommodations" for individuals with disabilities to include (1) making existing facilities accessible to and usable by individuals with disabilities and (2) job restructuring, modified work schedules, and acquisition or modification of equipment or devices. Employers are not obligated under the ADA to make accommodations that would be an "undue hardship" on the employer, as set forth in Section 102(b)(5)(A).

In *Lyons v. the Legal Aid Society*, presented in this section, the U.S. Court of Appeals for the Second Circuit held that it was improper for a federal district court to dismiss an ADA claim of discrimination based on an employer's failure to accommodate an employee's handicap, in refusing to provide and pay for a parking space near work in Manhattan. The court of appeals believed that there was nothing inherently unreasonable in the employee's request, and left the matter to be resolved by a properly developed evidentiary record at trial.

In *Vande Zande v. Wisconsin Department of Administration*,[14] the U.S. Court of Appeals for the Seventh Circuit rejected a claim of a state secretarial worker, who was paralyzed from the waist down as a result of a spinal tumor, that the employer did not fully accommodate her "reasonable accommodation" request. To accommodate her disability, the state modified the bathroom, built a ramp for her wheelchair, provided special adjustable furniture, paid half the cost of a cot, and modified her schedule to accommodate her medical appointments. Her supervisor refused her request for full-time work at home while recovering during an eight-week bout with pressure ulcers, and refused to install a desktop computer at her home. The supervisor advised her that he would have a maximum of 20 hours a week for her to work at home, and advised her to use her laptop computer at home. In finding for the employer, the court determined that the employer had done more than was required to accommodate the employee's disability under the ADA.

---

[14] 3 AD Cases 1636 (7th Cir. 1994).

LYONS v. THE LEGAL AID SOCIETY

United States Court of Appeals, 4 AD Cases 1694 (2d Cir. 1995).

[Beth Lyons was employed as a staff attorney by the Legal Aid Society. She was severely injured when struck by an automobile, and had to take a disability leave for a four year period while she underwent multiple reconstructive surgeries and received constant physical therapy. Before returning to work she asked Legal Aid to accommodate her disability, which included the necessity to wear a knee brace and an inability to climb stairs and walk long distances without difficulty, by paying for a parking space near her office and the courts in which she would practice. Her physician advised Legal Aid by letter that such a parking space was necessary to enable her to return to work. Legal Aid declined to pay for a parking space for her, and Lyons has had to pay up to $520 a month for parking which represents 26 percent of her net salary. The U.S. District Court dismissed her complaint against the employer under the Rehabilitation Act and the ADA, and she appealed.]

BEARSE, C.J. . . .

. . . under either the ADA or the Rehabilitation Act, a plaintiff can state a claim for discrimination based upon her employer's failure to accommodate her handicap by alleging facts showing (1) that the employer is subject to the statute under which the claim is brought, (2) that she is an individual with a disability within the meaning of the statute in question, (3) that, with or without reasonable accommodation, she could perform the essential functions of the job, and (4) that the employer had notice of the plaintiff's disability and failed to provide such accommodation. There is no question here with respect to the first, second, and fourth elements. The only question is whether Lyons's request that Legal Aid provide her with a parking space near work is, as a matter of law, not a request for a "reasonable" accommodation.

Neither the ADA nor the Rehabilitation Act provides a closed-end definition of "reasonable

accommodation." The ADA sets out a nonexclusive list of different methods of accommodation encompassed by that term, stating that

> [t]he term "reasonable accommodation" may include—
> (A) making existing facilities used by employees readily accessible to and usable by individuals with disabilities, and
> (B) job restructuring, part-time or modified work schedules, reassignment to a vacant position, acquisition or modification of equipment or devices, appropriate adjustment or modifications of examinations, training materials or policies, the provision of qualified readers or interpreters, and other similar accommodations for individuals with disabilities. . . .

The accommodation obligation does not require the employer to make accommodations that are "primarily for the [individual's] personal benefit," such as an "adjustment or modification [that] assists the individual throughout his or her daily activities, on and off the job," or to provide "any amenity or convenience that is not job-related." *Id.* at 412.

In support of the order of dismissal in the present case, Legal Aid argues that Lyons's claim for financial assistance in parking her car amounts to a demand for unwarranted preferential treatment because the requested accommodation is merely "a matter of personal convenience that she uses regularly in daily life." Legal Aid asserts that it does not provide parking facilities or any other commuting assistance to its nondisabled employees and that Lyons's special needs in getting to work must therefore lie outside the scope of its obligations under the federal disability statutes. We find Legal Aid's contentions to be an inappropriate foundation for the Rule 12(b)(6) dismissal. . . .

. . . It is clear that an essential aspect of many jobs is the ability to appear at work regularly and on time, *see, e.g., Carr v. Reno*, 23 F.3d

525, 530 (D.C. Cir. 1994) ("an essential function of any government job is an ability to appear for work"), and that Congress envisioned that employer assistance with transportation to get the employee to and from the job might be covered. Thus, the report of the House of Representatives Committee on Education and Labor noted that a qualified person with a disability seeking employment at a store that is "located in an inaccessible mall" would be entitled to reasonable accommodation in helping him "get to the job site." H.R. Rep. No. 485, 101st Cong., 2d Sess., pt. 2, at 61 (1990). . . . Similarly, the EEOC has stated that possible required accommodations other than those specifically listed in the statute include "making employer provided transportation accessible, and *providing reserved parking spaces.*" EEOC Interpretive Guidance at 407 (emphasis added). So far as we are aware, there has been no judicial interpretation of this EEOC guideline, which may have been intended to mean that the provision of parking spaces can be required, or that the reservation of employer-provided parking spaces can be required, or both.

Whatever the guideline intended, we think that the question of whether it is reasonable to require an employer to provide parking spaces may well be susceptible to differing answers depending on, *e.g.*, the employer's geographic location and financial resources, and that the determination of the reasonableness of such a requirement will normally require some development of a factual record. . . . Further, we have noted that while reasonableness depends upon "a common-sense balancing of the costs and benefits" to both the employer and the employee, *Borkowski v. Valley Central School District*, 63 F.3d at 140, an accommodation may not be considered unreasonable merely because it requires the employer "to assume more than a *de minimis* cost,"

id. at 138 n.3, or because it will cost the employer more overall to obtain the same level of performance from the disabled employee, *see id.*

Finally, we reject Legal Aid's contention that Lyons's request for a parking space amounts to no more than a demand for an additional fringe benefit in the nature of a "personal amenity" unrelated to the "essential functions" of her job. According to the complaint, whose factual allegations must be taken as true, Lyons cannot fulfill her responsibilities as a staff attorney at Legal Aid without being able to park her car adjacent to her office. Lyons's ability to reach her office and the courts is an essential prerequisite to her work in that position. There is no suggestion in the complaint that the requested parking space near the Legal Aid office and the courts was sought for any purpose other than to allow Lyons to reach and perform her job.

Plainly there is nothing inherently unreasonable, given the stated views of Congress and the agencies responsible for overseeing the federal disability statutes, in requiring an employer to furnish an otherwise qualified disabled employee with assistance related to her ability to get to work. We conclude that Lyons's complaint stated a claim on which relief can be granted under the ADA and the Rehabilitation Act. . . .

CASE QUESTIONS

1. State the basis of Ms. Lyons's claim against Legal Aid.
2. Does the ADA set forth an exclusive listing of the different methods of accommodations to be used by employers?
3. Is it inherently "unreasonable" and thus not a "reasonable" accommodation for an employer to be required to pay up to $6,000 per year for a parking space for a disabled employee when the employer does not have a parking facility and does not provide parking for any other employee?

SECTION 27—WORKERS' COMPENSATION: RELATIONSHIP TO THE ADA

At common law the employer is not liable to an injured employee if the employee is harmed by a fellow employee. Nor is the employer liable if the employee is harmed by an ordinary hazard of the work, because the employee assumed such risks. If the injured employee is contributorily negligent, regardless of the employer's negligence, the employer is not liable at common law. The rising incidence of industrial accidents due to the use of more powerful machinery and the growth of the industrialized labor force led to the statutory modification of common law rules relating to liability of employers for industrial accidents. Workers' compensation statutes have been adopted in every state.[15] These laws entitle workers or their dependents to compensation for work-related injuries, occupational diseases, or work-related deaths, without regard to fault or negligence as to the cause of the injuries, diseases, or deaths.

In exchange for compensation under workers' compensation statutes, workers lose their right to sue their employers in court, except for intentional torts. Thus even if an injury is caused by an employer's clear negligence, the employee's sole remedy is limited to that provided in the workers' compensation statute. Recoveries under these statutes are much less than what could be recovered in comparable common law lawsuits. The *Halliman v. Los Angeles School District* case, presented in this section, is an example of the application of the exclusive remedy rule. However, the exclusive remedy provisions in workers' compensation laws do not bar employees from pursuing ADA claims.

Benefits

For most injuries and occupational diseases, "arising out of and in the course of employment," the workers' compensation statutes usually provide (1) immediate medical benefits, (2) prompt periodic wage replacement, very often computed as a percentage of weekly wages (ranging from 50 percent to 80 percent of the injured employee's wage) for a specified number of weeks, (3) if applicable, a death benefit of a limited amount, (4) payment for loss of function or disfigurement (for example, loss of function and disfigurement payment due to a loss of an arm may be set at $31,000 by statute), and (5) vocational retraining services if the employee is unable to return to the former employment as a result of an injury.

A body of law continues to be developed concerning whether or not an employee received an injury "arising out of and in the course of employment." In *Carrillo v. Liberty Northwest Insurance*,[16] an office worker was struck by an automobile after she left her office building for a two-minute walk. She walked to a nearby building to obtain a gift for a co-worker during a paid, authorized fifteen-minute coffee break. Her injuries were found to have arisen "in the course of her employment" and thus were covered by

---

[15] Workers' compensation statutes do not cover railroad workers, longshore workers, and federal employees. Railroad workers are covered by the Federal Employers' Liability Act (FELA) 45 U.S.C. §§ 51–59; longshore and harbor workers are covered by the Longshoremen's and Harbor Workers' Compensation Act (LHWCA) 33 U.S.C. §§ 901–950; and federal employees are covered by the Federal Employees' Compensation Act (FECA) 5 U.S.C. §§ 8101 *et seq.* One example of the developing common law applicable to FELA suits is found in *Consolidated Rail Corporation v. Gottshall*, 114 S.Ct. 2396 (1994), when the Supreme Court held that a claim for negligent infliction of emotional distress is a valid legal theory under FELA, with a "zone of danger test" to be used for determining who may recover under the theory.

[16] 922 P.2d 1189 (Mont. 1996).

workers' compensation. Injuries suffered off the premises during unpaid lunch breaks are not covered by workers' compensation, however, since the employee is free from the control and obligations of employment during this period of time. Injuries occurring off premises while going and coming to work are generally not compensable. However, as will be seen in the *Quaker Oats Co. v. Ciha* case, presented in this section, an exception exists which provides for coverage of employees who are injured while on a "special errand" for the employer.

Proceedings

Workers' compensation proceedings are brought before a special administrative agency called a workers' compensation or industrial accident board. Workers' compensation laws, being remedial in purpose, are broadly and liberally construed and embrace all activities which can reasonably be included within their coverage. The *Gacioch v. Stroh Brewery Co.* case, presented in this section, is an illustration of the liberal application of a workers' compensation statute.

ADA Impact on Workers' Compensation

Under the Americans with Disabilities Act, employers may no longer inquire about job applicants' physical and mental conditions or their workers' compensation histories. Prior to the ADA it was common for employers to ask job applicants about their medical history and whether or not the applicants had received compensation for injuries. In some states, if an applicant intentionally misrepresented a preexisting disability in his or her employment application, the employer was allowed to raise this misrepresentation as a complete defense to a later workers' compensation claim by the individual. Since employers may no longer ask such questions, it appears that such misrepresentation defenses are no longer viable.

Many workers' compensation claimants fall within the definition of a "qualified individual with a disability" under the ADA. In a workers' compensation case, once an injured worker recovers and wishes to return to work, the employer may require that individual to take a medical examination to see if the individual can safely perform the essential functions of the job, with or without reasonable accommodation. Such a medical evaluation must be job related and consistent with business necessity. That is, instead of administering general strength tests, only functional capacities relating to the job in question can be tested. If the recovered worker can perform the essential job functions, the worker must be returned to work under the ADA.

Prior to the ADA many employers had the policy of requiring that employees be capable of performing the "full duties of a position, 100 percent" in order to be returned to work. Under the ADA employers must make reasonable accommodation for those workers who can otherwise perform the essential functions of the job.[17] However, employers are not required to provide accommodation that represents undue hardship.

---

[17] EEOC, *Technical Assistance Manual on the Employment Provisions of the ADA*, at IX-4 (January 1992).

Thus, a supermarket meat cutter, who was out on workers' compensation for a back injury, and who is released to return to work by his or her physician, may be found to be able to perform all of the functions of a job, except for being unable to carry meat from the loading dock to the processing area. The supermarket can no longer flatly refuse to return this individual to work without being in violation of the ADA. It would have to make available a cart or device to enable this worker to perform the unloading function. This "accommodation" may cost the employer $300–$500 for the cart or device. Such an accommodation on its face would be reasonable for a large supermarket chain. However, if the employer of the meat cutter was a small store and the owner had very limited financial resources, such an accommodation may be an undue hardship which the employer could lawfully refuse to make.

An employer may recognize a special obligation to create a light duty position for an employee who suffered an occupational injury while performing service for the employer and as a consequence is unable to do his or her regular duties. The employer is not legally obligated to create a light duty position for a nonoccupationally injured employee with a disability as a reasonable accommodation. The ADA does not require employers to create positions as a form of reasonable accommodation.[18]

The ADA, through the "accommodation" process, may return many injured workers to their prior jobs, which in the past would not be open to them. This may well reduce the overall amount of time workers are out on disabilities and may result in substantial reductions in the overall cost of workers' compensation.

HALLIMAN v. LOS ANGELES UNIFIED SCHOOL DISTRICT

California Court of Appeals, 163 Cal App 3d 46, 209 Cal Rptr 175 (1984).

[Robert Halliman was employed as a teacher by the Los Angeles Unified School District at Milliken Junior High School. On November 4, 1982, a minor student, Louis "R," intentionally threw a rock at him, hitting him on the head and seriously injuring him. The same student had committed previous assaults on the school grounds, including an assault earlier that very day. Halliman and his wife brought suit against the Los Angeles Unified School District and the student's parents, seeking damages. Halliman contended that the defendants had the power and ability to prevent the student's conduct by appropriate disciplinary action but did not do so, ignoring their duty to protect students and teachers. The school district filed a motion for a summary judgment on the ground that the Workers' Compensation Act provided the exclusive remedy for Halliman's injury. From a summary judgment in favor of the school district, Halliman appealed.]

ARGVELLES, A.J.

In this appeal from a judgment favoring a school district, we are called upon to determine whether workers' compensation is the exclusive remedy for a teacher's injuries caused by a student's unprovoked assault while the teacher is acting within the scope of his employment. . . .

---

[18] See *EEOC Enforcement Guidance: Workers' Compensation and the ADA* issued by the EEOC on Sept. 3, 1996, Questions and Answers 23, 24, 26, and 27.

We find . . . that plaintiffs have failed to state facts negating application of the exclusive remedy provision of the workers' compensation laws in their complaint. . . .

We disagree with plaintiffs' contention that *Meyer v. Graphic Arts International Union* (1979) 88 Cal. App. 3d 176, 151 Cal. Rptr. 597, is dispositive of the issue in their favor. *Meyer* involved injury by a coemployee of plaintiff, and there had been reported prior acts of aggression by that person against the complaining employee followed by the employer's ratification or acquiescence in failing to discipline, censure, criticize, suspend or discharge the offending coemployee. Here, as defendant correctly points out, the assailant was not a coemployee but a student for whom the plaintiff teacher, among other employees at the school, was responsible. The record before us discloses no reports of prior assaults upon plaintiff teacher by the same student. Additionally, the student's school records indicated that he had, indeed, been previously suspended and otherwise disciplined for prior assaults.

In *Adler v. Los Angeles Unified School Dist.* (1979) 98 Cal. App. 3d 280, 288, 159 Cal. Rptr. 528, though the case was decided on other grounds, the court presumed that where a teacher was injured in a classroom attack by a student, the available workers' compensation remedy barred a civil lawsuit for damages against the employer by virtue of Labor Code section 3601. Under the facts of this case, we so hold.

Plaintiffs argue that a student in this context is akin to an employer's agent or a coemployee who is "under the control" of the employer; and, therefore, the school district "employer" comes within the statutory exception to the exclusive remedy provisions of the workers' compensation laws for intentional acts of agents and coemployees. But, teacher and student are not equals, standing shoulder to shoulder in the classroom or on the play-

ground, with the same status, rights, duties, responsibilities, maturity, judgment, knowledge and skill. If an analogy is to be drawn, a more appropriate one would liken the student to raw material which must be wrought by the employee into a finished product.

Thus, we find it helpful in addressing plaintiff's contentions to refer to those cases where the alleged intentional misconduct of the employer does not go beyond failure to assure a safe working environment. The California Supreme Court in *Johns-Manville Products Corp. v. Superior Court* (1980) 27 Cal. 3d 465, 165 Cal. Rptr. 858, 612 P.2d 948, reviewed cases where the employer concealed inherent dangers in the material its employees were required to handle, or made false representations in that regard, or allowed an employee to use a machine without proper instruction. Workers' compensation was held to be the exclusive remedy for any injuries thus suffered. The Supreme Court concluded that the workers' compensation laws provided "the sole remedy for additional compensation against an employer whose employee is injured in the first instance as the result of a deliberate failure to assure that the physical environment of the workplace is safe."

The facts of the present case do not justify a departure from such precedent.

[Judgment affirmed]

CASE QUESTIONS

1. State the issue before the court.
2. Why did the Hallimans bring an action for damages in a court of law when Halliman was clearly entitled to benefits under the workers' compensation law?
3. When an employee is injured as a result of an employer's deliberate failure to provide a safe workplace, may the employee sue the employer for damages in a court of law?
4. Is there an exception to the exclusive remedy provisions of the workers' compensation laws for intentional acts of agents or "co-employees"?

QUAKER OATS CO. v. CIHA

Supreme Court of Iowa, 552 N.W. 2d 143 (1996).

[Bradley Ciha was assigned as the on call maintenance supervisor for the Memorial Day weekend. After completing call-in service at the employer's plant he returned home by a scenic, less direct route, and was seriously injured in a motorcycle accident. Quaker Oats, the employer, believed it was not responsible for the injuries of an employee going or coming to work; but if an exception existed for a special errand, the employer believed Ciha deviated from this errand by taking the indirect route home. Quaker Oats did not believe that "reasonable appliances" under the workers' compensation law included modifications to Ciha's home costing $20,788 and a van conversion costing $24,509, nor did it believe Ciha's wife should be paid for nursing care expenses. Finally, the employer did not believe that Ciha was 80 percent "permanent partial" disabled, since the employer modified the workplace and continued to provide full-time employment for Ciha. The matter was appealed from the industrial commissioners' office to the district court, to the state supreme court.]

MCGIVERIN, C.J. . . .
In May 1991, petitioner Bradley Ciha was employed by defendant Quaker Oats Company at its Cedar Rapids plant as an area maintenance supervisor. Quaker Oats employed twenty to twenty-five such supervisors. In that position, he was responsible for the planning, scheduling, and supervising of plant maintenance in a designated area of the plant's operation. . . . Ciha was considered an excellent employee. Ciha's normal work week . . . was Monday through Friday. On a typical weekend including Saturday and Sunday, Ciha was not on duty and was not expected to be on call to drive to the plant for emergency maintenance purposes.

For the first forty-eight hours on Memorial Day weekend in 1991, Ciha was assigned as "204 supervisor" for Quaker Oats. In that capac-ity, he was required to be on call for mechanical emergencies anywhere in the plant. On that particular Memorial Day weekend, Quaker Oats engaged in periodic heat sterilization of the plant for pest control purposes.

While preparing dinner at his home on Sunday, May 26, Ciha was contacted at approximately 4:15 p.m. through a company electronic paging device. He was informed that several large cooling fans at the plant were malfunctioning. Ciha responded to the breakdown by electing to drive his motorcycle to the plant to remedy the problem himself. To reach the plant, Ciha drove a direct route (of approximately four and a half miles) on Johnson Avenue. After reaching the plant without incident, he personally remedied the problem by cooling the fans with an air hose. At approximately 5:45 p.m., Ciha telephoned his wife and informed her that she could resume dinner preparations because he was about to return home.

Ciha drove a different route from the plant to home than he drove earlier from his home to the plant. The return-home route was on Ellis road and was admittedly not the most direct route from the plant to Ciha's home. The Ellis road route (approximately nine miles) was scenic and subject to less traffic and traffic signals than the direct route Ciha commonly drove from home to the plant. Apparently, the Ellis road route took approximately five to seven minutes longer to drive than the direct, Johnson road route. Ciha chose to drive this route home only during the spring, summer, and fall seasons as the road could become treacherous during the winter months.

On his return trip from the plant to home along Ellis road, Ciha was involved in a serious motor vehicle accident in which he suffered a broken neck and was rendered a quadriplegic. At the time of the accident, Ciha was married and resided in a home in Cedar Rapids with his wife, Kim.

Following the accident, Ciha was admitted to St. Luke's Hospital in Cedar Rapids until June 12, 1991, when he requested transfer to a specialized care facility, Craig Hospital, located in Englewood, Colorado. Kim accompanied Ciha to Colorado and she remained with him for the duration of his stay.

In addition to the health care Ciha received while at Craig, the hospital also provided Kim specialized training in order for her to be able to care for Ciha upon his return home. Kim received specialized training in areas including suprapubic catheterization, bowel care, skin care, and recognizing potentially dangerous or life threatening conditions that may confront Ciha as a quadriplegic.

Ciha was discharged from Craig Hospital on September 14, 1991, to his home in Cedar Rapids. Since his discharge, Kim has performed necessary, extensive home nursing services. Ciha requires assistance in dressing, changing urine bags, and transferring between his wheelchair and his bed. At night, he must be repositioned in bed one to four times in order to prevent him from developing pressure sores. Also, Kim must perform digital stimulation of Ciha for approximately ninety minutes every other day to induce bowel movements.

Ciha first returned to work at Quaker Oats in January 1992 in a new position as materials supervisor. In this position, he works at a computer (with the aid of an adaptive device and telephone headset) in the company's purchasing department. With the aid of a modified computer, Ciha analyzes inventory and makes purchases on behalf of Quaker Oats. Quaker Oats greatly aided in Ciha's return to work by adapting the workplace and position in order for Ciha to be able to perform the job.* It is apparent Ciha has progressed well in the new position.

In his position as materials supervisor, he receives the same base salary, not including raises, as that of an area maintenance supervisor. Ciha no longer has the same opportunity, however, to earn overtime as he had as an area maintenance supervisor. . . .

In order to return to work, Ciha relied on the county's disabled persons transportation service to and from Quaker Oats. Based on the hours of the transportation service, however, Ciha was not able to return to work full-time.

Ciha was readmitted to Craig for one week in March 1992 for a comprehensive evaluation. At the time of his readmittance, Ciha did not own a van and did not drive. While at Craig, Ciha had his driving potential assessed. A driving specialist from the hospital concluded Ciha would need to purchase a specially modified van in order to be able to drive independently. At some time thereafter, Ciha purchased the recommended van.

Many of Ciha's medical expenses from the accident were paid for through a group health and accident insurance plan available to Ciha through his employer Quaker Oats. However, there were significant limitations in coverage under the group plan. For example, in addition to a lifetime cap on medical expenses, the group plan did not provide Ciha coverage for necessary home health care services, home modifications, or motor vehicle conversions. . . .

[e]very employer, not specifically excepted by the provisions of [Iowa Code chapter 85], shall provide, secure, and pay compensation according to the provisions of this chapter for any and all personal injuries sustained by an employee arising out of and in the course of the employment. . . .

Iowa Code § 85.3(1); *see id.* § 85.61(7). To obtain such compensation, an injured employee has the burden of proving by a preponderance of the evidence that his injuries arose out of and in the course of his employment. *See 2800 Corp. v.*

---

* Upon Ciha's return to work, Quaker Oats installed an automatic door specifically for his use. Also, a group of five Quaker Oats employees were responsible for assisting Ciha with transportation throughout the plant, changing his catheter bags, and knowing of his whereabouts at all times.

Fernandez, 528 N.W.2d 124, 128 (Iowa 1995). An injury arises "out of" the employment when there is a causal relationship between the employment and the injury. *Fernandez*, 528 N.W.2d at 128. "In the course of" the employment concerns the time, place, and circumstances of the injury. *Id*. . . .

First and foremost, Quaker Oats contends Ciha did not sustain his injury in the course of his employment because the injury was sustained away from the employer's premises and while Ciha was on his way home from the plant. The employer relies on the well established "going and coming" rule which generally provides: "[A]bsent special circumstances, injuries occurring off the employer's premises while the employee is on the way to or from work are not compensable." . . .

Under the going and coming rule, Ciha admittedly did not sustain an injury in the course of his employment: he was injured while driving his motorcycle home from the Quaker Oats plant.

There are, however, several exceptions to the going and coming rule that " 'extend the employer's premises under certain circumstances when it would be unduly restrictive to limit coverage of compensation statutes to the physical perimeters of the employer's premises.' " . . .

. . . The first exception to the going and coming rule relied on by the commissioner is the "special errand" exception.

Under the exception, if an employee is on a special errand or mission for his or her employer at the time of the injury, the injury is held to have arisen in the course of employment. . . .

After considering all arguments raised by the parties, we believe substantial evidence supports the commissioner's conclusion that Ciha was on a special errand at the time of his injury. . . .

. . . The fact that Ciha was contacted on Sunday while he was on 204 duty was truly "special:" it was unusual, sudden, and unexpected. . . .

. . . Notwithstanding our conclusion that the special errand exception to the going and coming rule applies in the present case, Quaker Oats contends Ciha had "deviated" from his trip home from the plant to such an extent that he abandoned his employment at the time of the accident. The commissioner and district court rejected this argument, and we do the same. . . .

. . . In concluding Ciha did not deviate from his special errand, the commissioner stated:

[Ciha] testified that he often took [the Ellis road] route home because it was more scenic, it had less traffic, it had fewer stop lights, and the actual difference in miles between this route and the more direct route was minimal. [Ciha's] call to his wife from the plant to start the grill for their meal shows that his purpose was to return home, and that he had no other destination other than to return to his residence. The record does not show a deviation from the course of the employment.

. . . Of the expenses awarded by the commissioner under Iowa Code section 85.27, Quaker Oats only challenges the award of costs for home modifications, van conversion, and home nursing services. The commissioner and district court found the home modification and van conversion expenses to be reasonable "appliances" under section 85.27. In addition, the commissioner found the claimed expenses for home nursing services and the claimed value of those services to be reasonable.

Iowa Code section 85.27 provides in pertinent part:

The employer, for all injuries compensable under this chapter or chapter 85A, shall furnish reasonable surgical, medical, dental, osteopathic, chiropractic, podiatric, physical rehabilitation, nursing, ambulance and hospital services and supplies therefor and shall allow reasonably necessary transportation expenses incurred for such services. The employer shall also furnish reasonable and necessary crutches, artificial members and appliances. . . .

. . . Quaker Oats does not dispute that the cost of Ciha's wheelchair is compensable under section 85.27; therefore, the question becomes whether the home modifications and van conversion completed to accommodate an admittedly covered appliance (a wheelchair) are compensable under the same statute.

An "appliance" is defined as hearing aids, corrective lenses, orthodontic devices, dentures, orthopedic braces, or any other artificial device used to provide function or for therapeutic purposes.

Appliances which are for the correction of a condition resulting from an injury . . . are compensable under Iowa Code section 85.27. . . .

We begin with the unusually strong medical evidence of necessity and of the record that [the claimant's] family status and past lifestyle reveal no other use for the van. That evidence refutes any contention that the van is a frill or luxury and reveals what can be described as an appliance, not greatly different from crutches or a wheelchair. The point is that a van is necessary in order to make [the claimant's] wheelchair fully useful. . . .

Under the unique facts of the present case, we conclude substantial evidence supports the commissioner's ruling that the home modifications and van conversion were reasonable appliances under Iowa Code section 85.27.

In addition to the claimed home modification and van conversion expenses, Ciha also sought $58,447 in home nursing services performed by his wife after his return home from the hospital in Colorado. At the arbitration hearing, Quaker Oats unsuccessfully contended the claimed home nursing services were not reasonable expenses under section 85.27, and also that the claimed amount of the services set forth in an affidavit prepared by Kim Ciha was unreasonable.

On appeal, Quaker Oats does not dispute that it had a duty under Iowa Code section 85.27 to provide reasonable nursing services to Ciha if his injury was compensable (which we have concluded it is). In addition, Quaker Oats agrees the services performed by Kim were "nursing" services as contemplated by section 85.27. Quaker Oats contends, however, that $58,447 in home nursing expenses claimed by Ciha is unreasonable. The commissioner and district court disagreed and we must affirm this decision if supported by substantial evidence.

In ordering Quaker Oats to pay Ciha's home nursing services, the commissioner stated the following:

The record shows that [Ciha's] wife received special training to perform the functions of a nurse for her husband, including digital manipulation to stimulate a bowel movement.

. . . .

In the instant case, [Ciha's] spouse, although not a nurse or LPN, did have to receive special training to perform the services. The services themselves are clearly medical nursing services and not general care services such as dressing, bathing, feeding, etc. [Ciha's] spouse's nursing services are held to be compensable under Iowa Code section 85.27. . . .

. . . We believe the affidavit and Kim's testimony establish the reasonableness of the claimed home nursing care expenses by a preponderance of the evidence. We conclude substantial evidence supports the commissioner's finding on this issue.

As a final issue, Quaker Oats contends the commissioner erred in ruling that Ciha had sustained an eighty percent permanent partial industrial disability. Quaker Oats argues Ciha's disability is only fifty to sixty percent because it, Ciha's employer, went to great lengths to accommodate claimant and also that claimant has suffered no loss of earnings.

As we have stated on many occasions, "[i]ndustrial disability measures an injured worker's lost earning capacity." . . . Factors that should be considered include the employee's functional disability, age, education, qualifications, experience, and the ability of the employee to engage in employment for which the employee is fitted. . . .

As a result of the accident and resulting quadriplegia, Ciha is wheelchair-bound, cannot control his bowel functions, and his lifestyle has been severely limited from that prior to the injury. He requires extensive, daily care and attention by his wife, relatives, and co-workers as he no longer has the ability to perform many basic daily living functions. Also, as a thirty-eight year old man, it cannot be reasonably disputed that Ciha's employability outside of the Quaker Oats workforce has been significantly and negatively affected by his injury. Although we applaud the efforts of Quaker Oats in modifying the workplace to accommodate Ciha's disability, such efforts are not determinative of Ciha's industrial disability rating. *See Thilges v. Snap-On Tools Corp.*, 528 N.W.2d 614, 617 (Iowa 1995) ("[W]e are satisfied that the commissioner was correct in viewing loss of earning capacity in terms of the injured worker's present ability to earn in the competitive job market without regard to the accommodation furnished by one's present employer.").

In finding eighty percent industrial disability, the commissioner concluded the following:

[D]efendant [Quaker Oats] has gone to great effort to accommodate claimant's [Ciha's] devastating disability. Defendant has set up a team of five co-employees to assist claimant, installed a special elevator, etc. These efforts are very appropriate, and defendant is to be commended for putting claimant back to work under difficult circumstances. However, defendant also obtains an advantage by doing so in that claimant's disability is reduced from what it otherwise would be.

Although claimant's position is not a "make work" job and involves a significant contribution to his employer, nevertheless if claimant were to be suddenly thrust into the job market, his ability to compete with other workers for positions would be limited in the most extreme sense. Clearly, without the accommodation, claimant's disability would be permanent and total. Claimant's industrial disability is found to be [eighty] percent.

We conclude there is substantial evidence to support the commissioner's decision on this issue.

Affirmed.

CASE QUESTIONS

1. Assess the extent of the accommodations the employer made to allow Ciha to be able to return to work.
2. Since Bradley Ciha suffered no loss of earnings, how can he be considered 80 percent permanent partial disabled?
3. Under Section 85.27, "The employer shall also furnish reasonable and necessary crutches, artificial members, and appliances. . . ." Did the legislature authorize a home modification ($20,788) and a van conversion ($24,509) under the term *appliances*?

GACIOCH v. STROH BREWERY CO.

Court of Appeals of Michigan, 466 N.W. 2d 303 (1991).

[Gacioch sought workers' compensation benefits for chronic alcoholism, asserting that the condition arose out of his employment with the brewery and resulted in his disability. The Workers' Compensation Appeal Board (WCAB) awarded benefits and the employer appealed.]

NEFF, J.

Defendants appeal from a decision of the Workers' Compensation Appeal Board, which essentially found that the decedent's alcoholism and the resulting disability were compensable under the Workers' Disability Compensation Act.

Reduced to its essence, the lengthy opinion of the appeal board reached the following conclusions:

1. The decedent clearly had the disease of alcoholism and whether this disease was an occupational disease or an ordinary disease of life is irrelevant if the disease was aggravated, accelerated, or contributed to by the employment, thereby resulting in disability. Aggravation or acceleration of or contribution to the decedent's underlying condition would constitute a personal injury under the Workers' Disability Compensation Act.

2. Alcoholism, like cardiovascular disease, is an ordinary disease of life, and the allegation

is that the course of the disease was contributed to by the employment. Therefore, *Kostamo v. Marquette Iron Mining Co.*, 405 Mich. 105, 274 N.W.2d 411 (1979), and *Miklik v. Michigan Special Machine Co.*, 415 Mich. 364, 329 N.W.2d 713 (1982), apply to the case at bar.

3. While the decedent was predisposed to alcoholism before he was hired by defendant, he was not an alcoholic when he was hired. The unique circumstances of the employment shaped the course of the decedent's disease, aggravating and accelerating the underlying predisposition to alcoholism to the point of uncontrolled addiction, thus constituting a personal injury under the act.

4. The aggravation or acceleration of the decedent's alcoholic propensities occurred as a circumstance of the employment relationship.

5. Whether a personal injury analysis or an occupational disease analysis is employed in this case, the decedent's condition is compensable.

An ordinary disease of life can be compensable as an occupational disease if exposure to the disease is increased by inherent characteristics of the employment, as existed in this case. *Mills v. Detroit Tuberculosis Sanitarium*, 323 Mich. 200, 35 N.W.2d 239 (1948).

After review of the record, the parties' briefs, and oral argument, we conclude that the WCAB correctly decided this case, and, accordingly, we affirm and adopt the board's opinion and order.

Affirmed.

CASE QUESTIONS

1. Can ordinary diseases of life be compensable as an occupational injury or disease under a workers' compensation act?
2. Based on a "common-sense viewpoint of the average person in society" test, do you believe that Gacioch's disability should be a compensable industrial accident or occupational disease?

Chapter Questions and Problems

1. Are individuals who are perceived as having handicaps, but in fact either have recovered from the disability or are not handicapped, covered by the Rehabilitation Act of the ADA?
2. Are all workers with occupational injuries protected by the ADA?
3. Mazir Coleman drove a school bus for the Casey County, Kentucky, Board of Education for four years. In 1978, Coleman's left leg was amputated. Coleman was fitted with an artificial leg and underwent extensive rehabilitation to relearn driving skills. When his driving skills had been sufficiently relearned over the course of four years, Coleman applied to the county board of education for a job as a school bus driver. The county refused to accept Coleman's application. The county board said that they had no alternative but to deny Coleman a bus-driving job because a Kentucky administrative regulation required it. That regulation states in part: "No person shall drive a school bus who does not possess both of these natural bodily parts: feet, legs, hands, arms, eyes, and ears. The driver shall have normal use of the above named body parts."

   Coleman brought an action under the Rehabilitation Act claiming discrimination based on his physical handicap. The county board of education denied this charge claiming that the reason they rejected Coleman was because of the requirement of the state regulation.

   May Coleman maintain an action of employment discrimination in light of the state regulation on natural body parts? What factors must be proved to establish his case? Decide the case. [*Coleman v. Casey County Board of Education*, 26 FEP 357 (D.C. N.D. Ky.)]

4. The New York City Police Department was a recipient of federal funds subject to the Rehabilitation Act of 1973. When Officer Heron, a three-year veteran of the department, began having attendance problems, a police psychologist suggested that Heron turn in his gun and be placed on nonpatrol duty. Despite these actions Heron's attendance problems continued, and it was eventually discovered that Heron was addicted to heroin.

   The department immediately initiated disciplinary proceedings against Heron and sought to dismiss him. After a hearing Heron was dismissed and denied eligibility for continuing health or pension benefits.

   Heron alleged that his condition was due to job-related stress and exposure to dangerous and violent incidents. He challenged his dismissal in federal court because the department had a policy of not dismissing alcoholic officers. He alleged that the initiation of disciplinary action against him was prohibited by Section 504 of the Rehabilitation Act of 1973 because he was an otherwise qualified person disciplined solely because of his handicap.

   What factors must the court consider in evaluating Heron's claim? What result should the court reach in this case? Decide. [*Heron v. McGuire*, 42 FEP 31 (2d Cir.)]

5. The collective bargaining contract between the National Machinists Union (NMU) and Life Bread Company set forth a "no fault" attendance program which assessed points for absences and tardiness, regardless of fault. Article XIII states in part:

ATTENDANCE POLICY AND GUIDE

PURPOSE

   In order for the company to meet its customer requirements and maintain a competitive position in the market, it is essential that an employee be at work on time.

   The purpose of this guide is to outline and define the company's objectives concerning attendance and the methods to be used in order to attain these objectives.

PROCEDURE

1. Effective November 1, 1995, all employees will have a clean record.
2. Records of absences and lateness will be maintained on all employees.
3. Each occurrence will have a point value:
   A. DOCUMENTED ABSENCE ....5 POINTS
   B. LATENESS ....5 POINTS
   C. *LEAVE EARLY ....5 POINTS
   D. EXCESSIVE LATENESS (Employees who punch in more than three hours after the start of their scheduled shift) ....10 POINTS
   E. UNEXCUSED ABSENCE ....15 POINTS
   F. UNEXCUSED ABSENCE WITHOUT NOTIFICATION .....25 POINTS
   G. PERFECT ATTENDANCE—FOR EACH MONTH OF PERFECT ATTENDANCE AN EMPLOYEE WILL RECEIVE ....5 POINTS CREDIT

4.   . . .
    C. When an employee reaches seventy-five (75) Points, final counseling session will be conducted between the employee, his/her supervisor, and the manufacturing manager and the company general manager. A written record will be made with a copy sent to the union. A union representative may be present.
    D. When an employee reaches one hundred (100) Points, the employee will be terminated.
5.   INDUSTRIAL ACCIDENT
When an employee is hurt and is absent as a result of an industrial accident, he/she will not be charged with an absence.

The contract provides a bonus for perfect attendance; and after a year, each assessment of points is removed from an employee's record.

John O'Reilly joined the company after graduation from high school and had nine years of service as of March 1998. He played softball and bowled for company teams; and often stayed out late having a "few beers" after these events. John was late for his 6:00 AM shift more than most employees. John also lost a lot of time due to a documented asthma condition he had all of his life. In the past John had come close to being assessed 100 points, which could allow for his discharge.

In March of 1997 John seriously injured his back while working on a bread molding machine. The injury resulted in two back operations and extensive physical therapy. John was assigned to light duty during this period of time, and no points were assessed for any loss of time or lateness due to this injury. However, due to some car problems, some oversleeping, and some asthma attacks, his attendance record was assessed 115 points in March of 1998, and he was terminated under Article XIII(4)(D) of the collective bargaining contract.

What is a "no fault" attendance program?

Was the termination of O'Reilly justified under the contract? Is the contract in compliance with the ADA?

6. Excellent Lumber Milling Corp. has created light duty assignments for three disabled workers seriously injured on the job when they could no longer perform their regular duties as a result of their job-related injuries. A fourth employee, Clare Patrick, can no longer perform the heavy labor duties of a lumber stacker at the mill because of a disability caused by a serious off-the-job auto accident. As a disabled individual she requests the employer to create a light duty position for her as a reasonable accommodation under the ADA. The company president denied Clare's request, pointing out that Clare had not been injured on the job. Did the company violate the ADA by treating individuals with job-related disabilities differently from an individual with a disability caused by an off-the-job accident? [See *EEOC Enforcement Guidance: Workers' Compensation and the ADA*, Question and Answer 27.]

7. Beverly C. was fired from her position as a clerk-typist for county government in Maryland because of outbursts and rude behavior directed at her supervisors. She had a manic depressive disorder, and believed that she should not have been fired, but rather because of her handicap, she believed the employer should have made

reasonable accommodations, including restructuring her job duties, changing her work schedule to alleviate stressful periods, relocating her from her current supervisor, and exempting her from normal performance reviews. The county had made efforts to accommodate Ms. C's problems through extensive training opportunities, job counseling, a medical leave, and offers to work with a psychiatrist. Did the employer violate the ADA by refusing to make the changes sought by the disabled individual, and by terminating her for her outbursts and rude behavior to her supervisors? [DLR No. 9, Jan. 13, 1995]

8. Robert Maddox served as an assistant football coach at the University of Tennessee. The university did not know that he was an alcoholic with three arrests, two of which involved alcohol, prior to his employment by the university. On May 26, Maddox, while intoxicated, backed his car across a major public highway at a high rate of speed, and was arrested and charged with driving under the influence and public intoxication. This incident received considerable attention from the regional press. Thereafter, the university investigated the charges and then sent him a written notice of termination, stating three reasons for the university's action: (1) his criminal acts, (2) the bad publicity, and (3) the university's determination that Maddox no longer possessed the qualifications necessary to serve as an assistant football coach.

    Maddox brought an action against the university alleging that his termination was discriminatory because of his alcoholism and thus violated his rights under both the Rehabilitation Act and the ADA. In support of his action, Maddox alleged that the drunk driving incident constituted a causally connected manifestation of his alcoholism. In response, the university filed a motion for summary judgment, alleging that it had terminated Maddox for his misconduct rather than his disability. Can a person have a disability because of alcoholism and thus be within the protection of the Rehabilitation Act and the ADA? Under a different scenario, suppose the athletic director (AD) indirectly found out that an assistant football coach was an alcoholic through admissions made by the coach at an Alcoholics Anonymous meeting; and when confronted by the AD, admitted to having a history of excessive use of alcohol. Could the AD terminate the at-will assistant coach based on the individual's own admissions? How would you decide the *Maddox* case under the two disabilities acts? [*Maddox v. University of Tennessee*, 62 F.3d 843 (6th Cir.)]

9. Bryant is the administrator of the estate of the deceased and the guardian of the deceased's minor child. Bryant sued Wal-Mart for damages following the death of the deceased based on the theory of unlawful false imprisonment. While working on the night restocking crew, the deceased suffered a stroke. Medical personnel arrived six minutes later but could not enter the store because management had locked all doors of the store, and no manager was present to open the door. By the time the medical crew entered the store to assist her, they were unable to revive her, and she died 15 minutes later. Bryant contends that false imprisonment occurred between the time the deceased became ill until the time the medical team was able to enter the store. Wal-Mart claimed that Bryant's exclusive remedy was under the Workers' Compensation Act. Is Wal-Mart incorrect? [*Bryant v. Wal-Mart Stores Inc.* (Ga App) 417 SE2d 688]

10. Overton suffered from depression and was made sleepy at work by medication taken for this condition. Also, because of his medical condition Overton needed a work area away from public access and needed substantial supervision to complete his tasks.

The employer terminated him because of his routinely sleeping on the job, his inability to maintain contact with the public, and his need for supervision. Overton defended that he is a disabled person under the ADA and the Rehabilitation Act, fully qualified to perform the essential functions of the job, and that the employer had an obligation to make reasonable accommodations, such as allowing some catnaps as needed and providing some extra supervision. Decide. [*Overton v. Reilly*, 977 F.2d 1190 (7th Cir.)]

5
Employment Relationships: Contractual and Tort Theories

SECTION 28—EMPLOYMENT AT WILL, EXCEPTIONS, AND DISCRIMINATION CLAIMS

The relationship of employer and employee exists when, pursuant to an express or implied agreement of parties, one person, the employee, undertakes to perform services or to do work under the direction and control of another, the employer, for compensation. In most instances of individual employment contracts the employment contract does not state any time or duration. It is an employment-at-will contract. In contrast, the employment contract may state that it shall last for a specified period of time; an example would be a contract to coach the state university basketball team for five years. An employer cannot terminate a contract for a definite period of time at an earlier date without justification as contemplated by the parties to that agreement. Under the classic at-will rule, both the employer and employee are free to terminate the relationship with or without cause.

The employment-at-will rule set forth in *Payne v. Western & Atlantic R.R. Co.* states:

> [M]en must be left, without interference to buy and sell where they please, and to discharge or retain employees at will for good cause or for no cause, or even for bad cause without thereby being guilty of an unlawful act per se. It is a right which an employee may exercise in the same way, to the same extent, for the same cause or want of cause as the employer.[1]

This rule, which gives an employer the right to terminate an employee for any reason— good cause, no cause, or bad cause—has been uniformly recognized throughout the country. However, judicial and, in some instances, legislative intervention has had an impact on the application of the rule in some 45 states. The court decisions that have carved out exceptions to the employment-at-will doctrine may be classified as follows:

1. The tort theory that a discharge violates established public policy (the so-called whistleblowing cases also are structured on public policy).
2. The tort theory of abusive discharge.
3. The contract theory of express or implied guarantee of continued employment except for just-cause terminations.
4. The theory of an implied covenant of good faith and fair dealing in employment contracts.

Common to the court decisions on these developing exceptions to the employment-at-will doctrine are the expressions of judicial warnings on the narrowness of each decision. The employment-at-will doctrine continues to be a viable doctrine, subject to the developing exceptions. In a few jurisdictions courts have stated that changes in the employment-at-will doctrine must await legislative action.

Most collective bargaining agreements contain a provision whereby the employer agrees that no employee subject to the agreement will be discharged without just cause. These agreements provide for arbitration on whether the employer had just cause for a discharge, with the burden of proof being on the employer. Over half of the approximately 15 million workers employed in the public sector by federal, state, and local governments are protected by tenure processes or civil service against termination of employment without good cause. Also, a small number of managerial and professional employees have been successful in negotiating individual employment contracts in which the employer and the individual agree that the employer cannot terminate the employment during the duration of the contract unless there is good and sufficient cause. In the private sector, workers covered by union collective bargaining contracts that protect against termination without just cause constitute some 16.4 percent of the nation's workforce.[2] Protected employees in the public sector and employees with employment contracts constitute less than 10 percent of the workforce. Thus some 74 percent of the nation's workforce is employed "at will" or for indefinite durations and does not have the "good-cause" or "just-cause" protection against terminations negotiated by unions, granted by governmental bodies, or negotiated by individuals.

---

[1] 82 Tenn. 507, 518–19 (1884).
[2] BLS *Newsletter*, Feb. 12, 1996.

The National Conference of Commissioners on Uniform State Laws recently adopted the Model Employment Termination Act, which individual states may adopt to protect the millions of "at-will" workers employed in the United States from being discharged without "good cause."

Individuals are protected against discriminatory discharges principally by Title VII of the Civil Rights Act, the Age Discrimination in Employment Act, and the Americans with Disabilities Act. An at-will employee who is terminated may believe that there was a discriminatory motive to the discharge. Also, that employee may believe that one or more of the emerging exceptions to the employment-at-will doctrine are applicable to that employee's discharge. The result is that a terminated individual may join claims based on exceptions to the employment-at-will doctrine and a claim based on discrimination. In *Murphy v. American Home Products Corporation*,[3] the New York Court of Appeals rejected four of the plaintiff's theories of wrongful discharge based on tort and contract law and reinstated the plaintiff's fifth theory, that of age discrimination. In *Marzano v. Computer Science Corp., Inc.*,[4] the plaintiff brought a lawsuit against her former employer alleging gender discrimination based on pregnancy, breach of an implied-in-fact-employment contract, and violation of a state Family and Medical Leave Act (FMLA). The court upheld her right to pursue the discrimination and FMLA claims.

A discussion of the four exceptions to the employment-at-will doctrine and the new model act follows.

Public Policy

The courts in a number of jurisdictions have carved out an exception to the employment-at-will doctrine when the discharge is contrary to established public policy. In *Palmateer v. International Harvester*,[5] a so-called whistleblowing case, the court awarded damages for the wrongful discharge of an employee who was discharged in retaliation for his reporting to the police that a co-employee was engaged in criminal activities. The court held that the discharge violated an important public policy. In *Sheets v. Teddy's Frosted Foods*,[6] the court held that a cause of action in tort existed for wrongful discharge from employment where a quality control director alleged that he had been dismissed in retaliation for his insistence that the employer comply with the Food, Drug, and Cosmetics Act.

In some states whistleblower laws have been enacted to protect employees who disclose employer practices that endanger public health and safety. The *Granser v. Box Tree South Ltd.*[7] case, presented in this section, illustrates the application of a state whistleblower statute.

---

[3] 461 N.Y.2d 232 (1983).
[4] *Marzano v. Computer Science Corp. Inc.*, 91 F.3d 497 (3d Cir. 1996).
[5] 85 Ill.2d 124, 421 N.E2d 876 (1981).
[6] 179 Conn. 471, 424 A.2d 385 (1980). see also *Lynch v. Blanke Baer Inc.*, 901 S.W. 2d 147 (Mo. App. 1995).
[7] 623 N.Y.S.2d 977(Sup. 1994).

In *Phipps v. Clark Oil & Refining Corp.*, presented in this section, the court found that an at-will employee could sue for wrongful termination after he was discharged for refusing his supervisor's directive in violation of the Clean Air Act to pump leaded gasoline into an automobile equipped to receive only unleaded gasoline.

The most frequent application of the public policy exception is in response to employees who are discharged in retaliation for filing workers' compensation claims.[8] The courts' concern in these cases is that the statute would not be effective if employees feared that the consequence of filing a compensation claim would be their discharge from employment. In most states the public policy exception to the employment-at-will doctrine is a narrow one and is applied only if the plaintiff can satisfy a two-part test: (1) the discharge must violate some well-established public policy expressed in a constitution, statutes, or regulations promulgated pursuant to the statutes and (2) there must be no other remedy available to protect the interest of the aggrieved individual or society.

Abusive Discharge

The leading case for the abusive discharge tort theory exception to the employment-at-will doctrine is *Monge v. Beebe Rubber Co.*[9] In this case a female employee was discharged for declining to date her supervisor. Such a discharge is against public policy. A similar situation today would be handled under the post-*Monge* Title VII theory of sexual harassment, with a remedy including reinstatement with back pay, and capped compensatory and punitive damages.

Express or Implied Guarantee of Continued Employment

Courts have begun to construe statements by employers concerning continued employment, which previously had been viewed as having no binding effect, as a contractual basis for requiring good cause for the discharge of an employee. Also, written personnel policies used as guidelines for the employer's supervisors have been interpreted as being rules restricting the employer's right to discharge at will without proof of good or just cause.[10] In *Toussaint v. Blue Cross and Blue Shield*,[11] two management employees had been told upon their hiring that they would be employed as long as they "did the job." The company's personnel policy manual represented that it was the employer's policy, applicable to all nonprobationary employees, to require good cause for discharge. The court held that such oral and written statements could give rise to an enforceable contractual provision requiring good cause for discharge.

In *Duldulao v. St. Mary Nazareth Hospital Center*,[12] an 11-year employee, Nora Duldulao, was fired without notice for unsatisfactory performance. The hospital's

---

[8] *Wallace v. Milliken & Co.*, 406 S.E.2d 358 (S.C. 1991); *King v. Halliburton Co.*, 813 P.2d 1055 (Ok. App. 1991).
[9] 114 N.H. 130, 316 A.2d 549 (1974).
[10] *Gaglidari v. Denny's Restaurants, Inc.*, 815 P.2d 1362 (Wash. 1991).
[11] 408 Mich. 579, 292 N.W2d 880 (1980).
[12] 115 Ill.2d 482, 505 NE2d 314 (1987).

Employee Handbook provided that an employee could be terminated for enumerated causes following "proper notice and investigation." Duldulao contended before the Supreme Court of Illinois that such a provision had a limiting effect on her at-will employment status and created an enforceable contract that barred the hospital from terminating her without following the safeguards of notice and an investigation. The court agreed, holding that an employee handbook or other policy statement created enforceable contractual rights if the traditional requirements for contract formation are present. The court set forth the requirements as follows: (1) the language must contain a promise clear enough that an employee would reasonably believe that an offer has been made, (2) the statement must be disseminated to the employee in such a manner that the employee is aware of its contents and reasonably believes it to be an offer, and (3) the employee must accept the offer by continuing to work after learning of the policy statement. According to the court, the employee's continued work constitutes consideration for the promise.

Good Faith and Fair Dealing

Another development in the law governing the employment relationship is the recognition of a covenant of good faith and fair dealing in the employment relationship. For example, in *Fortune v. National Cash Register Co.*,[13] the court for the first time in Massachusetts recognized a common law contract action of "wrongful" or "bad faith" termination for an at-will employee. This case involved an employer's termination of a commission salesperson in order to deprive him of benefits and bonuses to which he was entitled. The court was offended by the overreaching and malicious acts of the company at the expense of the employee for the sole benefit of the employer. The court held that there existed an implied covenant of good faith and fair dealing in certain employment relationships.

In *Foley v. Interactive Data Corp.*,[14] the Supreme Court of California held that an employee who claims to be fired in violation of a covenant of good faith and fair dealing is limited to a contract claim and remedies such as reinstatement and lost wages. The court held that the covenant of good faith and fair dealing applies to employment contracts and that breach of covenant may give rise to contract but not tort damages.[15] Thus Foley could obtain reinstatement and back pay under a contract theory but was not eligible for the much greater damages that can be recovered under a tort theory, including recovery for emotional distress and punitive damages.

The Model Act

The Model Employment Termination Act, if adopted by all states, would extend relief to an estimated 150,000 to 200,000 terminated workers annually who could make claims

---

[13] 373 Mass. 96, 364 NE2d 1251 (1977). See also *Cleary v. American Airlines, Inc.*, 111 Cal. App. 3d 443, 168 Cal Rptr. 722 (1980), and *Khanna v. Microdata Corp.*, 170 Cal. App. 3d 250, 215 Cal. Rptr. 860 (1985).
[14] 47 Cal. App. 3d 654 (1988).
[15]*Id* p. 663; see also p. 700.

for wrongful termination under a "good-cause" standard. The model act defines an "employee" as an individual who works for the employer for at least one year, and includes within its protection supervisors, managers, and confidential employees. Employers continue to have the right to terminate employees for serious misconduct and to lay off employees for economic reasons and to otherwise exercise "honest business judgment."

In exchange for good-cause protection, the Act extinguishes all common law rights against the employer, including "violation of public policy" tort claims and related claims such as defamation actions and claims for intentional infliction of emotional distress.[16] Civil Rights Act theories and actions under collective bargaining agreements are not affected by the model act.

Under the model act a terminated employee may file for arbitration up to 180 days after the effective date of the termination. The ordinary remedy for termination without good cause is reinstatement with back pay. Thus, the act eliminates jury trials and compensatory and punitive damages.

The act, if widely adopted by the states, will provide American workers protection against wrongful termination that is presently afforded workers in the European Union, as well as Japan and Canada.

Employer Reactions

As a result of cases such as *Toussaint* and *Duldulao*, some nonunion employers have inserted in employment applications for applicants to sign conspicuous statements that the employment offered is "at will." Employers have revised their personnel manuals and employee handbooks and issued directives to all employees that no assurances of continued employment exist and that the employers are not obligated to have good cause to terminate employees, just as employees are free to leave their positions with the employers. However, such employers have had some difficulties in hiring and retaining quality craft, professional, and managerial employees in the aftermath of such actions. Such actions have provided the impetus for the organization of employees by unions.

Most employers have no interest in terminating employees without good and sufficient cause. They have taken steps to assure that terminations are in fact for good cause and that a solid case exists for each termination should the employee in question sue on an unjust dismissal theory. Employers have standardized their termination methods. Employers often now require that every disciplined employee be advised in writing of the infraction, the expected corrective action, and the fact that further misconduct could lead to additional discipline up to and including discharge. When a termination appears to be warranted, most employers require that at least two supervisors be involved and that they take care to ensure that the reasons for the termination are accurate and consistent with the documentation concerning the employee's deficiencies. Moreover, employers should inform the employee of the basis of the proposed termination and give the employee an opportunity to be heard before issuing the dismissal notice.

---

[16] See for example *Russ v. TRW*, 59 Ohio St.3d 42, 570 N.E.2d 1076 (1991), where evidence supported the conclusion that the employer had inflicted emotional harm by assuring an employee that certain contracting practices were legitimate, and subsequently discharged him for following those practices and gave his name to federal authorities in connection with a contract fraud investigation.

PHIPPS v. CLARK OIL & REFINING CORP.

Court of Appeals of Minnesota, 396 N.W. 2d 588 (1986).

[The complaint stated that Mark Phipps was employed as a cashier at a Clark gas station. On November 17, 1984, a customer drove into the station and asked him to pump leaded gasoline into her 1976 Chevrolet—an automobile equipped to receive only unleaded gasoline. The station manager told Phipps to comply with the request, but he refused, believing that his dispensing leaded gasoline into the gas tank was a violation of law. Phipps stated that he was willing to pump unleaded gas into the tank, but the manager immediately fired him. Phipps sued Clark for wrongful termination, and the trial court decided the case in favor of Clark, stating that Minnesota law allowed Phipps, an employee at-will, to be terminated for any reason or for no reason. Phipps appealed.]

LANSING, J.

Does Minnesota law recognize a cause of action for wrongful discharge if an employee is terminated for refusing to violate a law? . . .

EMPLOYMENT-AT-WILL DOCTRINE AND THE PUBLIC POLICY EXCEPTION

The parties concede that there is no formal agreement governing the employment relationship between Phipps and Clark Oil. Thus, Phipps is an at-will employee. The at-will employment doctrine in Minnesota is generally traced to the early case of *Skagerberg v. Blandin Paper Co.*, 197 Minn. 291, 266 N.W. 872 (1936). The *Skagerberg* court interpreted a contract for permanent employment as being merely a contract for employment at will. *Skagerberg* set forth the general rule in Minnesota that employment at will "may be terminated by either party at any time, and no action can be sustained in such case for a wrongful discharge." *Id.* at 301–02, 266 N.W. at 877 (quoting *Minter v. Tootle, Campbell Dry Goods, Co.*, 187 Mo.App. 16, 27–28, 173 S.W. 4, 8 (1915)).

The employer's absolute right of discharge has been tempered during the last 50 years. The majority of jurisdictions have adopted, and numerous commentators have advocated, exceptions to the employment-at-will doctrine. Three general exceptions have been judicially created to relieve employees from the strict application of the employment-at-will doctrine:

1. a contract cause of action based on implied-in-fact promises of employment conditions, generally derived from personnel manuals;
2. an implied covenant of "good faith and fair dealing" under both contract and tort theories; and
3. a "public policy" exception, based in tort, which permits recovery upon the finding that the employer's conduct undermines some important public policy.

Although the Minnesota Supreme Court has declined to imply a covenant of good faith and fair dealing into every employment contract, it has followed the modern trend in recognizing exceptions to employment at will.

In *Pine River State Bank v. Mettille*, 333 N.W.2d 622 (Minn. 1983), the Supreme Court recognized the implied-in-fact contract exception. The *Pine River* court held that an employee manual may constitute an employment contract with enforceable terms preventing termination at will. . . .

Among other states, the most widely adopted exception to the doctrine is the public policy exception. Simply stated, the exception provides that an employer becomes subject to tort liability if its discharge of an employee contravenes some well-established public policy. Although the adoption of this exception has not been addressed in Minnesota, the majority of jurisdictions recognize this exception to the employment-at-will doctrine.*

---

*At least 25 jurisdictions have adopted the public policy exception.

The exception began as a narrow rule permitting employees to sue their employers when a statute expressly prohibited their discharge. The rule later expanded to include any discharge in violation of a statutory expression of public policy. The broadcast formulation of the rule permits recovery even in the absence of a specific statutory prohibition.

Courts have reached the public policy exception to accommodate competing interests of society, the employee, and the employer. The Illinois Court of Appeals stated:

With the rise of large corporations conducting specialized operations and employing relatively immobile workers who often have no other place to market their skills, recognition that the employer and employee do not stand on equal footing is realistic. In addition, unchecked employer power, like unchecked employee power, has been seen to present a distinct threat to the public policy carefully considered and adopted by society as a whole. As a result, it is now recognized that a proper balance must be maintained among the employer's interest in operating a business efficiently and profitably, the employee's interest in earning a livelihood, and society's interest in seeing its public policies carried out.

Palmateer v. International Harvester Co., 85 Ill.2d 124, 129 52 Ill.Dec. 13, 15, 421 N.E. 2d 876, 878 (1981) (citation omitted).

These courts have also recognized that important societal interests oppose an employer's conditioning employment on required participation in unlawful conduct.

Although employers generally are free to discharge at-will employees with or without cause at any time, they are not free to require employees, on pain of losing their jobs, to commit unlawful acts or acts in violation of a clear mandate of public policy expressed in the constitution, statutes, and regulations promulgated pursuant to statute. The at-will employment doctrine does not depend upon the employer having such a right. The employer is bound to know the public policies of the state and nation as expressed in their constitutions, statutes, judicial decisions and administrative regulations, particularly, as here, those bearing directly upon the employer's business. . . .

The at-will employment doctrine does not include, contemplate or require a privilege in the employer to subject its employee to the risks of civil and criminal liability that participation in such activities entails.

Boyle v. Vista Eyewear, Inc., 700 S.W.2d 859, 877–78 (Mo.Ct.App. 1985).

We find the reasoning of the cases adopting a public policy exception to be persuasive. An employer's authority over its employee does not include the right to demand that the employee commit a criminal act. An employer therefore is liable if an employee is discharged for reasons that contravene a clear mandate of public policy.

Employers may have a legitimate concern that such an exception will allow fraudulent or frivolous suits by disgruntled employees who are discharged for valid reasons. In order to prevent this, the employee should have the burden of proving the dismissal violates a clear mandate of public policy, either legislatively or judicially recognized. Once the employee has demonstrated that the discharge may have been motivated by reasons that contravene a clear mandate of public policy, the burden then shifts to the employer to prove that the dismissal was for reasons other than those alleged by the employee. This structure, obviously, is a tort-based analysis rather than a contract-based analysis. A significant difference between these theories is the measure of damages. From the standpoint of damages and the conceptual framework which supports the action, we believe it is properly based on tort.

We also believe the reasons supporting recognition of the public policy exception are consistent with principles expressed by the Minnesota Supreme Court. In *Lewis* [389 N.W.2d 876 (Minn. 1986)] the court characterized its decisions on exceptions to the employment-at-will doctrine as following the modern trend. Although recovery in *Lewis* was based on an implied contract theory, we believe that a public policy exception to the employment-at-will doctrine would assist in maintaining the integrity and limitations of other causes of action. Rather than attempting to reach a grievous wrong, repugnant to an ordered society, through the artificial expansion of other doctrines, it is preferable to recognize it in its individual posture.

Clark Oil argues that the decision to adopt the public policy exception should be left to the legislature, citing *Murphy v. American Home Products Corp.*, 58 N.Y.2d 293, and *Hunt v. IBM Mid America Employees Federal Credit Union*, 384 NW2d 853 (Minn. 1986). In rejecting the implied covenant of good faith and fair dealing, the court in *Hunt* adverted to the problem of defining the amorphous concept of bad faith and the extent of the intrusion in imposing this concept on the employment relationship.

We see a public policy exception as significantly different from a covenant of good faith and fair dealing. A public policy exception can be reasonably defined by reference to clear mandates of legislative or judicially recognized public policy. In addition, courts have historically interpreted the effect of illegality on contracts. The at-will doctrine is a creation of common law. Other exceptions to the doctrine have been considered and adopted or rejected by the courts. The judiciary may properly extend or limit a judicially created doctrine. . . .

APPLICATION OF THE PUBLIC POLICY EXCEPTION

On appeal from a judgment on the pleadings, this court assumes as true all material facts which are well pleaded. Phipps' complaint alleges that he was terminated for refusing to violate the Federal Clean Air Act, 42 U.S.C. §§ 7401–7642.

Clark Oil argues that this is not the proper case to apply this exception because the penalty for violating this provision is imposed only upon the retailer, not the retailer's employees or agent.

We hold that Phipps has stated a cause of action for wrongful termination under the public policy exception to the at-will employment doctrine. It is not determinative that the employee would not have suffered any monetary loss by violating the law. The law clearly states:

[N]o retailer or his employee . . . shall introduce or allow the introduction of leaded gasoline into any motor vehicle which is labeled "unleaded gasoline only," or which is equipped with a gasoline tank filler inlet which is designed for this introduction of unleaded gasoline.

40 C.F.R. § 80.22(a) (1984) (emphasis added). . . .

Complaint which alleges that an at-will employee was terminated for refusing to violate a law states a cause of action in Minnesota for wrongful discharge. . . .

Reversed and remanded.

CASE QUESTIONS

1. What is the most common exception to the employment-at-will doctrine?
2. How does the court expect to cut down on frivolous lawsuits by disgruntled former employees based on the public policy exception?
3. Is the public policy exception a tort-based or contract-based analysis?
4. Did the court hold that the public policy exception would apply only to clear mandates of legislative or judicially recognized public policy?

GRANSER v. BOX TREE SOUTH LTD.

Supreme Court, New York County, 623 N.Y.S. 2d 977 (1994).

[Rudolf Granser sued the owner of the Box Tree restaurant and hotel, Augustine Paege, alleging that his termination by Paege violated the state whistleblower law. Paege made a motion for a summary judgment, contending that Granser quit and was not fired, and that Granser was an accomplice and thus could not recover under the act.]

GOODMAN, J.

The plaintiff Rudolf Granser was employed as chef and general manager by the defendant Box Tree South LTD. ("Box Tree") over two apparently tempestuous terms, from 1974–85 and 1991–92. The defendant Augustine Paege ("Paege") is the chief executive officer and sole shareholder of Box Tree. The complaint alleges that Paege fired plaintiff because plaintiff threatened to report various health and safety violations to the Department of Buildings. The alleged violations included that the hotel portion of the business was unlicensed; fireplaces were installed in hotel rooms without obtaining a certificate of occupancy; construction work was performed without appropriate permits; the restaurant regularly violated its certificate of occupancy by serving 60 patrons instead of 26; and the premises had inadequate safety exits. Labor Law 740 prohibits retaliatory personnel action by an employer against an employee who discloses or threatens to disclose an activity of the employer that is in violation of law, rule or regulation when the violation creates and presents a substantial and specific danger to the public health or safety.

Defendants move to dismiss, claiming that (1) plaintiff was not fired, but that he quit; (2) plaintiff, as a manager with control over some of the activities is an accomplice in the activities who may not recover under the Whistleblower Law; (3) plaintiff has not presented sufficient proof of actual violations; (4) there is no provision in 740(5) for punitive damages; and (5) Paege as an individual is not a proper defendant.

In opposition to the motion, plaintiff argues that he suffered a retaliatory demotion which defendants concede is included in the definition of a retaliatory personnel action (Labor Law 740[1][e]) and also that the demotion is actionable as a constructive discharge; that the complaint, answers to interrogatories and affidavits show proof of violations; that plaintiff was not an accomplice; that punitive damages are recoverable; and that a controlling party of a thinly capitalized corporation is a proper defendant under Labor Law 740.

Plaintiff swears in his Affidavit in Opposition to Defendant's Motion that in December 1992 he "confronted" Paege with various violations of the New York City Administrative Code that had come to his attention, including the lack of a certificate of occupancy, the lack of fire exits and signs and the failure to obtain construction permits. . . . The Affidavit states that Granser advised Paege that unless the problems were immediately rectified, he "would be forced to report them to the authorities", and that, "instead, Paege terminated my services."

Defendants fail to submit an affidavit from Paege denying Granser's allegations that the incident between the parties which led to the termination of Granser's employment occurred after Granser threatened to "blow the whistle" about the violations. Paege denies that he fired Granser, but he does not deny that he demoted Granser; in fact, Paege testified at his deposition that he told Granser that he was going to reduce Granser's salary because Paege would be taking a larger cut and that thereupon Granser left the room and never returned. . . .

. . . None of the exhibits contradict Granser's allegations that he threatened to blow the whistle on conditions at the restaurant. The relevant portions of Paege's testimony are as follows:

Q. *Let me bring you back to the conversation you had when he left the employment of the Box Tree. You asked him to go and become the chef?*

A. *Yes, I said, to take over the kitchen. Get in the whites.*

He said, he did not want to do that. Then he said, okay, I will do that, but I want to be paid the same. I said, I cannot pay you the same because I am taking a bigger part of it, at which point I was expected to negotiate with him a pay somewhat lower, not necessarily much, much lower, but somewhat lower. Since the other responsibilities will be taken away from him, there was no room for that. He ran out of the room, and today is the first time I have seen him since.

The relevant pages of Granser's testimony are as follows:

Q. *Can you tell me the circumstances under which you left the Box Tree.*
A. *The date when I was told to leave?*
Q. *Did you have a conversation with Mr. Paege regarding your leaving the Box Tree?*
A. *That day, yes.*
Q. *On December 14th?*
A. *Yes.*
Q. *Tell me about that conversation.*
A. *We had a meeting, he wanted to restructure the Box Tree, things are not working.*
   He thought that the food is not adequate. He offered me the position as a chef. I asked him. "Are they the same terms?"
   And he said, "No," and I said, "I consider myself fired," and I left.
Q. *Did he ever say to you that you were fired?*
A. *I do not recall.*
Q. *Did you discuss what conditions, what salary, he would offer you to stay on as chef?*
A. *No, but he refused when I asked him if the terms are the same.*
Q. *You didn't take that discussion any further though; is that correct?*
A. *No.*
Q. *You left on the spot?*
A. *Yes.*

Thus, on the record before the Court, we must assume that Granser did threaten to blow the whistle on various administrative code violations and that Granser was demoted and left his position after the whistle blowing threat. . . .

. . . Both sides agree that plaintiff was working as the chef and manager and that on December 14, 1992 Paege told Granser he would no longer be the general manager and that he would be the chef. As noted above, defendants have not disputed that Paege's statements came after Granser's whistleblower threats. Thus, this Court must find that plaintiff was removed as

general manager after he complained about various violations . . . .

A constructive discharge occurs when "the employer has made working conditions so difficult that a reasonable person will feel forced to resign . . ." *Fischer v. KPMG Peat Marwick*, 195 A.D.2d 222, 607 N.Y.S.2d 309 (1st Dept.1994). In *Fischer*, the plaintiff, a partner in Peat Marwick, argued that the significant diminution of his role in the partnership pursuant to a reorganization constituted a constructive discharge or expulsion from the firm. The plaintiff conceded that "(a true constructive discharge occurs only when an employer 'deliberately makes an employee's working conditions so intolerable that the employee is forced to an involuntary termination') (citations omitted)." The plaintiff argued that "dashing an employee's reasonable expectations of advancement may create intolerable conditions rising to a level of constructive discharge." The First Department agreed and held that whether an employer has made working conditions so difficult that a reasonable person would feel forced to resign is a question of fact that should be left to the trier of fact. . . . Here, Granser alleges that he was the "General Manager" of the Box Tree on December 14, 1992 when Paege informed Granser that he wanted to restructure the Box Tree and offered Granser a position as chef. It must be left to the trier of fact to determine whether a reasonable person in Granser's place would have felt forced to resign under such circumstances. . . .

. . . Under *Fischer*, the allegations in the complaint that Granser was terminated as general manager is a sufficient pleading of constructive discharge.

Section 740 prohibits an employer from taking any retaliatory personnel action against an employee who threatens to disclose any "practice of the employer that is in violation of law, rule or regulation which violation creates and presents a substantial and a specific danger to the public health or safety." It is apparent from the plain words of the statute that violations which would create hazardous fire conditions are within the statute's purview.

. . . This Court disagrees with defendant's attorney's statement that plaintiff has not offered any evidence that these violations actually occurred. Plaintiff worked on the premises on a daily basis. He observed the conditions to which the public was exposed. Plaintiff's observation of the absence of fire exit signs alone, without any denial by defendants, is sufficient. The purpose of the Whistleblower Law will not be served by requiring employees with personal knowledge of obviously dangerous unlawful conditions to submit additional proof of the existence of the conditions. Such a requirement would make it more difficult for employees to state a cause of action under Section 740, a result that is clearly inappropriate to a statute enacted for the public benefit. Therefore, this Court finds that plaintiff's sworn statements as to his observation of dangerous unlawful conditions is a sufficient showing of violations which present an actual and substantial present danger to the public health.

Defendants also argue that plaintiff may not recover under section 740 because plaintiff was an accomplice in the illegal acts of the employer. . . .

This Court disagrees that an absentee employer may avoid liability under Section 740 by delegating to its employee responsibility for enforcement of safety laws, or that such a delegation would render the employee an "accomplice" in the employer's failure to comply with the law. Section 740 does not exclude "supervisors" from the protection of the Labor Law. . . .

Additionally, Subsection 2(c) protects employees who refuse to participate in unlawful activities that present a substantial and specific

danger to the public health or safety. *Remba v. Federation*, 149 A.D.2d 131, 135, 545 N.Y.S.2d 140. There is no exception for employees who may initially participate in an alleged unlawful activity and then, at a subsequent point, refuse to engage in such activities and seek the protection of the law. In today's economic climate of high unemployment and uncertain job security it is not difficult to imagine that an employee may avoid confronting an employer when first observing questionable or even unlawful practices. An employee in that position, who subsequently places his job in jeopardy by speaking out in the interest of public health and safety is to be commended, not punished, for overcoming his or her initial reticence at blowing the whistle. There simply is no basis to interpret the statute to exclude from its protection, employees who go along with an employer's unlawful scheme prior to the employee's asserting the rights afforded under the Whistleblower Law.

Defendants next argue that plaintiff is not entitled to an award of punitive damages if he prevails under Section 740. Defendants are correct. . . .

Motion for summary judgment denied.

CASE QUESTIONS

1. Can an owner who is not present at a work location avoid liability under the whistleblower law by delegating responsibility for enforcement of safety laws to a supervisor located at the work site?
2. From 1991 until December of 1992, Granser was a general manager and chef, and did nothing to correct the illegal conduct at the Box Tree. Should such an individual be allowed to claim protection under the whistleblower act?
3. On the facts given, do you believe a constructive discharge took place?

SECTION 29—EMPLOYER LIABILITY FOR TORTS OF EMPLOYEES

The legal concept of imposing liability on an employer for the wrongs of its employees is known as vicarious liability, and is sometimes called the doctrine of *respondeat superior*—let the master (employer) respond. It imposes liability, however, only when an employee is acting within the course of employment. The concept is justified on the grounds that the business should pay for the harm caused in the undertaking of the business, that the employer will be more careful in the selection of employees if made responsible for their actions, and that the employer is in a position to obtain liability insurance to protect against claims of third persons.

Employee or Independent Contractor

If the work is done by an independent contractor rather than an employee, the owner is generally not liable for harm caused by the contractor to third persons or their property. An exception exists, however, when the work undertaken by the contractor is inherently dangerous.

In *Studebaker v. Nettie's Flower Garden, Inc.*, presented in this section, Judith Studebaker sued a florist for her injuries caused when a van driven by James Ferry collided with her car. The florist asserted that Ferry was an independent contractor; however, Studebaker established that the florist either controlled or had the right to control Ferry at the time of the accident, thus making the florist responsible for the harm caused by Ferry.

STUDEBAKER v. NETTIE'S FLOWER GARDEN, INC.

Missouri Court of Appeals (Mo App) 842 SW2d 227 (1992).

[Judith Studebaker was injured when a van driven by James Ferry collided with her vehicle. She brought an action against Nettie's Flower Garden, Inc. (Nettie's) on a *respondeat superior* theory on the belief that Ferry was Nettie's employee at the time of the accident. Nettie's defended that Ferry was an independent contractor, not an employee. From a judgment in favor of Studebaker for $125,000, Nettie's appealed.]

CRANDALL, P. J.

. . . Ferry delivered flowers for Nettie's from its main shop on Grand Avenue in the City of St. Louis. Ferry was paid, not by the hour, but at a rate of $2.50 to $3.00 per delivery. If there were no deliveries, he was not paid. He delivered only in an area of St. Louis which Nettie's designated as his territory. Nettie's required him to make two runs each day: one in the morning at 9:30 A.M.; one in the afternoon at 1:30 P.M. When he arrived at the shop, he set up his own route based upon the location of the deliveries in his area. He generally got to work at 8:00 A.M. to

prepare for the morning run and at 12:00 P.M. to prepare for the afternoon run. Nettie's also required Ferry to stop by its shop in downtown St. Louis at St. Louis Centre before noon each day to pick up items which needed to be transported to the Grand Avenue shop. After this stop, Ferry proceeded to the Grand Avenue shop for his afternoon run. Nettie's paid Ferry $5.00 for this stop, whether or not there was anything for him to take to the Grand Avenue shop.

Ferry used his own van for the deliveries; Nettie's required that it be heated and air-conditioned to protect the flowers and plants. Although he did not wear a uniform, Nettie's directed that Ferry be neat in appearance and that he conduct himself in a certain manner when on the job. If his behavior or appearance fell below its standards, Nettie's reprimanded Ferry. Ferry paid his own expenses and received no fringe benefits from Nettie's.

On August 9, 1989, the date of the accident in question, Ferry made his morning run and then his mid-day stop at the downtown shop at about 11:00 A.M. There was nothing for him to transport to the Grand Avenue shop. After Ferry left the downtown shop, he stopped at a pawn shop to conduct personal business. He then proceeded to the Grand Avenue shop to prepare for his afternoon run. On the way to the Grand Avenue shop, at approximately 11:45 A.M., Ferry's van collided with plaintiff's automobile. . . .

Under the doctrine of respondeat superior an employer is liable for those negligent acts or omissions of his employee which are committed within the scope of his employment. . . . Liability based on respondeat superior requires some evidence that a master-servant relationship existed between the parties. . . . The test to determine if respondeat superior applies to a tort is whether the person sought to be charged as master had the right or power to control and direct the physical conduct of the other in the performance of the act. . . . If there was no right to control there is no liability; for those rendering services but retaining control over their own movements are not servants. . . . The master-servant relationship arises when the person charged as master has the right to direct the method by which the master's service is performed. . . . An additional inquiry is whether the person sought to be charged as the servant was engaged in the prosecution of his master's business and not simply whether the accident occurred during the time of employment. . . . Whether a party is liable under the doctrine of respondeat superior depends on the facts and circumstances in evidence in each particular case and no single test is conclusive of the issue of the party's interest in the activity and his right of control. . . .

Nettie's first asserts that, when the accident in question occurred, Ferry was not driving his vehicle to serve Nettie's business interests. It argues that Ferry was on his own time, conducting his own business. . . .

Ferry's slight detour prior to the accident to conduct personal business did not mean that he was using his van exclusively for his independent purposes. . . . The object of Ferry's trip was not just to go to the pawn shop. At the time of the accident, Ferry was doing Nettie's business because he was returning to the Grand Avenue shop after making his routine mid-day stop at the downtown shop. This stop was so encompassed within his daily routine that it would be difficult to segregate it from his morning and afternoon runs.

There was sufficient evidence for the jury to determine that at the time of the accident, Ferry was engaged primarily in advancing the business interests of Nettie's and thus was acting within the scope of his employment. Nettie's first point is denied.

Nettie's further contends that there was no substantial evidence that Nettie's controlled or had the right to control Ferry at the time of the collision. Whether or not the right of control existed in a particular case is ordinarily a question of fact for the jury. . . .

In the instant action, Ferry furnished his own means of transportation; but it was mandatory that he have a vehicle to carry out his job responsibilities. Nettie's required that his vehicle be equipped with heating and air-conditioning systems. Nettie's also set standards for Ferry's dress and conduct while he was on the job, and monitored his compliance with these standards. In addition, although Ferry mapped out his own route to deliver the flowers, Nettie's gave him the list of customers and determined his territory. Nettie's directed Ferry to make the mid-day stop at its downtown shop on a daily basis and paid him for that stop. Ferry incorporated that stop into his route. The stop usually occurred after his morning run and prior to his return trip to the Grand Avenue shop for his afternoon run. In addition, Nettie's always paid him for this stop, whether or not he transported anything. There was substantial evidence from which a jury reasonably could have found that, at the time of the accident in question, Nettie's either controlled or had the right to control the manner in which Ferry performed the duties for which he was employed. Nettie's second point is denied.

　　　　[*Judgment affirmed*]

CASE QUESTIONS

1. Did Nettie's control or have the right to control Ferry at the time of the collision?

2. Is not the fact that Ferry, just prior to the accident, had gone to a pawn shop compelling evidence he was using his van exclusively for his independent purposes and was not acting within the course of his employer's business?

3. Give your opinion on the ethics of businesses converting employees to independent contractors to reduce or eliminate costs, such as health and retirement benefits, vacations, overtime, and maintenance and proper insurance of motor vehicles.

SECTION 30—PROPER CLASSIFICATION OF WORKERS

In the *Studebaker* case, presented in the previous section, the employer did not consider its delivery person an employee; yet it turned out that the employer was held responsible for $125,000 in damages caused by the driver. It is critical therefore to properly assess whether an individual is an employee or independent contractor so the employer may purchase appropriate liability insurance, and may exercise proper care in the selection and supervision of the individual(s) in question.

Other considerations exist as well. If the individual is an independent contractor who has earned over $600, the employer must supply an IRS 1099 form to each contractor stating the amount of money paid the contractor during the year, and must turn in a summary sheet to the IRS. If the employer hires "employees," the employer must have an IRS employer identification number; pay state and federal unemployment taxes; supply workers' compensation insurance; withhold payroll taxes, both federal and state, and submit payroll tax returns monthly or quarterly; and pay Social Security taxes equal to the amount withheld and paid by the employee. The employer may also provide benefits to employees, such as vacations, sick days, medical and dental plans, and a retirement plan. Benefits are not provided to independent contractors.

Substantial penalties exist for employers who attempt to misclassify their employees as independent contractors to avoid paying taxes and benefits. For example, the penalty for an employer who does not provide a 1099 form and has misclassified an employee as an independent contractor is 40 percent of the Social Security (FICA) tax owed and 3 percent of wages paid. If overtime is not paid employees because they are willfully misclassified as independent contractors, it is a violation of the Fair Labor Standards Act and the employer is subject to a fine of $10,000 and imprisonment of up to six months. Figure 5-1 provides questions that can be used to determine if an individual is an independent contractor or an employee. You will note that the degree of control the employer exercises over the individual's work is pivotal in making the proper determination.

SECTION 31—NEGLIGENT HIRING AND RETENTION OF EMPLOYEES

In addition to a complaint against the employer based on the doctrine of *respondeat superior*, a lawsuit may often raise a second theory, that of negligent hiring or retention of

FIGURE 5–1   Questions for Ascertaining Independent Contractor or Employee Status

	Independent Contractor	Employee
1. Does the employer control the manner and means of accomplishing the work? (A worker who is required to follow the employer's instruction on when, where, and how and with what tools is generally considered an employee.)	No	Yes
2. Does the employer set the hours of employment?	No	Yes
3. Does the employer provide substantial training or schooling?	No	Yes
4. Does the employer provide tools, supplies, and equipment?	No	Yes
5. Does the individual have a continuing relationship with the employer and maintain regular hours of work at the employer's business?	No	Yes
6. Is the employer the individual's sole source of income?	No	Yes
7. Does the employer have other "employees" on the payroll doing the same kind of work?	No	Yes
8. Does the individual have an office rented at fair value from a party unrelated to the employer?	Yes	No
9. Does the individual work as a professional or skilled technician?	Yes	No
10. Does the individual have business stationery, advertise, have a written contract, and send bills for work performed?	Yes	No

an employee.[17] Unlike the *respondeat superior* theory by which the employer may be vicariously liable for the tort of an employee, the negligent hiring theory is based upon the negligence of the employer in the hiring process. Under the *respondeat superior* rule the employer is only liable for those torts committed within the scope of employment or in the furtherance of the employer's interests. The negligent hiring theory has been used to impose liability in cases where an employee commits an intentional tort, almost invariably outside the scope of employment, against a customer or the general public, where the employer knew or should have known that the employee was incompetent, violent, dangerous, or criminal. In *Harrison v. Tallahassee Furniture Company*,[18] the employer hired John Turner to deliver furniture to customers' houses without having him fill out a job application form and without conducting an interview and checking references. It turned out that Turner had a juvenile record for armed robbery and burglary, a conviction involving cutting his former wife's face with a knife, and a voluntary hospitalization for

---

[17] *Medina v. Graham's Cowboys, Inc.*, 827 P.2d 859 (N.M.App. 1992).
[18] 583 So. 2d 744 (Fla. App. 1991).

psychiatric problems. He was an intravenous drug user, and he had been fired from his former employment. The court held the employer liable for damages that resulted when Turner attacked a customer (Harrison) in her home under a negligent hiring theory.

Need for Due Care in Hiring

An employer may be liable on a theory of negligent hiring when it is shown that the employer knew, or in the exercise of ordinary care should have known, that the job applicant would create an undue risk of harm to others in carrying out job responsibilities. Moreover, it must also be shown that the employer could have reasonably foreseen injury to the third party. Thus, an employer who knows of an employee's preemployment drinking problems and violent behavior may be liable to customers assaulted by that employee.

Employers might protect themselves from liability for negligent hiring by having each prospective employee fill out an employment application form and then checking into the applicant's work experience, background, character, and qualifications. This would be evidence of due care in hiring. Generally, the scope of preemployment investigation should correlate to the degree of opportunity the prospective employee would have to do harm to third persons. A minimum investigation consisting of the filling out of an application form and a personal interview would be satisfactory for the hiring of an outside maintenance person, but a full background inquiry would be necessary for the hiring of a security guard.[19] However, such inquiry does not bar *respondeat superior* liability.

Employees with Criminal Records

The hiring of an individual with a criminal record does not by itself establish the tort of negligent hiring.[20] An employer who knows that an applicant has a criminal record has a duty to investigate to determine if the nature of the conviction in relationship to the job to be performed creates an unacceptable risk to third persons.

Negligent Retention

Courts assign liability under negligent retention on a basis similar to negligent hiring. That is, the employer knew, or should have known, that the employee would create an undue risk of harm to others in carrying out job responsibilities. The *Bryant v. Livigni* case, presented in this section, involves *respondeat superior* liability as well as negligent retention liability.

A hospital is liable for negligent retention when it continues the staff privileges of a physician that it knew or should have known had sexually assaulted a female patient in the past.[21]

---

[19] Often employers desire to evaluate a potential employee's credit standing when hiring for a responsible position. The federal Fair Credit Reporting Act (FCRA) 15 U.S.C.§§ 1681–1681(t) defines the employment context for creditworthiness reporting. If an applicant is denied employment because of a credit report, under the FCRA the employer must notify the applicant and give the name of the consumer credit company making the report.
[20] *Connes v. Molalla Transportation Systems*, 831 P.2d 1316 (1992).
[21] *Capithorne v. Framingham Union Hospital*, 401 Mass. 860, 520 N.E.2d 139 (1988).

BRYANT v. LIVIGNI

Illinois Court of Appeals, 250 Ill. App. 3d 303 (1994).

[Mark Livigni was manager of the National Super Markets, Inc., store in Cahokia, Illinois. After drinking alcoholic beverages one evening he stopped by the store to check the operation when he observed a ten-year-old boy's unacceptable behavior outside the store. Livigni chased the boy to a car, where he then pulled a four-year-old child named Farris Bryant from the car and threw him through the air. A multicount lawsuit was brought against National and Livigni. A verdict was rendered against National for $20,000 on a *respondeat superior* theory of the battery of Farris Bryant. A verdict was also rendered against National for $15,000 in negligent retention of Livigni and for $115,000 punitive damages for willful and wanton retention. National appealed the trial court's denial of its motions for directed verdicts on these courts.]

MAAG, J. . . .

On March 18, 1987, while off duty, Livigni stopped by the Cahokia National store. As manager, he was authorized to check and supervise the operation of the store even during off-duty hours. He was intoxicated at the time of his visit, which was a violation of National rules. . . . Livigni observed a young man urinating on the store wall outside the east exit doors. He hollered at the young man and followed the fleeing youth to the parked vehicle of Diana Bryant.

Livigni pulled four-year-old Farris Bryant from the automobile, . . . throwing the child through the air.

Farris was taken to Centreville Township Hospital's emergency room for medical treatment. Farris was admitted to the hospital and was released after four days. He was released from all medical treatment approximately one month after the battery. . . .

At trial, Livigni's supervisor testified that during Livigni's 17-year tenure with National,

Livigni had been a good employee. This supervisor never received any reports from customers or employees that Livigni had "violent-related" problems, although he was aware of a report that Livigni threw an empty milk crate which struck a coworker.

Evidence was offered of two batteries committed by Livigni prior to his attack of Farris. In 1980, Livigni had a disagreement with a subordinate employee resulting in Livigni throwing an empty milk crate at the employee striking him on the arm and necessitating medical treatment. At the time of this battery, Livigni was an assistant store manager. A workers' compensation claim was filed against National by the injured employee. A short time after the workers' compensation claim was resolved, Livigni was promoted to store manager by National in spite of this incident.

The second battery occurred in 1985 when Livigni, while disciplining his 13-year-old son, threw the boy into a bed causing the boy to sustain a broken collar bone. In June 1986 Livigni pleaded guilty to aggravated battery to a child and was sentenced to two years' probation. He was still on probation at the time he attacked Farris.

Livigni testified at the trial that he had not told any of his supervisors at National about the battery of his son. He admitted to telling employees of equal or lesser positions than himself about the battery. He considered these people to be his friends. . . .

According to National, there was no evidence that it knew or had reason to know that Livigni was anything other than "an excellent store manager, fit for his position." To support this argument, National claims that there was conflicting evidence regarding the 1980 incident where Livigni threw a milk crate at a coworker causing injury. It argues that the 1980 incident was of uncertain origin since differing versions of the incident and its cause were presented in the evidence. It asserts that due to this conflicting evidence the incident could not form the basis for a negligent retention claim. . . .

Rather than disciplining Livigni after he injured a subordinate employee in an unprovoked attack, National promoted him following the resolution of the injured employee's workers' compensation claim.

National further argues that it had no knowledge of the incident involving Livigni's son that resulted in Livigni's felony conviction for aggravated battery of a child. Relying upon *Campen v. Executive House Hotel, Inc.* (1982), 105 Ill.App.3d 576, 61 Ill.Dec. 358, National points to the general rule which states that to impute knowledge of this occurrence to National a showing was required that an agent or employee of National had notice or knowledge of the incident and that the knowledge concerned a matter within the scope of the agent's authority. According to National, evidence of such knowledge was lacking. . . .

National first admits that Livigni told employees of equal or lesser rank within the corporation about the battery involving his son. However, it claims that this is insufficient notice to the corporation. It argues that the people Livigni told were his "friends" and that as mere "coworkers" of equal or subordinate position no notice could legally be imputed to National. We disagree. . . .

Viewing the evidence in the light most favorable to the plaintiff (*Pedrick*), we believe that a reasonable jury could have concluded that the information concerning the battery of Livigni's son, learned by these coworkers, was within the scope of their authority to act upon. Whether reported to higher authorities or not, the information still constitutes "corporate knowledge". (*Campen,* 105 Ill. App.3d at 586. . . .) In such a case, their knowledge is chargeable to National. . . .

We conclude that the circuit court did not err in denying National's motion for a directed verdict, nor did it err in refusing to grant a judgment *n.o.v.* on plaintiff's claim of negligent retention. Viewing the evidence in the light most favorable to the plaintiff, we cannot state that the evidence so overwhelmingly favored National that this verdict cannot stand.

National next claims that the circuit court should have directed a verdict in its favor or granted a judgment *n.o.v.* on the plaintiff's punitive damages claim. This count alleged that National's retention of Mark Livigni as a management employee constituted willful and wanton misconduct. . . .

The Restatement (Second) of Torts, section 909, at 467 (1977) provides:

"Punitive damages can properly be awarded against a master or other principal because of an act by an agent if, but only if,

*   *   *

(b) the agent was unfit and the principal or a managerial agent was reckless in . . . retaining him."

This count did not seek to impose liability upon the defendant vicariously. Rather, the plaintiff's cause of action alleged wrongful conduct on the part of National itself. Section 909(b) of the Restatement (Second) of Torts speaks directly to the issue under discussion. So too does the case of *Easley v. Apollo Detective Agency, Inc.* (1979), 69 Ill.App.3d 920, 26 Ill.Dec. 313, 387 N.E.2d 1241.

Easley recognized that it is settled law that a cause of action exists in Illinois for negligent hiring of an employee, and that if the defendant's conduct could properly be characterized as willful and wanton then punitive damages are recoverable. (*Easley,* 69 Ill.App.3d at 931, 26 Ill. Dec. at 320, 387 N.E.2d at 1248). We see little difference between a punitive damages claim for willfully and wantonly hiring an employee in the first instance and a claim for willfully and wantonly retaining an unfit employee after hiring. In both instances, the interest to be protected is the same. Employers that wrongfully (whether negligently or willfully and wantonly) hire or retain unfit employees expose the public to the acts of these employees. In such cases it is not unreasonable to hold the employer accountable when the employee causes injury or damage to another. The principle at issue is not *respondeat superior*, although that may also be implicated. Rather, the cause of action is premised upon the wrongful conduct of the employer itself. (*Easley*, 69 Ill.App.3d at 931, 26 Ill.Dec. at 320, 387 N.E.2d at 1248). For this reason, the cause of action is distinguishable from the situation in *Mattyasovszky v. West Towns Bus Co.* (1975), 61 Ill.2d 31, 330 N.E.2d 509, where the plaintiff sought to hold the employer responsible for an employee's acts based upon principles of vicarious liability.

The jury heard evidence that Livigni attacked a fellow employee in 1980 and was then promoted. He injured his own son, he was convicted of aggravated battery in a criminal proceeding, and members of National's management admittedly knew of that incident. National took no action. Then while a store manager, in an intoxicated state, he attacked a four-year-old child and threw him through the air, resulting in his hospitalization. National itself characterizes this attack on young Farris as outrageous. We cannot say the jury was unjustified in concluding the same and also concluding that retaining this man as a managerial employee constituted willful and wanton misconduct. . . .

. . . The circuit court did not err in refusing to grant a directed verdict, not did it err in refusing to grant a judgment *n.o.v.* on plaintiff's punitive damages claim.

Finally, National asks that a judgment *n.o.v.* be entered in its favor on the plaintiff's *respondeat superior* claims.

In order to impose liability upon National, it was not necessary that Livigni be motivated *solely* by a desire to further National's interest. It is sufficient if his actions were prompted only *in part* by a purpose to protect store property or further the employers business. (*Wilson v. Clark Oil & Refining Corp.* (1985), 134 Ill.App.3d 1084, 1089, 90.) The evidence was sufficient to justify such a conclusion by the jury.

Finally, the actions of Livigni in attacking Farris were committed within the constraints of the authorized time and location of his employment, thus bolstering a finding that the battery occurred within the course and scope of his employment. *Sunseri v. Puccia* (1981), 97 Ill. App. 3d 488. . . .

CONCLUSION

For the foregoing reasons, the judgment of the circuit court of St. Clair County is affirmed. *Affirmed.*

Justice WELCH, concurring in part and dissenting in part:

I concur with the majority's opinion with respect to, and would affirm the judgment of the circuit court on the jury verdict against National Food Stores on, the *respondeat superior* counts of plaintiff's complaint. With respect to the majority's opinion concerning the judgment against National on the negligent and willful and wanton retention counts of plaintiffs' complaint, however I must respectfully dissent. . . .

From a practical standpoint, the majority's opinion sends a message to all employers that in order to insulate themselves from liability for negligent or willful and wanton retention any employee who has ever had an altercation on or off the workplace premises must be fired. Moreover, the majority opinion places an unreasonable investigative burden upon the employer by forcing the employer to discover, retain, and analyze the criminal records of its employees. Is not the majority's opinion then at cross-purposes with the established public policy and laws of Illinois protecting the privacy of citizens and promoting the education and rehabilitation of criminal offenders? See Ill.Rev. Stat. 1991, ch. 68, par. 2–103 (making it a civil rights violation to ask a job applicant about an arrest record); see also Ill.Rev.Stat.1991, ch. 38, par. 1003–12–1 *et seq.* (concerning correctional employment programs whose function is to teach marketable skills and work habits and responsibility to Illinois prisoners).

I would have granted defendant National Food Stores' motion for judgment *non obstante veredicto.* . . .

CASE QUESTIONS

1. Was there *respondeat superior* liability in this case?
2. Should National have reasonably known about Livigni's "violent-related" problems? And if so, did it act negligently in retaining him as an employee?
3. From Judge Welch's dissent, will the *Livigni* case hurt the employment prospects of individuals with criminal records involving violence?

Chapter Questions and Problems

1. List the four types of exception to the classic employment-at-will rule.
2. Five years after Kathy Small began her employment with Spring Industries, the company distributed an employee handbook to all employees setting forth the company's termination procedure. It outlined a four-step disciplinary process consisting of a verbal reprimand, a written warning, a final written warning, and discharge. Small was discharged after only one written warning and sued the company for breach of contract.

   Small contended that the company was bound by the plain language of the handbook and that it would be unjust for an employer to issue a handbook and not be held to its contents. Moreover, she contended that if company policies were not worth the paper on which they were printed, then it would be better not to mislead employees by distributing them.

   The company contended that Small did not present evidence that the parties agreed the handbook was to become part of her employment contract and that if Small were to succeed, it would result in the removal of employee handbooks from the workforce and stifle economic growth in the state.

   Did Small have an enforceable contract? Comment on whether handbooks will be removed from the workplace because of cases like this. What can an employer do to avoid liability under similar circumstances? [*Small v. Spring Industries, Inc.*, Sup. Ct. S.C., 357 SE 2d 452]
3. Under an oral contract of indefinite duration, Marlene S. Gates worked as a cashier for Life of Montana Insurance Company for over three years prior to October 19, 1979, when she was called in to meet with her supervisor, Roger Syverson. Without any prior warning, she was given the option of resigning or being fired. She testified that while in a distraught condition and under duress, she signed a letter of resignation that was handed to her by Syverson. Gates stated that she signed the letter of resignation because she thought it would be better for her record and because Syverson told her he would give her a letter of recommendation so that she could be reemployed. Gates went home and discussed the situation with her husband who advised her to retrieve the letter of resignation and inform her supervisor that she was not resigning. Appellant stated that she immediately called Mr. Syverson and demanded the letter be returned and that he promised to do so. Syverson testified that she only requested a photocopy of the letter. Syverson testified that he offered to give Gates a letter of recommendation if she resigned. However, he testified that he only planned to give her a letter that would state that appellant was employed by Life of Montana Insurance Company; he

never intended to provide appellant with a favorable letter of recommendation. There was evidence from which a jury might infer that Gates understood she was to receive a favorable letter of recommendation and that Syverson allowed her to resign on this basis. The company contended that Gates was discharged for incompetence and insubordination. The evidence indicated that a resignation rather than a discharge may protect an employer from immediately becoming liable for unemployment compensation benefits in Montana and by obtaining a letter of resignation an employer may be insulating itself against a claim for wrongful discharge.

Montana law allows for the litigation of the question of whether there was a breach of an implied covenant of fair dealing where an employee is discharged without warning and an opportunity for a hearing. Montana law holds that a breach of the covenant of fair dealing is imposed by operation of law; therefore, its breach should find a remedy in tort for which punitive damages can be recovered if the defendant's conduct is sufficiently culpable, that is, if there was fraud, oppression, or malice.

The company contended that it was a legislative rather than a judicial function to create a cause of action that would apply a just-cause standard for the discharge of at-will employees and that, in any event, the company should not be liable for punitive damages if new legal rights are granted Gates, which rights could not have been known by the company at the time it terminated her.

Did the company breach its implied covenant of fair dealing to Gates when it terminated her? Should the company be held liable for punitive damages? [*Gates v. Life of Montana Insurance Co.*, 668 P.2d 213 Mont., DLR No. 162]

4. Michael Hauck claims that he was discharged by his employer, Sabine Pilot Service, Inc., because he refused his employer's direction to perform the illegal act of pumping the bilges of his employer's vessel into the waterways. Hauck was an employee at will, and Sabine contends that it therefore had the right to discharge him without having to show cause. Hauck brought a wrongful discharge action against Sabine. Decide. [*Sabine Pilot Service Inc. v. Hauck*, 687 S.W.2d 733 (Tex)]

5. Steven Trujillo was told by the assistant door manager of Cowboys Bar "to show up to work tonight in case we need you as a doorman." He came to the bar that evening, wearing a jacket with the bar logo on it. Trujillo "attacked" Rocky Medina in the parking lot of the bar, causing him serious injury. Prior to working for Cowboys, Trujillo was involved in several fights at that bar and in the parking lot; and Cowboys knew of these matters. Medina sued Cowboys on two theories of liability: (1) *respondeat superior* and (2) negligent hiring of Trujillo. Cowboys defends that the *respondeat superior* theory should be dismissed because the assault was clearly not within the course of Trujillo's employment. Concerning the negligent hiring theory, Cowboys asserts that Trujillo was not on duty that night as a doorman. Decide. [*Medina v. Graham's Cowboys Inc.*, 827 P.2d 859 (NM App)]

6. Neal Rubin, while driving his car in Chicago, inadvertently blocked the path of a Yellow Cab Co. taxi driven by Robert Ball, causing the taxi to swerve and hit Rubin's car. Angered by Rubin's driving, Ball got out of his cab and hit Rubin over the head and shoulders with a metal pipe. Rubin sued the Yellow Cab Co. for the damages caused by this beating, contending that the employer was vicariously liable for the beating under the doctrine of *respondeat superior*, since the beating occurred in furtherance of the employer's business, which was to obtain fares without delay. The company defended that Ball's beating of Rubin was not an act undertaken to further

the employer's business. Is the employer liable under *respondeat superior*? [*Rubin v. Yellow Cab Co.*, 154 Ill App 3d 336, 107 Ill Dec 450, 507 NE2d 114]

7. On July 11, Jose Padilla was working as a vacation-relief route salesperson for Frito-Lay. He testified that he made a route stop at Sal's Beverage Shop. He was told by Mrs. Ramos that she was dissatisfied with Frito-Lay service and no longer wanted the products in the store. He asked if there was anything he could do to change her mind. She said no and told him to pick up his merchandise. He took one company-owned merchandise rack to his van and was about to pick up another rack when Mr. Ramos said that the rack had been given to him by the regular route salesperson. Padilla said the route salesperson had no authority to give away Frito-Lay racks. A confrontation occurred over the rack, and Padilla pushed Mr. Ramos against the cash register, injuring Ramos's back. Frito-Lay has a company policy, clearly communicated to all employees, that prohibits them from getting involved in any type of physical confrontation with a customer. Frito-Lay contended that Padilla was not acting within the course and scope of his employment when the pushing incident took place, and that the company was therefore not liable to Ramos. Ramos contended that Frito-Lay was responsible for the acts of its employee Padilla. [*Frito-Lay Inc. v. Ramos*, (Tex Civ. App), 770 S.W.2d 887]

8. Hewlett-Packard has an employee manual called *The H-P Way* which states the corporate philosophy of "belief in people." The manual stated the company goal ". . . to provide job security based on their [employees'] performance. . . ." The manual stated on its first page that its contents do not present a contract, and it was intended only for distribution among managers. The manual described a discipline process. The company did not follow the process set forth in the manual when it terminated Orbach, and the at-will employee sued H-P for wrongful termination. Did the discipline process set forth in the manual have a limiting effect on Orbach's at-will employment status and bar H-P from terminating him without following the procedures? [*Orbach v. Hewlett-Packard Co.*, 97 F.3d 429 (10th Cir.)]

6
Employee Privacy Topics

SECTION 32—HISTORICAL BACKGROUND, INTRODUCTION TO EMPLOYEE PRIVACY

In *Robertson v. Rochester Folding Box Co.*,[1] a 1902 decision by New York state's highest court, the court, by a 4–3 margin, refused to grant injunctive relief based on an asserted violation of a young woman's right to privacy. The defendant had used a picture of Ms. Abigail Robertson on 25,000 posters advertising Franklin Mills' flour without her consent. The court majority indicated that the right to privacy was nonexistent at common law, since mention of it was "not to be found in Blackstone, Kent, or any of the great commentators on the law." The majority also stated:

---

[1] 171 N.Y. 538(1902).

. . . While most persons would much prefer to have a good likeness of themselves appear in a responsible periodical or leading newspaper, rather than upon an advertising card or sheet, the doctrine which the courts are asked to create for this case would apply to one publication as to the other, for the principle which a court of equity is asked to assert in support of recovery in this action is that the right of privacy exists and is enforceable in equity. . . .

The dissenting opinion was less fearful of recognizing such a doctrine. It stated:

Security of person is as necessary as the security of property; and for that complete personal security which will result in the peaceful and wholesome enjoyment of one's privileges as a member of society there should be afforded protection, not only against the scandalous portraiture and display of one's features and person, but against the display and use thereof for another's commercial purposes or gain. The proposition is to me, an inconceivable one that these defendants may, unauthorizedly, use the likeness of this young woman upon their advertisement as a method of attracting widespread public attention to their wares, and that she must submit to the mortifying notoriety without right to invoke the exercise of the preventive power of a court of equity.

Outraged by the decision, and persuaded by the thought-provoking law review article written over a decade before by Samuel D. Warren and Louis D. Brandeis which concluded that a right to privacy existed in the common law,[2] the New York legislature passed a statutory right to privacy in 1903.[3]

The common law right of privacy goes beyond the mere unauthorized use of one's portrait. It extends to any unreasonable intrusion on one's private life. The Restatement of Torts provided that "any person who unreasonably and seriously interferes with another's interest in not having his affairs known to others or his likeness exhibited to the public is liable to the other."[4] Early applications of the doctrine provided recovery in situations ranging from eavesdropping by tapping a telephone line to barging into a woman's stateroom on a steamship. It should also be made clear that the common law right to privacy was never intended to interfere with the constitutional guarantees of freedom of speech and freedom of the press, including the public's right to know about matters of legitimate public interest and to be informed about the lives of public figures. Although not specifically spelled out in the U.S. Constitution, the Supreme Court has recognized that there is a federal constitutional right to personal privacy. The Court found in *Griswold v. Connecticut*[5] that the right to privacy is implicit in the Bill of Rights, which prohibits various types of unreasonable governmental intrusion upon personal freedom.

Employers may desire to monitor employee telephone conversations in the ordinary course of their business in order to evaluate employee performance and customer service, or document business transactions between employees and customers, or meet special security, efficiency, or other needs. Employers may likewise desire to monitor E-mail for what employers perceive to be sound business reasons. Or employers may

---

[2] Warren & Brandeis, *The Right to Privacy*, 4 Harv. L. Rev. 193 (1890).
[3] Civil Rights Law of New York, Sec. 50, 51; N.Y. Laws 1903, ch. 132 Sec. I, 2.
[4] Restatement of Torts, Sec. 867.
[5] 381 U.S. 479 (1965).

seek to test employees for drug use, or search employees' lockers for illicit drugs. Employers need to make personnel decisions based on medical reports by physicians about employees, and management needs to fully discuss the strengths and weaknesses of employees for hiring, promotion, and retention decisions. Employers are called upon to provide evaluations for their former employees. Litigation may result because employees may believe that such activities violate their right to privacy. The focus of this chapter will be on the extent of employee rights to privacy in the public and private sectors. Recommendations will be made for employers on reasonable steps to take to avoid violating employee privacy rights.

The Bill of Rights contained in the United States Constitution, including the First Amendment's protection of the freedom to associate and the Fourth Amendment's protection against unreasonable search and seizure, provides a philosophical and legal basis for individual privacy rights for federal employees. The Fourteenth Amendment applies this privacy protection to actions taken by state and local governments affecting their employees. The privacy rights of individuals working in the private sector are not directly controlled by the Bill of Rights, however, because challenged employer actions are not governmental actions. Limited employee privacy rights in the private sector are provided by state constitutions, statutes, case law, and collective bargaining agreements.[6]

SECTION 33—PUBLIC EMPLOYEES' PRIVACY RIGHTS

Federal employees have certain protections against disclosures under the Privacy Act of 1974. Federal and state employees have privacy protection against unreasonable searches under the federal Constitution.

The Privacy Act

The Privacy Act of 1974 provides federal employees limited protection from the dissemination of personal records without the prior written consent of the employee. Eleven exceptions exist including use by officers or employees of the agency which maintains the records who have a need for the records in the performance of their agency duties, and court orders for the records. The Privacy Act also bars disclosure of information about federal employees unless it would be required under the Freedom of Information Act. In *U.S. Department of Defense v. FLRA*,[7] the Federal Labor Relations Authority directed federal agencies to provide unions with home addresses of all agency employees eligible to be represented by unions, including nonunion members. The Department of Defense refused to comply because it believed that such an order violated the Privacy Act. The U.S. Supreme Court, applying a balancing test

---

[6] An example of the establishment of privacy rights by a state constitution is found in Article 1, Section 1, of the Constitution of the State of California which was amended in 1972 to provide as follows:

> All people are by nature free and independent and have inalienable rights. Among these are enjoying and defending life and liberty, acquiring, possessing, and protecting property, and pursuing and obtaining safety, happiness and *privacy*. (Emphasis added).

[7] 114 S.Ct. 1006 (1994).

between the privacy interests of employees and the relevant public interest, determined that the nonunion members who for whatever reason have chosen not to give unions their addresses had a nontrivial privacy interest in nondisclosure which outweighed any public interest in disclosure. The privacy interest of federal employees thus prevailed.

Property Searches in the Public Sector

As set forth previously, the Fourth Amendment's provision against unreasonable searches and seizures protects federal employees, and the Fourteenth Amendment extends this protection to state employees. In *O'Connor v. Ortega*, presented in this section, the Supreme Court set forth the parameters for property searches in the public sector. The case involved the search of a Dr. Ortega's office, desk, and files in connection with possible impropriety in the management of a residency program. The Court majority determined that Dr. Ortega had a reasonable expectation of privacy in his office desk and file cabinets but the state had a public interest in the supervision, control, and efficient operation of the workplace. The Court directed that searches conducted by public employers be evaluated under a "reasonableness" standard which balances the employee's expectation of privacy against the employer's legitimate business needs.[8]

O'CONNOR v. ORTEGA

Supreme Court of the United States, 480 U.S. 710 (1987).

[The respondent, Dr. Magno Ortega, a physician and psychiatrist, was an employee of a state hospital and had primary responsibility for training physicians in the psychiatric residency program. Hospital officials including the executive director of the hospital, Dr. Dennis O'Connor, became concerned about possible improprieties in Dr. Ortega's management of the program, particularly with respect to his acquisition of a computer and charges against him concerning sexual harassment of female hospital employees and inappropriate disciplinary action against a resident. While he was on administrative leave pending investiga-

tion of the charges, hospital officials, allegedly in order to inventory and secure state property, searched his office and seized personal items from his desk and file cabinets that were used in administrative proceedings resulting in his discharge. No formal inventory of property in the office was ever made, and all the other papers in the office were merely placed in boxes for storage. Dr. Ortega filed an action against the hospital officials under 42 U.S.C. § 1983, alleging that the search of his office violated the Fourth Amendment. On cross-motions for summary judgment, the District Court granted judgment for the hospital, con-

---

[8]The *O'Connor* principles apply as well to closed-circuit television monitoring of a public employer's workplace, with a critical inquiry being whether employees have a reasonable expectation of privacy in the areas under surveillance. If the employer uses cameras to detect wrongdoing in hallways, lunchrooms, or other public areas, there is no employee privacy violation because there is no reasonable expectation of privacy in such areas. However, surreptitious visual surveillance of restrooms or dressing rooms would be a privacy violation, absent a specific advisory of the surveillance program to employees. In *Thornton v. University Aire Services Board*, (9 IER Cases (BNA) 338 (Conn. 1994)), the use of a hidden video camera installed in a public university's police station was held not to be a privacy violation in a lawsuit over the discipline of a police officer shown on the video to be involved in unlawful gambling.

cluding that the search was proper because there was a need to secure state property in the office. Affirming in part, reversing in part, and remanding the case, the Court of Appeals concluded that Dr. Ortega had a reasonable expectation of privacy in his office, and that the search violated the Fourth Amendment. The court held that the record justified a grant of partial summary judgment for him on the issue of liability for the search, and it remanded the case to the District Court for a determination of damages. The Supreme Court granted certiorari.]

O'CONNOR, J. . . .

. . . We accept the conclusion of the Court of Appeals that Dr. Ortega had a reasonable expectation of privacy at least in his desk and file cabinets. . . .

In our view, requiring an employer to obtain a warrant whenever the employer wished to enter an employee's office, desk, or file cabinets for a work-related purpose would seriously disrupt the routine conduct of business and would be unduly burdensome. . . .

The governmental interest justifying work-related intrusions by public employers is the efficient and proper operation of the workplace. Government agencies provide myriad services to the public, and the work of these agencies would suffer if employers were required to have probable cause before they entered an employee's desk for the purpose of finding a file or piece of office correspondence. Indeed, it is difficult to give the concept of probable cause, rooted as it is in the criminal investigatory context, much meaning when the purpose of a search is to retrieve a file for work-related reasons. Similarly, the concept of probable cause has little meaning for a routine inventory conducted by public employers for the purpose of securing state property. . . . To ensure the efficient and proper operation of the agency, therefore, public employers must be given wide latitude to enter employee offices for work-related, noninvestigatory reasons.

We come to a similar conclusion for searches conducted pursuant to an investigation of work-related employee misconduct. Even when employers conduct an investigation, they have an interest substantially different from "the normal need for law enforcement." *New Jersey v. T.L.O., supra,* 469 U.S. at 351, 105 S.Ct., at 748 (BLACKMUN, J., concurring in judgment). Public employers have an interest in ensuring that their agencies operate in an effective and efficient manner, and the work of these agencies inevitably suffers from the inefficiency, incompetence, mismanagement, or other work-related misfeasance of its employees. Indeed, in many cases, public employees are entrusted with tremendous responsibility, and the consequences of their misconduct or incompetence to both the agency and the public interest can be severe. In contrast to law enforcement officials, therefore, public employers are not enforcers of the criminal law; instead, public employers have a direct and overriding interest in ensuring that the work of the agency is conducted in a proper and efficient manner. In our view, therefore, a probable cause requirement for searches of the type at issue here would impose intolerable burdens on public employers. The delay in correcting the employee misconduct caused by the need for probable cause rather than reasonable suspicion will be translated into tangible and often irreparable damage to the agency's work, and ultimately to the public interest. . . .

Balanced against the substantial government interests in the efficient and proper operation of the workplace are the privacy interests of government employees in their place of work which, while not insubstantial, are far less than those found at home or in some other contexts. As with the building inspections at *Camara,* the employer intrusions at issue here "involve a relatively limited invasion" of employee privacy. 387 U.S., at 537, 87 S.Ct., at 1735. Government offices are provided to employees for the sole purpose of facilitating the work of an agency. The employee may avoid exposing personal belongings at work by simply leaving them at home.

In sum, we conclude that the "special needs, beyond the normal need for law enforcement make the . . . probable-cause requirement impracticable," 469 U.S., at 351, 105 S.Ct., at 748 (BLACKMUN, J., concurring in judgment), for legitimate work-related, noninvestigatory intrusions as well as investigations of work-related misconduct. A standard of reasonableness will neither unduly burden the efforts of government employers to ensure the efficient and proper operation of the workplace, nor authorize arbitrary intrusions upon the privacy of public employees. We hold, therefore, that public employer intrusions on the constitutionally protected privacy interests of government employees for noninvestigatory, work-related purposes, as well as for investigations of work-related misconduct, should be judged by the standard of reasonableness under all circumstances. Under this reasonableness standard, both the inception and the scope of the intrusion must be reasonable:

"Determining the reasonableness of any search involves a twofold inquiry: first, one must consider 'whether the . . . action was justified at its inception.' Terry v. Ohio, 392 U.S. [1], at 20 [88 S.Ct. 1868, 1879, 20 L.Ed.2d 889 (1968)]; second, one must determine whether the search as actually conducted 'was reasonable related in scope to the circumstances which justified the interference in the first place,' ibid." New Jersey v. T.L.O., supra, at 341, 105 S.Ct., at 742–743.

Ordinarily, a search of an employee's office by a supervisor will be "justified at its inception" when there are reasonable grounds for suspecting that the search will turn up evidence that the employee is guilty of work-related misconduct, or that the search is necessary for a noninvestigatory work-related purpose such as to retrieve a needed file. . . . The search will be permissible in its scope when "the measures adopted are reasonably related to the objectives of the search and not excessively intrusive in light of . . . the nature of the [misconduct]." 469 U.S., at 342.

In the procedural posture of this case, we do not attempt to determine whether the search of Dr. Ortega's office and the seizure of his personal belongings satisfy the standard of reasonableness we have articulated in this case. No evidentiary hearing was held in this case because the District Court acted on cross-motions for summary judgment, and granted petitioners summary judgment. The Court of Appeals, on the other hand, concluded that the record in this case justified granting partial summary judgment on liability to Dr. Ortega.

We believe that both the District Court and the Court of Appeals were in error because summary judgment was inappropriate. . . .

. . . A search to secure state property is valid as long as petitioners had a reasonable belief that there was government property in Dr. Ortega's office which needed to be secured, and the scope of the intrusion was itself reasonable in light of this justification. Indeed, petitioners have put forward evidence that they had such a reasonable belief; at the time of the search, petitioners knew that Dr. Ortega had removed the computer from the Hospital. The removal of the computer—together with the allegations of mismanagement of the residency program and sexual harassment—may have made the search reasonable at its inception under the standard we have put forth in this case. As with the District Court order, therefore, the Court of Appeals conclusion that summary judgment was appropriate cannot stand.

On remand, therefore, the District Court must determine the justification for the search and seizure, and evaluate the reasonableness of both the inception of the search and its scope.

Accordingly, the judgment of the Court of Appeals is reversed, and the case is remanded to that court for further proceedings consistent with this opinion.

It is so ordered.

Justice SCALIA, concurring in the judgment.

Justice BLACKMUN, with whom Justice BRENNAN, Justice MARSHALL, and Justice STEVENS join, dissenting.

The facts of this case are simple and straightforward. Dr. Ortega had an expectation of privacy in his office, desk, and file cabinets, which were the target of a search by petitioners that can be characterized only as investigatory in nature. Because there was no "special need," see *New Jersey v. T.L.O.*, 469 U.S. 325, 351, 105 S.Ct. 733, 748, 83 L.Ed.2d 720 (1985) (opinion concurring in judgment), to dispense with the warrant and probable-cause requirements of the Fourth Amendment, I would evaluate the search by applying this traditional standard. Under that standard, this search clearly violated Dr. Ortega's Fourth Amendment rights.

CASE QUESTIONS

1. Did Dr. Ortega have a reasonable expectation of privacy, at least as to his desk and file cabinets?
2. Why didn't the Supreme Court require that the employer have a warrant based on probable cause to search an employee's desk and files when investigating work-related misconduct?
3. What did the Court decide in this case?

SECTION 34—PRIVATE-SECTOR EMPLOYEES

Private-sector employers are not subject to the same restrictions imposed on public-sector employers by the federal Constitution. Private employers, then, are generally less restricted in conducting searches on company property. However, some restrictions exist on employer searches in some states based on state constitution, statutes, or the common law.

In *K-Mart Corp. v. Trotti*,[9] the court determined that a private-sector employer may create a reasonable expectation of privacy in the workplace by providing an employee with a locker and allowing the employee to provide his or her own lock and key. A search of lockers under such circumstances could be an invasion of privacy. Or a search of lockers where the employer has a "respect of the privacy rights of employees" policy in effect could be an invasion of privacy. An employer may minimize the risk of liability for invasion of privacy if it formulates and disseminates a written company policy to all employees stating that due to security problems, concern for a drug-free environment, or other managerial concerns it is company policy that it may search all lockers, desks, purses, briefcases, and lunch boxes as it deems necessary at any time. Employers should provide all locks used on company property and prohibit the use of employee-owned locks. Each employee should be required to acknowledge receipt of the company's search policy.

SECTION 35—CONFIDENTIALITY OF MEDICAL RECORDS; UNREASONABLE PUBLICITY OF THE PRIVATE LIFE OF ANOTHER

The right to privacy protects employees' interests in not disclosing personal matters. Medical records, which may contain intimate facts of a personal nature, are well within the orbit of materials entitled to privacy protection. Indeed, disclosing a list of names with specific medications being used by the named employees may reveal the nature of

---

[9] 677 S.W.2d 632 (Tex. Civ. App. 1984).

the employee illnesses, where, for example, certain drugs are used exclusively to treat HIV infections.

The Americans with Disabilities Act (ADA) requires that any information relating to the medical condition or history of a job applicant or employee be collected and maintained by employers on separate forms, and kept in medical files separate and distinct from general personnel files. Disclosure of medical records or information is allowed only in three situations under the ADA: (1) when supervisors need to be informed regarding necessary restrictions on the duties of an employee, or necessary accommodations; (2) when the employer's medical staff needs to be informed about a disability that might require emergency treatment; and (3) when government officials investigating compliance with the ADA request access to such records or information.[10]

State laws may also require employers and health care providers to establish and maintain appropriate procedures to ensure that employee medical information remains confidential, and such laws may prohibit disclosure of medical information without a signed authorization from the employee. Not only must the employer protect the confidentiality of employees' medical records in its possession, but providers paid by the employer to make medical evaluations of employees cannot divulge details of the employees' personal lives to the employer without the written consent of the employees, and can only report on the functional limits of patients. The *Doe v. Southeastern Pennsylvania Transportation Authority (SEPTA)* decision, a public-sector case presented in this section, is illustrative of the hardships that can be caused by improper handling of medical and prescription records. The district court's decision was overturned by a divided panel of the Third Circuit Court of Appeals. Excerpts from the district court and the court of appeals decisions are presented to show the difficulty of the issues faced by these courts.

Invasion of privacy by the unreasonable publicity given to the private life of another is a recognized tort in some 30 jurisdictions that have considered this question.[11] Disclosure and publicity of the private facts of a private person's exposure to the HIV virus and his homosexual lifestyle is an actionable tort in these jurisdictions.

DOE v. SOUTHEASTERN PENNSYLVANIA TRANSPORTATION AUTHORITY (SEPTA)

United States District Court, 1995 WL 4290 (E.D. Pa. 1995).
United States Court of Appeals, 72 F.3d 1133 (3d Cir. 1995).

[John Doe was employed by the Southeastern Pennsylvania Transportation Authority (SEPTA), a state-operated transportation authority, as the Manager of the Employee Assistance Program. Dr. Richard Press was the head of the Medical Department and was Doe's supervisor. Judith

Pierce was SEPTA's Chief Administrative Officer, Jacob Aufschauer served as Director of Benefits, and Dr. Louis Van de Beek was an employee in the Medical Department. Doe was HIV-positive, and before using the SEPTA prescription plan to fill a prescription for AZT, an anti-viral drug used exclu-

---

[10] 42 U.S.C. § 12112 (c)(3)(B).
[11] *Borquez v. Ozer*, 923 P.2d 166 (Colo. App. 1995).

sively to treat HIV illness, he was assured by an informed SEPTA official that names would not be associated with the drugs they were taking. Judith Pierce did not have a need to know the names on the report of its drug supply contractor Rite Aid, but Pierce continued to look at names, and as a result Doe's diagnosis was disclosed to her. Nor did the Director of Benefits have to know Doe's name and medications, yet it was disclosed; nor was there any reason that Doe's supervisor, Dr. Press, would need to know Doe's name and medications, and it was disclosed. Dr. Van de Beek told Doe that he had received a call from Judith Pierce who appeared to be reading from a list of Doe's medications. Van de Beek also told Doe that he had concluded that as a result of the conversation, Pierce now knew that Doe was HIV-positive. Van de Beek was aware of the medications that Doe was taking because he had discussed them with Doe previously, as Van de Beek had some expertise regarding AIDS. Doe, who specifically did not wish Pierce to know he was HIV-positive, was upset to discover that Pierce had acquired this information. Doe then went to Dr. Press with his concern that Pierce now knew. Press told Doe that Pierce had asked him to audit a list of prescriptions which contained employees' names and which had HIV medications, including Doe's, highlighted. Doe was even further upset by this information. Doe sued SEPTA and Pierce under 42 U.S.C. § 1983 for deprivation of his constitutional right to privacy. From a judgment for Doe for $125,000 SEPTA appealed.]

FROM THE DISTRICT COURT'S OPINION . . . YOHN, J. . . .

Doe's claims against Pierce individually and as a SEPTA policymaker asserted that her actions with regard to the Rite Aid report violated Doe's constitutional right to privacy. As the court explained in its memorandum disposing of the defendants' motion for summary judgment, the constitutional right to privacy as defined by the Supreme Court protects "the individual interest in avoiding disclosure of personal matters." *Whalen v. Roe*, 429 U.S. 589, 598-99 (1977). Ini-

tially, the court must determine whether particular information is a "private matter" protected by the constitutional privacy right. The Third Circuit has noted that "[t]he more intimate or personal the information, the more justified is the expectation that it will not be subject to public scrutiny." In *Westinghouse* the court stated that "[t]here can be no question that an employee's medical records, which may contain intimate facts of a personal nature are well within the ambit of materials entitled to privacy protection." *Id.*

The defendants . . . contend that the court erroneously held and instructed the jury that as a matter of law the prescription information at issue in this case was protected by the constitutional right to privacy. In *F.O.P.* [*v. City of Philadelphia*, 812 F.2d 105 (3d Cir. 1987)] the Third Circuit held that question 19 in the questionnaire at issue, which asked; "Are you presently using any prescription drugs? If yes, state the drug, the need for it and the dosage," among other medical information questions, implicated the plaintiffs' constitutional privacy rights. *Id.* at 113. The court cited, *inter alia*, *Whalen v. Roe*, 429 U.S. 589, 599-600 (1977), *In re Search Warrant (Sealed)*, 810 F.2d 67 (3d Cir.), *cert. denied*, 483 U.S. 1007 (1987), as recognizing the constitutionally protected status of medical information. 812 F.2d at 113. In addition to these cases recognizing the constitutionally protected status of prescription information, at least one court within the Third Circuit has held that an AIDS diagnosis is similarly protected. *Doe v. Borough of Barrington*, 729 F. Supp. 376, 382 (D.N.J. 1990) (finding that "the Constitution protects plaintiffs from governmental disclosure of their husband's and father's infection with the AIDS virus").

To determine whether particular information was protected, the Third Circuit looked at whether the information sought was "within an individual's reasonable expectations of confidentiality." Given that certain prescription medications are used exclusively to treat HIV infection, the information that someone is taking such drugs clearly reveals his or her diagnosis. Particularly in view of the hysteria surrounding

HIV and AIDS at the time of the events in question, *see generally Doe*, 729 F. Supp. at 380-81, and Doe's documented efforts to keep the information confidential, the court affirms its prior holding that, under the standards set forth by the Supreme Court and the Third Circuit, the information contained in the prescription benefit utilization report, linking Doe's name with HIV-specific medications, was well within his reasonable expectations of confidentiality and thus was protected by the constitutional right to privacy. In other words, this information was a "private matter" into which the government, here Pierce and SEPTA, could not intrude without sufficient cause.

Violation of the Constitutional Right to Privacy

If the government is to intrude into such protected information, the Third Circuit has indicated that a balancing test must be applied to determine whether the government's interest in access to the information outweighs the individual's interest in keeping the matter private; if not, the intrusion violates the constitutional right to privacy. *United States v. Westinghouse Elec. Corp.*, 638 F.2d 570, 577 (3d Cir. 1980), *cited in F.O.P.*, 812 F.2d at 110. In *Westinghouse*, the Third Circuit listed seven factors to be considered in this balancing test:

The factors which should be considered in deciding whether an intrusion into an individual's privacy is justified are the type of record requested, the information it does or might contain, the potential for harm in any subsequent nonconsensual disclosure, the injury from disclosure to the relationship in which the record was generated, the adequacy of safeguards to prevent unauthorized disclosure, the degree of need for access, and whether there is an express statutory mandate, articulated public policy, or other recognizable public interest militating toward access.

638 F.2d at 578. Having found that Doe had established genuine issues of material fact with regard to the application of these factors in this

case, the court denied summary judgment to the defendants. At trial, the application of the *Westinghouse* factors was a question of fact for the jury; the court read the *Westinghouse* factors twice to the jury as part of the charge. (Tr. 12/5/94 at 92, 97.) . . .

. . . Even using the defendants' "need-to-know" analysis, the evidence supports a reasonable jury finding that a constitutional violation occurred. It was undisputed that the names on the report were unnecessary for Pierce's review of the Rite Aid report and that knowing this, she nevertheless continued to look at the report, and that as a result, Doe's diagnosis was disclosed to her. Similarly, there was no need for Aufschauer to know Doe's name and medications as disclosed to him as a result of his assisting Pierce in reviewing the Rite Aid report. Lastly, there was no reason for Press to know Doe's name and medications as disclosed to him when Pierce showed him the marked up page of the report which contained that information. None of these people had a business need to know the names contained in that report. Accordingly, Pierce's use of that report, without covering or obliterating the names, violated Doe's constitutional right to privacy. . . .

. . . There was evidence that the "type of record requested" was prescription utilization data; furthermore there was evidence that the actual record *received* was a report which listed employees' names on a line with the medications they were taking. The jury reasonably could have found that it was possible to learn Doe's diagnosis from the information contained in the prescription benefit utilization report. Pierce testified that she did learn his condition in that manner, and both Press and Aufschauer testified that she pointed out Doe's name to them and that they knew what the drugs Doe was taking were used for. The jury could clearly find that such linking names with drugs, which in turn inevitably reveals diagnoses, weighs heavily in favor of the individual privacy interest here. . . .

... The court concludes that with the information before it, the jury could have taken all of the *Westinghouse* factors into account and weighed SEPTA's interest in having the information in the form it did and in using it in the way it did against Doe's privacy interest in the information and reasonably could have concluded that a constitutional violation occurred. Furthermore, the court concludes that, as to this issue, the jury's verdict was not against the weight of the evidence. . . .

Doe presented evidence that Pierce knew that she might come across a name she knew on the Rite Aid report and that she saw Doe's name and medications on the report. Pierce testified that she felt that she had a right to look at all the information she was given by Rite Aid because SEPTA's prescription benefit program was self-insured. There was evidence that Pierce knew that she was asking about Doe's medications in that Van de Beek testified that she was upset to learn that the drug she had asked about was used exclusively to treat HIV infection. . . . Pierce further testified that she was not concerned that by asking Van de Beek about Doe's medications that she would be learning Doe's medical condition without his knowledge. Aufschauer testified that Pierce pointed Doe's name out to him while they were reviewing the report. Doe presented evidence in addition that the Rite Aid reports were voluminous, but that the individual report she showed Press was the one which contained Doe's name and medications. Moreover, there was evidence that Pierce had highlighted the report, including Doe's name and medications, before showing it to Press. Pierce testified that she knew from the expression on Press' face that he had seen Doe's name and had recognized his diagnosis. Press testified that Pierce asked him whether he knew if Doe was being treated for AIDS.

First, from the testimony regarding Pierce's reaction to the use of Doe's medication, a reasonable jury could infer that she learned his condition intentionally, recklessly or with deliberate indifference to Doe's constitutional right to privacy in that she knew that she was asking about Doe's medications and that she would thereby learn his diagnosis. Second, because there was evidence that Pierce pointed out Doe's name to Aufschauer, and that he could see the report as she called and queried Van de Beek over a speakerphone, a reasonable jury could infer that Pierce caused Aufschauer to learn Doe's condition intentionally, recklessly or with deliberate indifference. Lastly, because Pierce knew that Press was Doe's direct supervisor and that he was a doctor who was likely to know what particular medications were used for, and because Pierce had the opportunity to use another individual report or to obliterate the names from the report she used, a reasonable jury was free to infer that Pierce disclosed Doe's condition to Press intentionally, recklessly or with deliberately indifference. Accordingly, the court finds that Doe presented sufficient evidence of state of mind to succeed on his claim against Pierce individually and against SEPTA as a result of Pierce's status as a SEPTA policy-maker. Further, the court concludes that a new trial on the issue of liability under these theories is not warranted as the verdict is not against the weight of evidence. . . .

Doe . . . testified that he was angry and frightened of what Pierce might do with the information. The jury could have inferred that learning that Pierce knew of his illness was particularly upsetting to Doe because he had consciously decided that he did not want her to know. He felt that Pierce was capricious and demonstrated a "marked lability in her emotions."* Doe testified that he perceived Pierce's attitude and behavior toward him to change after the incident. He also testified that the attitudes and behavior of other people at SEPTA toward him changed after

---

* Doe explained that the term "labile" or "lability" meant, "in layman's terms, [that] she would be calm one moment and screaming at you the next, screaming obscenities." (*Id.* at 43.)

the incident, albeit subtly.** Doe is a trained psychologist. When he recognized himself to be suffering from depression shortly after the incident, he asked his physician to prescribe an antidepressant medication, and the physician did so. . . .

FROM THE COURT OF APPEALS
OPINION . . . *ROSENN, J.* . . .

. . . Based upon this testimony, the court readily concludes that Doe established a "reasonable probability" that he did indeed suffer emotional distress damages as a result of defendants' actions. Accordingly, the court will not order a remittitur of Doe's damages to nothing. . . .

As a result of the hysteria surrounding AIDS when this incident occurred, the impact of the defendants' invasion of Doe's privacy was greater than had Doe's illness been anything else: this was perhaps the most private information Doe possessed [end of district court's opinion].

. . . Because SEPTA is an agency subsidized by the state and federal government, its operating costs are substantially borne by the public who use its facilities and the taxpayers who pay its subsidies. Keeping fares and taxes low, and preserving the public fisc are genuine, recognizable public interests. Therefore, Pierce's need for access, factor six of *Westinghouse*, also articulates a recognizable public policy encouraging access, as noted in factor seven.

As Chief Administrative Officer for SEPTA, Pierce had responsibility for health costs. Her ability over a period of three years to successfully reduce prescription drug and dental costs by a combined total of over $42,000,000 gives us some idea of the immensity of her task and the money at stake. The new contract between

SEPTA and Rite-Aid gave strong financial incentives to cut costs if possible. There can be no serious argument that Pierce could do this monitoring without being able to audit reports of the actual costs and the drugs purchased. It is true that the names of the individual employees were unnecessary for this purpose. It is equally true that Pierce did not request such names, nor did she disclose those names, or any of the information contained in the report, in anything other than a legitimate manner. Except for Dr. Press, who had the information directly from Doe, the only other person to whom Pierce disclosed the information was Aufschauer. As they requested only information for which they had a legitimate and compelling need, and used the information received in a legitimate, careful and confidential manner, it cannot be said that they violated Doe's right to privacy merely because the first report from Rite-Aid contained unnecessary, unrequested information in which he had a privacy interest. . . .

We hold that a self-insured employer's need for access to employee prescription records under its health insurance plan, when the information disclosed is only for the purpose of monitoring the plans by those with a need to know, outweighs an employee's interest in keeping his prescription drug purchases confidential. Such minimal intrusion, although an impingement on privacy, is insufficient to constitute a constitutional violation. The district court should have granted defendants' Rule 50 motion for judgment as a matter of law.

SEPTA demonstrated important interests in the prescription information furnished by its supplier, and disclosed such information only to people with a right to know. This outweighs the minimal intrusion into Doe's privacy. The district court erred in its analysis of the *Westinghouse* factors, and should have granted defendant's motion for judgment under Rule 50.

Accordingly, the judgment of the district court will be reversed, and the matter will be remanded to the district court for entry of judg-

---

** Specifically, Doe testified that he was concerned that a proposed expansion of his job duties would not take place, which it did not. He also testified that he was afraid he might be forced to stop seeing patients because of the hysteria regarding HIV-positive health care workers. Finally, he was afraid that he would be fired. (*Id.* at 66-67.)

ment for the defendants as a matter of law. Each side to bear its own costs.

GREENBERG, *Circuit Judge, concurring.*

Although I agree with Judge Rosenn's conclusions, I have a few reservations about his opinion that I note here. . . .

I join in Judge Rosenn's opinion because I believe that, even viewed in the light most favorable to Doe, the verdict winner in the district court, the facts of this case cannot, as a matter of law, support the jury's verdict. I support this holding because factors six and seven of the balancing test announced in *United States v. Westinghouse Elec. Corp.*, 638 F.2d 570, 578 (3d Cir.1980), namely SEPTA's need for access to the prescription information and "whether there is an express statutory mandate, articulated public policy, or other recognizable public interest militating toward access," outweigh Doe's limited privacy interests in the information. . . .

However, I do not believe that Judge Rosenn's opinion reflects the facts of the case in the light most favorable to Doe. For example, in describing Pierce's actions with respect to the Rite-Aid report, he states that she highlighted the names on the report whose medications she was unfamiliar with "for her research purposes," *see* majority opinion at 1139, and that she "discreetly never mentioned Doe by name" to Dr. Van de Beek. Yet, Pierce's motivations for highlighting the names of the employees, in particular Doe's, was a primary factual issue in the case, as was her possible carelessness. Clearly, Doe did not claim that Pierce highlighted the names merely for her research purposes, nor would he have described her behavior as "discreet." The jury's verdict for Doe, then, might reflect its agreement with his assertions that her motivations, as well as her conduct, were improper. In any case, it does not seem that Judge Rosenn's opinion paints the issue in the light most favorable to a verdict for Doe. Although I regard this point as somewhat academic because of my analysis of the *Westinghouse* factors, it is worth noting because of our clear man-

date to view the facts in the most favorable light to the verdict-winner in reviewing a denial of a motion for judgment as a matter of law. . . .

LEWIS, *Circuit Judge, concurring and dissenting.* . . .

With respect to the sixth factor, which addresses the degree of need for access to the information, I note initially that at Doe's trial, Ms. Pierce, the SEPTA administrator responsible for auditing the company's health benefits plan, testified that for her purposes the employee names on the Rite-Aid printout were irrelevant. In fact, the district court specifically noted that "it was undisputed that the names on the report were unnecessary for Pierce's review of the Rite Aid report." While it is true that SEPTA could have legitimately requested these names for auditing purposes, the fact is that in this case it neither required nor requested such information. Thus, the jury had no factual basis upon which to conclude that SEPTA needed its employees' names in order effectively to audit its health plan. . . .

With respect to the seventh *Westinghouse* factor, I agree that there is an important public interest in allowing companies such as SEPTA, which administer their own health plans, to have access to the prescription drug records of their employees. In general, I would agree that such employers have a legitimate need for this information. Nevertheless, I do not believe that this interest, standing alone, is sufficient to overcome the other *Westinghouse* factors, which in this case weigh largely in Doe's favor. . . .

But I am particularly troubled by the potential implications of the majority's position. I hope I am wrong, but I predict that the court's decision in this case will make it far easier in the future for employers to disclose their employees' private medical information, obtained during an audit of the company's health benefits plan, and to escape constitutional liability for harassment or other harms suffered by their employees as a result of that disclosure.

For the above reasons, I respectfully concur and dissent.

2. Carefully review the district court's opinion and extract what that court required the plaintiff to establish in order to win his case.
3. What did the court of appeals decide?

CASE QUESTIONS

1. What does the constitutional right to privacy as defined by the Supreme Court protect from government action?

SECTION 36—MONITORING EMPLOYEE TELEPHONE CONVERSATIONS AND E-MAIL

The Federal Wiretapping Act[12] makes it unlawful to intercept oral and electronic communications, and provides for both criminal liability and civil damages against the violator. There are two major exceptions, however. The first allows an employer to monitor a firm's telephones in the "ordinary course of business" through the use of extension telephones; a second exception applies where there is prior consent to the interception. If monitoring by the employer results in intercepting a business call, it is within the ordinary course of business exception. Personal calls can be monitored, however, only to the extent necessary to determine that the call is personal, and then the employer must cease listening. To illustrate, in the *Deal v. Spears* case presented in this section, Newell Spears taped all phone conversations at his store to try to find out if an employee was connected to a theft at the store. He listened to virtually all 22 hours of intercepted and recorded telephone conversations between his employee Sibbie Deal and her boyfriend Calvin Lucas without regard to the conversations' relation to Spears's business interest. While Spears might well have legitimately monitored Deal's calls to the extent necessary to determine that the calls were personal and made or received in violation of store policy, the scope of the interception in this case was well beyond the boundaries of the "ordinary course of business exception," and thus in violation of the Act.

Employer monitoring of employee phone calls can be accomplished without fear of violating the Act if consent is established. Consent may be established by prior written notice to employees of the employer's monitoring policy. It is prudent as well for the employer to give customers notice of the policy through a recorded message as part of the employer's phone answering system.

E-Mail Monitoring

Electronic mail (E-mail) network systems are a primary means of communication in many of today's businesses, and are deemed alternatives to fax, telephone, or the Postal Service by some employers. Employers seek to monitor the E-mail messages of their employees for the purpose of evaluating the efficiency and effectiveness of the employees, or for corporate security purposes, including the protection of trade secrets and

---

[12] Title III of the Omnibus Crime Control and Safe Streets Act of 1968, 18 U.S.C. §§ 2510–2520.

other intangible property interests. When employees are disciplined or terminated for alleged wrongful activities discovered as a result of E-mail searches, the privacy issue may be raised.

The Electronic Communications Privacy Act (ECPA)[13] amended the Federal Wiretapping Act and was intended, in part, to apply to E-mail. However, "ordinary course of business" and "consent" exceptions apply to E-mail, and it would appear that employers have broad latitude to monitor employee E-mail use. Alana Shoars, an E-mail administrator for Epson America Inc., was fired after complaining about her supervisor's reading of employee E-mail messages. Her state court invasion of privacy case was unsuccessful.[14] Very few cases involving E-mail issues have been adjudicated to date under the ECPA.

An employer can place itself within the "consent" exception to the Act by issuing a policy statement to all employees, informing them of the monitoring program and its purposes and justification.

DEAL v. SPEARS

United States Court of Appeals, 980 F.2d 1153 (8th Cir. 1992).

[Sibbie Deal and Calvin Lucas brought a civil action for damages under the federal wiretapping statute against Deal's former employers, Newell and Juanita Spears, doing business as the White Oak Package Store, for the intentional interception and disclosure of their telephone conversations. The District Court awarded statutory damages to Deal and Lucas in the amount of $40,000 and granted their request for attorney's fees. Newell and Juanita Spears appealed. Deal and Lucas cross-appealed the court's refusal to award punitive damages.]

BOWMAN, C. J. . . .
Newell and Juanita Spears have owned and operated the White Oaks Package Store near Camden, Arkansas, for about twenty years. The Spearses live in a mobile home adjacent to the store. The telephone in the store has an extension in the home, and is the only phone line into either location. The same phone line

thus is used for both the residential and the business phones.

Sibbie Deal was an employee at the store from December 1988 until she was fired in August 1990. The store was burglarized in April 1990 and approximately $16,000 was stolen. The Spearses believed that it was an inside job and suspected that Deal was involved. Hoping to catch the suspect in an unguarded admission, Newell Spears purchased and installed a recording device on the extension phone in the mobile home. When turned on, the machine would automatically record all conversations made or received on either phone, with no indication to the parties using the phone that their conversation was being recorded. Before purchasing the recorder, Newell Spears told a sheriff's department investigator that he was considering this surreptitious monitoring and the investigator told Spears that he did not "see anything wrong with that."

---

[13] 18 U.S.C. § 2510–2520 (1988); the Act was amended in 1994 to apply to cellular phones.
[14] See *Shoars v. Epson America, Inc.*, 1994 Cal. Lexus 3670 (Cal. June 29, 1994).

Calls were taped from June 27, 1990, through August 13, 1990. During that period, Sibbie Deal, who was married to Mike Deal at the time, was having an extramarital affair with Calvin Lucas, then married to Pam Lucas. Deal and Lucas spoke on the telephone at the store frequently and for long periods of time while Deal was at work. (Lucas was on 100% disability so he was at home all day.) Based on the trial testimony, the District Court concluded that much of the conversation between the two was "sexually provocative." Deal also made or received numerous other personal telephone calls during her workday. Even before Newell Spears purchased the recorder, Deal was asked by her employers to cut down on her use of the phone for personal calls, and the Spearses told her they might resort to monitoring calls or installing a pay phone in order to curtail the abuse.

Newell Spears listened to virtually all twenty-two hours of the tapes he recorded, regardless of the nature of the calls or the content of the conversations, and Juanita Spears listened to some of them. Although there was nothing in the record to indicate that they learned anything about the burglary, they did learn, among other things, that Deal sold Lucas a keg of beer at cost, in violation of store policy. On August 13, 1990, when Deal came in to work the evening shift, Newell Spears played a few seconds of the incriminating tape for Deal and then fired her. Deal and Lucas filed this action on August 29, 1990, and the tapes and recorder were seized by a United States deputy marshal pursuant to court order on September 3, 1990. . . .

The Spearses challenge the court's finding of liability. They admit the taping but contend that the facts here bring their actions under two statutory exceptions to civil liability. . . .

The elements of a violation of the wire and electronic communications interception provisions (Title III) of the Omnibus Crime Control and Safe Streets Act of 1968 are set forth in the section that makes such interceptions a criminal offense. 18 U.S.C. § 2511 (1988). Under the relevant provisions of the statute, criminal liability attaches and a federal civil cause of action arises when a person intentionally intercepts a wire or electronic communication or intentionally discloses the contents of the interception. *Id.* §§ 2511(1)(a), (c), 2520(a). The successful civil plaintiff may recover actual damages plus any profits made by the violator. If statutory damages will result in a larger recovery than actual damages, the violator must pay the plaintiff "the greater of $100 a day for each day of violation or $10,000." *Id.* § 2520(c)(2)(B) (1988). Further, punitive damages, attorney fees, and "other litigation costs reasonably incurred" are allowed. *Id.* § 2520(b)(2), (3) (1988).

The Spearses first claim they are exempt from civil liability because Sibbie Deal consented to the interception of calls that she made from and received at the store. Under the statute, it is not unlawful "to intercept a wire, oral, or electronic communication . . . where one of the parties to the communication has given prior consent to such interception," 18 U.S.C. § 2511(2)(d), and thus no civil liability is incurred. The Spearses contend that Deal's consent may be implied because Newell Spears had mentioned that he might be forced to monitor calls or restrict telephone privileges if abuse of the store's telephone for personal calls continued. They further argue that the extension in their home gave actual notice to Deal that her calls could be overheard, and that this notice resulted in her implied consent to interception. We find these arguments unpersuasive.

There is no evidence of express consent here. Although constructive consent is inadequate, actual consent may be implied from the circumstances. *See Griggs-Ryan v. Smith*, 904 F.2d 112, 116 (1st Cir. 1990). Nevertheless, "[c]onsent under Title III is not to be cavalierly implied. . . . [K]nowledge of the *capability* of monitoring alone cannot be considered implied consent." *Watkins v. L. M. Berry & Co.*, 704 F.2d 577, 581 (11th Cir. 1983) (citations omitted).

We do not believe that Deal's consent may be implied from the circumstances relied upon in the Spearses' arguments. The Spearses did not inform Deal that they were monitoring the phone, but only told her they might do so in order to cut down on personal calls. Moreover, it seems clear that the couple anticipated Deal would not suspect that they were intercepting her calls, since they hoped to catch her making an admission about the burglary, an outcome they would not expect if she knew her calls were being recorded. As for listening in via the extension, Deal testified that she knew when someone picked up the extension in the residence while she was on the store phone, as there was an audible "click" on the line.

Given these circumstances, we hold as a matter of law that the Spearses have failed to show Deal's consent to the interception and recording of her conversations.

The Spearses also argue that they are immune from liability under what has become known as an exemption for business use of a telephone extension. . . .

We do not quarrel with the contention that the Spearses had a legitimate business reason for listening in: they suspected Deal's involvement in a burglary of the store and hoped she would incriminate herself in a conversation on the phone. Moreover, Deal was abusing her privileges by using the phone for numerous personal calls even, by her own admission, when there were customers in the store. The Spearses might legitimately have monitored Deal's calls to the extent necessary to determine that the calls were personal and made or received in violation of store policy.

But the Spearses recorded twenty-two hours of calls, and Newell Spears listened to all of them without regard to their relation to his business interests. Granted, Deal might have mentioned the burglary at any time during the conversations, but we do not believe that the Spearses' suspicions justified the extent of the intrusion. *See Watkins*, 704 F.2d at 583 ("We hold that a personal call may not be intercepted in the ordinary course of business under the exemption in section 2510(5)(a)(i), except to the extent necessary to guard against unauthorized use of the telephone or to determine whether a call is personal or not."); *Briggs v. American Air Filter Co.*, 630 F.2d 414, 420 n. 9 (5th Cir. 1980) ("A general practice of surreptitious monitoring would be more intrusive on employees' privacy than monitoring limited to specific occasions."). We conclude that the scope of the interception in this case takes us well beyond the boundaries of the ordinary course of business.

For the reasons we have indicated, the Spearses cannot avail themselves of the telephone extension/business use exemption of Title III. . . .

We agree with the District Court that defendants' conduct does not warrant the imposition of punitive damages.

The judgment of the District Court is affirmed in all respects.

CASE QUESTIONS

1. It is not unlawful to monitor the telephone conversation of an employee if the employee has given prior consent. Did Deal give her employer consent in this case?
2. Because of the recent burglary of the store, did the employer have a legitimate business reason to record and review the employee's phone calls made or received while at work?
3. Under the *Watkins* precedent what is the extent to which an employer can monitor personal phone calls to employees within the ordinary course of business exemption of the federal wiretapping law?

SECTION 37—DRUG TESTING

It is estimated that some six million Americans currently use cocaine and that some 23 million Americans use marijuana. The outward signs of drug use and impairment are sometimes not as evident as is impairment due to the abuse of alcohol. Employee drug users themselves often believe that they are not impaired while at work. For example, in a study of ten experienced pilots who were trained for eight hours on a flight simulator for landing tasks, when each smoked a marijuana cigarette containing 19 milligrams of THC, 24 hours after smoking the cigarettes their mean performance on flight tasks showed trends towards impairment on all variables. Moreover, each experienced significant impairment in "distance off center" in landing and vertical and lateral deviation on approach to landing.[15] Despite these deficiencies the pilots reported no awareness of impaired performance. Such a study conducted by the Stanford University School of Medicine, and other studies, indicates that there is a need for concern about the performance of those entrusted with complex behavioral and cognitive tasks within 24 hours after smoking marijuana.

Governmental Testing

Employee drug use costs the United States government alone an estimated $33 billion per year. The seriousness of the problem at all levels of government has led to efforts to combat drug use by the use of drug testing by public employers. Constitutional challenges of the testing programs have been made in courts by individual employees and public-sector unions. Certain patterns have emerged as to the legality of various types of testing.

The most common challenge to governmental employers' drug testing programs is that the tests violate the Fourth Amendment prohibition against unreasonable searches and seizures. Courts uniformly have found that requiring an individual to submit urine samples for drug analysis constitutes a search and seizure within the meaning of the Fourth Amendment. The *Patchogue-Medford Congress of Teachers v. Board of Education* decision of New York State's highest court, reported in this section, makes very clear that such testing constitutes a search. The next question for a court is whether the search was reasonable under the Fourth Amendment. This question is answered on a case by case basis by balancing the social and governmental need for the testing in question against the invasion of personal privacy rights that the search entails.

In *Skinner v. Railway Labor Executives' Association*[16] and *National Treasury Employees Union v. Von Raab*,[17] the Supreme Court established a "special needs" exception to the Fourth Amendment's protections against warrantless and suspicionless drug

---

[15] A. Yesauage, M. D., et al., "Carry-over Effects of Marijuana Intoxication on Aircraft Pilot Performances: A Preliminary Report," *Am. J. Psychiatry* 142 (1985): 1325–29.
[16] 109 S.Ct. 1402 (1989).
[17] 109 S.Ct. 1384 (1989).

testing of public employees or the testing of private railroad employees under a federal administrative agency's regulations.

In the *Skinner* case, certain railroad unions challenged Federal Railway Administration (FRA) regulations that mandated warrantless, suspicionless breath, blood, and urinalysis testing of railroad employees involved in rail accidents resulting in deaths, injuries, or property damage. The FRA contended that the long history of drug and alcohol abuse in the railroad industry justified the random testing mandates. The Supreme Court recognized to collect blood, urine, or breath for analysis is a search and seizure under the Fourth Amendment. But the Court stated that the Fourth Amendment does not prohibit all searches and seizures, but only those that are unreasonable based upon a review of the surrounding circumstances. The Court determined that the special need for the protection of public safety in rail transportation made the typical prerequisites of search warrants or individualized suspicion impracticable.

Once the special need has been shown, the Supreme Court indicated that a balancing test must be used that weighs the intrusion on the individual's privacy rights against the promotion of legitimate governmental objectives. The Court determined that railroad employees holding safety-sensitive positions within a heavily regulated industry possess a diminished expectation of privacy. The Court also determined that there was only a minimum intrusion on individual privacy under the FRA regulations. Balanced against these considerations was the government interest in protecting the public from the immediate potential for catastrophic railway accidents. The Court determined that the government interest outweighed employee interests.

In the *Von Raab* case, presented in this section, the Supreme Court found special needs beyond mere law enforcement, and applying a balancing test, determined that the governmental interests of protecting national borders and the public safety outweighed employee privacy interests. The Court then justified the warrantless, suspicionless drug testing utilized by the Customs Service.

Testing in the Private Sector

The federal constitutional protections of privacy, to whatever extent they exist, apply only to the actions of the state.[18] Thus constitutional defenses may be raised against public employers, as set forth previously. Private-sector employers may have collective bargaining agreements that restrict employer testing to "reasonable-cause" situations. These employers may have to meet just-cause standards in disciplinary matters. However, unless restricted or prohibited by collective bargaining contracts or state or local law, private employers have a right to require employees to submit to drug testing.[19]

---

[18] *Jackson v. Metropolitan Edison Co.*, 419 U.S. 345 (1974).

[19] In New Jersey, for example, where the New Jersey Constitution protects individuals' right to privacy, the state's supreme court approved random drug testing in the private sector. The court held that the right of privacy was outweighed by the competing public interest in safety, where an employee who attempts to perform his or her duties impaired by drugs would pose a threat to co-workers, the workplace, or the public at large. *Hennessey v. Costal Eagle Point Oil Co.*, 129 N.J. 81, 609 A.2d 611.

It is common for private-sector employers to test applicants for employment for drug use as one of the numerous tests given in a preemployment physical examination. Past drug users may be protected by certain state and federal laws from discrimination; however, if they test positive for drugs in a preemployment drug test, they lose protection under the Americans with Disabilities Act of 1990 and the Rehabilitation Act of 1973. Job applicants ordinarily have no protection under collective bargaining contracts, and unions have no standing to bring suit against the employers since union members do not face the risk of exposure to the testing.[20] Government regulations may require notice of testing. However, private-sector employers generally have wide latitude in testing job applicants for drug use. Job applicants who test positive for drug use simply are not offered a position.

Private-sector employers have an obligation to bargain with their unions about new drug testing programs for their current employees unless the employers have expressly reserved rights to make changes in these programs in their current collective bargaining contracts.

Testing Procedures and Methods

Questions may be raised at an arbitration or in a wrongful-discharge lawsuit as to the integrity of the chain of custody of the test sample, the accuracy of the type of test(s) performed, and the reliability of the testing laboratory. It is widely accepted that the gas chromatography/mass spectrometry (GC/MS) test is highly accurate. This expensive test is used as a second or confirmatory test if the "EMIT" test yields a positive result. Some employers and unions have reached agreements on testing protocols, which help eliminate testing issues. Thus the Teamsters and a committee of employers have reached a reasonable-cause testing agreement as part of a Master Freight Agreement. The agreement designates the testing laboratory and procedures and covers such details as the amount of urine to be taken and the type of tests to be performed.

PATCHOGUE-MEDFORD CONGRESS OF TEACHERS v. BOARD OF EDUCATION

New York State Court of Appeals, 517 N.Y. 2d 456 (1987).

[On May 3, 1985, the Patchogue-Medford School District notified all of its twenty-two teachers completing their probationary terms that they must submit to urinalysis examination. The letter stated that "the district is requiring a urine sample for all employees eligible for tenure." The sample would be collected by the school nurse and then forwarded to a laboratory for testing. It was conceded that the sole purpose of this examination was to determine whether any of the teachers were using drugs illegally. The teachers' union challenged the testing, and an injunction against the testing

---

[20] *APWU v. Frank*, 968 F.2d 1373 (1st Cir. 1992).

was issued. The action of the lower court was affirmed by the Appellate Division of the New York Supreme Court.]

WACHTLER, C. J.

. . . It is unrealistic to argue, as the School District and the United States Attorney General do, that a person has no reasonable expectation of privacy with respect to urine because it is a waste product periodically eliminated from the body. Although it is a waste product, it is not generally eliminated in public or in such a way that the public or government officials can gain access to it in order to "read" its contents. That is why the School District is requiring the teachers to preserve it and deliver it for inspection. It is settled that a person can have no reasonable expectation of privacy in things which are intentionally abandoned or discarded. But it does not follow from this rule that a person has no privacy interests in a waste product before it is abandoned and therefore no right to dispose of it in a way which maintains privacy. If that were true, documents which individuals and businesses periodically destroy would be entitled to no constitutional protection from government scrutiny.

We also reject the School District's contention that no search is involved when a person is required to provide a urine sample because urine, unlike blood, may be obtained without invading the person's body. That is not the only privacy interest the Constitution protects. The act of discharging urine is a private, indeed intimate one and the product may contain revealing information concerning an individual's personal life and habits for those capable of analyzing it. There is no question that requiring a person to disrobe and expose his body or body cavities, or to empty the contents of his pockets, involves a sufficient intrusion on privacy to constitute a search (*Bell v. Wolfish*, 441 US 520, 558). Requiring a person to urinate in the presence of a government official or agent, as is sometimes required in these cases, is at least as intrusive as a strip search. Even when the individual is permitted to perform the act in private, at the command and supervision of a person designated by the State, privacy interests are implicated. Ordering a person to empty his or her bladder and produce the urine in a container for inspection and analysis by public officials is no less offensive to personal dignity than requiring an individual to empty his pockets and produce a report containing the results of a urinalysis examination. In short, we conclude that the government's act of requiring a person to submit to urinalysis for drug abuse constitutes a search and seizure. The remaining question is what standard of reasonableness the State must meet before it can require an employee to submit to such a test.

Reasonableness generally requires that the State have probable cause and obtain a warrant before conducting a search and seizure. Under certain special circumstances, however, it may be reasonable to permit the government to search without a warrant on grounds not amounting to probable cause. In such instances the court must assess the reasons for the search and the extent to which it intrudes on legitimate privacy interests to determine whether, on balance, the government's action is reasonable.

. . . The School District has an interest in seeing that its teachers are fit and that drug abuse does not impair their ability to deal with the students. Teachers in this state are generally required to submit to an examination to determine their physical and mental fitness to perform their duties (Education Law, § 613). They therefore have a diminished expectation of privacy with respect to State inquiries into their physical fitness to perform as teachers, and it is not unreasonable to require teachers to submit to further testing when school authorities have reason to suspect that they are currently unfit for teaching duties. Thus we agree with the courts below that reasonable suspicion is an appropriate standard, and that probable cause and a warrant are not required before school officials can demand that a teacher submit to a urinalysis for potential drug abuse. . . .

The School District concededly did not have reasonable suspicion to believe that all or any of its probationary teachers were engaged in drug abuse. It claims, however, that reasonable suspicion is not required when a public employer chooses to test all employees in a particular category for potential drug abuse. . . .

The State has a legitimate interest in seeing that its employees are physically fit and that their performance is not impaired by illegal drug usage. The State also has a manifest interest in preventing crime and seeing that those who violate the law are brought to justice. There is little question that these goals would be more attainable if the State were able to search everyone periodically in an all-inclusive dragnet. If random searches of those apparently above suspicion were not effective, there would be little need to place constitutional limits upon the government's power to do so. By restricting the government to reasonable searches, the State and Federal Constitutions recognize that there comes a point at which searches intended to serve the public interest, however effective, may themselves undermine the public's interest in

maintaining the privacy, dignity, and security of its members. Thus random searches conducted by the State without reasonable suspicion are closely scrutinized, and generally only permitted when the privacy interests implicated are minimal, the government's interest is substantial, and safeguards are provided to ensure that the individual's reasonable expectation of privacy is not subjected to unregulated discretion (*People v. Scott, supra*). In this case those requirements have not been satisfied. . . .

Accordingly, the order of the Appellate Division should be
Affirmed.

CASE QUESTIONS

1. Was the testing required by the school district individualized-suspicion testing?
2. Did the court find that the testing constituted a search and seizure?
3. Must there be probable cause and a warrant before school officials can demand that an individual teacher submit to urinalysis for suspected drug abuse?
4. Why would a court prohibit random testing when it is an effective method of protecting the public interest against drug abuse?

NATIONAL TREASURY EMPLOYEES UNION v. VON RAAB

Supreme Court of the United States, 109 S.Ct. 1384 (1989).

[The United States Customs Service, which has as a primary enforcement mission the interdiction and seizure of illegal drugs smuggled into the country, has implemented a drug-screening program requiring urinalysis tests from Service employees seeking transfer or promotion to positions having a direct involvement in drug interdiction or requiring the incumbent to carry firearms or to handle "classified" material. Among other things, the program requires that an applicant be notified that selection is contingent upon

successful completion of drug screening. Petitioners, a federal employees' union, filed suit on behalf of Service employees alleging that the drug-testing program violated the Fourth Amendment. The District Court agreed and enjoined the program. The Court of Appeals vacated the injunction, holding that, although the program effects a search within the meaning of the Fourth Amendment, such searches are reasonable in light of their limited scope and the Service's strong interest in detecting drug use among employees in covered positions. The Supreme Court granted certiorari.]

KENNEDY, J. . . .

I.

. . . After an employee qualifies for a position covered by the Customs testing program, the Service advises him by letter that his final selection is contingent upon successful completion of drug screening. An independent contractor contacts the employee to fix the time and place for collecting the sample. On reporting for the test, the employee must produce photographic identification and remove any outer garments, such as a coat or a jacket, and personal belongings. The employee may produce the sample behind a partition, or in the privacy of a bathroom stall if he so chooses. To ensure against adulteration of the specimen, or substitution of a sample from another person, a monitor of the same sex as the employee remains close at hand to listen for the normal sounds of urination. Dye is added to toilet water to prevent the employee from using the water to adulterate the sample.

Upon receiving the specimen, the monitor inspects it to ensure its proper temperature and color, places a tamper-proof custody seal over the container, and affixes an identification label indicating the date and the individual's specimen number. The employee signs a chain-of-custody form, which is initialed by the monitor, and the urine sample is placed in a plastic bag, sealed, and submitted to a laboratory.

The laboratory tests the sample for the presence of marijuana, cocaine, opiates, amphetamines, and phencyclidine. Two tests are used. An initial screening test uses the enzyme-multiplied-immunoassay technique (EMIT). Any specimen that is identified as positive on this initial test must then be confirmed using gas chromatography/mass spectrometry (GC/MS). Confirmed positive results are reported to a "Medical Review Officer," "[a] licensed physician . . . who has knowledge of substance abuse

disorders and has appropriate medical training to interpret and evaluate the individual's positive test result together with his or her medical history and any other relevant biomedical information." HHS Reg. § 1.2, 53 Fed.Reg. 11980 (1988); HHS Reg. § 2.4(g), id., at 11983. After verifying the positive result, the Medical Review Officer transmits it to the agency.

Customs employees who test positive for drugs and who can offer no satisfactory explanation are subject to dismissal from the Service. Test results may not, however, be turned over to any other agency, including criminal prosecutors, without the employee's written consent.

II.

In *Skinner v. Railway Labor Executives Assn.*, 109 S.Ct. 1402, 1412–1413, decided today, we hold that federal regulations requiring employees of private railroads to produce urine samples for chemical testing implicate the Fourth Amendment, as those tests invade reasonable expectations of privacy. Our earlier cases have settled that the Fourth Amendment protects individuals from unreasonable searches conducted by the Government, even when the Government acts as an employer, and, in view of our holding in *Railway Labor Executives* that urine tests are searches, it follows that the Customs Service's drug testing program must meet the reasonableness requirement of the Fourth Amendment.

While we have often emphasized, and reiterate today, that a search must be supported, as a general matter, by a warrant issued upon probable cause, our decision in *Railway Labor Executives* reaffirms the long-standing principle that neither a warrant nor probable cause, nor, indeed, any measure of individualized suspicion, is an indispensable component of reasonableness in every circumstance.

As we note in *Railway Labor Executives*, our cases establish that where a Fourth Amendment intrusion serves special governmental needs, beyond the normal need for law enforcement, it is necessary to balance the individual's privacy expectations against the Government's interest to determine whether it is impractical to require a warrant or some level of individualized suspicion in the particular context. *Ante*, at 1413–1414.

It is clear that the Customs Service's drug testing program is not designed to serve the ordinary needs of law enforcement. Test results may not be used in a criminal prosecution of the employee without the employee's consent. The purposes of the program are to deter drug use among those eligible for promotion to sensitive positions within the Service and to prevent the promotion of drug users to those positions. These substantial interests, no less than the Government's concern for safe rail transportation at issue in *Railway Labor Executives*, present a special need that may justify departure from the ordinary warrant and probable cause requirements. . . .

Even where it is reasonable to dispense with the warrant requirement in the particular circumstances, a search ordinarily must be based on probable cause. *Ante*, at 1416. Our cases teach, however, that the probable-cause standard " 'is peculiarly related to criminal investigations.' " *Colorado v. Bertine*, 479 U.S. 367, 371, 107 S.Ct. 738, 741, 93 L.Ed.2d 739 (1987). In particular, the traditional probable-cause standard may be unhelpful in analyzing the reasonableness of routine administrative functions, *Colorado v. Bertine, supra*, 479 U.S., at 371.

. . . The Customs Service is our Nation's first line of defense against one of the greatest problems affecting the health and welfare of our population. We have adverted before to "the veritable national crisis in law enforcement caused by smuggling of illicit narcotics." *United States v. Montoya de Hernandez*, 473 U.S. 531, 538, 105 S.Ct. 3304, 3309, 87 L.Ed.2d 381 (1985). Our cases also reflect the traffickers' seemingly inexhaustible repertoire of deceptive practices and elaborate schemes for importing narcotics. . . .

It is readily apparent that the Government has a compelling interest in ensuring that frontline interdiction personnel are physically fit, and have unimpeachable integrity and judgment. . . .

A drug user's indifference to the Service's basic mission or, even worse, his active complicity with the malefactors, can facilitate importation of sizable drug shipments or block apprehension of dangerous criminals. The public interest demands effective measures to bar drug users from positions directly involving the interdiction of illegal drugs.

The public interest likewise demands effective measures to prevent the promotion of drug users to positions that require the incumbent to carry a firearm, even if the incumbent is not engaged directly in the interdiction of drugs. Customs employees who may use deadly force plainly "discharge duties fraught with such risks of injury to others that even a momentary lapse of attention can have disastrous consequences." *Ante*, at 1419. We agree with the Government that the public should not bear the risk that employees who may suffer from impaired perception and judgment will be promoted to positions where they may need to employ deadly force. Indeed, ensuring against the creation of this dangerous risk will itself further Fourth Amendment values, as the use of deadly force may violate the Fourth Amendment in certain circumstances.

Against these valid public interests we must weight the interference with individual liberty that results from requiring these classes of employees to undergo a urine test. The interference with individual privacy that results from the collection of a urine sample for subsequent chemical analysis could be substantial in some circumstances. *Ante*, at 1418. We have recognized, however, that the "operational realities of the workplace" may render entirely reasonable certain work-related intrusions by supervisors and co-workers that might be viewed as unreasonable in other contexts. While these operational realities will rarely affect an employee's expectations of privacy with respect to searches of his person, or of personal effects that the employee may bring to the workplace, *id.*, at 716, 725, 107 S.Ct., at 1498, 1502, it is plain that certain forms of public employment may diminish privacy expectations even with respect to such personal searches. Employees of the United States Mint, for example, should expect to be subject to certain routine personal searches when they leave the workplace every day. . . .

We think Customs employees who are directly involved in the interdiction of illegal drugs or who are required to carry firearms in the line of duty likewise have a diminished expectation of privacy in respect to the intrusions occasioned by a urine test. Unlike most private citizens or government employees in general, employees involved in drug interdiction reasonably should expect effective inquiry into their fitness and probity. Much the same is true of employees who are required to carry firearms. Because successful performance of their duties depends uniquely on their judgment and dexterity, these employees cannot reasonably expect to keep from the Service personal information that bears directly on their fitness. Cf. In re *Caruso v. Ward*, 72 N.Y.2d 433, 441, 534 N.Y.S.2d 142, 146–148, 530 N.E.2d 850, 854–855 (1988). While reasonable tests designed to elicit this information doubtless infringe some privacy expectations, we do not believe these expectations outweigh the Government's compelling interests in safety and in the integrity of our borders.*

III.

Where the Government requires its employees to produce urine samples to be analyzed for evidence of illegal drug use, the collection and subsequent chemical analysis of such samples are searches that must meet the reasonableness requirement of the Fourth Amendment. Because the testing program adopted by the Customs Service is not designed to serve the ordinary needs of law enforcement, we have balanced the public interest in the Service's testing program against the privacy concerns implicated by the tests, without reference to our usual presumption in favor of the procedures specified in the Warrant Clause, to assess whether the tests required by Customs are reasonable.

We hold that the suspicionless testing of employees who apply for promotion to positions directly involving the interdiction of illegal drugs, or to positions which require the incumbent to carry a firearm, is reasonable. The Government's compelling interests in preventing the promotion of drug users to positions where they might endanger the integrity of our Nation's borders or the life of the citizenry outweigh the privacy interests of those who seek promotion to these positions, who enjoy a diminished expectation of privacy by virtue of the

---

*The procedures prescribed by the Customs Service for the collection and analysis of the requisite samples do not carry the grave potential for "arbitrary and oppressive interference with the privacy and personal security of individuals," United States v. Martinez-Fuerte, 428 U.S. 543, 554, 96 S.Ct. 3074, 3081, 49 L.Ed.2d 1116 (1976), that the Fourth Amendment was designed to prevent. Indeed, these procedures significantly minimize the program's intrusion on privacy interests. Only employees who have been tentatively accepted for promotion or transfer to one of the three categories of covered positions are tested, and applicants know at the outset that a drug test is a requirement of those positions. Employees are also notified in advance of the scheduled sample collection, thus reducing to a minimum any "unsettling show of authority." Delaware v. Prouse, 440 U.S. 648, 657, 99 S.Ct. 1391, 1398, 59 L.Ed.2d 660 (1979), that may

be associated with unexpected intrusions on privacy. Cf. United States v. Martinez-Fuerte, *supra*, 428 U.S., at 559, 96 S.Ct. at 3083 (noting that the intrusion on privacy occasioned by routine highway checkpoints is minimized by the fact that motorists "are not taken by surprise as they know, or may obtain knowledge of, the location of the checkpoints and will not be stopped elsewhere"); Wyman v. James, 400 U.S. 309, 320–321, 91 S.Ct. 381, 387–388, 27 L.Ed.2d 408 (1971) (providing a welfare recipient with advance notice that she would be visited by a welfare caseworker minimized the intrusion on privacy occasioned by the visit). There is no direct observation of the act of urination, as the employee may provide a specimen in the privacy of a stall.

Further, urine samples may be examined only for the specified drugs. The use of samples to test for any other substances is prohibited. See HHS Reg. § 2.1(c), 53 Fed.Reg. 11980 (1988). And, as the court of appeals noted, the combination of EMIT and GC/MS tests required by the Service is highly accurate, assuming proper storage, handling, and measurement techniques. 816 F.2d at 181. Finally, an employee need not disclose personal medical information to the Government unless his test result is positive, and even then any such information is reported to a licensed physician. Taken together, these procedures significantly minimize the intrusiveness of the Service's drug screening program.

special, and obvious, physical and ethical demands of those positions. We do not decide whether testing those who apply for promotion to positions where they would handle "classified" information is reasonable because we find the record inadequate for this purpose.

The judgment of the Court of Appeals for the Fifth Circuit is affirmed in part and vacated in part, and the case is remanded for further proceedings consistent with this opinion.

It is so ordered.

Justice MARSHALL, with whom Justice BRENNAN joins, dissenting.

For the reasons stated in my dissenting opinion in *Skinner v. Railway Labor Executives Association,* I also dissent from the Court's decision in this case. Here, as in *Skinner,* the Court's abandonment of the Fourth Amendment's express requirement that searches of the person rest on probable cause is unprincipled and unjustifiable. . . .

Justice SCALIA, with whom Justice STEVENS joins, dissenting.

The issue in this case is not whether Customs Service employees can constitutionally be denied promotion, or even dismissed, for a single instance of unlawful drug use, at home or at work. They assuredly can. The issue here is what steps can constitutionally be taken to *detect* such drug use. The Government asserts it can demand that employees perform "an excretory function traditionally shielded by great privacy," *Skinner v. Railway Labor Executives' Assn.,* 109 S.Ct., at 1418, while "a monitor of the same sex . . . remains close at hand to listen for the normal sounds," *ante,* at 1388, and that the excretion thus produced be turned over to the Government for chemical analysis. The Court agrees that this constitutes a search for purposes of the Fourth Amendment—and I think it obvious that it is a type of search par-

ticularly destructive of privacy and offensive to personal dignity.

Until today this Court had upheld a bodily search separate from arrest and without individualized suspicion of wrongdoing only with respect to prison inmates, relying upon the uniquely dangerous nature of that environment. Today, in *Skinner,* we allow a less intrusive bodily search of railroad employees involved in train accidents. I joined the Court's opinion there because the demonstrated frequency of drug and alcohol use by the targeted class of employees, and the demonstrated connection between such use and grave harm, rendered the search a reasonable means of protecting society. I decline to join the Court's opinion in the present case because neither frequency of use nor connection to harm is demonstrated or even likely. In my view the Customs Service rules are a kind of immolation of privacy and human dignity in symbolic opposition to drug use. . . .

Those who lose because of the lack of understanding that begot the present exercise in symbolism are not just the Customs Service employees, whose dignity is thus offended, but all of us—who suffer a coarsening of our national manners that ultimately give the Fourth Amendment its content, and who become subject to the administration of federal officials whose respect for our privacy can hardly be greater than the small respect they have been taught to have for their own.

CASE QUESTIONS

1. Summarize the testing procedures utilized by the Customs Service.
2. Is the GC/MS test almost always accurate?
3. What "special needs" were identified by the Court that could justify departure from the ordinary warrant and probable cause requirements?
4. In your own words, explain Justice Scalia's concern about those "who lose because of the lack of understanding that begot the present exercise in symbolism. . . ."

SECTION 38—ALCOHOL ABUSE AND EMPLOYEE ASSISTANCE PROGRAMS

Alcohol abuse in the workplace is the cause of many deaths, injuries, and lost workdays and much unsatisfactory worker performance. The economic costs to employers are significant. Most employers publicize and enforce plant or company rules prohibiting the use or possession of alcoholic beverages (and drugs) while on duty or subject to duty. Through the observations of an employee, such as an unsteady or staggering walk, slurred speech, bloodshot eyes, and the odor of alcohol on the breath, supervisors are often able to identify an employee who has been apparently violating the employer's no-alcohol rule. Commonly employers require two supervisors to observe the employee, and where their observations indicate a rule violation, the supervisors will confront the employee and offer the employee the opportunity to vindicate himself or herself by taking a blood-alcohol test. Employees who violate an employer's no-alcohol rule are subject to major discipline up to and including discharge.

Most employers have made major investments in the selection and training of their employees. It is in the employer's best interest to retain valuable employees by providing a rehabilitation program for those employees who suffer from alcohol abuse. Employee assistance programs (EAPs) exist in most major companies to help troubled employees overcome difficulties such as drug and alcohol abuse, work and family tensions, eating disorders, gambling addictions, and financial and other problems.

The recovery rate from alcohol abuse under EAPs has been determined to be as high as 80 percent. Employers, cooperating unions, and the individual participants are pleased with the success of the EAPs in dealing with alcohol problems. Instead of disciplining or discharging employees for the no-alcohol rule violation on a first offense, the matter is commonly handled through the EAP, with the employee signing a conditional reinstatement agreement under which the employee, after a period of hospitalization at a rehabilitation facility, promises to abide by the rehabilitation program. Should the employee fail to do so, the employee agrees and acknowledges that she or he may be subject to termination.

Where an employee is unwilling to participate in an employee assistance program and where there is a collective bargaining agreement with a just-cause provision restricting the employer's right to discharge, the employee may be discharged for the no-alcohol rule violation. If the observations of two supervisors indicate a problem concerning the demeanor of an employee and if the odor of alcohol is present on the employee's breath, as discussed above, there is probable cause for the employer to seek a blood-alcohol test. Under such circumstances no serious challenge to the decision to test can be raised at an arbitration hearing. Absent mitigating or unusual circumstances, the discharge of the employee will likely be upheld in arbitration.

Incidents such as accidents or major safety rule violations may also trigger an employer's testing program, and where impairment due to alcohol is found through a test, the EAP procedures may also be followed. In the case of serious accidents or injuries caused by alcohol or drug impairment, reinstatement to employment may not be offered, absent an agreement to the contrary.

The misconduct involved in the *Brotherhood of Locomotive Engineers* arbitration decision, presented in this section, led to the criminal conviction of the engineer. The misconduct stirred a national dialogue on the issue of alcohol and drug testing for operating employees in the transportation industries.

BROTHERHOOD OF LOCOMOTIVE ENGINEERS AND ILLINOIS CENTRAL GULF RAILROAD

PLB 3538, No. 2 (NMB, July 3, 1984).

FROM THE FINDINGS OF THE ARBITRATION BOARD:

The record before the Board indicates that on September 27, 1982, the Claimant, Engineer E. P. Robertson and crew went on duty about 7:00 P.M. at McComb, Mississippi, to take a train to Baton Rouge, Louisiana. They went off duty at 10:40 P.M. at Baton Rouge and were immediately transported to their designated lodging at the Prince Murat Inn to rest because, according to the usual routine of their assignment, they would be required after the rest period to work the return assignment back to McComb. The crew was thereafter called at 2:30 A.M., September 28, and listed for work at 3:30 A.M.

The testimony indicates that Mr. Robertson did not take his rest when he arrived at the motel; and that he and Brakeman Reeves went to the motel bar and stayed until midnight. He drank at least one drink and ordered a drink to go in a plastic cup, according to the testimony of the bartender Mr. J. D. Morales and the waitress Ms. K. M. Sword. Sometime after midnight, he and Mr. Reeves met with Clerk Janet Byrd, and it developed that he, Brakeman Reeves, and Ms. Byrd boarded the cab of the locomotive together. The crew had been called at 2:30 A.M., listed for work at 3:30 A.M., and departed Baton Rouge at 4:15 A.M. Ms. Byrd later told company officials that Mr. Robertson invited Ms. Byrd to "run" the engine.

At approximately 5:05 A.M. on September 28, 1982, the train Extra 9629 East (GS-2-28) derailed 43 cars on the single main track of the Hammond District in Livingston, Louisiana. Of the derailed cars, 36 were tank cars; 27 of these cars contained various regulated hazardous materials, and 5 contained flammable petroleum products. Fires broke out in the wreckage, and smoke and toxic gases were released into the atmosphere. Explosions of two tank cars that had not been punctured caused them to rocket violently. Some 3000 persons living within a five-mile radius of the derailment site were evacuated for as long as two weeks. Nineteen residences and other buildings in Livingston were destroyed or severely damaged. Toxic chemical products were spilled and absorbed into the ground requiring extensive excavation of contaminated soil and its transportation to a distant dump site. This caused the closing of the track for a year; and the derailment costs to the Carrier are presently over $25,000,000, with several lawsuits pending.

The Carrier does not hold that Mr. Robertson caused the derailment, for its experts determined that the derailment was caused by equipment failure. The Carrier did, however, find that Mr. Robertson was responsible for three serious rule violations: (1) drinking while subject to duty [Rule G], (2) speeding at several locations during his trip, and (3) allowing an unauthorized passenger to ride in the locomotive. We find that substantial evidence of record exists to support the Carrier's findings in this case.

Two employees from the Prince Murat Inn, J. D. Morales and Kelly M. Sword, testified that two drinks were served to Mr. Robertson containing one and one-half ounces of alcohol, one he drank at the bar and the other was put in a plastic glass to go. Mr. Robertson knew full well that he was on a short layover and that he was subject to duty, after a limited rest period. When an engineer, entrusted with the responsibility for a train, and particularly when entrusted with responsibility for a train containing hazardous chemicals, spends a portion of his short layover in a bar drinking any amount of alcohol, he is guilty of the highest degree of irresponsibility. Such is a clear violation of Rule G, for that employee is "subject to duty" within the explicit language of that rule. Clearly one drink by an employee subject to duty causes some impairment of that individual, and the Carrier and the public have a right not to have a train operated by an individual impaired to any degree. Mr. Robertson acted in a most irresponsible manner by purchasing alcoholic beverages while subject to duty and he was clearly in violation of Rule G.

The evidence of record, including the testimony of Supervisor of Communications R. L. Mont and Supervisor Instructor A. J. Puth, make it evident that Mr. Robertson's train was operated well beyond the timetable authorized at several locations during the trip. . . .

. . . Mr. Robertson's widely publicized misconduct not only caused a national embarrassment to the Illinois Central Gulf Railroad, but tarnished the high professional reputation of locomotive engineers throughout the Country. The discipline of dismissal is appropriate.

Claim denied.

CASE QUESTIONS

1. Company Rule G prohibits the use of alcohol or drugs not only while on duty but also while "subject to duty." Give your opinion as to whether an employer can properly regulate the actions of its employees when they are off duty and not being paid.
2. Should Engineer Robertson be returned to service upon successful completion of the EAP alcohol rehabilitation program?

SECTION 39—POLYGRAPH EXAMINATIONS

Law enforcement and security agencies do not want to hire individuals who have sold or who use illegal drugs because drug-impaired judgment would adversely affect law enforcement duties and may lead to compromised operations. A large segment of society believes that there is an inherent contradiction in lawbreakers being hired to enforce the law. Some law enforcement and security agencies believe that preemployment polygraph testing is an effective tool in finding out whether certain applicants should be disqualified for employment. The applicants may truthfully admit drug sales or drug use during the polygraph examination, or where no admissions are made during the examination, the polygraph examiners may find that certain applicants are "deceptive."

Employers believe that polygraph examinations are one of the best tools that management has at its disposal to investigate thefts and related workplace misconduct. The problem is that there is no widely accepted evidence establishing the scientific validity of polygraph testing, and the utility of such testing is debatable and, indeed, is much debated.[21]

---

[21] See *Anderson v. Philadelphia*, 845 F.2d 1216 (3d Cir. 1988).

In a polygraph examination a relative increase in heart rate, respiration, and perspiration when theft-related or economic-loss-related questions are asked is interpreted as a sign of guilt. Opponents of polygraph testing point out that errors may result when an innocent person, who believes that the test could be wrong, out of fear exhibits an increase in heart rate, respiration, and perspiration when asked such incident-related questions.[22]

State Laws

Some 25 states and the District of Columbia either prohibit or restrict the use of polygraphs in employment matters. In the *Anderson v. Philadelphia* decision, presented in this section, the United States Court of Appeals rejected employment applicants' constitutional challenges to a state law that forbade preemployment polygraph testing except for public law enforcement agencies. The court deferred to the state legislature's judgment to allow polygraph testing in the limited circumstances of law enforcement. Where a state statute prohibits requiring a polygraph as a condition of employment, an employer who terminates or adversely affects employees who refuse to take such examinations may be found liable under a "public policy" tort theory for back pay, damages for emotional distress, and punitive damages.[23]

Polygraph Examinations and the Right to Privacy

In *Thorne v. City of El Segundo*,[24] the Ninth Circuit Court of Appeals held that Thorne's First Amendment rights to privacy and free association were abridged when she was denied the opportunity to become a city police officer after she was required to disclose information regarding personal sexual matters during a polygraph examination.

Federal Laws

The federal Employee Polygraph Protection Act of 1988 (EPPA)[25] makes it unlawful for private employers to use preemployment lie detector (polygraph) tests while screening applicants for employment or to take any disciplinary action or deny employment or promotion to any individual who refuses to take a polygraph test. However, federal, state, and local government employers are exempt from any restrictions on the use of polygraph tests, and the federal government may also test private consultants under contract to the Defense Department, CIA, FBI, the National Security Agency, or the Department of Energy. The law also permits private security firms and drug companies to administer polygraph tests to job applicants and employees.

Under the law a limited exemption exists that allows employers to request an employee to submit to a polygraph test if (1) the test is administrated in connection with an ongoing investigation involving economic loss or injury to an employer's business,

---

[22] P. Ekman, *Telling Lies* (New York: Berkley, 1985), 201–206.
[23] *Moniodis v. Cook*, 1 ITER Cases 441 (Md. Ct. Spec. App. 1985).
[24] 726 F.2d 459 (9th Cir. 1983).
[25] Public Law No. 100-347, signed into law on June 27, 1988.

such as theft or embezzlement; (2) the employee had access to the property in question; (3) the employer has "reasonable suspicion" of the employee; and (4) the employer gives a written statement to the employee of the basis for its reasonable suspicion.

The EPPA also deals with a number of objections to the testing process itself. To avoid short, incomplete, and unfair tests, the law requires that tests last at least 90 minutes.[26] Because examiners have sometimes asked offensive questions about sexual preferences and practices, racial matters, religious beliefs, or political or union affiliations or beliefs, the law prohibits questions on such topics.[27] Section 8 of the EPPA sets forth detailed procedures that must be followed prior to, during, and following any lie detector test permitted under the limited exception for "ongoing investigations."

The law authorizes civil suits to enforce the Act and to make whole adversely affected individuals, including the payment of lost wages and benefits. An employer who violates the Act may also be assessed a civil penalty of up to $10,000 as determined by the Secretary of Labor.[28]

The law does not preempt any state or local law or collective bargaining agreement that prohibits lie detector tests or is more restrictive than the federal law.

ANDERSON v. PHILADELPHIA

United States Court of Appeals, 845 F.2d 1216 (3d Cir. 1988).

[Pennsylvania law forbids the use of polygraph testing for preemployment screening by any private or public employer. An exception exists, however, for public law enforcement agencies. The City of Philadelphia police and prison departments base their hiring on the results of a competitive civil service examination with individuals passing this test being placed on a certified eligibility list. As openings occur, individuals ranked high on the eligibility lists are notified and must then pass a number of additional tests before being found qualified for employment. These additional tests include a medical examination, a psychiatric examination, a background investigation, and, usually last in the process, a polygraph test. As part of the background investigation, candidates must fill out a Personal Data Questionnaire (PDQ), which includes questions about family and financial status;

driving record; educational and employment history; criminal record; use of alcoholic beverages; and the use, sale, and possession of illicit drugs. Candidates are given prior notification of the content of the PDQ, including the questions relating to illicit drugs. Candidates are also informed that deception or falsification in answering PDQ/polygraph questions may result in rejection. The police and prison departments will hire otherwise qualified individuals who admit that they have used or possessed drugs over six months before completing the PDQ and taking the polygraph. The plaintiffs claim that the use of the polygraph test results in order to deny them employment deprives them of their constitutional rights to procedural and substantive due process and equal protection of law. After a bench trial the district court held in favor of the plaintiffs, and the city appealed.]

---

[26] Section 8(b)(5).
[27] Section 8(b)11(c).
[28] Section 6(a).

STAPLETON, C. J.

I.

... The polygraph testing procedures currently used by both the police and prison departments were developed in 1983 in the course of settling class actions by blacks and Hispanics who had brought suit alleging that the Philadelphia Police Department's hiring and promotion policies were discriminatory. These settlements require the above-described prior notification concerning the PDQ/polygraph questions, and require that if during the test the polygraph examiner finds the applicant "deceptive," the applicant must be told immediately and given a chance to explain, deny, or admit the deception. If the applicant denies being deceptive, or if the explanation is found unsatisfactory by the examiner, the applicant must have the opportunity to retake the test with a second examiner. The second examiner does not review the results of the first prior to readministering the polygraph. If the second examiner finds no deception, the applicant is considered to have passed; if the second examiner also finds the applicant deceptive, that finding is ordinarily final and preclusive of employment. The applicant may, however, appeal to either the Police Department's Review Panel or to the Superintendent of Prisons or the prison review panel, and the reviewers may decide to give the applicant the opportunity to take a third test. If the applicant is found deceptive on a third test, he or she will not be hired. Deception is found on about half of all the tests given.

During a pre-test interview, applicants are asked if there is any other information they would like to provide. During a post-test review, if deception is indicated, they are asked again if there is any information they are withholding. Admissions to disqualifying information were made during these interviews by 315 of the 1028 applicants for positions with the Police Department in 1985, and 251 of the 619 applicants in 1986.

... The results of the tests are not made public, but are used only within the departments for evaluating the suitability of the applicant for employment.

There is considerable controversy about the validity and reliability of polygraph testing. The polygraph measures stress or anxiety, which in many cases may not correlate very well with deception. In 1983, Congress' Office of Technology Assessment put out a Technical Memorandum on polygraph testing, which read in part as follows:

There are two major reasons why an overall measure of validity is not possible. First, the polygraph test is, in reality, a very complex process that is much more than the instrument. Although the instrument is essentially the same for all applications, the types of individuals tested, training of the examiner, purpose of the test, and types of questions asked, among other factors, can differ substantially. A polygraph test requires that the examiner infer deception or truthfulness based on a comparison of the person's physiological responses to various questions. . . . Second, the research on polygraph validity varies widely in terms of not only results, but also in the quality of research design and methodology. Thus, conclusions about scientific validity can be made only in the context of specific applications and even then must be tempered by the limitations of available research evidence.

. . . OTA concluded that the available research evidence does not establish the scientific validity of the polygraph test for personnel security screening.

. . . [D]espite many decades of judicial, legislative, and scientific discussion, no consensus has emerged about the accuracy of polygraph tests.

App. at 618, 652, Professor Leonard Saxe, who headed the OTA group, testified as an expert witness for the plaintiffs. According to Professor Saxe, polygraph tests are likely to find many truthful applicants deceptive (false positives) and some unknown lesser, though "potentially large," number of deceptive applicants truthful (false negatives). App. at 344. When polygraphs are used for pre-employment screening, the risk of false positive results is generally thought to be higher than that of false negative results.

The City's law enforcement departments consider polygraph tests reliable and valid. An additional advantage of using the polygraph test, in the department's view, is that it encourages applicants to be candid in responding to questions on the PDQ. The departments do not believe that this secondary advantage can be separated from the trustworthiness that they consider to be the main advantage of the polygraph. Both advantages, the departments believe, enable them to acquire necessary information about potential employees.

The department's experts do admit that polygraph testing is not perfect. While they recognize the impossibility of conducting error-free polygraph testing, however, they correctly point out that there is no evidence establishing that the polygraph is not valid. Moreover, they point out that there must be some method of acquiring the information necessary to make choices among applicants and stress that the decision to utilize a polygraph examination must be evaluated in light of the available alternatives. One of the department's experts, Dr. Frank Horvath, noted that

there is also little scientific support for many of the procedures which are used in employment screening. There is little "scientific" evidence, for instance, to show that background investigations actually yield accurate information or that psychiatric interviews accurately discriminate between "good" and "bad" candidates. On the other hand, there is considerable scientific data to show that personal interviews as generally used in employment screening are unreliable; yet, employers continue to carry out such interviews. Written psychological tests, moreover, have received considerable research attention which, according to many, shows little scientific support for their use.

App. at 398. . . .

II.

. . . In *Board of Regents v. Roth*, the Supreme Court made it clear that "[t]he requirements of procedural due process apply only to the deprivation of interests encompassed by the Four-teenth Amendment's protection of liberty and property." 408 U.S. 564, 569 (1972). According to the Court, "to determine whether due process requirements apply in the first place, we must look . . . to the *nature* of the interest at stake." *Id.* at 571. In this case, the plaintiffs have alleged that they have been deprived of both property and liberty interests by the City departments' use of the polygraph test to disqualify them from employment.

Property Interest.

. . . While the departments were bound to consider the plaintiffs for employment, they were by no means bound to hire the plaintiffs. The plaintiffs can cite to no section of the Pennsylvania statutes which sets an objective standard for the hiring or rejection of applicants from the eligibility lists, and which might thereby create a legitimate claim of entitlement to employment. On the contrary, under the state law applicable here, agencies such as the defendant departments may and do exercise broad discretion in hiring. . . .

[W]e find nothing in the departmental hiring practices or in Pennsylvania law that establishes a legitimate claim of entitlement to employment in applicants like the plaintiffs. We therefore conclude that the plaintiffs' interest in the civil service positions they sought did not rise to the level of a property interest protected by the Constitution.

Liberty Interest.

On the subject of liberty interests in employment, this court has stated that

[a]n employment action implicates a fourteenth amendment liberty interest only if it (1) is based on a "charge against [the individual] that might seriously damage his standing and associations in the community . . . for example, [by implying] that he had been guilty of dishonesty, or immorality," or (2) "impose[s] on him a stigma or other disability that forecloses his freedom to take advantage of other employment opportunities."

Robb, 733 F.2d at 294 (citing *Roth*, 408 U.S. at 573)....

In this case, plaintiffs assert that they have been "branded as liars" on account of their failure to pass the polygraph examination. While the polygraph results might conceivably be viewed as stigmatizing the plaintiffs or damaging their reputations, the plaintiffs have not alleged that any of their polygraph test results were made public. Rather, the departments' assertion that the polygraph results are kept confidential and undisclosed stands unchallenged. Given that, we find untenable the plaintiffs' claim that they have been deprived of a liberty interest.

We conclude that the City's polygraph requirement does not violate the plaintiffs' right to procedural due process, since no protected property or liberty interest of the plaintiffs is at stake.

III.

We next address the plaintiff's argument that they have been denied equal protection of the law.... The plaintiffs bear the burden of proof on this issue, and so must show that the requirements imposed by law or regulation "so lack rationality that they constitute a constitutionally impermissible denial of equal protection." Rogin v. Bensalem Township, 616 F.2d 680, 688 (3d Cir. 1980). In considering this issue, we bear in mind the Court's statement that a statute or regulation should not be overturned on equal protection grounds "unless the varying treatment of different groups or persons is so unrelated to the achievement of any combination of legitimate purposes that we can only conclude that the legislature's actions were irrational." Vance v. Bradley, 440 U.S. 93, 97 (1979).

The defendants stress, and the plaintiffs acknowledge, that the public has a legitimate and, indeed, compelling interest in hiring applicants who are qualified for employment as public law enforcement officers. It is this interest that the polygraph requirement is said to serve. The key question we confront here, therefore, is whether the requirement that applicants pass a polygraph test can arguably be said to result in a better-qualified group of new employees. The defendant City departments need not show that the polygraph requirement does in fact result in the selection of a better-qualified group of new employees. Rather, the burden is on the plaintiff applicants to show that the department's use of the polygraph could not reasonably be believed to produce a better-qualified group of new hires than would be chosen absent the polygraph requirement.

It is clear that the district court placed the burden on the wrong party in this case, since a necessary stepping-stone to that court's holding was its conclusion that "[t]he testimony, exhibits and evidence presented at the trial failed to prove the reliability of polygraph tests in general." App. at 706, 709....

Professor Saxe's testimony supports the proposition that the validity and reliability of polygraph testing as a device to screen prospective employees have not been scientifically established. It does not demonstrate, however, that it is irrational to believe that the polygraph has utility in connection with the selection of law enforcement officers. First, Professor Saxe acknowledges that "virtually no research has been conducted on the validity of polygraph tests to screen prospective employees." App. at 354, and it is, accordingly, apparent that such testing has not been empirically established as invalid or unreliable. Moreover, Professor Saxe does not dispute that preemployment polygraph screening is widely used by intelligence and law enforcement agencies which consider it useful in eliminating unqualified candidates. The record indicates that such screening is used by the National Security Administration, the Central Intelligence Agency, and approximately 50% of police departments throughout the nation. Finally, Professor Saxe does not dispute Dr. Horvath's assertion that "both proponents and opponents maintain that such testing can distinguish between truthful and deceptive persons with an accuracy greater than chance." App. at 394....

. . . As Dr. Horvath put it,

the important practical issue is not whether polygraph testing is 95% or 90% or even 70% accurate but whether relative to other methods it yields a reasonable degree of accuracy and whether there is another more suitable method of accomplishing the same objective.

App. at 397. The record in this case provides no basis for concluding that superior alternatives are available.

. . . [W]e think it rational for the departments to believe that the polygraph requirement results in fuller, more candid disclosures on the PDQ and thus provides additional information that is helpful in selecting qualified law enforcement officers.

In sum, from the plaintiffs' perspective, the most that can be said on the basis of this record is that the utility of polygraph testing in the pre-employment screening of candidates for law enforcement positions is a debatable and much-debated issue. In such situations, legislators and administrators are free to exercise their judgment regarding the manner in which the public interest will best be served. *Ginsberg v. New York*, 390 U.S. 629, 642–43 (1967) (where causal link between pornography and impaired ethical and moral development of youth is debatable, courts "do not demand of legisla-

tures 'scientifically certain criteria of legislation' " and will not overturn the legislative judgment). Accordingly, we conclude that in the absence of a scientific consensus, reasonable law enforcement administrators may choose to include a polygraph requirement in their hiring process without offending the equal protection clause. . . .

IV.

For the foregoing reasons, we reverse the judgment of the district court and remand with instructions that judgment be entered for the defendants.

CASE QUESTIONS

1. Did the congressional Office of Technology Assessment (OTA) Memorandum conclude that the evidence established the scientific validity of polygraph tests for personnel security screening?
2. Does the city believe that polygraph tests encourage applicants to be candid in responding to questions on the PDQ?
3. Did the court conclude that the city's polygraph test requirement violated the plaintiff's right to procedural due process having been deprived of a "liberty interest"?
4. Was it important to the outcome of this case that the plaintiffs had the burden of proof?

SECTION 40—EMPLOYEE DEFAMATION CLAIMS

Individuals whose employment is terminated by their employers may join claims based on exceptions to the employment-at-will doctrine and a claim based on Title VII, the ADEA, or a violation of their constitutional right to privacy. In addition, such individuals may also pursue a claim based on "defamation." Employee defamation claims commonly stem from unfavorable evaluations, investigations of workplace misconduct, and negative references. In the *Michaelson v. Minnesota Mining and Manufacturing Co.* case, presented in this section, the plaintiff brought an action against his employer based on exceptions to the employment-at-will doctrine, and in addition thereto, he brought a defamation suit resulting from a letter identifying deficiencies in his job performance.

Defamation consists of a false statement about the plaintiff which is communicated—"published"—to a third party and which tends to harm the plaintiff's reputation or standing in the community. Thus, falsely accusing an employee in front of others of improper conduct such as theft or dishonesty on the job is defamatory per se. While heavily veiled references to "certain parties" stealing from the company may not be actionable because a specific individual is not reasonably identifiable in such a statement, the statement "a certain head of the accounting department is skimming from the till" is clearly actionable.[29]

Absolute and Conditional Privileges

An *absolute privilege* provides a complete defense against a defamation suit, even though the statement turns out to be false or is in reckless disregard for the rights of the defamed person. This privilege is ordinarily limited to statements made in the course of litigation, legislative proceedings, or administrative agency hearings.

A *conditional privilege* exists in situations where the publisher of the statement and the recipient share a legitimate business interest in the information exchanged, provided it is made in good faith and without a willful design to defame. Employers have a conditional privilege concerning employee evaluations, investigations of misconduct, and references.

Employee Evaluations

Employers and their managers are conditionally privileged to communicate frankly about the skills, performance, and qualifications of their employees. The employer is entitled to appraisals of employees' character, as well. However, sound business judgment dictates that sensitive communications should be strictly confined to those who need to know. The burden of proof is on the employee to show that the defamatory statements were made recklessly or that they were excessively published.

Investigation of Misconduct in the Workforce

Employers have a duty to maintain safe and healthful working conditions under OSHA. They also have a duty to maintain a workforce free of sexual harassment. Employers thus have a duty to conduct investigations into safety and sexual harassment matters. Numerous other circumstances arise where either the employer has a duty to investigate or sound business judgment requires an investigation into possible workplace wrongdoing. The employer has a conditional privilege to conduct prudent, discreet, and well-meaning investigations into such matters. Where defamatory facts result, the publisher-employer's actual belief in their truth, or the absence of recklessness in holding and expressing the belief, will generally preserve the conditional privilege.

References

Where prospective employers make inquiries to a former employer about the character and capabilities of a former employee, the former employer has a conditional privilege

---

[29] *McCallum v. Lambie*, 145 Mass. 234, 238 (1887).

to communicate this information. When the former employer discloses defamatory information in such a privileged situation, the statement may turn out not to be true, but truth or falsehood is not material if there is no abuse of the privilege or if no actual malice is shown. Employers' false accusations are not privileged, however, if they did not act on their honest belief that the statements were true. While frank opinions about a former employee's work habits, competence, and character are well protected by the employer's conditional privilege, many employers desiring to steer clear of possible litigation give very limited reference information, such as the former employee's job title, a job description, and rates of pay and employment dates.

MICHAELSON v. MINNESOTA MINING AND MANUFACTURING CO.
Court of Appeals of Minnesota, 474 N.W. 2d 174 (1991).

[Victor Michaelson sued the employer for tort and contract claims under exceptions to the employment-at-will doctrine. Additionally, he brought suit for defamation based on a letter identifying deficiencies in his job performance. From a judgment for the employer, Michaelson appealed.]

SCHULTZ, J.

FACTS

In 1974, respondent Minnesota Mining and Manufacturing Company hired appellant Victor Michaelson, an attorney specializing in labor issues, to work in their office of general counsel. Appellant alleges respondent made assurances to him that if he did good work he could work until retirement. In addition, appellant points to three documents which respondent distributed to its employees as making promises which created a unilateral employment contract. Those documents were the *3M Guide to Conduct*, the *3M Office Operating Manual*, and the *Corrective Action* guide.

In his early years with respondent, appellant experienced serious financial problems, a fact which is uncontested here. Respondent helped appellant solve those problems. In addition, the Minnesota Lawyers Professional Responsibility Board twice limited appellant's license to practice due to disciplinary problems. As a result, respondent's practice is limited to his representation of respondent. Although respondent had supported appellant through these difficult times, it began to feel that appellant's problems "reflected adversely" on respondent.

Appellant worked primarily with the respondent's Human Resources department as an employment lawyer dealing with equal employment opportunity (EEO) issues. On several occasions, respondent sought appellant's evaluation and advice on employment problems and situations. Appellant counseled respondent on the law and gave his opinion as to the appropriate measures that respondent should have taken. On several of those occasions, respondent chose not to follow appellant's advice.

Annual performance reviews show that respondent found appellant's work to be consistently above average. These favorable reviews continued until September 1987 when an interim performance review reported a decline due to appellant's lack of proper time management, attention to cases and special projects, and a lack of communication with management. Respondent reviewed appellant early in order to give him the opportunity to correct the situation before the next formal performance review came due. That report, followed by a meeting between appellant and his supervisors, modified appellant's job responsibilities.

Respondent reassigned appellant to develop an educational and training program for the Human Resources department on issues regarding EEO and employment law. This reassignment of duties did not change appellant's status as respondent's legal advisor on EEO and employment law matters, but rather transferred the burden of litigation from appellant to another attorney in the department. Appellant maintained the same status, title, salary and benefits as he had before the reassignment. Respondent never terminated the employment relationship; it merely reassigned appellant's duties.

Appellant sent respondent a letter on October 19, 1987 which announced that appellant found the transition into his new assignment to be difficult and met with resistance from respondent. Appellant took a two-week vacation after which he never returned to work. Currently, appellant remains on long-term disability leave and receives disability compensation from respondent. . . .

The court determined that the trial court properly granted summary judgment in favor of the employer on the employment-at-will issues.

Appellant argues the trial court erred as a matter of law when it concluded that appellant's claims failed to create a cause of action for defamation. Common law defamation consists of a false statement about the plaintiff which is communicated ("published") to a third party and which tends to harm the plaintiff's reputation or standing in the community. *Stuempges v. Parke, Davis & Co.*, 297 N.W.2d 252, 255 (Minn. 1980). Truth is a complete defense to a claim of defamation. *Id.*

As basis for this claim, appellant cites the letter of September 10, 1987, in which respondent enumerated deficiencies in appellant's job performance and the company's decision to reassign him to new duties. We cannot agree with appellant that respondent defamed him when it sent a copy of the letter to two of appellant's su-

pervisors and discussed his performance in the presence of these two men. Preparation of and distribution of a letter to a personnel file and to other officers may constitute publication sufficient to support a cause of action. *Frankson v. Design Space Int'l*, 394 N.W.2d 140, 144 (Minn. 1986). Such a cause of action may be defeated, however, by a showing that the publication is protected by a qualified privilege. *Lewis*, 389 N.W. 2d at 889–90.

[A] communication, to be privileged, must be made upon a proper occasion, from a proper motive, and must be based upon reasonable or probable cause. When so made in good faith, the law does not imply malice from the communication itself, as in the ordinary case of libel. Actual malice must be proved, before there can be a recovery, and in the absence of such proof the plaintiff cannot recover.

Stuempges, 297 N.W.2d at 256–57 (quoting Hebner v. Great N. Ry., 78 Minn. 289, 292, 80 N.W. 1128, 1129 (1899)). In order to prove actual malice, appellant must show "actual ill will, or a design causelessly and wantonly to injure" appellant. Frankson, 394 N.W.2d at 144 (quoting *McBride v. Sears, Roebuck & Co.*, 306 Minn. 93, 98, 235 N.W.2d 371, 375 (1975)).

The letter from respondent candidly addresses its concerns with appellant's job performance and its reasons for reassigning his duties. Although publication did occur through distribution of the letter to third parties, the record does not establish that respondent made false statements nor that it made those statements with the requisite malice to create a cause of action. The trial court properly concluded that these statements did not constitute defamation and, if they had, that they were privileged under *Lewis*, 389 N.W.2d at 889–90.

DECISION

The trial court properly granted summary judgment in favor of respondent on all common law claims.

Affirmed.

CASE QUESTIONS

1. Did the fact that the employer "reviewed" Michaelson earlier than other employees indicate that the employer had malice towards him?

2. When is a communication privileged, under the *Lewis* rule?

3. Did Michaelson prove that the employer had the requisite actual malice to create a cause of action?

Chapter Questions and Problems

1. Why does the law differ between public-sector employers and private-sector employers in their testing of employees for drug use?

2. Local 1 of the Association of Western Pulp and Paper Workers was the bargaining representative for employees at Boise-Cascade Corporation's paper mill in St. Helen's, Oregon. Workers at the mill worked with heavy equipment, pressurized vessels, and hazardous chemicals. As a result, injuries were common.

    The labor agreement in effect between Local 1 and Boise-Cascade allowed the company unilaterally to introduce work rules that were consistent with the agreement. The union could challenge the reasonableness of a rule through grievance arbitration. In an effort to combat on-the-job injuries, Boise-Cascade unilaterally implemented a drug and alcohol testing program. The company announced that the testing program would apply to employees suspected by their supervisor of being under the influence of drugs or alcohol, employees who suffered on-the-job injuries that required more than first aid, and all employees involved in accidents at the mill. A positive result could result in discipline or discharge. In addition, refusal to submit to a test under the circumstances outlined above would result in discipline.

    The union objected to the drug and alcohol testing program as "illegal" and "unconstitutional." The union has asked you for advice on how to challenge the testing program.

    Should the union bring the issue to arbitration? The NLRB? The courts? Advise the union and explain. [*Paper Workers v. Boise-Cascade Corp.*, 1 ITER Cases 1072 (D. Oregon)]

3. The Nebraska Public Power District (NPPD) operated the Cooper Nuclear Station and instituted a "fitness for duty" program that required all employees who had access to protected areas at the Cooper plant to undergo random annual urine tests for drugs.

    The employees challenged the testing program on the grounds that it was contrary to the Fourth Amendment's ban on unreasonable searches and seizures since there was no individualized suspicion. They also argued that through tampering or mistakes in the testing process, employees could be wrongly accused of drug use.

    The NPPD stated that its testing program was "reasonable" and that its "chain of custody" rules and confirmatory tests protected employees from mistakes in the test results. Decide. [*Rushton v. Nebraska Public Power District*, 653 F. Supp. 1513 (D. Neb)]

4. Prior to 1988 Marguerite Cook and other former employees of Rite Aid of Maryland Inc. were directed to submit to polygraph examinations regarding inventory shortages or "shrinkage" at certain Rite Aid stores. Cook and others refused to take the examination. After her refusal Cook had her hours cut, had her store keys taken away, and was transferred to a distant store. When Cook refused to comply with the transfer

and schedule changes, she was terminated for refusing the directives of management. The state polygraph statute prohibits employers from requiring individuals or employees to take polygraph examinations and authorizes the attorney general to bring suit on behalf of "any aggrieved applicant for employment."

Cook brought a common law tort action for "discharge contrary to public policy" against Rite Aid, seeking compensatory and punitive damages from Rite Aid. Cook contended that Rite Aid improperly challenged her trustworthiness by ordering her to take a polygraph and then aggravated the injury by attempting to force her to resign by giving her undesirable work hours at an undesirable work location. She stated that when she refused the new assignment, she was wrongfully discharged.

Rite Aid contended that the common law action must be dismissed because the polygraph statute includes a civil remedy, and such is Cook's exclusive remedy. Rite Aid contended that while the polygraph statute prohibits the discharge of employees who refuse to take a polygraph test, it did not prohibit a transfer or a reduction in hours for an employee who refused to take such an examination. Rite Aid contended that it terminated Cook because she failed to follow a proper directive of management, which was its right, and that chaos would result if an employer were not allowed to terminate insubordinate employees.

Was Cook precluded from bringing a wrongful discharge case on her own rather than seeking a remedy under the polygraph statute? Will the EPPA of 1988 preclude similar public policy wrongful discharge actions? Did the employer have a right to terminate Cook for failure to comply with the assignment and hours given to her? [*Moniodis v. Cook*, 64 Md. App. 1]

5. Ms. Gay, a nurse's aide at the William Hill Manor Nursing Home, was discharged by her employer for placing a pillow on a resident's face to keep her from shouting. Following her termination, she was escorted through the facility to her car by three managers. Gay filed a defamation claim alleging her reputation was severely harmed by being publicly escorted out of the home. She also contended that a report submitted to the state unemployment agency, which gave "physical mistreatment of a resident" as the reason for termination, was defamatory publication which fell outside the scope of the home's qualified privilege.

Was defamatory information about Ms. Gay disseminated to employees and patients by the fact that three supervisors had escorted her to her car? If it is established that Ms. Gay had applied minimum pressure to the resident to stop her from shouting and disrupting the peace and quiet of the home, will she succeed in her defamation suit based on the employer's published reason for termination of "physical mistreatment of a resident"? [*Gay v. William Hill Manor, Inc.*, 3 IER Cases 744]

6. From June 25, 1982, to February 5, 1987, Brent Jennings was employed as a police officer/dispatcher for the city of Warrensville Heights. As a dispatcher, Jennings was required to answer incoming phone calls requesting police or fire department assistance and to dispatch the proper persons to meet those requests. On February 5, 1987, Jennings was called into the office of Warrensville Heights Police Chief Craig Merchant. Merchant was concerned about Jennings's involvement in "some drug incident in another community." In October 1986, Jennings had been arrested by Highland Heights police after he was found with two friends in a restroom stall at a theater, with cocaine and marijuana in the stall's toilet bowl. Jennings stated that he was not formally charged in the incident, and that the record of his arrest in the

incident was eventually expunged. At the meeting on February 5, Jennings gave Merchant his account of the incident. However, Merchant was not satisfied, particularly in light of Jennings's admissions during a preemployment polygraph test that he had previously used marijuana. Merchant testified that he told Jennings it was necessary for Jennings to take a polygraph test to confirm his account and to make certain he was not involved in the drug incident. Jennings testified that he knew the sole purpose of the polygraph test was to determine whether he had been involved with any drugs. Merchant told Jennings that he was not "after any criminal prosecution" and that the results of the polygraph test would not be used in any criminal proceeding. He also told Jennings that he must take the polygraph test or otherwise be discharged. Jennings refused to take the polygraph test. To avoid being discharged, Jennings submitted his resignation. Jennings later submitted an application for unemployment compensation. Under state law individuals can be denied unemployment benefits if terminated for "just cause in connection with their work." A department rule prohibited any member from illegally taking, possessing, or using any controlled substances both on and off duty. Jennings argued that polygraph tests are unreliable and thus a refusal to take one cannot serve as a basis for a "just-cause" discharge. Moreover, the conduct being questioned was off-duty, not work-related, conduct. The city responded that a police dispatcher is the "hub" of the department, and an impaired dispatcher could undermine the public safety. It states that polygraph tests, while not admissible in evidence at court, can be a useful internal investigative device; and failure to take the test was insubordination.

Decide, answering the contentions of the parties. [*City of Warrensville Heights v. Jennings*, 569 N.E.2d 489 (Ohio)]

7. Borquez was hired by the Ozer law firm as an associate in May 1990. He did not disclose his sexual orientation to Ozer or to anyone else at the firm. Also, because he was concerned about Ozer's acknowledged dislike of homosexuals, he kept his personal life confidential. Borquez was well respected and well liked, and performed capably as an attorney with the firm. He was awarded three merit raises in his salary, including one just 11 days before he was fired. On February 19, 1992, Borquez learned for the first time that his companion had been diagnosed with AIDS. Upset by that news and having been advised by his physician that he should be tested immediately for AIDS, Borquez concluded that he could not represent a client effectively in a deposition that afternoon, nor could he participate in an arbitration hearing the following day. In an effort to locate another attorney to handle the deposition and the hearing, Borquez discussed the matter with Ozer and disclosed facts about his personal life including his sexual orientation, his homosexual relationship, and his need for immediate AIDS testing. Borquez asked Ozer to keep this information confidential, but Ozer made no reply. However, Ozer agreed to handle the deposition and hearing. Shortly thereafter, Ozer told his wife, who is another shareholder in the firm, and others of Borquez's disclosures. Within two days, all employees and shareholders in the firm had learned about Borquez's personal life and his need for AIDS testing. Two days later, Ozer met with Borquez and told him that he had not agreed to keep the disclosures confidential. Ozer also made derogatory comments about people with AIDS. On February 26, Ozer fired Borquez. The reason for the firing was disputed, with Ozer maintaining that it had been for economic reasons. Those economic reasons stemmed from a pending bankruptcy which had been filed by the Ozer law firm in August 1991.

Does Borquez have a basis to bring an action against Ozer? If so, on what theory? Decide. [*Borquez v. Ozer*, 923 P.2d 166 (Colo. App.)]

8. Louis Pettus was employed by the DuPont Company for some 22 years. He sought time off from work under the company's short-term disability leave policy due to work-related stress. As required by the company policy, in order to qualify for the leave Pettus had to submit to a DuPont-selected doctor to confirm the necessity for the leave. This company-selected doctor recommended that Pettus be evaluated by a psychiatrist, Dr. Cole; and Dr. Cole recommended that Pettus see a chemical dependency specialist, Dr. Unger. Drs. Cole and Unger submitted reports to DuPont stating that Pettus's stress condition might be caused by misuse of alcohol. Dr. Cole telephoned Pettus's supervisor after his evaluation of Pettus, and Dr. Unger prepared a written report that was sent to DuPont's employee relations manager containing information about Pettus's family and work histories, his drinking habit, and his emotional condition. When Pettus refused to enter a 30-day inpatient alcohol rehabilitation program, DuPont terminated him. Pettus sued DuPont and the doctors for violation of California's Confidentiality of Medical Information Act. He believed that the doctors would only report their medical conclusions on whether or not he was entitled to the unpaid short-term leave, since he did not authorize the doctors to disclose full details. The company believes that it acted in good faith and for Mr. Pettus's own good and for the safety of co-workers by providing and paying for a full medical evaluation of his problems. The company asserts that once the alcohol problem was ascertained, its insistence that it be corrected before the company could safely allow him to return to work was a sound business judgment. Decide. [*Pettus v. Cole*, 57 Cal.Rptr.2d 46]

9. Michael Smyth was an operations manager at the Pillsbury Co., and his employment status was that of an employee at will. Smyth received certain E-mail messages at home, and he replied to his supervisor by E-mail. His E-mail messages contained some provocative language including a reference to "kill the backstabbing bastards" and a reference to an upcoming company party as the "Jim Jones Koolaid affair." Later Smyth was given two weeks' notice of his termination, and he was told that his E-mail remarks were inappropriate and unprofessional. Smyth believes that he is the victim of invasion of privacy because the E-mail messages caused his termination, and the company had promised that E-mail communications would not be intercepted and used as a basis for discipline or discharge. The company denies that it intercepted the E-mail messages and points out that Smyth himself sent the unprofessional comments to his supervisor. Is Smyth entitled to reinstatement and back pay because of the invasion of privacy? [*Smyth v. Pillsbury Co.*, 914 F. Supp. 97 (E.D.PA.)]

10. Patricia Rue, an employee with 12 years of service at K-Mart, was discharged for "eating and concealing" a bag of K-Mart's potato chips while on the job. When news of her termination spread throughout the workplace and caused a slowdown in productivity as employees discussed the incident, a K-Mart manager called a meeting and informed the employees that Rue had been fired for "eating and concealing a bag of potato chips." Following the discharge an unemployment compensation referee ruled that she did not steal the chips. She sued K-Mart for defamation. At the trial it was learned that a security officer's identification of Rue was not based on personal recognition of her as the one who stole the potato chips. K-Mart believes it

was not liable for defamation because of a privilege whereby it reasonably relied upon a report from its security department that Rue had stolen the chips and because of the necessity to assuage co-worker anxiety, whereby it had a right to tell co-workers why it discharged Rue. Is K-Mart liable to Rue for defamation? If so, what should the damages be? [*Rue v. K-Mart Corp.*, 11 IER Cases 1543 (Pa. Super. Ct.)]

11. Officers John Bohach and Jon Catalono, of the Reno, Nevada, Police Department, communicated with each other on the Alphapage computer system, typing messages on a keyboard and sending them to each other by use of a "send" key. The computer dials a commercial paging company which receives the message by modem, and the message is sent to the pager by radio broadcast. When the system was installed, the police chief warned that every Alphapage message is logged on the network. The chief barred messages critical of department policy and messages that were discriminatory in nature. The two police officers sought to block a department investigation into their messages and to prevent disclosure of the content of the messages. The officers claimed the messages should be treated the same as telephone calls under federal wiretap laws. The department contended that the system is essentially a form of E-mail, which messages are by definition stored in a computer, and the storage is itself not part of the communication. Were the federal wiretap laws violated? [*Bohach v. City of Reno*, D.C. Nev. 96-ECR]

7
Developing Topics

SECTION 41—DEVELOPING LAW REGULATING WAGES AND HOURS

On January 3, 1938, President Franklin Roosevelt declared in his annual message to Congress:

> The people of this country by an overwhelming vote are in favor of having Congress—this Congress—put a floor below which individual wages shall not fall, and a ceiling beyond which the hours of individual labor shall not rise.

Within six months of the president's message, Congress passed a federal wage and hour law called the Fair Labor Standards Act (FLSA). It was signed into law on June 25, 1938.[1] The FLSA has three broad objectives:

---

[1] Public Law No. 718, 75th Cong., 52 Stat. 1060.

1. The establishment of minimum wages, a floor under which wages would not fall that would provide a basic minimum standard of living for workers.[2]
2. The encouragement of a ceiling on the number of hours of labor for individual workers in a workweek, the ultimate purpose of which was to put financial pressure on employers to spread employment opportunities and hire additional workers to avoid the extra pay required for overtime hours (time worked in excess of 40 hours per week).[3]
3. The discouragement of "oppressive child labor."[4]

Coverage and Exemptions

Workers at enterprises engaged in interstate commerce are covered by the FLSA. Moreover, the Act has been amended to cover domestic service workers, including day workers such as housekeepers, chauffeurs, cooks, and full-time baby-sitters. The FLSA applies to most federal employees as well as to state and local government workers.[5]

Workers exempt from both the minimum wage and overtime provisions of the law include executive, administrative, and professional employees and outside salespersons. Also exempt are employees of certain small farmers and casual baby-sitters.

Certain highly paid commissioned employees of retail and service businesses are exempt from the overtime pay provision, as are farm workers and domestic service workers residing in their employer's homes.

The Wage and Hour Division (Wage-Hour Office) of the U.S. Department of Labor administers and enforces the FLSA. Detailed information about coverage and exemptions is beyond the scope of this section but is available at local Wage-Hour Offices.

The *Patel v. Quality Inn South* decision, presented in this section, shows the far-reaching scope of coverage of the FLSA: It upheld an undocumented alien's right to sue an employer for violations of the minimum wage and overtime provisions of the FLSA.

Subminimum Wage Provisions

The FLSA provides for the employment of certain individuals at wage rates below the statutory minimum, including full-time students at institutions of higher education. Under the 1996 amendments to the FLSA a special youth subminimum wage can be paid to employees under 20 years of age for their first 90 consecutive calendar days of employment with an employer.

Individuals whose productive capacity is impaired by age or physical or mental deficiency or injury may also be employed at less than the minimum wage in order to prevent the curtailment of work opportunities for these individuals. However, such employment is permitted only under certificates issued by the appropriate Wage-Hour

---

[2] The minimum wage as of September 1, 1997, is $5.15 per hour.
[3] See Section 7(a) of the FLSA and *Overnight Motor Transportation Co. v. Missel*, 316 U.S. 572 (1942).
[4] See Section 12(a) of the FLSA.
[5] See *Garcia v. San Antonio Metropolitan Transit Authority*, 469 U.S. 528 (1985).

Office. Compliance officers closely scrutinize practices in regard to the issuance and reissuance of certificates allowing subminimum wages.

Basic Wage Standards

Wages required by the FLSA are due on the regular payday for the period covered. Deductions made from wages for such items as cash or merchandise shortages, employer-required uniforms, and tools of a trade are not legal if they reduce wages below the minimum wage or reduce the amount of overtime pay due under the FLSA. Moreover, should an employer require employees to provide uniforms or tools on their own, to the extent that they reduce wages below the minimum wage, such is also a violation of the law. Thus nursing homes that require their nurse's aides to wear either white dresses or white pantsuits to work each day but pay these individuals the minimum wage are in violation of the FLSA. The employer nursing homes must, in addition to the minimum wage, compensate these employees for the value of such uniforms.

Overtime Pay

Overtime must be paid at a rate of at least 1½ times the employee's regular rate of pay for each hour worked in a workweek in excess of 40 hours. Thus an employee whose regular rate of pay is $10 per hour who works 44 hours in a workweek is entitled to $400 for the first 40 hours plus $15 for each of the four hours over 40—the overtime hours— for a total of $460 pay for the workweek.

The Wage-Hour Office provides regulations for employers to guide them in the calculation of overtime for piecework and salaried workers. Executive, administrative, and professional employees, as well as outside salespeople, are exempt from the overtime provisions. In *Freeman et al. v. NBC, Inc.*,[6] Jacob Freeman was the domestic news writer for *NBC Nightly News with Tom Brokaw*. He wrote headlines, teasers, transitions, voice-overs, lead-ins, and stories to be read by the news anchor, and was one of only two news writers assigned to *Nightly News*. Under a collective bargaining agreement, NBC paid him overtime at 1½ times his hourly rate for time worked in excess of 40 hours. Under the FLSA overtime pay is based on one's hourly rate and fees paid per hour. Freeman and others sued NBC for the difference in overtime pay calculated by inclusion of fees in the rate. NBC responded that Congress had expressly exempted persons employed in a "professional" capacity from the FLSA's overtime provisions. The Second Circuit Court of Appeals rejected the application of the Department of Labor's guidelines that the reporting of news must be considered nonexempt work, and concluded that Freeman and certain others at NBC who hold some of the most coveted jobs in broadcast journalism were "artistic professionals," exempt from the FLSA's overtime provisions.

---

[6] 3 WH2d 289 (2d Cir. 1996).

In *Auer v. Robbins*,[7] the Supreme Court upheld the Secretary of Labor's determination that certain police sergeants and a lieutenant were not entitled to overtime pay because they were within the "executive, administrative or professional" employees' exemption from the overtime provisions.

Under the Portal-to-Portal Act,[8] activities of employees that take place either before an employee begins or after the employee completes the productive activities for which the employee was hired are not to be included in "working time" for compensation purposes unless required by a collective bargaining contract or by past practice. Examples of nonproductive activities for which no pay is due under the FLSA are walking from the plant gate to the work site and changing clothes for the employees' convenience.

Child Labor Provisions

The FLSA child labor provisions are designed to protect the educational opportunities of minors and prohibit their employment in occupations detrimental to their health and well-being. The FLSA restricts hours of work for minors under 16 and lists hazardous occupations too dangerous for minors to perform.

Record Keeping

Employers are required by the Act to keep records on wages and hours for each employee for three years from the date of last entry.[9] Should an employer have to defend a wage or overtime suit under the FLSA, adequate records are essential for the employer's defense.

Enforcement

Enforcement of the FLSA is carried out by wage-hour compliance officers. Wage-hour officers may supervise the recovery and payment of back wages. Either the Secretary of Labor or an employee may file suit for back wages plus an equal amount as liquidated damages against employers who violate the FLSA. A two-year statute of limitations applies to the recovery of back pay except in the case of willful violations in which a three-year statute applies.

In *McLaughlin v. Richland Shoe Co.*, presented in this section, the Supreme Court held that a violation of the FLSA is "willful" for purposes of triggering the three-year statute of limitations if the employer either knew that or showed reckless disregard for whether the employer's conduct was prohibited by the FLSA.

---

[7] 34 DLR E-1 (Feb. 20, 1997).
[8] Public Law No. 49, 80th Cong., 29 USC § 251–263.
[9] Section 11(c) of the FLSA and regulations 29 CFR, Ch. V, Sec 516.5.

PATEL v. QUALITY INN SOUTH

United States Court of Appeals, 846 F.2d 700 (8th Cir. 1988).

[On June 1, 1982, Rajni Patel came to the United States from India on a visitor's visa. Although the visa expired after six weeks, Patel remained in the United States. In July 1983 he began working for the Sumani Corporation's Quality Inn South in Birmingham, Alabama. Patel performed maintenance and janitorial work at the hotel until October 1985. In August 1986 Patel brought an FLSA suit against the hotel seeking to recover unpaid back wages of $47,132 and an equivalent amount as liquidated damages plus attorney's fees. The district court granted the defendant's motion from summary judgment, holding that undocumented aliens could not recover for violations of the FLSA. Patel appealed.]

VANCE, C. J.

A.

. . . In deciding whether undocumented aliens are entitled to the protections of the FLSA we begin by examining the act itself. Congress enacted the FLSA in 1938 to eliminate substandard working conditions. *See* 29 U.S.C. § 202. It requires covered employers to pay their employees a statutorily prescribed minimum wage, *Id.* § 206, and prohibits employers from requiring their employees to work more than forty hours per week unless the employees are compensated at one and one half times their regular hourly rate. *Id.* § 207(a)(1). For violations of its provisions the FLSA imposes criminal sanctions and allows employees to bring an action to recover any unpaid minimum wages and overtime plus liquidated damages and attorney's fees. *Id.* § 216(a), (b).

In section 3(e) of the FLSA, *Id.* § 203(e), Congress defined the term "employee" for the purpose of determining who would be covered by the act. It would be difficult to draft a more expansive definition. The term "employee" was defined to include "any individual employed by an employer." *Id.* § 203(e)(1). . . . This definitional framework—a broad general definition followed by several specific exceptions—strongly suggests that Congress intended an all encompassing definition of the term "employee" that would include all workers not specifically excepted.

That Congress intended a broad definition of the term "employee" is also apparent from the FLSA's legislative history. One representative described the act as "the most momentous and far-reaching measure that [Congress has] considered for many years." 83 Cong. Rec. 9262 (1938)(statement of Rep. Fish). The remarks of then Senator Hugo Black, the FLSA's chief legislative sponsor, are even more instructive. During debate over the act Senator Black declared that its "definition of employee . . . is the broadest definition that has ever been included in any one act. . . ." 81 Cong. Rec. 7656-57 (1937).

Given the unequivocal language of the FLSA and its legislative history, it is not surprising that the Supreme Court has adopted an expansive definition of the term "employee" in its decisions under the act. Although it has never faced the question of whether undocumented aliens are covered by the FLSA, the Court consistently has refused to exempt from coverage employees not within a specific exemption. As the Court explained in *Powell v. United States Cartridge Co.*, 339 U.S. 497, 70 S. Ct. 755, 94 L.Ed. 1017 (1950):

Breadth of coverage was vital to [the FLSA's] mission. . . . Where exceptions were made, they were narrow and specific. [Congress] included as employees "any individual employed by an employer" § 3(e), and . . . devoted § 13 to listing exemptions of specific classes of employees. . . . Such specificity in stating exemptions strengthens the implication that employees not thus exempted . . . remain within the Act.

. . . In *Sure-Tan, Inc. v. NLRB*, 467 U.S. 883, 104 S. Ct. 2803, 81 L.Ed.2d 732 (1984), the Court used similar reasoning when it held that undocumented aliens are "employees" within the meaning of the National Labor Relations Act (NLRA). The Court stated:

The breadth of § 2(3)'s definition is striking: the Act squarely applies to "any employee." The only limitations are specific exemptions. . . . Since undocumented aliens are not among the few groups of workers expressly exempted by Congress, they plainly come within the broad statutory definition of "employee."

. . . The Department of Labor also supports Patel's position. It first interpreted the FLSA to cover undocumented aliens in 1942, when the Wage and Hour Administrator opined that alien prisoners of war were covered by the act and therefore were entitled to be paid the minimum wage. Since that time the Department of Labor has enforced the FLSA on behalf of undocumented workers on numerous occasions. *See, e.g., Donovan v. Burgett Greenhouses, Inc.*, 759 F.2d 1483 (10th Cir. 1985); *Brennan v. El San Trading Corp.*, 73 Lab. Cas. (CCH) ¶ 33,032 (W.D. Tex. 1973). To be sure, we are not bound by the Department of Labor's interpretation of the FLSA. As the agency charged with implementing the act, however, the Department's interpretation is entitled to considerable deference. . . . .

In short, the defendants' contention that Congress did not intend to protect undocumented workers when it passed the FLSA is contrary to the overwhelming weight of authority. Nothing in the FLSA or its legislative history suggests that Congress intended to exclude undocumented workers from the act's protections. The defendants conceded as much during oral argument. The defendants, however, . . . argue that in light of the IRCA undocumented aliens are no longer entitled to the protections of the FLSA. . . .

B.

We first consider the effect of the IRCA on the rights of undocumented aliens under the FLSA.

As we noted earlier, the district court relied heavily on the IRCA in granting the defendants' motion for summary judgment.

We begin our analysis by noting the familiar principle that amendments by implication are disfavored. Only when Congress' intent to repeal or amend is clear and manifest will we conclude that a later act implicitly repeals or amends an earlier one. *See, e.g., Rodriguez v. United States*, 107 S. Ct. 1391, 1392, 94 S. Ct. 1391 (1987). Here, nothing in the IRCA or its legislative history suggests that Congress intended to limit the rights of undocumented aliens under the FLSA. To the contrary, the FLSA's coverage of undocumented aliens is fully consistent with the IRCA and the policies behind it. . . .

[T]he FLSA's coverage of undocumented aliens goes hand in hand with the policies behind the IRCA. Congress enacted the IRCA to reduce illegal immigration by eliminating employers' economic incentive to hire undocumented aliens. To achieve this objective the IRCA imposes an escalating series of sanctions on employers who hire such workers. *See* 8 U.S.C. § 1324a. The FLSA's coverage of undocumented workers has a similar effect in that it offsets what is perhaps the most attractive feature of such workers—their willingness to work for less than the minimum wage. If the FLSA did not cover undocumented aliens, employers would have an *incentive* to hire them. Employers might find it economically advantageous to hire and underpay undocumented workers and run the risk of sanctions under the IRCA. . . .

. . . Nothing in the FLSA suggests that undocumented aliens cannot recover unpaid minimum wages and overtime under the act, and we can conceive of no other reason to adopt such a rule. We therefore conclude that Patel is entitled to the full range of available remedies under the FLSA without regard to his immigration status.

Reversed and remanded.

CASE QUESTIONS

1. Did the court agree with Quality Inn's contention that Congress did not intend to protect illegal aliens when it passed the FLSA? Explain.
2. Is it true that in light of the Immigration Reform and Control Act of 1986, undocu-

mented aliens are not entitled to the protection of the FLSA?

3. Could the FLSA's coverage of undocumented aliens go hand in hand with the policies behind the IRCA?

MCLAUGHLIN v. RICHLAND SHOE CO.

Supreme Court of the United States, 108 S.Ct. 1677 (1988).

[The respondent, a manufacturer of shoes and boots, employed seven mechanics to maintain and repair its equipment. In 1984 the Secretary of Labor (Secretary) filed a complaint alleging that "in many workweeks" the respondent had failed to pay those employees the overtime compensation required by the FLSA. As an affirmative defense the respondent pleaded the two-year statute of limitations. The district court rejected the respondent's claim that the two-year statute of limitations applied, finding the three-year exception applicable under the standard of *Coleman v. Jiffy June Farms, Inc.,* 458 F.2d 1139, whereby an action is "willful" if there is substantial evidence that the employer "knew or suspected that his actions might violate the FLSA," i.e., if the employer merely knew that the FLSA was "in the picture." Vacating the judgment against the respondent and remanding, the court of appeals rejected the *Jiffy June* standard in favor of the test employed in *Trans World Airlines, Inc. v. Thurston,* 469 U.S. 111. The Supreme Court granted certiorari to resolve the conflict between the circuit courts regarding the meaning of the word *willful* in the FLSA.]

STEVENS, J.

. . . Because no limitations period was provided in the original 1938 enactment of the FLSA, civil actions brought thereunder were governed by state statutes of limitations. In the Portal-to-Portal Act of 1947, 61 Stat. 84, 29 U.S.C. §§ 216, 251–262, however, as part of its response

to this Court's expansive reading of the FLSA, Congress enacted the 2-year statute to place a limit on employers' exposure to unanticipated contingent liabilities. As originally enacted, the 2-year limitations period drew no distinction between willful and nonwillful violations.

In 1965, the Secretary proposed a number of amendments to expand the coverage of the FLSA, including a proposal to replace the two-year statute of limitations with a three-year statute. The proposal was not adopted, but in 1966, for reasons that are not explained in the legislative history, Congress enacted the three-year exception for willful violations.

The fact that Congress did not simply extend the limitations period to three years, but instead adopted a two-tiered statute of limitations, makes it obvious that Congress intended to draw a significant distinction between ordinary violations and willful violations. It is equally obvious to us that the *Jiffy June* standard of willfulness—a standard that merely requires that an employer knew that the FLSA "was in the picture"—virtually obliterates any distinction between willful and nonwillful violations. As we said in *Trans World Airlines, Inc. v. Thurston, supra,* at 128, "it would be virtually impossible for an employer to show that he was unaware of the Act and its potential applicability." Under the *Jiffy June* standard, the normal two-year statute of limitations would seem to apply only to ignorant employers, surely not a state of affairs intended by Congress.

In common usage the word "willful" is considered synonymous with such words as "voluntary," "deliberate," and "intentional." See *Roget's International Thesaurus* § 622.7, p. 479; § 653.0, p. 501 (4th ed. 1977). The word "willful" is widely used in the law, and, although it has not by any means been given a perfectly consistent interpretation, it is generally understood to refer to conduct that is not merely negligent. The standard of willfulness that was adopted in *Thurston*—that the employer either knew or showed reckless disregard for the matter of whether its conduct was prohibited by the statues—is surely a fair reading of the plain language of the Act. . . .

Ordinary violations of the FLSA are subject to the general two-year statute of limitations. To obtain the benefit of the three-year exception, the Secretary must prove that the employer's conduct was willful as that term is defined in both *Thurston* and this opinion.*

The judgment of the Court of Appeals is *Affirmed.*

CASE QUESTIONS

1. Summarize the *Jiffy June* standard of "willfulness."
2. What did the Supreme Court find to be wrong with the *Jiffy June* standard of "willfulness"?
3. State the rule of the case.

---

*Of course, we express no view as to whether, under the proper standard, respondent's violation was "willful." That determination is for the District Court to make on remand from the Court of Appeals.

SECTION 42—FAMILY AND MEDICAL LEAVES OF ABSENCE

The federal Family and Medical Leave Act of 1993 (FMLA) entitles an eligible employee, whether male or female, to a total of 12 workweeks of unpaid leave during any 12-month period: (1) due to the birth or adoption of the employee's son or daughter; (2) in order to care for the employee's spouse, son, daughter, or parent with a serious health condition; or (3) because of a serious health condition that makes the employee unable to perform the functions of the employee's position. In the case of an employee's serious health condition or that of a covered family member, an employer may require that the employee use any accrued paid vacation, personal, medical, or sick leave toward any part of the 12-week leave provided by the Act. When an employee requests leave due to the birth or adoption of a child, the employer may require that the employee use all available paid personal, vacation, and family leave, but not sick leave, toward any FMLA leave.

To be eligible for FMLA leave, an employee must have been employed by a covered employer for at least 12 months and worked at least 1,250 hours during the 12-month period preceding the leave. Upon return from FMLA, the employee is entitled to be restored to the same or an equivalent position, with equivalent pay and benefits.

The FMLA does not set forth a notice period for the employee to notify the employer of the need for an FMLA leave. The Department of Labor has instituted a regulation on this matter requiring an employee to give the employer 30 days' notice if the leave is foreseeable, and "as soon as practicable" when it is not foreseeable. The leave may be taken intermittently or on a reduced schedule basis, and notice need only be given at one time.

In the first case brought by the Department of Labor against an employer, the termination of the employee for absenteeism was upheld by the court, because the evidence showed the employee had gone to a bank on her fifth day out of work, and that she was at least "practically" able to notify the employer of her condition at that time in sufficient detail to make it evident to the employer that she had a serious health condition which required an FMLA qualifying leave.[10]

SECTION 43—PLANT CLOSING LAWS: THE WARN ACT

All areas of the United States have experienced the closing of manufacturing facilities in recent years. Often these closings were the result of decisions made by large corporations that the benefits to the corporations of moving to new facilities in other areas of the country or moving to foreign countries were more economically advantageous than remaining in their older unprofitable or less profitable facilities.

It is argued by some that such decisions, which were made solely by looking at "private" costs and benefits to the firms, ignored the "external" costs to the community and industry, worker unemployment, economic hardships on community businesses and others, decreases in tax revenues of the community, the loss of real estate values in the community, and numerous significant social costs. These individuals advocate laws to restrict plant closings. It is argued by others that to impose restrictions on plant closings would inhibit the economy's ability to grow and apply new manufacturing technology and would inhibit businesses' ability to be efficient producers in today's worldwide marketplace.

Through collective bargaining, unions and employers have often agreed in their labor agreements to provide limited notice to their employees of layoffs at their plants, and they have agreed to pay severance pay to employees who are permanently laid off. Where no plant closing language exists in a collective bargaining contract, the employer has an obligation to bargain over the "effects" of its decision to close the plant under *First National Maintenance Corp. v. NLRB.*[11]

In 1988 Congress enacted the first federal plant closing law, the Worker Adjustment and Retraining Notification Act (WARN Act).[12] It requires employers who have 100 or more employees to give a 60-day notice of a plant closing if 50 or more workers at one site are to lose their jobs. A "mass layoff" provision of the law requires a 60-day notice of layoffs to affected workers if the affected workers make up at least 33 percent of the workforce at the site (with a minimum of 50 affected workers). If 500 or more employees are to be laid off, notice is required regardless of the percentage of the workforce to be laid off at the site.

---

[10] *Reich v. Midwest Plastic Engineering, Inc.*, 2 WH2d 1409 (W.D. MI. 1995). During the first two years under the FMLA the Department of Labor brought just three enforcement cases to court, including the *Midwest* case. The other two cases were settled in the employees' favor. The Department of Labor has been successful in resolving nearly 60 percent of the cases filed during the past year of the Act in favor of employees. It will not seek enforcement if the employee did not have a serious health condition to justify the leave and did not give proper notice or if the employee tried to use the FMLA as an excuse for a poor attendance record (DLR 151, p. AA-2 Aug. 7, 1995).

[11] 452 U.S. 666 (1981).

[12] 29 U.S.C. §§ 2101–2109.

In the *UPIU v. Alden Corrugated Container Corp.* decision, reported in this section, two different corporations with common ownership and management were considered a "single business entity" under federal law standards, thus bringing them within the 100-employee requirement triggering the WARN Act notice requirements. The remedy for the notice violation was back pay and benefits for each of the 60-day notice periods.

Exceptions to the notice requirement exist for unforeseen business circumstances, faltering companies, closures or layoffs from temporary projects, and closures due to legitimate strike and lockout activity.

Congress did not set a time limit for filing WARN Act lawsuits. In *North Star Steel Co. v. Thomas,*[13] the U.S. Supreme Court determined that the appropriate time limit for filing a lawsuit for failure to give proper notice of a plant closing or a mass layoff under the Act is to be determined by borrowing a time limit from an analogous state law, such as the two-year limitation period for civil penalties and a three-year period for state wage payment actions. Certain employers felt that the time limit should have been the six-month deadline of the NLRA. The Court's ruling allowed a lawsuit to proceed which would have been untimely if the NLRA time limits applied. The suit was on behalf of workers at a plant in Pennsylvania who claimed that the steel company had laid off 270 workers without giving 60 days' advance notice.

In *United Food Commercial Workers v. Brown Shoe Co.,*[14] the U.S. Supreme Court held that a union has standing to bring a WARN Act lawsuit against an employer on behalf of its workers. This decision revived a lawsuit against the shoe company based on the union's belief that the employer had already begun the layoff of workers at a plant it was closing before giving the closing notice required by the Act to the union.

A small number of states have passed laws regulating plant closings. A state plant closing law may require that the employer give advance notice to employees that the plant will be closing.[15] Such would allow employees to have a reasonable period of time, while still employed, to find another job. The law may also require that notice be given to a designated state agency, whereby a program to provide placement counseling, retraining, and other services could be set up for the benefit of employees.[16] Moreover, a state may enact laws that provide severance pay for qualifying employees[17] or provide for the continuation of employer-provided health insurance benefits for a certain number of months after the closing.[18] Under COBRA former workers can stay in group health care plans commonly for up to 18 months, but they can be required to pay the full cost of their coverage.

In *Fort Halifax Packing Co. v. Coyne,*[19] the United States Supreme Court upheld Maine's law requiring employers to pay severance pay to employees who lose their jobs because of a plant closing.

---

[13] 115 S.Ct. 1927 (1995).
[14] 116 S.Ct. 1529 (1996).
[15] Wis. Stat. Ann. § 109.07.
[16] Mass. Stat. Ann. 151 A § 71 B(a).
[17] Me. Rev. Stat. Ann. Tit. 26 § 625 B-2-3.
[18] Mass. Stat. Ann. 151 A § 71 G.
[19] 107 S.Ct. 2211 (1987).

UPIU v. ALDEN CORRUGATED CONTAINER CORP.

United States District Court, 10 IER Cases 1700 (D.C. Mass. 1995).

[Sixty days prior to the plant closing at Alden corrugated Container Corp., it employed some 51 workers; and Bates Corrugated Box Corp. employed some 93 workers sixty days prior to the Bates plant closing. The companies were interconnected, sharing certain officers and directors, and stock of both companies was owned by a common holding company, Alden Holdings Corporation. The companies did not believe that a WARN Act notice was required because neither company employed 100 employees 60 days prior to the plant closings. The United Paperworkers International Union (UPIU) believed that collectively the companies formed a "single business enterprise" under the act and that notice was required.]

COLLINGS, U.S.M.J. . . .

There is no dispute that the closings of the Alden and Bates Plants constitute plant closings under § 2101 (a)(2) of the Act in that each was a permanent shutdown of a single site as a consequence of which over fifty employees suffered the loss of employment. However, in order to establish both the applicability of the WARN Act and the defendants' liability thereunder, the plaintiffs must prove that Alden and Bates were "employers" as defined by § 2101 (a)(1) of the statute, i.e., that they were business enterprises that employed one hundred (100) or more employees.

According to the regulations, "[t]he point in time at which the number of employees is to be measured for the purpose of determining coverage is the date the first notice is required to be given." 20 C.F.R. § 639.5 (a)(3). Thus, the relevant date for determining whether Alden was an employer is December 25, 1990, sixty days prior to the Alden Plant closing on February 22, 1991. At that time, Alden employed at least fifty-one (51) full time workers. On November 18,

1990, sixty days before the Bates Plant closing on January 18, 1991, ninety-three (93) employees were working for Bates. *See, e.g., United Electrical, Radio and Machine Workers of America (UE) and UE Local 291 v. Maxim, Inc.* 1990 WL 66578, *1–*2 (D. Mass.).

Although neither Alden nor Bates per se had the requisite number of employees working at their respective plants on the relevant dates, the plaintiffs advance several theories pursuant to which they contend that the corporations could be considered employers within the meaning of the WARN Act. The plaintiffs' primary argument is that the defendants are so interconnected that, collectively, they constituted a single business enterprise. There is no dispute that if the Alden and Bates workers were aggregated, the threshold number of one hundred (100) employees on the relevant dates would be met.

The term "business enterprise" is not defined in the statute. The pertinent regulation provides:

Under existing legal rules, independent contractors and subsidiaries which are wholly or partially owned by a parent company are treated as separate employers or as a part of the parent or contracting company depending upon the degree of their independence from the parent. Some of the factors to be considered in making this determination are (i) common ownership, (ii) common directors and/or officers, (iii) de facto exercise of control, (iv) unity of personnel policies emanating from a common source, and (v) the dependency of operations.

20 C.F.R. § 639.3 (a)(2).

To further clarify the definition of "independent contractors and subsidiaries" as used in § 639.3 (a)(2), the Department of Labor has stated:

The intent of the regulatory provision relating to independent contractors and subsidiaries is not to create a

special definition of these terms for WARN purposes; the definition is intended only to summarize existing law that has developed under State Corporations laws and such statutes as the NLRA, the Fair Labor Standards Act (FLSA) and the Employee Retirement Income Security Act (ERISA). The Department does not believe that there is any reason to attempt to create new law in this area especially for WARN purposes when relevant concepts of State and federal law adequately cover the issue. Thus, no change has been made in the definition. Similarly, the regulation is not intended to foreclose any application of existing law or to identify the source of legal authority for determinations of whether related entities are separate. To the extent that existing law recognizes the joint employer doctrine or the special situation of the garment industry, nothing in the regulation prevents application of that law. Nor does the regulation preclude recognition of the National Mediation Board as an authoritative decision maker for entities covered by the RLA. Neither does the regulation preclude treatment of operating divisions as separate entities if such divisions could be so defined under existing law.

54 Fed. Reg. 16045 (April 10, 1989) . . .

The factors suggested to be weighed in the WARN regulations are quite similar to those in the single employer analysis. The facts of common ownership and management of the corporate defendants have already been established, and need not be repeated. Similarly, the centralized control of labor negotiations has been discussed, as has the interdependency of the Alden and Bates operations. The final factor to be examined is de facto control.

A number of facts underscore the control that Alden Holdings had, and exercised, over Alden and Bates. Alden Holdings owned all the stock of Alden and ninety-one percent (91%) of the stock of Bates. The primary stockholders of Alden Holdings, Walter Zuckerman, Benjamin Gottlieb and Frederic M. Gottlieb, with one exception, were each officers and directors of Alden Holdings, Alden and Bates. Three of the four directors of Alden Holdings supervised the labor negotiations of Alden and Bates. Alden

Holdings secured financing for Alden and Bates. Two of the officers/directors of Alden Holdings determined the allocation of Stanley Jacobson's salary between Alden and Bates. Representatives of Alden Holdings attended the meeting of Alden's and Bates' paper suppliers. De facto control of Alden and Bates by Alden Holdings is amply supported by the record.

Considering the factors set forth in the WARN regulations, the plaintiffs have proven that defendants Alden Holdings, Alden and Bates were a single business enterprise.

To summarize, a conclusion in favor of the separateness of defendants is reached under state common law. However, when the tests predicated on federal law are applied, Alden Holdings, Alden and Bates must be deemed to be a single business enterprise. Given these disparate results, it is important to bear in mind that the WARN Act,

. . . like other federal labor statues, has as its goal the protection of workers, and therefore, the single employer test and the factors enumerated in the D.O.L. regulations, which echo and expand the single employer test, are persuasive.

Local 397 II, 779 F.Supp. at 800.

Consequently, Alden Holdings, Alden and Bates are found to be a single business enterprise. Together, their aggregate number of workers surpasses the minimum number of employees required for the provisions of the WARN Act to apply. As a matter of law, Alden Holdings, Alden and Bates were a single employer and, as such, are liable for the established violations of the WARN Act.

Title 29 U.S.C. § 2102(b)(1) provides for a reduction in the notification period as follows:

An employer may order the shutdown of a single site of employment before the conclusion of the 60-day period if as of the time that notice would have been required the employer was actively seeking capital or business which, if obtained, would have enabled the employer

to avoid or postpone the shutdown and the employer reasonably and in good faith believed that giving the notice required would have precluded the employer from obtaining the needed capital or business.

From and after the business reorganization in May of 1990, its financial losses continued to mount as Bates proved unable to manage effectively the finished box business transferred from Alden. Although a decision was made to attempt to sell the Bates operation in November, 1990, no interested buyers could be found. There is absolutely no evidence in the record with regard to what specific steps Bates took to sell its business.

After receipt of Bates' 1990 year-end figures, the Bank of Boston called the company's loan effective January 18, 1991. Again, there is no objective proof in the record to demonstrate that Bates' expectation that its operation could be maintained was held reasonably and in good faith.

Based on this record, the Court finds that Bates has failed to carry its burden of proof that the conditions for the "faltering company" exception have been met.

2. The Unforeseeable Business Circumstances Exception

As a second exception to the notification requirement, the WARN Act provides:

An employer may order a plant closing or mass layoff before the conclusion of the 60-day period if the closing or mass layoff is caused by business circumstances that were not reasonably foreseeable as of the time that notice would have been required.

29 U.S.C. § 2102 (b) (2) (A). . . .

The regulations are instructive in interpreting and applying this exception, stating in relevant part:

An important indicator of a business circumstance that is not reasonably foreseeable is that the circumstance is caused by some sudden, dramatic, and unexpected action or condition outside the employer's control.

The test for determining when business circumstances are not reasonably foreseeable focuses on an employer's business judgment. The employer must exercise

such commercially reasonable business judgment as would a similarly situated employer i[n] predicting the demands of its particular market. . . .

20 C.F.R. §§ 639.9(b)(1) and (2).

Both Alden and Bates contend that the decision by the Bank of Boston to call their loans and order that they cease operations was an unforeseen business circumstance.

The fiscal misfortunes of both companies were apparent even before May of 1990, as evidenced by the ever increasing losses they sustained beginning in 1988 as well as the fact that their loans were in a workout mode with the Bank of Boston. The slide continued unabated after the business reorganization as reflected by the C.O.D. decision of their paper suppliers in September, 1990. The extremely poor year end figures demonstrate that both Alden's and Bates' financial decline accelerated dramatically in the latter part of 1990.

In light of this deepening downward fiscal spiral, the Bank of Boston's ultimate order to cease operations cannot be viewed as an unforeseen business circumstance within the meaning of the WARN Act. While certainly dramatic, the decision was neither unforeseen or sudden, but rather the culmination of the continuing, and admittedly worsening, financial devastation of Alden and Bates. In the exercise of commercially reasonable business judgment, Alden and Bates could have anticipated by the end of 1990 that their plants would be forced to close, and, therefore, could have given the notification required by the WARN Act.

An employer found to have violated the WARN Act shall be liable to each aggrieved employee for back pay for each day of violation as well as benefits under an employee benefit plan. 29 U.S.C. § 2104(1). Given that no notices were provided in these cases, liability is calculated based on the maximum allowable period of violation, i.e., sixty days. *Id.*

The amounts of back pay and benefits are the subject of stipulation by the parties. Based on an eight hour day, the collective daily pay of the twenty-four Union members who were terminated by Alden in the Alden Plant closing was one thousand eight hundred seventy-six dollars and fifty-six cents ($1,876.56) (Stip. [f]) The collective daily pay multiplied by the sixty-day period of violation equals one hundred twelve thousand five hundred ninety-three dollars and sixty cents ($112,593.60). The value of sixty days of benefits for these same Union members is twelve thousand eight hundred ninety-six dollars and eighty-eight cents ($12,896.88).

The total amount of collective daily pay and employee benefits for the members of Local 996 laid off and/or terminated at Bates or a sixty-day period is four hundred eighty-six thousand, three hundred ninety-six dollars and ninety-two cents ($486,396.92). The value of sixty days collective pay and employee benefits for the eleven non-union Bates employees terminated when the Bates Plant closed is ninety-five thousand eight hundred fifty dollars and thirty-eight cents ($95,850.38).

CASE QUESTIONS

1. Did either Alden or Bates have the 100 employees necessary for the WARN Act to apply?
2. Were the shutdowns caused by "business circumstances that were not reasonably foreseeable" as of the time that notice would have been required?
3. What are the damages owed the employees who did not receive notice?

SECTION 44—UNEMPLOYMENT COMPENSATION

As set forth in the previous section, federal and state laws require notice to workers of impending unemployment due to plant shutdowns, in some situations. A federally mandated unemployment compensation system exists for the benefit of unemployed workers. Over 96 percent of wage and salary workers in the United States may qualify for unemployment benefits.

Unemployment compensation is provided primarily through a federal–state system under the unemployment insurance provisions of the Social Security Act of 1935. All states have laws that provide benefits under the broad federal standards of the 1935 law. The states are largely free to prescribe the amount and durations of benefits and the conditions for eligibility. Weekly benefits are paid at approximately 50 percent of the worker's wage, up to set maximums; and "regular benefits" commonly continue for a period of up to 26 weeks. The unemployed person must be available for placement in a similar position at comparable pay. Individuals may be disqualified from receiving benefits if the individual quits a job without good cause, or is fired for misconduct.

Employers are taxed for unemployment benefits based on each employer's "experience rating" account. Thus employers with a stable workforce with no layoffs, who thus do not draw upon the state unemployment insurance fund, pay favorable tax rates. Employers whose experience ratings are higher pay higher rates. Motivated by the desire to avoid higher unemployment taxes, employers may challenge the state's payment of unemployment benefits to individuals whom they believe are not properly entitled to benefits.

Misconduct

Like workers' compensation statutes, unemployment compensation statutes are humanitarian in nature and are liberally construed. In determining an individual's entitlement to unemployment compensation benefits, the issue is not whether the employer was justified in discharging the employee, but, rather, whether the employee committed "misconduct." Misconduct resulting in disqualification for unemployment benefits is conduct resulting in a willful or wanton substantial disregard of the employer's interests.[20] Mere negligence or incompetence will not suffice.

In *McCourtney v. Imprimis Technology, Inc.,*[21] an individual who was discharged for frequent absences from work, while properly dismissed by her employer, nevertheless was not disqualified from unemployment benefits because her absences did not amount to "misconduct" under the Act. The dismissed individual was unable to obtain child care for her sick infant and her missing of work was thus not "in wanton disregard of her employer's interests," but motivated by her child's interests.

In *Hill v. Commissioner of Labor,*[22] Mr. Hill had been returned to work under a "last chance" drug treatment agreement. The evidence established that he had failed to follow through with the drug treatment program and tested positive for drugs. As a result, the employer dismissed him. The court ruled that Mr. Hill was disqualified from receiving unemployment benefits because of his "misconduct."

In some states and employee's off-duty use of illegal drugs is not considered work-connected misconduct.[23] Such decisions are narrow, however, and there must not be work-connected rules violations that result from the off-duty use of drugs. In *Weyerhauser Co. v. Employment Division,*[24] the Oregon Court of Appeals held that a worker's poor attendance record, related to his off-duty use of alcohol and drugs, was willful misconduct making him ineligible for unemployment compensation.

Voluntary Quits

Every state disqualifies individuals from receiving benefits when they voluntarily leave their jobs, without good cause. Exceptions to this voluntary quit rule exist in some states for employees who elect voluntary termination under a voluntary termination plan (VTP) adopted by the employer, whereby an employer purchases employees' employment and seniority rights in exchange for separation packages. In *Ford Motor Co. v. Ohio Bureau of Employment Services,*[25] the Supreme Court of Ohio ruled that an employee who was voluntarily terminated under a VTP, even though she had sufficient seniority to avoid the layoff in question, was entitled to unemployment compensation benefits.

A voluntary quit because of sex discrimination or sexual harassment constitutes "good cause" for leaving employment where the victim makes reasonable efforts to resolve the matter before leaving the employment. In *Umbarger v. Virginia Employment Commission,* presented in this section, the court held that an employee who reasonably believed that she was the victim of sexual discrimination, and had exhausted all reasonable alternatives for redress, was not disqualified from receiving unemployment benefits.

---

[20] *Boynton Cab Co. v. Newbeck,* 296 N.W.2d 636 (Wis. 1941).
[21] *McCourtney v. Imprimis Technology, Inc.* (Minn. App.), 465 N.W.2d 74 (1991).
[22] *Hill v. Commissioner of Labor,* 172 A.D.2d 954, 568 N.Y.S.2d 235 (1991).
[23] *Glide Lumber Products Co. v. Employment Division,* 86 Or.App. 669, 741 P.2d 907 (1987).
[24] 107 Or. App. 505, 812 P.2d 44 (1991).
[25] 571 N.E.2d 727 (Ohio 1991).

Availability

In most states the unemployed person must be available for placement in a similar job and be willing to take such employment at a comparable rate of pay. Full-time students generally have difficulty proving that they are "available" for work once they become unemployed. In *Evjen v. Employment Agency*,[26] full-time student Robert Evjen was laid off from his full-time employment at Boise Cascade Co. The court decided that Evjen was entitled to benefits because he had overcome the inference of nonavailability that exists for full-time students by his uncontroverted testimony that he never missed work in order to go to classes, and that his education was secondary to his employment.

UMBARGER v. VIRGINIA EMPLOYMENT COMMISSION

Court of Appeals of Virginia, 404 S.E.2d 380 (Va. App. 1991).

[Kathy Umbarger was disqualified from receiving unemployment benefits based on her separation from Glenn Roberts Tire and Recapping, Inc., and she appealed the decision ultimately to the Court of Appeals.]

KOONTZ, C. J. . . .
From November 28, 1978 until her resignation on August 8, 1988, Ms. Umbarger worked as a bookkeeper for Glenn Roberts Tire and Recapping, ultimately earning $5.10 per hour. Glenn Roberts Tire and Recapping has two stores, one in Big Stone Gap and one in Norton, and is owned by Appalachian Tire Products in Charleston, West Virginia. During the latter part of her employment, Ms. Umbarger became increasingly anxious about the future of her job since the business was doing poorly. On July 1, 1988, the manager of the Big Stone Gap store retired. Shortly thereafter, the service manager of this store resigned, and with three male employees from the service department, started his own business. In an unsuccessful attempt to retain some of those employees, Glenn Roberts offered them raises but they declined the offers. As a result of those departures, the Glenn Roberts store

in Big Stone Gap was left with one male employee in the service department and Ms. Umbarger in the office.

Subsequently, a salesman from the Norton store was made manager of the Big Stone Gap store. The new manager retained sales responsibilities that required him to be away from the Big Stone Gap store on a regular basis. During the latter part of July and without notice to Ms. Umbarger, Glenn Roberts hired Tim Mack to oversee inventory at the Big Stone Gap store and potentially become a store manager. Mack was paid $5.50 per hour for this newly created position titled "Supervisor in Inventory Control." Mack had prior inventory control experience at Westmoreland Coal Company where he recently had been laid off, but no prior experience in the tire business.

Ms. Umbarger was displeased with the fact that Mack was doing some of the work that she had performed for Glenn Roberts for nearly the ten previous years. On August 8, 1988, she discovered Mack was earning forty cents per hour more than she was earning. Upon returning from lunch that day, Ms. Umbarger approached Leonard Canfield, Glenn Roberts' operations

---

[26] 22 Or. App. 372, 539 P.2d 662 (1975).

manager for the two stores. She demanded an explanation of the pay differential. Canfield told her that Mack was in a different classification than her and would possibly become store manager someday. She responded that she did not think it was fair and demanded a pay raise, which Canfield told her conditions would simply not permit. At that point, Ms. Umbarger told Canfield she felt she was the victim of sex discrimination and left the store. The next day she removed her personal belongings and filed her claim for unemployment compensation. . . .

An individual is disqualified from receiving unemployment benefits if the commission finds that individual voluntarily left work without good cause. The corollary to that rule is that an individual may receive unemployment benefits if the commission finds that individual voluntarily left work with good cause. The determination of what constitutes "good cause" is a mixed question of law and fact, and therefore is subject to review on appeal. In *Lee v. Virginia Employment Comm'n*, 335 S.E.2d 104, 106 (1985), we considered the requirement of "good cause" in the context of an employee who voluntarily leaves employment and stated: "[B]efore relinquishing his employment . . . the claimant must have made every effort to eliminate or adjust with his employer the differences or conditions of which he complains. He must take those steps that could be reasonably expected of a person desirous of retaining his employment before hazarding the risks of unemployment." *Id.* In other words, a claimant must take all reasonable steps to resolve his conflicts with his employer and retain his employment before voluntarily leaving that employment.

. . . [W]hen determining whether good cause existed for a claimant to voluntarily leave employment, the commission and the reviewing courts must first apply an objective standard to the reasonableness of the employment dispute and then to the reasonableness of the employee's efforts to resolve that dispute before leaving the employment. In making this two-part analysis,

the claimant's claim must be viewed from the standpoint of a reasonable employee. "Factors that . . . are peculiar to the employee and her situation are factors which are appropriately considered as to whether good cause existed. . . ." *Id.* 382 S.E.2d at 481.

In the present case, the commission and Glenn Roberts contend Ms. Umbarger's evidence fails to show she had no reasonable alternative except to quit her job. . . .

We interpret the circuit court's finding that Ms. Umbarger "felt she was . . . discriminated against in view of the recently hired higher paid male employee" as a determination that she reasonably believed she was a victim of sexual discrimination. The record supports such a determination. Without notifying her or allowing her to apply, Glenn Roberts hired a male, Tim Mack, who lacked any apparent experience in the tire business, to fill a newly created position that entailed performing many of her current duties. Mack's starting salary was forty cents per hour more than Ms. Umbarger's salary even though she had been employed at Glenn Roberts for nearly ten years. Finally, she was denied a raise after Glenn Roberts recently had offered several male employees raises. The combination of these factors demonstrates the reasonableness of Ms. Umbarger's belief that she was the victim of sexual discrimination. The determination that Ms. Umbarger reasonably believed that she was a victim of sexual discrimination negates an assertion that her belief was a purely subjective perception on her part, even though she may have erroneously held this belief. Consequently, the commission's finding in this case that Ms. Umbarger did not demonstrate she was in fact discriminated against is immaterial.

Based upon the initial determination that Ms. Umbarger reasonably believed she was being discriminated against, we also must decide whether she took those steps that could be reasonably expected of a person desirous of retaining her employment. Unlike *Lee*, there is no evidence that Ms. Umbarger had the benefit of an established, designated procedure for addressing employee grievances. The evidence shows that Glenn Roberts was owned by an out-of-state corporation, Appalachian Tire Products, and that Mr. Canfield, the operations manager in charge of the two Glenn Roberts stores, was one of the top officers, if not the top officer, in Glenn Roberts available to review Ms. Umbarger's complaint. Nothing in the record indicates or suggests that Appalachian Tire Products took an active role in the management of Glenn Roberts or in any way oversaw employee affairs. In a situation such as this, we find, as a matter of law, that Ms. Umbarger exhausted all reasonable alternatives within Glenn Roberts to resolve her complaint of discrimination when she confronted Mr. Canfield and he failed to respond to that complaint.

Based on our findings, we hold Ms. Umbarger is not disqualified from receiving unemployment benefits. Accordingly, the decision of the circuit court is reversed and the case is remanded for entry of an order consistent with this opinion.

Reversed and remanded.

CASE QUESTIONS

1. May an individual receive unemployment benefits if that individual voluntarily left work with good cause?
2. What analysis must the commission and reviewing courts pursue in order to determine if a claimant who voluntarily leaves employment does so for "good cause"?
3. Did Ms. Umbarger have a reasonable basis to believe she was the victim of sex discrimination?
4. Did Ms. Umbarger make a sufficient effort to resolve the dispute before leaving the job?

SECTION 45—EMPLOYMENT-RELATED IMMIGRATION LAWS: INTRODUCTION

The Immigration Reform and Control Act of 1986[27] (IRCA) addressed problems associated with illegal immigration to the United States through a broad amnesty program and the initiation of both criminal and civil sanctions against employers who employ undocumented aliens.

The Immigration Act of 1990[28] reformed legal immigration to the United States. The 1990 Act provides for 140,000 visas annually for employer-sponsored immigrants. The Act includes aliens with extraordinary ability such as outstanding professors and researchers, as well as aliens who are members of the professions, holding advanced degrees. Some 10,000 annual visas will be available for entrepreneurs who invest at least $1,000,000 and create at least ten new jobs. Congress provided the largest increase in visas for those aliens with the greatest skills, who could stimulate the American economy through their employment and job-creating investment.

SECTION 46—EMPLOYER SANCTIONS AND VERIFICATION RESPONSIBILITIES

The availability of jobs and the higher pay scales in the United States have been a principal factor in drawing illegal immigrants to the country. The IRCA is structured on the

---

[27] Pub. L. N. 99-603, 100 Stat. 3359, 8 U.S.C. §§ 1324a.
[28] Pub. L. N. 101-949, 101 Stat. 4978. A 1996 immigration law doubled the size of the Border Patrol, and introduced procedures to speed up the deportation of immigrants without proper travel documents in an effort to reduce illegal immigration.

premise that if employer sanctions are applied and employers are enlisted to help enforce the immigration laws, employment opportunities for illegal immigrants will be drastically diminished and so will illegal immigration. The employer sanctions and verification responsibilities under the law are covered below.

Employer Sanctions

Section 101 of the IRCA makes it illegal to hire, recruit, or refer for a fee unauthorized aliens. The law also makes it illegal for an employer to employ an alien in the United States knowing that the alien is (or has become) an unauthorized alien with respect to employment. An employer who violates the law is subject to civil penalties of $250 to $2,000 for each unauthorized alien. This penalty is increased to $2,000 to $5,000 for each alien for a second violation.[29] Criminal penalties where a "pattern or practice" of unlawful hiring exists can include a fine of not more than $3,000 for each unauthorized alien and imprisonment for up to six months.[30]

Employer Verification

The law requires employers to verify that each new employee hired after November 6, 1986, is authorized to work in the United States. The Immigration and Naturalization Service (INS) has designated Form I-9, Immigration Eligibility Verification Form, as the official verification form to comply with the IRCA.

The prospective employee must complete the initial portion of Form I-9 attesting under the penalty of perjury that she or he is a U.S. citizen or is authorized by the INS to work in the United States, and that the verification document(s) presented to the employer are genuine and relate to the signer. The employer must then review the documents that support the individual's right to work in the United States. Documents that both identify and support an individual's eligibility to work are a U.S. passport, a certificate of U.S. citizenship, a certificate of naturalization, an unexpired foreign passport with attached visa authorizing U.S. employment, or an Alien Registration Card with photograph. Where the individual does not have one of the above documents, the individual may provide a document evidencing his or her identity and another document evidencing the right to employment. Thus, a state-issued driver's license is sufficient to provide identity and a Social Security card or official birth certificate issued by a municipal authority is sufficient to prove employment eligibility. Numerous other documents exist that will satisfy the identity and employment eligibility documentation requirements.

The employer has three days to complete the I-9s. I-9s must be completed for all employees hired after November 6, 1986, including employees who are U.S. citizens. I-9s must be kept for three years after the date of hire.[31] Fines of between $100 and

---

[29] IRCA § 101(a)(1), 8 U.S.C. § 1324 A(e)(4).
[30] IRCA § 101(a)(1), 8 U.S.C. § 1324 A(f).
[31] 52 Fed. Reg. 8765 (Mar. 19, 1987).

$1,000 may be assessed for each individual employee for failure to comply with the paperwork verification requirements.

Burden of Proof and Affirmative Defenses

In an action against the employer under the IRCA, the government must establish that the employer had "actual knowledge" that the employee was unauthorized to work in the United States. This standard is one of the highest standards of proof under law.

The IRCA provides an affirmative defense for an employer if the employer, in good faith, simply complies with the verification requirements of the Act. This is accomplished "if the document reasonably appears on its face to be genuine."[32] However, an employer who is informed by the INS that named employees may have used fraudulent green cards, but takes no investigative or corrective action whatsoever, cannot avail itself of the good faith defense.[33]

SECTION 47—EMPLOYER DISCRIMINATION

Under Section 102 of the IRCA and Title VII of the Civil Rights Act, it is an unfair practice to discriminate against a person in employment situations on the basis of national origin. Additionally, Section 102 of the IRCA makes it an unfair immigration-related practice to discriminate against an individual in hiring, discharging, recruiting, or referring for a fee because of an individual's national origin or, in the case of a citizen or intending citizen, because of that individual's citizenship status.

Since the IRCA imposes employer sanctions for violations of the Act, Congress was concerned that the IRCA might lead to employment discrimination against "foreign-looking" or "foreign-sounding" persons or against persons who, although not citizens, are legally in the United States. In order to prevent the occurrence of such practices, Congress enacted Section 102 and established enforcement measures including the creation of a "Special Counsel for Immigration-Related Unfair Employment Practices" within the Department of Justice. Among the special counsel's statutory responsibilities is the investigation of unfair immigration-related employment practices either on the counsel's own initiative or in response to charges filed with the Office of Special Counsel by aggrieved individuals, their representatives, or officers of the Immigration and Naturalization Service.

The Immigration Act of 1990 strengthened the antidiscrimination provisions of the IRCA by prohibiting employers from demanding overdocumentation. Section 535(a) of the 1990 Act provides that employers' requests for more or different documents than required under the IRCA or refusal to honor documents that on their face reasonably appear to be genuine shall be treated as an unfair immigration-related employment practice.[34]

---

[32] IRCA § 101(a)(1) and 8 U.S.C. § 1324 A(b)(1)(A).
[33] *Mester Manufacturing Co. v. INS*, 879 F.2d 561 (9th Cir. 1989).
[34] 8 U.S.C. § 1324 B(a)(6).

In *Jones v. DeWitt Nursing Home*,[35] Jones, a newly hired employee, gave DeWitt Nursing Home a Social Security card and a driver's license to show work authorization in conjunction with the I-9 form requirements. The employer asked to see Jones's birth certificate. Jones, a U.S. citizen, refused to provide the additional document, and the employer fired him. The employer was found to have violated the IRCA and was ordered to reinstate Jones with back pay.

SECTION 48 — BUSINESS VISAS

Nonimmigrant B–1 business visas are issued by a U.S. consular office abroad after it has been shown that the visitor (1) has an unabandoned foreign residence, (2) intends to enter the United States for a limited period of time, and (3) will engage solely in legitimate business activities for which the visitor will not be paid in the United States.[36]

Certain investors qualify for E–2 business visas. Principal foreign investors responsible for development and direction of an enterprise in the United States are granted such a visa. An E visa is very desirable because it is issued for extended periods of time, usually four to five years, and may be renewed indefinitely so long as the alien maintains her or his role with respect to the investment. An E–2 visa will not be issued to an applicant who has invested "a relatively small amount of capital in a marginal enterprise solely for the purpose of earning a living."[37]

L–1 visas allow qualifying multinational businesses to make intracompany transfers of foreign persons to the United States when the individuals are employed in management or have "specialized knowledge." L–1 visas are good for up to seven years for executives and managers. "Specialized knowledge" personnel may stay for five years.[38]

H–1 classification visas allow aliens of "distinguished merit and ability" to enter and work in the United States on a temporary basis. These persons include architects, engineers, lawyers, physicians, and teachers.

Temporary agricultural workers are admissible to the United States under the H–2A category of the 1990 Act. An H–2B nonagricultural worker is an alien who is coming temporarily to the United States to perform temporary services or labor, is not displacing U.S. workers capable of performing such services or labor, and whose employment is not adversely affecting the wages and working conditions of a U.S. worker.[39]

The 1990 Act places an annual limit on the number of H–2B visas at 66,000.

The 1990 Act created new categories of visas. The R visa facilitates the temporary entry of religious workers into the United States. The Q visa allows private businesses to bring individuals into the country for cultural events. The O and P visas apply to professional entertainers and athletes.

---

[35] 67 Interpreter Releases, 88-86 (Aug. 13, 1990).
[36] Department of State, 9 *Foreign Affairs Manual*, § 41.25.
[37] 22 C.F.R. § 41:51 (b)(1) (1996).
[38] Pub. L. N. 101-649, § 206(b)(2) (1990). See DLR No. 249 (12-29-95) pc-1 for a special report on how U.S. employers are using immigration laws to meet staffing needs.
[39] 8 C.F.R. § 214.2(h)(5)(i) (1996).

The *International Union of Bricklayers v. Meese* decision, presented in this section, is an example of the complicated employment issues an employer faces in meeting the needs of its business.

INTERNATIONAL UNION OF BRICKLAYERS v. MEESE

United States District Court, 616 F. Supp. 1387 (D.C. Cal. 1985).

[The International Union of Bricklayers (Union) brought an action against U.S. Attorney General Edwin Meese, Secretary of State George Schultz, the INS, and the Homestake Mining Co., which owned the McLaughlin Gold Project in Lake County, California. The Union challenges the INS instruction that allowed B-1 "temporary visitor for business" visas to be issued to ten West Germans to come to the United States temporarily to do certain bricklaying and other work. The Union contends that the instruction is in violation of the INA. The defendants disagree.]

LEGGE, D. J.

I.

Statutory and Regulatory Overview.

The Act generally charges the Attorney General and the Secretary of State with the administration and enforcement of the immigration laws of the United States. *See* 8 U.S.C. §§ 1103(a), 1104(a). Primary responsibility, however, rests with the Attorney General, and his "determination and ruling . . . with respect to all questions of [immigration] law [is] controlling." 8 U.S.C. § 1103(a).

Under the Act, an alien seeking to enter the United States is categorized either as an "immigrant" or "nonimmigrant." In most instances, an immigrant seeks permanent residence, and a nonimmigrant seeks only a temporary stay. . . . The distinction between immigrant and nonimmigrant aliens is significant. The Act contains numerical limitations and strict documentary requirements for certain classes of immigrant

aliens. In contrast, there are no numerical limitations placed upon the classes of nonimmgrant aliens.

The dispute in the present case centers on the Act's provisions regarding nonimmigrant aliens. Section 101(a)(15) of the Act, 8 U.S.C. § 1101(a)(15), sets forth thirteen classes of aliens entitled to nonimmigrant status. The parties have stipulated, however, that only two of those classes are germane to this case.

A.

Temporary Visitors for Business.

The first class of nonimmigrant aliens relevant here is the "temporary visitor for business" class. Section 101(a)(15)(b) of the Act defines a "temporary visitor for business" as:

an alien (other than one coming for the purpose of study or of performing skilled or unskilled labor or as a representative of foreign press, radio, film, or other foreign information media coming to engage in such vocation) having a residence in a foreign country which he has no intention of abandoning and who is visiting the United States temporarily for business. . . .

8 U.S.C. § 1101(a)(15)(B). An alien qualifying for this nonimmigrant status is entitled to receive a "B–1" visa. *See* 8 U.S.C. § 1201(a)(2).

Pursuant to his authority under the Act, *see* 8 U.S.C. § 1104(a), the Secretary of State has promulgated a regulation defining the term "business" for purposes of the B–1 "temporary visitor for business" class:

The term "business," as used in section 101(a)(15)(B) of the Act, refers to legitimate activities of a commercial or professional character. It does not include purely lo-cal employment or labor for hire. An alien seeking to enter as a nonimmigrant for employment or labor pur-suant to a contract or other prearrangement shall be re-quired to qualify under the provisions of [22 C.F.R.] § 41.55.

22 C.F.R. § 41.25(b)(1985). *See also* C.F.R. § 41.25(a)(1985) (specifying factors considered by consular officer in determining whether an alien is classifiable as a "temporary visitor for business").

Among the criteria utilized to determine an alien's eligibility for B-1 "temporary visitor for business" status is INS Operations Instruction 214.2(b)(5), an INS internal agency guideline that is the subject of this dispute. The Opera-tions Instruction provides:

Each of the following may also be classified as a B-1 nonimmigrant if he/she is to receive no salary or other remuneration from a United States source (other than an expense allowance or other reimbursement for ex-penses incidental to the temporary stay): . . .

(5) An alien coming to install, service, or repair commercial or industrial equipment or machinery pur-chased from a company outside the U.S. or to train U.S. workers to perform such service, provided: the con-tract of sale specifically requires the seller to perform such services or training, the alien possesses specialized knowledge essential to the seller's contractual obliga-tion to provide services or training, the alien will receive no remuneration from a U.S. source, and the trip is to take place within the first year following the purchase.

Pursuant to the Operations Instruction, B-1 visas have been issued to the foreign labor-ers who came to the United States to work on the project owned by Homestake, and to foreign la-borers to do other work throughout the United States. The central issue in this case is whether the Operations Instruction violates the Act and the regulations promulgated under the Act.

B.

Temporary Workers.

The second class of nonimmigrant aliens involved here is the "temporary worker" class.

Section 101(a)(15)(H)(ii) of the Act defines a "temporary worker" as:

an alien having a residence in a foreign country which he has no intention of abandoning . . . [and] who is coming temporarily to the United States to perform temporary services of labor, if unemployed persons ca-pable of performing such service or labor cannot be found in this country. . . .

8 U.S.C. § 1101(a)(15)(H)(ii). An alien qualify-ing for this nonimmigrant status is entitled to re-ceive an "H-2" visa. *See* 8 U.S.C. § 1201(a)(2).

The Attorney General is authorized to make the determination concerning the admissibility of an H-2 "temporary worker" applicant after consulting with other government agencies. . . .

II.

The Present Case.

Factual Background.

Homestake began construction in early 1984 on its McLaughlin Gold Project in order to open a new gold mine. Due to metallurgical problems in the Lake County region, Homes-take concluded that it was necessary to employ technology not used previously in the gold min-ing industry. Davy McKee Corporation ("Davy McKee"), Homestake's construction manager, therefore conducted a search to locate the ap-propriate technology.

On behalf of Homestake, Davy McKee agreed to purchase a newly-designed gold ore processing system from Didier-Werke ("Didier"), a West German manufacturing company. Al-though the purchase agreement required Didier to supply an integrated processing system, it was not possible to premanufacture the entire sys-tem in West Germany. The purchase agreement was therefore made contingent upon Didier's West German employees completing the work on the system at the project site in Lake County.

In September 1984, Didier submitted B-1 "temporary visitor for business" visa petitions on behalf of ten of its West German employees to United States consular officers in Bonn, West Germany. Relying upon INS Operations Instruction 214.2(b)(5), consular officers approved the petitions and issued B–1 visas to the West Germans. In January 1985, the West Germans entered the United States to work on the processing system. The work involves the installation of the interior linings of the system's auto-claves, and requires certain technical bricklaying skills. . . .

III.

The Validity of the Operations Instruction under the Act.

Plaintiffs contend that INS Operations Instruction 214.2(b)(5) violates the Act, because the Operations Instruction is inconsistent with specific provisions of the Act, and with the legislative intent underlying those provisions.

In testing the Operations Instruction against the Act, the court's task is to interpret the Act in light of the purposes Congress sought to achieve in enacting it. *Dickerson v. New Banner Institute, Inc.*, 460 U.S. 103 (1983). The starting point must be the language employed by *Congress. I.N.S. v. Phinpathya*, 464 U.S. 183 (1984). Absent a clearly expressed legislative intention to the contrary, the statutory language is to be regarded as conclusive. *Escondido Mutual Water Co. v. Mission Indians*, 466 U.S. 765 (1984).

The Language of the Act and the Operations Instruction.

The court must begin its analysis by comparing the language of the Act with the language of the Operations Instruction. In particular, the court must focus on the nonimmigrant visa provisions in sections 101(a)(15)(B) and 101(a)(15)(H)(ii) of the Act.

Section 101(a)(15)(B) of the Act defines a "temporary visitor for business" nonimmigrant as:

an alien (other than one coming for the purpose of study or of performing skilled or unskilled labor *or as a representative of foreign press, radio, film, or other*

foreign information media coming to engage in such vocation) having a residence in a foreign country which he has no intention of abandoning and who is visiting the United States temporarily for business. . . .

8 U.S.C. § 1101(a)(15)(B) (emphasis added). A "temporary visitor for business" nonimmigrant is entitled to receive a B–1 visa. *See* 8 U.S.C. § 1201(a)(2). Under section 101(a)(15)(B), however, an alien coming to the United States for the purpose of "performing skilled or unskilled labor" is expressly *excluded* from the "temporary visitor for business" class.

Section 101(a)(15)(H)(ii) of the Act defines a "temporary worker" nonimmigrant as:

an alien *having a residence in a foreign country which he has no intention of abandoning . . . [and] who is* coming temporarily to the United States to perform temporary services or labor, if unemployed persons capable of performing such service or labor cannot be found in this country. . . .

8 U.S.C. § 1101(a)(15)(H)(ii) (emphasis added). A "temporary worker" nonimmigrant is entitled to receive an H–2 visa.

INS Operations Instruction 214.2(b)(5) provides that an alien may be classified as a "temporary visitor for business" nonimmigrant if:

he/she is to receive no salary or other remuneration from a United States source (other than an expense allowance or other reimbursement for expenses incidental to the temporary stay) . . . [and is] coming to install, service, or repair commercial or industrial equipment or machinery purchased from a company outside the U.S. *or to train U.S. workers to perform such service.* . . .

A comparison of the language of section 101(a)(15)(B) of the Act with the language of INS Operations Instruction 214.2(b)(5) demonstrates that the Operations Instruction contravenes that section of the Act. Section 101(a)(15)(B) unequivocally excludes from the B–1 "temporary visitor for business" classification an alien who is "coming for the purpose of . . . performing skilled or unskilled labor." 8 U.S.C. § 1101(a)(15)(B). . . .

INS Operations Instruction 214.2(b)(5), however, does not contain an exclusion for an alien seeking to enter the United Sates to perform skilled or unskilled labor. The Operations Instruction provides that an alien may be classified as a "temporary visitor for business" if the alien is "coming to install, service, or repair commercial or industrial equipment or machinery." The effect of this language is to authorize the issuance of a B–1 visa to an alien coming to this country to perform skilled or unskilled labor. In the present case, for example, the West Germans undeniably are performing labor—whether it be deemed skilled or unskilled—in connection with the installation of the gold ore processing system at the McLaughlin Gold Project.

Similarly, a comparison of the language of section 101(a)(15)(H)(ii) of the Act with the language of INS Operations Instruction 214.2(b)(5) shows that the Operations Instruction also contravenes that section of the Act. Section 101(a)(15)(H)(ii) classifies an H–2 "temporary worker" as an alien "coming . . . to perform temporary services or labor, if unemployed persons capable of performing such service or labor cannot be found in this country." 8 U.S.C. § 1101(a)(15)(H)(ii). Because the Act requires the Attorney General to consult other agencies of the government concerning "temporary worker" visas, *see* 8 U.S.C. § 1184(c), the Attorney General has established H–2 labor certification procedures. Thus, an H–2 visa petition cannot be approved unless the alien's employer obtains either "[*a*] *certification from the Secretary of Labor* . . . stating *that qualified persons in the United States are not available and that the employment* of the beneficiary *will not adversely affect wages and working conditions of workers in the United States* similarly employed . . . [*or*] notice that such certification *cannot* be made." 8 C.F.R. § 214.2(h)(3) (1985) (emphasis added).

In contrast, INS Operations Instruction 214.2(b)(5) does not require an alien to seek labor certification prior to obtaining a nonimmigrant visa. More importantly, the Operations Instruction authorizes the issuance of a nonimmigrant visa to a person performing skilled or unskilled labor, though qualified Americans may be available to perform the work involved. The Operations Instruction therefore lacks the safeguards contained in section 101(a)(15)(H)(ii) of the Act and the regulation promulgated under that section. Again, the present case illustrates this point, because the parties have stipulated that neither the West Germans nor their employer was required to seek labor certification from the Secretary of Labor prior to the issuance of the visas to the West Germans.

In summary, it is apparent that the language of INS Operations Instruction 214.2(b)(5) is inconsistent with the language of sections 101(a)(15)(B) and 101(a)(15)(H)(ii) of the Act. First, the Operations Instruction ignores the provision in section 101(a)(15)(B) *excluding* skilled or unskilled labor. Second, the Operations Instruction ignores the provision in section 101(a)(15)(H)(ii) concerning the availability of qualified American workers. . . .

The court concludes from both the language and legislative intent of the Act that the federal defendants' interpretation embodied in the Operations Instruction contravenes the Act. The court therefore decides that INS Operations Instruction 214.2(b)(5) violates sections 101(a)(15)(B) and 101(a)(15)(H)(ii) of the Act. . . .

It is so ordered.

CASE QUESTIONS

1. Summarize the facts of this case.
2. What rule of statutory construction did the court follow in assessing the validity of the INS instruction in question?
3. Was INS Operations Instruction 214.2(b)(5) consistent with the law that provides for "temporary visitor for business" B–1 visas?
4. May an H–2 visa be obtained as easily as a B–1 visa?

Chapter Questions and Problems

1. A plant closing law entitles employees to a 60-day notice of the closing of the plant. Present an employer's view of such a law. Present an employee's view of such a law.

2. Under the IRCA verification procedures, may an employer insist that a prospective employee with a foreign accent produce either a certificate of naturalization or an Alien Registration Card?

3. Knifepersons performed butchering operations at the King Packing Co. Various knives and three types of electric saws were used in the butchering operation. Some of the knives were furnished by the employees. The saws and the more expensive knives were furnished by the employer. All the knives, as well as the saws, had to be razor-sharp for the proper performance of work. A dull knife slowed down production, which was conducted on an assembly line basis; affected the appearance of the meat, as well as the quality of the hides; and caused waste and accidents. The knifepersons were required to sharpen their own knives outside the scheduled shift of eight hours, and they were not paid for the time so spent.

    The Secretary of Labor contended that the time spent sharpening knives was compensable working time under the FLSA. King Packing Co. contended that such is noncompensable preliminary activity under the Portal-to-Portal Act. Decide. [*Mitchell v. King Packing Co.*, 350 U.S. 260]

4. Mester Manufacturing Co. makes furniture at facilities in San Diego, California. INS Agent Shanks made an educational visit to the facilities in July of 1987. On September 2, 1987, INS agents inspected I–9s on file at the facility. The INS then made a computer search of its records, which showed that the numbers on the green cards used by three employees belonged to other aliens. On September 3, 1987, Shanks gave Barry Mester, the company president, a handwritten list identifying the three employees in question. Mester took no investigative or corrective actions. On September 25 INS agents returned to again inspect Mester's I–9s, and found that the three named individuals suspected of using false green cards were still employed by Mester. Mester was penalized a total of $1,500 for continuing to employ the three individuals. Mester appealed, contending that INS did not give it proper notice that it suspected green card fraud and that the evidence did not support a finding of green card fraud. Which party has the burden of proof? Decide. [*Mester Manufacturing Co. v. INS*, (CA 9 Cal) 879 F2d. 561]

5. Workers at the Greeley, Colorado, beef processing plant of Montfort Inc. are required to spend time before and after their shift putting on and removing special safety equipment, and at the end of the shift cleaning the special gear worn by these knifepersons. The workers believe that they are entitled to be paid for this "work." The employer believes that it is not "work" for which they should be paid. Is there a governmental agency that employees may turn to that has the power to evaluate their claim for additional pay, and, if appropriate, seek a remedy on their behalf? Are the employees entitled to pay for the functions performed before and after their shifts? And if so, at what rate? [*Reich v. Montfort*, DC Colo, No.92-M-2456 11/15/96]

6. The American Friends Service Committee (AFSC) is a Quaker organization that employs some 400 individuals in charitable and relief work. The Immigration Reform and Control Act prohibits employers from hiring aliens not authorized to work in the

United States, and requires examination of documents evidencing identity and work authorization. The AFSC seeks declaratory relief, alleging that the IRCA violates its free exercise of religion, which religion requires its members to welcome and not show hostility to strangers, the poor, and the dispossessed. The U.S. Attorney General contends that the law is neutral and not directed at religious beliefs. Should an injunction be issued? [*American Friends Service Committee v. Thornburg*, 941 F.2d 808 (9th Cir.)]

7. While on FMLA related to the birth of her son, Catherine Marzano was notified in writing that her position was being eliminated as a result of a reduction in force (RIF) caused by financial difficulties. Shortly thereafter in October of 1993 she went to see her boss and he told her "how his wife had collected unemployment so that she could stay at home with their kids, and how [Ms. Marzano] might be better off if she could stay at home with her son and collect unemployment." On November 1, 1993, her boss circulated a memo advertising three positions. Ms. Marzano was never advised of or considered for these positions. Ms. Marzano asserts that pregnancy is the kiss of death with the employer, with many employees being terminated after taking maternity leave. The employer asserts that it acted out of legitimate business and economic considerations when it eliminated nine out of some fifty positions in the unit, including Ms. Marzano's. Ms. Marzano responded that it was a reshuffling of employees, not a legitimate RIF. Did the employer violate the FMLA by terminating Ms. Marzano during her leave? [See *Marzano v. Computer Science Corp. Inc.*, 91 F3d 497 (3d Cir.)]

8. The Fort Halifax Packing Co. closed its poultry packaging and processing plant and laid off its employees. The director of Maine's Bureau of Labor Standards, Daniel Coyne, filed suit to enforce the provisions of a state statute. This statute provided that any employer that terminates operations at a plant with 100 or more employees, or relocates those operations more than 100 miles away, must provide one week's pay for each year of employment to all employees who have worked in the plant at least three years. The employer has no such liability if the employee accepts employment at the new location, or if the employee is covered by a contract that deals with the issue of severance pay. The employer contended that the state statute was preempted by the Employee Retirement Income Security Act of 1974 (ERISA) and by the National Labor Relations Act (NLRA). Decide. [*Fort Halifax Packing Co. v. Coyne*, 107 S.Ct. 2211]

Appendixes

Appendix A

Excerpts from Title VII of the Civil Rights Act of 1964 as Amended by the Equal Employment Opportunity Act of 1972

DISCRIMINATION BECAUSE OF RACE, COLOR, RELIGION, SEX, OR NATIONAL ORIGIN

Section 703. (a) It shall be an unlawful employment practice for an employer—

(1) to fail or refuse to hire or to discharge any individual, or otherwise to discriminate against any individual with respect to his compensation, terms, conditions, or privileges of employment, because of such individual's race, color, religion, sex, or national origin; or

(2) to limit, segregate, or classify his employees or applicants for employment in any way which would deprive any individual of employment opportunities or otherwise adversely affect his status as an employee, because of such individual's race, color, religion, sex, or national origin. (As amended by P.L. 92-261, eff. March 24, 1972.)

(b) It shall be an unlawful employment practice for an employment agency to fail or refuse to refer for employment, or otherwise to discriminate against, any individual because of his race, color, religion, sex, or national origin, or to classify or refer for employment any individual on the basis of his race, color, religion, sex, or national origin.

(c) It shall be an unlawful employment practice for a labor organization—

(1) to exclude or to expel from its membership, or otherwise to discriminate against, any individual because of his race, color, religion, sex, or national origin;

(2) to limit, segregate, or classify its membership or applicants for membership or to classify or fail or refuse to refer for employment any individual, in any way which would deprive or tend to deprive any individual of employment opportunities, or would limit such employment opportunities or otherwise adversely affect his status as an employee or as an applicant for employment, because of such individual's race, color, religion, sex, or national origin; or

(3) to cause or attempt to cause an employer to discriminate against an individual in violation of this section.

(d) It shall be an unlawful employment practice for any employer, labor organization, or joint labor-management committee controlling apprenticeship or other training or retraining, including on-the-job training programs to discriminate against any individual because of his race, color, religion, sex, or national origin in admission to, or employment in, any program established to provide apprenticeship or other training.

(e) Notwithstanding any other provision of this title, (1) it shall not be an unlawful employment practice for an employer to hire and employ employees, for an employment agency to classify, or refer for employment any individual, for a labor organization to classify its membership or to classify or refer for employment any individual, or for an employer, labor organization, or joint labor-management committee controlling apprenticeship or other training or retraining programs to admit or employ any individual in any such program, on the basis of his religion, sex, or national origin in those certain instances where religion, sex, or national origin is a bona fide occupational qualification reasonably necessary to the normal operation of that particular business or enterprise, and (2) it shall not be an unlawful employment practice for a school, college, university, or other educational institution or institution of learning to hire and employ employees of a particular religion if such school, college, university or other educational institution or institution of learning is, in whole or in substantial part, owned, supported, controlled, or managed, by a particular religion or by a particular religious corporation, association, or society, or if the curriculum of such school, college, university, or other educational institution or institution of learning is directed toward the propagation of a particular religion.

(f) As used in this title, the phrase "unlawful employment practice" shall not be deemed to include any action or measure taken by an employer, labor organization, join labor-management committee or employment agency with respect to an individual who is a member of the Communist Party of the United States or of any other organization required to register as a Communist-action or Communist-front organization by final order of the Subversive Activities Control Board pursuant to the Subversive Activities Control Act of 1950.

(g) Notwithstanding any other provision of this title, it shall not be an unlawful employment practice for an employer to fail or refuse to hire and employ any individual for any position, for an employer to discharge an individual from any position, or for an employment agency to fail or refuse to refer any individual for employment in any position, or for a labor organization to fail or refuse to refer any individual for employment in any position, if—

(1) the occupancy of such position, or access to the premises in or upon which any part of the duties of such position is performed or is to be performed, is subject to any requirement imposed in the interest of the national security of the United States under any security program in effect pursuant to or administered under any statute of the United States or any Executive order of the President; and

(2) such individual has not fulfilled or has ceased to fulfill that requirement.

(h) Notwithstanding any other provision of this title, it shall not be an unlawful employment practice for an employer to apply different standards of compensation, or different terms, conditions, or privileges of employment pursuant to a bona fide seniority or merit system, or a system which measures earnings by quantity or quality of production or to employees who work in different locations, provided that such differences are not the result of an intention to discriminate because of race, color, religion, sex, or national origin; nor shall it be an unlawful employment practice for an employer to give and to act upon the results of any professionally developed ability test provided that such test, its administration or action upon the results is not designed, intended, or used to discriminate because of race, color, religion, sex, or national origin. It shall not be an unlawful employment practice under this title for any employer to differentiate upon the basis of sex in determining the amount of the wages or compensation paid to employees of such employer if such differentiation is authorized by the provisions of Section 6(d) of the Fair Labor Standards Act of 1938 as amended (29 USC 206(d)).

(i) Nothing contained in this title shall apply to any business or enterprise on or near an Indian reservation with respect to any publicly announced employment practice of such business or enterprise under which a preferential treatment is given to any individual because he is an Indian living on or near a reservation.

(j) Nothing contained in this title shall be interpreted to require any employer, employment agency, labor organization, or joint labor-management committee subject to this title to grant preferential treatment to any individual or to any group because of the race, color, religion, sex, or national origin of such individual or group on account of an imbalance which may exist with respect to the total number or percentage of persons of any race, color, religion, sex, or national origin employed by any employer, referred or classified for employment by any employment agency or labor organization, admitted to membership or classified by any labor organization, or admitted to, or employed in, any apprenticeship or other training program, in comparison with the total number or percentage of persons of such race, color, religion, sex, or national origin in any community, State, section, or other area, or in the available work force in any community, State, section, or other area. (As amended by P.L. 92-261, eff. March 24, 1972.)

OTHER UNLAWFUL EMPLOYMENT PRACTICES

Section 704. (a) It shall be an unlawful employment practice for an employer to discriminate against any of his employees or applicants for employment, for an employment agency or joint labor-management committee controlling apprenticeship or other training or retraining, including on-the-job training programs, to discriminate against any individual, or for a labor organization to discriminate against any member thereof or applicant for membership, because he has opposed any practice, made an unlawful employment practice by this title, or because he has made a charge, testified, assisted, or participated in any manner in an investigation, proceeding, or hearing under this title. (As amended by P.L. No. 92-261, eff. March 24, 1972.) . . .

Excerpts from Civil Rights Act of 1991

Public Law 102–166, 105 Stat. 1071, 42 U.S.C. 1981
November 21, 1991

Be it enacted by the Senate and House of Representatives of the United States of America in Congress assembled,

SHORT TITLE

Section 1. This Act may be cited as the "Civil Rights Act of 1991".

FINDINGS

Section 2. The Congress finds that—

(1) additional remedies under Federal law are needed to deter unlawful harassment and intentional discrimination in the workplace;

(2) the decision of the Supreme Court in Wards Cove Packing Co. v. Atonio, 490 U.S. 642 (1989) has weakened the scope and effectiveness of Federal civil rights protections; and

(3) legislation is necessary to provide additional protections against unlawful discrimination in employment.

PURPOSES

Section 3. The purposes of this Act are—

(1) to provide appropriate remedies for intentional discrimination and unlawful harassment in the workplace;

(2) to codify the concepts of "business necessity" and "job related" enunciated by the Supreme Court in Griggs v. Duke Power Co., 401 U.S. 424 (1971), and in the other Supreme Court decisions prior to Wards Cove Packing Co. v. Atonio, 490 U.S. 642 (1989);

(3) to confirm statutory authority and provide statutory guidelines for the adjudication of disparate impact suits under title VII of the Civil Rights Act of 1964 (42 U.S.C. 2000e et seq.); and

(4) to respond to recent decisions of the Supreme Court by expanding the scope of relevant civil rights statutes in order to provide adequate protection to victims of discrimination.

TITLE I—FEDERAL CIVIL RIGHTS REMEDIES

PROHIBITION AGAINST ALL RACIAL DISCRIMINATION IN THE MAKING AND ENFORCEMENT OF CONTRACTS

Section 101. Section 1977 of the Revised Statutes (42 U.S.C. 1981) is amended—

(1) by inserting "(a)" before "All persons within"; and

(2) by adding at the end the following new subsections:

"(b) For purposes of this section, the term 'make and enforce contracts' includes the making, performance, modification, and termination of contracts, and the enjoyment of all benefits, privileges, terms, and conditions of the contractual relationship.

"(c) The rights protected by this section are protected against impairment by nongovernmental discrimination and impairment under color of State law."

DAMAGES IN CASES OF INTENTIONAL DISCRIMINATION

Section 102. The Revised Statutes are amended by inserting after section 1977 (42 U.S.C. 1981) the following new section:

DAMAGES IN CASES OF INTENTIONAL DISCRIMINATION IN EMPLOYMENT

Section 1977A. '(a) Right of Recovery.—

'(1) Civil rights.—In an action brought by a complaining party under section 706 or 717 of the Civil Rights Act of 1964 (42 U.S.C. 2000e-5) against a respondent who engaged in unlawful intentional discrimination (not an employment practice that is unlawful because of its disparate impact) prohibited under section 703, 704, or 717 of the Act (42 U.S.C. 2000e-2 or 2000e-3), and provided that the complaining party cannot recover under section 1977 of the Revised Statutes (42 U.S.C. 1981), the complaining party may recover compensatory and punitive damages as allowed in subsection (b), in addition to any relief authorized by section 706(g) of the Civil Rights Act of 1964, from the respondent.

'(2) Disability.—In an action brought by a complaining party under the powers, remedies, and procedures set forth in section 706 or 717 of the Civil Rights Act of 1964 (as provided in section 107(a) of the Americans with Disabilities Act of 1990 (42 U.S.C. 12117(a)), and section 505(a)(1) of the Rehabilitation Act of 1973 (29 U.S.C. 794a(a)(1)), respectively) against a respondent who engaged in unlawful intentional discrimination (not an employment practice that is unlawful because of its disparate impact) under section 501 of the Rehabilitation Act of 1973 (29 U.S.C. 791) and the regulations implementing section 501, or who violated the requirements of section 501 of the Act or the regulations implementing section 501 concerning the provision of a reasonable accommodation, or section 102 of the Americans with Disabilities Act of 1990 (42 U.S.C. 12112), or committed a violation of section 102(b)(5) of the Act, against an individual, the complaining party may recover compensatory and punitive damages as allowed in subsection (b), in addition to any relief authorized by section 706(g) of the Civil Rights Act of 1964, from the respondent.

'(3) Reasonable accommodation and good faith effort.—In cases where a discriminatory practice involves the provision of a reasonable accommodation pursuant to section 102(b)(5) of the Americans with Disabilities Act of 1990 or regulations implementing section 501 of the Rehabilitation Act of 1973, damages may not be awarded under this section where the covered entity demonstrates good faith efforts, in consultation with the person with the disability who has informed the covered entity that accommodation is needed, to identify and make a reasonable accommodation that would provide such individual with an equally effective opportunity and would not cause an undue hardship on the operation of the business.

"(b) Compensatory and Punitive Damages.—

"(1) Determination of punitive damages.—A complaining party may recover punitive damages under this section against a respondent (other than a government, government agency or political subdivision) if the complaining party demonstrates that the respondent engaged in a discriminatory practice or discriminatory practices with malice or with reckless indifference to the federally protected rights of an aggrieved individual.

"(2) Exclusions from compensatory damages.—Compensatory damages awarded under this section shall not include backpay, interest on backpay, or any other type of relief authorized under section 706(g) of the Civil Rights Act of 1964.

"(3) Limitations.—The sum of the amount of compensatory damages awarded under this section for future pecuniary losses, emotional pain, suffering, inconvenience, mental anguish, loss of enjoyment of life, and other nonpecuniary losses, and the amount of punitive damages awarded under this section, shall not exceed, for each complaining party—

"(A) in the case of a respondent who has more than 14 and fewer than 101 employees in each of 20 or more calendar weeks in the current or preceding calendar year, $50,000;

"(B) in the case of a respondent who has more than 100 and fewer than 201 employees in each of 20 or more calendar weeks in the current or preceding calendar year, $100,000; and

"(C) in the case of a respondent who has more than 200 and fewer than 501 employees in each of 20 or more calendar weeks in the current or preceding calendar year, $200,000; and

"(D) in the case of a respondent who has more than 500 employees in each of 20 or more calendar weeks in the current or preceding calendar year, $300,000.

"(4) Construction.—Nothing in this section shall be construed to limit the scope of, or the relief available under, section 1977 of the Revised Statutes (42 U.S.C. 1981).

"(c) Jury Trial.—If a complaining party seeks compensatory or punitive damages under this section—

"(1) any party may demand a trial by jury; and

"(2) the court shall not inform the jury of the limitations described in subsection (b)(3).

"(d) Definitions.—As used in this section:

"(1) Complaining party.—The term 'complaining party' means—

"(A) in the case of a person seeking to bring an action under subsection (a)(I), the Equal Employment Opportunity Commission, the Attorney General, or a person who may bring an action or proceeding under title VII of the Civil Rights Act of 1964 (42 U.S.C. 2000e et seq.); or

"(B) in the case of a person seeking to bring an action under subsection (a)(2), the Equal Employment

Opportunity Commission, the Attorney General, a person who may bring an action or proceeding under section 505(a)(1) of the Rehabilitation Act of 1973 (29 U.S.C. 794a(a)(1), or a person who may bring an action or proceeding under title I of the Americans with Disabilities Act of 1990 (42 U.S.C. 12101 et seq.).

"(2) Discriminatory practice.—The term 'discriminatory practice' means the discrimination described in paragraph (1), or the discrimination or the violation described in paragraph (2), of subsection (a).

ATTORNEY'S FEES

Section 103. The last sentence of section 722 of the Revised Statutes (42 U.S.C. 1988) is amended by inserting, "1977A" after "1977".

DEFINITIONS

Section 104. Section 701 of the Civil Rights Act of 1964 (42 U.S.C. 2000e) is amended by adding at the end the following new subsections:

"(1) The term 'complaining party' means the Commission, the Attorney General, or a person who may bring an action or proceeding under this title.

"(m) The term 'demonstrates' means meets the burdens of production and persuasion.

"(n) The term 'respondent' means an employer, employment agency, labor organization, joint labor-management committee controlling apprenticeship or other training or retraining program, including an on-the-job training program, or Federal entity subject to section 717."

BURDEN OF PROOF IN DISPARATE IMPACT CASES

Section 105. (a) Section 703 of the Civil Rights Act of 1964 (U.S.C. 2000e-2) is amended by adding at the end the following new subsection:

"(k)(1)(A) An unlawful employment practice based on disparate impact is established under this title only if—

"(i) a complaining party demonstrates that a respondent uses a particular employment practice that causes a disparate impact on the basis of race, color, religion, sex, or national origin and the respondent fails to demonstrate that the challenged practice is job related for the position in question and consistent with business necessity; or

"(ii) the complaining party makes the demonstration described in subparagraph (C) with respect to an alternative employment practice and the respondent refuses to adopt such alternative employment practice.

"(B)(i) With respect to demonstrating that a particular employment practice causes a disparate impact as described in subparagraph (A)(i), the complaining party shall demonstrate that each particular challenged employment practice causes a disparate impact, except that if the complaining party can demonstrate to the court that the elements of a respondent's decisionmaking process are not capable of separation for analysis, the decisionmaking process may be analyzed as one employment practice.

"(ii) If the respondent demonstrates that a specific employment practice does not cause the disparate impact, the respondent shall not be required to demonstrate that such practice is required by business necessity.

"(C) The demonstration referred to by subparagraph (A)(ii) shall be in accordance with the law as it existed on June 4, 1989, with respect to the concept of 'alternative employment practice'.

"(2) A demonstration that an employment practice is required by business necessity may not be used as a defense against a claim of intentional discrimination under this title.

"(3) Notwithstanding any other provision of this title, a rule barring the employment of an individual who currently and knowingly uses or possesses a controlled substance, as defined in schedules I and II of section 102(6) of the Controlled Substances Act (21 U.S.C. 802(6)), other than the use or possession of a drug taken under the supervision of a licensed health care professional, or any other use or possession authorized by the Controlled Substances Act or any other provision of Federal law, shall be considered an unlawful employment practice under this title only if such rule is adopted or applied with an intent to discriminate because of race, color, religion, sex, or national origin.".

(b) No statements other than the interpretive memorandum appearing at Vol. 137 Congressional Record S 15276 (daily ed. Oct. 25, 1991) shall be considered legislative history of, or relied upon in any way as legislative history in construing or applying, any provision of this Act that relates Wards Cove-Business necessity/cumulation/alternative business practice.

PROHIBITION AGAINST DISCRIMINATORY USE OF TEST SCORES

Section 106. Section 703 of the Civil Rights of 1964 (42 U.S.C. 2000e-2) (as amended by section 105) is further amended by adding at the end the following new subsection:

"(1) It shall be an unlawful employment practice for a respondent, in connection with the selection or referral of applicants or candidates for employment or promotion, to adjust the scores of, use different cutoff scores for, or otherwise alter the results of, employment related tests on the basis of race, color, religion, sex, or national origin.".

CLARIFYING PROHIBITION AGAINST IMPERMISSIBLE CONSIDERATION OF RACE, COLOR, RELIGION, SEX, OR NATIONAL ORIGIN IN EMPLOYMENT PRACTICES

Section 107. (a) In General.—Section 703 of the Civil Rights Act of 1964 (42 U.S.C. 2000e-2) (as amended by sections 105 and 106) is further amended by adding at the end the following new subsection:

"(m) Except as otherwise provided in this title, an unlawful employment practice is established when the complaining party demonstrates that race, color, religion, sex, or national origin was a motivating factor for any employment practice, even though other factors also motivated the practice.".

(b) Enforcement Provisions.—Section 706(g) of such Act (42 U.S.C. 2000e-5(g)) is amended—

(1) by designating the first through third sentences as paragraph (1);

(2) by designating the fourth sentence as paragraph (2)(A) and indenting accordingly; and

(3) by adding at the end the following new subparagraph:

"(B) On a claim in which an individual proves a violation under section 703(m) and a respondent demonstrates that the respondent would have taken the same action in the absence of the impermissible motivating factor, the court—

"(i) may grant declaratory relief, injunctive relief (except as provided in clause (ii)), and attorney's fees and costs demonstrated to be directly attributable only to the pursuit of a claim under section 703(m); and

"(ii) shall not award damages or issue an order requiring any admission, reinstatement, hiring, promotion, or payment, described in subparagraph (A).".

FACILITATING PROMPT AND ORDERLY RESOLUTION OF CHALLENGES TO EMPLOYMENT PRACTICES IMPLEMENTING LITIGATED OR CONSENT JUDGMENTS OR ORDERS

Section 108. Section 703 of the Civil Rights Act of 1964 (42 U.S.C. 2000e-2) (as amended by sections 105, 106, and 107 of this title) is further amended by adding at the end the following new subsection:

"(n)(1)(A) Notwithstanding any other provision of law, and except as provided in paragraph (2), an employment practice that implements and is within the scope of a litigated or consent judgment or order that resolves a claim of employment discrimination under the Constitution or Federal civil rights laws may not be challenged under the circumstances described in subparagraph (B).

"(B) A practice described in subparagraph (A) may not be challenged in a claim under the Constitution or Federal civil rights laws—

"(i) by a person who, prior to the entry of the judgment or order described in subparagraph (A), had—

"(I) actual notice of the proposed judgment or order sufficient to apprise such person that such judgment or order might adversely affect the interests and legal rights of such person and that an opportunity was available to present objections to such judgment or order by a future date certain; and

"(II) a reasonable opportunity to present objections to such judgment or order; or

"(ii) by a person whose interests were adequately represented by another person who had previously challenged the judgment or order on the same legal grounds and with a similar factual situation, unless there has been an intervening change in law or fact.

"(2) Nothing in this subsection shall be construed to—

"(A) alter the standards for intervention under rule 24 of the Federal Rules of Civil Procedure or apply to the rights of parties who have successfully intervened pursuant to such rule in the proceeding in which the parties intervened;

"(B) apply to the rights of parties to the action in which a litigated or consent judgment or order was entered, or of members of a class represented or sought to be represented in such action, or of members of a group on whose behalf relief was sought in such action by the Federal Government;

"(C) prevent challenges to a litigated or consent judgment or order on the ground that such judgment or order was obtained through collusion or fraud, or is transparently invalid or was entered by a court lacking subject matter jurisdiction; or

"(D) authorize or permit the denial to any person of the due process of law required by the Constitution.

"(3) Any action not precluded under this subsection that challenges an employment consent judgment or order described in paragraph (1) shall be brought in the court, and if possible before the judge, that entered such judgment or order. Nothing in this subsection shall preclude a transfer of such action pursuant to section 1404 of title 28, United States Code.".

PROTECTION OF EXTRA-TERRITORIAL EMPLOYMENT

Section 109. (a) Definition of Employee. — Section 701(f) of the Civil Rights Act of 1964 (42 U.S.C. 2000e(f)) and section 101(4) of the Americans with Disabilities Act of 1990 (42 U.S.C. 12111(4)) are each amended by adding at the end the following "With respect to employment in a foreign country, such term includes an individual who is a citizen of the United States.".

(b) Exemption. —

(1) Civil Rights Act of 1964. — Section 702 of the Civil Rights Act of 1964 (42 U.S.C. 2000e-1) is amended —

(A) by inserting "(a)" after "Sec. 702"; and

(B) by adding at the end of the following:

"(b) It shall not be unlawful under section 703 or 704 for an employer (or a corporation controlled by an employer), labor organization, employment agency, or joint labor-management committee controlling apprenticeship or other training or retraining (including on-the-job training programs) to take any action otherwise prohibited by such section, with respect to an employee in a workplace in a foreign country if compliance with such section would cause such employer (or such corporation), such organization, such agency, or such committee to violate the law of the foreign country in which such workplace is located.

"(c)(1) If an employer controls a corporation whose place of incorporation is a foreign country, any practice prohibited by section 703 or 704 engaged in by such corporation shall be presumed to be engaged in by such employer.

"(2) Sections 703 and 704 shall not apply with respect to the foreign operations of an employer that is a foreign person not controlled by an American employer.

"(3) For purposes of this subsection, the determination of whether an employer controls a corporation shall be based on —

"(A) the interrelation of operations;

"(B) the common management;

"(C) the centralized control of labor relations; and

"(D) the common ownership or financial control, of the employer and the corporation.".

(2) Americans with Disabilities Act of 1990. — Section 102 of the Americans with Disabilities Act of 1990 (42 U.S.C. 12112) is amended —

(A) by redesignating subsection (c) as subsection (d); and

(B) by inserting after subsection (b) the following new subsection:

"(c) Covered Entities in Foreign Countries. —

"(1) In general. — It shall not be unlawful under this section for a covered entity to take any action that constitutes discrimination under this section with respect to an employee in a workplace in a foreign country if compliance with this section would cause such covered entity to violate the law of the foreign country in which such workplace is located.

"(2) Control of corporation. —

"(A) Presumption. — If an employer controls a corporation whose place of incorporation is a foreign country, any practice that constitutes discrimination under this section and is engaged in by such corporation shall be presumed to be engaged in by such employer.

"(B) Exception. — This section shall not apply with respect to the foreign operations of an employer that is a foreign person not controlled by an American employer.

"(C) Determination.—For purposes of this paragraph, the determination of whether an employer controls a corporation shall be based on—

"(i) the interrelation of operations;

"(ii) the common management;

"(iii) the centralized control of labor relations; and

"(iv) the common ownership or financial control, of the employer and the corporation.".

"(c) Application of Amendments.—The amendments made by this section shall not apply with respect to conduct occurring before the date of the enactment of this Act.

TECHNICAL ASSISTANCE TRAINING INSTITUTE

Section 110. (a) Technical Assistance.—Section 705 of the Civil Rights Act of 1964 (42 U.S.C. 2000e-4) is amended by adding at the end the following new subsection.

"(j)(1) The Commission shall establish a Technical Assistance training Institute, through which the Commission shall provide technical assistance and training regarding the laws and regulations enforced by the Commission.

"(2) An employer or other entity covered under this title shall not be excused from compliance with the requirements of this title because of any failure to receive technical assistance under this subsection.

"(3) There are authorized to be appropriated to carry out this subsection such sums as may be necessary for fiscal year 1992.".

"(b) Effective Date.—The amendment made by this section shall take effect on the date of the enactment of this Act.

EDUCATION AND OUTREACH

Section 111. Section 705(h) of the Civil Rights Act of 1964 (42 U.S.C. 2000e-4(h)) is amended—

(1) by inserting "(1)" after "(h)"; and

(2) by adding at the end the following new paragraph:

"(2) In exercising its powers under this title, the Commission shall carry out educational and outreach activities (including dissemination of information in languages other than English) targeted to—

"(A) individuals who historically have been victims of employment discrimination and have not been equitably served by the Commission; and

"(B) individuals on whose behalf the Commission has authority to enforce any other law prohibiting employment discrimination, concerning rights and obligations under this title or such law, as the case may be.".

EXPANSION OF RIGHT TO CHALLENGE DISCRIMINATORY SENIORITY SYSTEMS

Section 112. Section 706(e) of the Civil Rights Act of 1964 (42 U.S.C. 2000e-5(e)) is amended—

(1) by inserting "(1)" before "A charge under this section"; and

(2) by adding at the end the following new paragraph:

"(2) For purposes of this section, an unlawful employment practice occurs, with respect to a seniority system that has been adopted for an intentionally discriminatory purpose in violation of this title (whether or not that discriminatory purpose is apparent on the face of the seniority provision), when the seniority system is adopted, when an individual becomes subject to the seniority system, or when a person aggrieved is injured by the application of the seniority system or provision of the system.".

AUTHORIZING AWARD OF EXPERT FEES

Section 113. (a) Revised Statutes.—Section 722 of the Revised Statutes is amended—

(1) by designating the first and second sentences as subsections (a) and (b), respectively, and indenting accordingly; and

(2) by adding at the end the following new subsection:

"(c) In awarding an attorney's fee under subsection (b) in any action or proceeding to enforce a provision of sections 1977 or 1977A of the Revised Statutes, the court, in its discretion, may include expert fees as part of the attorney's fee.".

"(b) Civil Rights Act of 1964.—Section 706(k) of the Civil Rights Act of 1964 (42 U.S.C. 2000e-5(k)) is amended by inserting "(including expert fees)" after "attorney's fee".

PROVIDING FOR INTEREST AND EXTENDING THE STATUTE OF LIMITATIONS IN ACTIONS AGAINST THE FEDERAL GOVERNMENT

Section 114. Section 717 of the Civil Rights Act of 1964 (42 U.S.C. 2000e-16) is amended—

(1) in subsection (c), by striking "thirty days" and inserting '90 days'; and

(2) in subsection (d), by inserting before the period ", and the same interest to compensate for delay in payment shall be available as in cases involving nonpublic parties.".

NOTICE OF LIMITATIONS PERIOD UNDER THE AGE DISCRIMINATION IN EMPLOYMENT ACT OF 1967

Section 115. Section 7(e) of the Age Discrimination in Employment Act of 1967 (29 U.S.C. 626(e)) is amended—

(1) by striking paragraph (2);

(2) by striking the paragraph designation in paragraph (1);

(3) by striking "Sections 6 and" and inserting "Section"; and

(4) by adding at the end the following: "If a charge filed with the Commission under this Act is dismissed or the proceedings of the Commission are otherwise terminated by the Commission, the Commission shall notify the person aggrieved. A civil action may be brought under this section by a person defined in section 11(a) against the respondent named in the charge within 90 days after the date of the receipt of such notice.".

LAWFUL COURT-ORDERED REMEDIES, AFFIRMATIVE ACTION, AND CONCILIATION AGREEMENTS NOT AFFECTED

Section 116. Nothing in the amendments made by this title shall be construed to affect court-ordered remedies, affirmative action, or conciliation agreements, that are in accordance with the law. . . .

Appendix C
Excerpts from the EEOC's Uniform Guidelines on Employee Selection Procedures (1978)

ADVERSE IMPACT

The fundamental principle underlying the guidelines is that employer policies or practices which have an adverse impact on employment opportunities of any race, sex, or ethnic group are illegal under title VII and the Executive order unless justified by business necessity.

If adverse impact exists, it must be justified on grounds of business necessity. Normally, this means by validation which demonstrates the relation between the selection procedure and performance on the job.

The guidelines adopt a "rule of thumb" as a practical means of determining adverse impact for use in enforcement proceedings. This rule is known as the "4/5ths" or "80 percent" rule.

WHERE ADVERSE IMPACT EXISTS: THE BASIC OPTIONS

Once an employer has established that there is adverse impact, what steps are required by the guidelines? As previously noted, the employer can modify or eliminate the procedure which produces the adverse impact, thus taking the selection procedure from the coverage of these guidelines. If the employer does not do that, then it must justify the use of the procedure on grounds of "business necessity." This normally means that it must show a clear relation between performance on the selection procedure and performance on the job.

General Principles
1. Relationship between validation and elimination of adverse impact, and affirmative action. Federal equal employment opportunity law generally does not require evidence of validity for a selection procedure if there is not adverse impact: e.g., *Griggs v. Duke Power Co.* Therefore, a user has the choice of complying either by providing evidence of validity (or otherwise justifying use in accord with Federal law), or by eliminating the adverse impact. These options have always been present under Federal law and the Federal Executive Agency Guidelines. The December 30 draft guidelines,

however, clarified the nature of the two options open to users.
2. The *"bottom line"* (section 4C). The guidelines provide that when the overall selection process does not have an adverse impact the Government will usually not examine the individual components of that process for adverse impact or evidence of validity. The concept is based upon the view that the Federal Government should not generally concern itself with individual components of a selection process, if the overall effect of that process is nonexclusionary. Many commenters criticized the ambiguity caused by the word "generally" in the December 30 draft of section 4C which provided, "the Federal enforcement agencies generally will not take enforcement action based upon adverse impact of any component" of a process that does not have an overall adverse impact. Employer groups stated the position that the "bottom line" should be a rule prohibiting enforcement action by Federal agencies with respect to all or part of a selection process where the bottom line does not show adverse impact. Civil rights and some labor union representatives expressed the opposing concerns that the concept may be too restrictive, that it may be interpreted as a matter of law, and that it might allow certain discriminatory conditions to go unremedied.

Sec. 5. *General Standards for validity studies.* A. Acceptable types of validity studies. For the purposes of satisfying these guidelines, users may rely upon criterion-related validity studies, content validity studies or construct validity studies, in accordance with the standards set forth in the technical standards of the guidelines. New strategies procedures will be evaluated as they become accepted by the psychological profession.

B. *Criterion-related content, and construct validity.* Evidence of the validity of a test or other selection procedure by a criterion-related validity study should consist of empirical data demonstrating that the selection procedure is predictive of or significantly correlated with important elements of job performance. Evidence of the validity of a test or other selection procedure by a content validity study should consist of data showing that the content of the selection procedure is representative of important aspects of performance on the job for which the candidates are to be evaluated. Evidence of the validity of a test or other selection procedure through a construct validity study should consist of data showing that the procedure measures the degree to which candidates have identifiable characteristics which have been determined to be important in successful performance in the job for which the candidates are to be evaluated.

C. *Guidelines are consistent with professional standards.* The provisions of these guidelines relating to validation of selection procedures are intended to be ·consistent with generally accepted professional standards for evaluating standardized tests and other selection .procedures, such as those described in the Standards for Educational and Psychological Tests prepared by a joint committee of the American Psychological Association, the American Educational Research Association, and the National Council on Measurement in Education (American Psychological Association, Washington, D.C., 1974) (hereinafter "A.P.A. Standards") and standard textbooks and journals in the field of personnel selection.

D. *Need for documentation of validity.* For any selection procedure which is part of a selection process which has an adverse impact and which selection procedure has an adverse impact, each user should maintain and have available such documentation as is described in section 15 below.

E. *Accuracy and standardization.* Validity studies should be carried out under conditions which assure insofar as possible the adequacy and accuracy of the research and the report. Selection procedure should be administered and scored under standardized conditions.

F. *Caution against selection on basis of knowledges, skills, or ability learned in brief orientation period.* In general, users should avoid making employment decisions on the basis of measures of knowledges, skills, or abilities which are normally learned in a brief orientation period, and which have an adverse impact.

G. *Method of use of selection procedures.* The evidence of both the validity and utility of a selection procedure should support the method the user chooses for operational use of the procedure, if that method of use has a greater adverse impact than another method of use. Evidence which may be suffi-

cient to support the use of a selection procedure on a pass/fail (screening) basis may be insufficient to support the use of the same procedure on a ranking basis under these guidelines. Thus if user decides to use a selection procedure on a ranking basis, and that method of use has a greater adverse impact than use on an appropriate pass/fail basis (see section 5H below), the user should have sufficient evidence of validity and utility to support the use on a ranking basis.

H. *Cutoff scores.* Where cutoff scores are used, they should normally be set so as to be reasonable and consistent with normal expectations of acceptable proficiency within the work force. Where applicants are ranked on the basis of properly validated selection procedures and those applicants scoring below a higher cutoff score than appropriate in light or no chance of being selected for employment, the higher cutoff score may be appropriate, but the degree of adverse impact should be considered.

Documentation of Impact and Validity Evidence
Sec. 15. *Documentation of impact and validity evidence.* A. *Required information.* Users of selection procedures other than those users complying with section 15 A(1) below should maintain and have available for each job information on adverse impact of the selection process for that job and, where it is determined a selection process has an adverse impact, evidence of validity as set forth below.

(1) *Simplified recordkeeping for users with less than 100 employees.* In order to minimize recordkeeping burdens on employers who employ one hundred (100) or fewer employees and other users not required to file EEO-1. et seq., reports, such users may satisfy the requirements of this section 15 if they maintain and have available records showing, for each year:

(a) The number of persons hired, promoted, and terminated for each job, by sex, and where appropriate by race and national origins;

(b) The number of applicants for hire and promotion by sex and where appropriate by race and national origin: and

(c) The selection procedures utilized (either standardized or not standardized).

These records should be maintained for each race or national group constituting more than two percent (2%) of the labor force in the relevant labor area. However, it is necessary to maintain records by race and/or national origin if one race or national origin group in the relevant labor area constitutes more than ninety-eight percent (98%) of the labor force in the area. If the user has reason to believe that a selection procedure has an adverse impact, the user should maintain any available evidence of validity for that procedure.

Definitions

Sec. 16. *Definitions.* The following definitions shall apply throughout these guidelines:

A. *Ability.* A present competence to perform an observable behavior or a behavior whi[ch] results in an observable product.

B. *Adverse impact.* A substantially different rate of selection in hiring, promotion, or other employment decisions which work to the disadvantage of members of a race, sex, or ethnic group.

C. *Compliance with these guidelines.* Use of a selection procedure is in compliance with these guidelines if such use has been validated in accord with these guidelines, or if such use does not result in adverse impact on any race, sex, or ethnic group, or, in unusual circumstances, if use of the procedure is otherwise justified in accord with Federal law.

D. *Content validity.* Demonstrated by data showing that the content of a selection procedure is representative of important aspects of performance on the job.

E. *Construct validity.* Demonstrated by data showing that the selection procedure measures the degree to which candidates have identifiable characteristics which have been determined to be important for successful job performance.

F. *Criterion-related validity.* Demonstrated by empirical data showing that the selection procedure is predictive of or significantly correlated with important elements of work behavior.

G. *Employer.* Any employer subject to the provisions of the Civil Rights Act of 1964, as amended, including State or local governments and any Federal agency subject to the provisions of section 717 of the Civil Rights Act of 1964, as amended, and any Federal contractor or subcontractor or federally assisted construction contractor or subcontractor by Executive Order 11246, as amended.

H. *Employment agency.* Any employment agency subject to the provisions of the Civil Rights Act of 1964, as amended.

I. *Enforcement action.* A proceeding by a Federal enforcement agency such as a lawsuit or an administrative proceeding leading to debarment from withholding, suspension, or termination of Federal Government funds; but not a finding of reasonable cause or a conciliation process or the issuance of right to sue letters under title VII or under Executive Order 11246 where such finding, conciliation, or issuance of notice of right to sue is based upon an individual complaint.

J. *Enforcement agency.* Any agency of the executive branch of the Federal Government which adopts these guidelines for purposes of the enforcement of the equal employment opportunity laws or which has responsibility for securing compliance with them.

K. *Job analysis.* A detailed statement of work behaviors and other information relevant to the job.

L. *Job descriptions.* A general statement of job duties and responsibilities.

M. *Knowledge.* A body of information applied directly to the performance of a function. Evidence for intermittent leave, or leave on a reduced leave schedule, for planned medical treatment, the dates on which such treatment is expected to be given and the duration of such treatment.

Appendix D

Excerpts from Americans with Disabilities Act of 1990
Public Law 101-336; 42 U.S.C. 12101; July 26, 1990

An Act to establish a clear and comprehensive prohibition of discrimination on the basis of disability.

Be it enacted by the Senate and House of Representatives of the United States of America in Congress assembled,

FINDINGS AND PURPOSES

Section 2. (a) FINDINGS. The Congress find that:

(1) some 43,000,000 Americans have one or more physical or mental disabilities, and this number is increasing as the population as a whole is growing older;

(2) historically, society has tended to isolate and segregate individuals with disabilities, and, despite some improvements, such forms of discrimination against individuals with disabilities continue to be a serious and pervasive social problem;

(3) discrimination against individuals with disabilities persists in such critical areas as employment, housing, public accommodations, education, transportation, communication, recreation, institutionalization, health services, voting, and access to public services;

(4) unlike individuals who have experienced discrimination on the basis of race, color, sex, national origin, religion, or age, individuals who have experienced discrimination on the basis of disability have often had no legal recourse to redress such discrimination;

(5) individuals with disabilities continually encounter various forms of discrimination, including outright intentional exclusion, the discriminatory effects of architectural, transportation, and communication barriers, overprotective rules and policies, failure to make modifications to existing facilities and practices, exclusionary qualification standards and criteria, segregation, and relegation to lesser services, programs, activities, benefits, jobs, or other opportunities;

(6) census data, national polls, and other studies have documented that people with disabilities, as a group, occupy an inferior status in our society, and are severely disadvantaged socially, vocationally, economically, and educationally;

(7) individuals with disabilities are a discrete and insular minority who have been faced with restrictions and limitations, subjected to a history of purposeful unequal treatment, and relegated to a position of political powerlessness in our society, based on characteristics that are beyond the control of such individuals and resulting from stereotypic assumptions not truly indicative of the individual ability of such individuals to participate in, and contribute to, society;

(8) the Nation's proper goals regarding individuals with disabilities are to assure equality of opportunity, full participation, independent living, and economic self-sufficiency for such individuals; and

(9) the continuing existence of unfair and unnecessary discrimination and prejudice denies people with disabilities the opportunity to compete on an equal basis and to pursue those opportunities for which our free society is justifiably famous, and costs the United States billions of dollars in unnecessary expenses resulting from dependency and nonproductivity.

(b) PURPOSE. It is the purpose of this Act:

(1) to provide a clear and comprehensive national mandate for the elimination of discrimination against individuals with disabilities;

(2) to provide clear, strong, consistent, enforceable standards addressing discrimination against individuals with disabilities;

(3) to ensure that the Federal Government plays a central role in enforcing the standards established in this Act on behalf of individuals with disabilities; and

(4) to invoke the sweep of congressional authority, including the power to enforce the fourteenth amendment and to regulate commerce, in order to address the major areas of discrimination faced day-to-day by people with disabilities.

DEFINITIONS

. . . (8) QUALIFIED INDIVIDUAL WITH A DISABILITY. The term "qualified individual with a disability" means an individual with a disability who, with or without reasonable accommodation, can perform the essential functions of the employment position that such individual holds or desires. For the purposes of this title, consideration shall be given to the employer's judgment as to what functions of a job are essential, and if an employer has prepared a written description before advertising or interviewing applicants for the job, this description shall be considered evidence of the essential functions of the job.

(9) REASONABLE ACCOMMODATION. The term "reasonable accommodation" may include:

(A) making existing facilities used by employees readily accessible to and usable by individuals with disabilities; and

(B) job restructuring, part-time or modified work schedules, reassignment to a vacant position, acquisition or modification of equipment or devices, appropriate adjustment or modifications of examinations, training materials or policies, the provision of qualified readers or interpreters, and other similar accommodations for individuals with disabilities.

(10) UNDUE HARDSHIP.

(A) IN GENERAL. The term "undue hardship" means an action requiring significant difficulty or expense, when considered in light of the factors set forth in subparagraph (B).

(B) FACTORS TO BE CONSIDERED. In determining whether an accommodation would impose an undue hardship on a covered entity, factors to be considered include:

(i) the nature and cost of the accommodation needed under this Act;

(ii) the overall financial resources of the facility or facilities involved in the provision of the reasonable accommodation; the number of persons employed at such facility; the effect on expenses and resources, or the impact otherwise of such accommodation upon the operation of the facility;

(iii) the overall financial resources of the covered entity; the overall size of the business of a covered entity with respect to the number of its employees; the number, type, and location of its facilities; and

(iv) the type of operation or operations of the covered entity, including the composition, structure, and functions of the workforce of such entity; the geographic separateness, administrative, or fiscal relationship of the facility or facilities in question to the covered entity.

DISCRIMINATION

Section 102. (a) GENERAL RULE. No covered entity shall discriminate against a qualified individual with a disability because of the disability of such individual in regard to job application procedures, the hiring, advancement, or discharge of employees, employee compensation, job training, and other terms, conditions, and privileges of employment.

(b) CONSTRUCTION. As used in subsection (a), the term "discriminate" includes:

(1) limiting, segregating, or classifying a job applicant or employee in a way that adversely affects the opportunities or status of such applicant or employee because of the disability of such applicant or employee;

(2) participating in a contractual or other arrangement or relationship that has the effect of subjecting a covered entity's qualified applicant or employee with a disability to the discrimination prohibited by this title (such relationship includes a relationship with an employment or referral agency, labor union, an organization providing fringe benefits to an employee of the covered entity, or an organization providing training and apprenticeship programs);

(3) utilizing standards, criteria, or methods of administration;

(A) that have the effect of discrimination on the basis of disability; or

(B) that perpetuate the discrimination of others who are subject to common administrative control;

(4) excluding or otherwise denying equal jobs or benefits to a qualified individual because of the known disability of an individual with whom the qualified individual is known to have a relationship or association;

(5) (A) not making reasonable accommodations to the known physical or mental limitations of an otherwise qualified individual with a disability who is an applicant or employee, unless such covered entity can demonstrate that the accommodation would impose an undue hardship on the operation of the business of such covered entity; or

(B) denying employment opportunities to a job applicant or employee who is an otherwise qualified individual with a disability, if such denial is based on the need of such covered entity to make reasonable accommodation to the physical or mental impairments of the employee or applicant;

(6) using qualification standards, employment tests or other selection criteria that screen out or tend to screen out an individual with a disability or a class of individuals with disabilities unless the standard, test or other selection criteria, as used by the covered entity, is shown to be job-related for the position in question and is consistent with business necessity; and

(7) failing to select and administer tests concerning employment in the most effective manner to ensure that, when such test is administered to a job applicant or employee who has a disability that impairs sensory, manual, or speaking skills, such test results accurately reflect the skills, aptitude, or whatever other factor of such applicant or employee that such test purports to measure, rather than reflecting the impaired sensory, manual, or speaking skills of such employee or applicant (except where such skills are the factors that the test purports to measure).

(c)   MEDICAL   EXAMINATIONS   AND INQUIRIES.

(1) IN GENERAL. The prohibition against discrimination as referred to in subsection (a) shall include medical examinations and inquiries.

(2) PREEMPLOYMENT.

(A) PROHIBITED EXAMINATION OR INQUIRY. Except as provided in paragraph (3), a covered entity shall not conduct a medical examination or make inquiries of a job applicant as to whether such applicant is an individual with a disability or as to the nature or severity of such disability.

(B) ACCEPTABLE INQUIRY. A covered entity may make preemployment inquiries into the ability of an applicant to perform job-related functions.

(3) EMPLOYMENT ENTRANCE EXAMINATION. A covered entity may require a medical examination after an offer of employment has been made to a job applicant and prior to the commencement of the employment duties of such applicant, and may condition an offer of employment on the results of such examination, if:

(A) all entering employees are subjected to such an examination regardless of disability;

(B) information obtained regarding the medical condition or history of the applicant is collected and maintained on separate forms and in separate medical files is treated as a confidential medical record, except that

(i) supervisors and managers may be informed regarding necessary restrictions on the work or duties of the employee and necessary accommodations;

(ii) first aid and safety personnel may be informed, when appropriate, if the disability might require emergency treatment; and

(iii) government officials investigating compliance with this Act shall be provided relevant information on request; and

(C) the results of such examination are used only in accordance with this title.

(4) EXAMINATION AND INQUIRY.

(A) PROHIBITED EXAMINATIONS AND INQUIRIES. A covered entity shall not require a medical examination and shall not make inquiries of an employee as to whether such employee is an individual with a disability or as to the nature or severity of the disability, unless such examination or inquiry is shown to be job-related and consistent with business necessity.

(B) ACCEPTABLE EXAMINATIONS AND INQUIRIES. A covered entity may conduct voluntary medical examinations, including voluntary medical histories, which are part of an employee health program available to employees at that work site. A covered entity may make inquiries into the ability of an employee to perform job-related functions.

(C) REQUIREMENT. Information obtained under subparagraph (B) regarding the medical condition or history of any employee is subject to the requirements of subparagraphs (B) and (C) of paragraph (3). . . .

ILLEGAL USE OF DRUGS AND ALCOHOL

Section   104. (a)   QUALIFIED   INDIVIDUAL WITH A DISABILITY. For purposes of this title, the term "qualified individual with a disability" shall not include any employee or applicant who is currently engaging in the illegal use of drugs, when the covered entity acts on the basis of such use.

(b) RULES OF CONSTRUCTION. Nothing in subsection (a) shall be construed to exclude as a qualified individual with a disability an individual who:

(1) has successfully completed a supervised drug rehabilitation program and is no longer engaging in the illegal use of drugs, or has otherwise been rehabilitated successfully and is no longer engaging in such use;

(2) is participating in a supervised rehabilitation program and is no longer engaging in such use; or

(3) is erroneously regarded as engaging in such use, but is not engaging in such use;

except that it shall not be a violation of this Act for a covered entity to adopt or administer reasonable policies or procedures, including but not limited to drug testing, designed to ensure that an individual described in paragraph (1) or (2) is no longer engaging in the illegal use of drugs. . . .

Appendix E
Excerpts from the EEOC's ADA Enforcement Guidance:
Pre-employment Disability-Related Questions and Medical Examinations

INTRODUCTION

Under the Americans with Disabilities Act of 1990 (the "ADA"), an employer may ask disability-related questions and require medical examinations of an applicant only after the applicant has been given a conditional job offer. This Enforcement Guidance explains these ADA provisions.

BACKGROUND

In the past, some employment applications and interviews requested information about an applicant's physical and/or mental condition. This information was often used to exclude applicants with disabilities before their ability to perform the job was even evaluated.

For example, applicants may have been asked about their medical conditions at the same time that they were engaging in other parts of the application process, such as completing a written job application or having references checked. If an applicant was then rejected, s/he did not necessarily know whether s/he was rejected because of disability, or because of insufficient skills or experience or a bad report from a reference.

As a result, Congress established a process within the ADA to isolate an employer's consideration of an applicant's non-medical qualifications from any consideration of the applicant's medical condition.

THE STATUTORY AND REGULATORY FRAMEWORK

Under the law, an employer may not ask disability-related questions and may not conduct medical examinations until *after* it makes a conditional job offer to the applicant. This helps ensure that an applicant's possible hidden disability (including a prior history of a disability) is not considered before the employer evaluates an applicant's non-medical qualifications. An employer may not ask disability-related questions or require a medical examination pre-offer even if it intends to look at the answers or results only at the post-offer stage.

Although employers may not ask disability-related questions or require medical examinations at the pre-offer stage, they *may* do a wide variety of things to evaluate whether an applicant is qualified for the job, including the following:

- Employers *may* ask about an applicant's ability to perform specific job functions. For example, an employer may state the physical requirements of a job (such as the ability to lift a certain amount of weight, or the ability to climb ladders), and ask if an applicant can satisfy these requirements.
- Employers *may* ask about an applicant's non-medical qualifications and skills, such as the applicant's education, work history, and required certifications and licenses.
- Employers *may* ask applicants to describe or demonstrate how they would perform job tasks.

Once a conditional job offer is made, the employer may ask disability-related questions and require medical examinations as long as this is done for all entering employees in that job category. If the employer rejects the applicant after a disability-related question or medical examination, investigators will closely scrutinize whether the rejection was based on the results of that question or examination.

If the question or examination screens out an individual because of a disability, the employer must demonstrate that the reason for the rejection is "job-related and consistent with business necessity."

In addition, if the individual is screened out for safety reasons, the employer must demonstrate that the individual poses a "direct threat." This means that the individual poses a significant risk of substantial harm to him/herself or others, and that the risk cannot be reduced below the direct threat level through reasonable accommodation.

Medical information must be kept confidential. The ADA contains narrow exceptions for disclosing specific, limited information to supervisors and managers, first aid and safety personnel, and government officials investigating compliance with the ADA. Employers may also disclose medical information to state workers' compensation offices, state second injury funds, or workers' compensation insurance carriers in accordance with state workers' compensation laws and may use the medical information for insurance purposes.

THE PRE-OFFER STAGE

What is a Disability-Related Question? Definition: "Disability-Related Question" means a question that is *likely* to *elicit* information about a disability.

At the pre-offer stage, an employer cannot ask questions that are *likely* to *elicit* information about a disability. This includes directly asking whether an applicant has a particular disability. It also means that an employer cannot ask questions that are *closely related* to disability.

On the other hand, if there are many possible answers to a question and only some of those answers would contain disability-related information, that question is not "disability-related."

Below are some commonly asked questions about this area of the law.

- May an employer ask **whether an applicant can perform the job?**

  Yes. An employer may ask whether applicants can perform any or all job functions, including whether applicants can perform job functions "with or without reasonable accommodation."

- May an employer ask applicants to **describe or demonstrate how they would perform the job** (including any needed reasonable accommodations)?

  Yes. An employer may ask applicants to describe how they would perform any or all job functions, as long as all applicants in the job category are asked to do this.

  Employers should remember that, if an applicant says that s/he will need a reasonable accommodation to do a job demonstration, the employer must either:

  - provide a reasonable accommodation that does not create an undue hardship; or

  - allow the applicant to simply describe how s/he would perform the job function.

- May an employer ask a **particular applicant to describe or demonstrate how s/he would perform the job,** if other applicants aren't asked to do this?

  When an employer could reasonably believe that an applicant will not be able to perform a job function because of a known disability, the employer may ask that particular applicant to describe or demonstrate how s/he would perform the function. An applicant's disability would be a "known disability" either because it is obvious (for example, the applicant uses a wheelchair), or because the applicant has voluntarily disclosed that s/he has a hidden disability.

- May an employer ask applicants **whether they will need reasonable accommodation for the hiring process?**

  Yes. An employer may tell applicants what the hiring process involves (for example, an interview, timed written test, or job demonstration), and may ask applicants whether they will need a reasonable accommodation for this process. . . .

- May an employer ask applicants **whether they will need reasonable accommodation to perform the functions of the job?**

  In general, an employer may not ask questions on an application or in an interview about whether an applicant will need reasonable accommodation for a job. This is because these questions are likely to elicit whether the applicant has a disability (generally, only people who have disabilities will need reasonable accommodations).

  Example: An employment application may not ask, "Do you need reasonable accommodation to perform this job?"

  Example: An employment application may not ask, "Can you do these functions with___without___reasonable accommodations? (Check One)"

  Example: An applicant with no known disability is being interviewed for a job. He has not asked for any reasonable accommodation, either for the application process or for the job. The employer may not ask him, "Will you need reasonable accommodation to perform this job?"

However, when an employer could reasonably believe that an applicant will need reasonable accommodation to perform the functions of the job, the employer may ask that applicant certain limited questions. Specifically, the employer may ask *whether s/he needs reasonable accommodation and what type of reasonable accommodation* would be needed to perform the functions of the job. The employer could ask these questions if:

- the employer reasonably believes the applicant will need reasonable accommodation because of an obvious disability;

- the employer reasonably believes the applicant will need reasonable accommodation because of a hidden disability that the applicant has voluntarily disclosed to the employer; or

- an applicant has voluntarily disclosed to the employer that s/he needs reasonable accommodation to perform the job.

Example: An individual with diabetes applying for a receptionist position voluntarily discloses that she will need periodic breaks to take medication. The employer may ask the applicant questions about the reasonable accommodation such as how often she will need breaks, and how long the breaks must be. Of course, the employer may not ask any questions about the underlying physical condition.

Example: An applicant with a severe visual impairment applies for a job involving computer work. The employer may ask whether he will need reasonable accommodation to perform the functions of the job. If the applicant answers "no," the employer may not ask additional questions about reasonable accommodation (although, of course, the employer could ask the applicant to describe or demonstrate performance). If the applicant says that he *will* need accommodation, the employer may ask questions about the type of required accommodation such as, "What will you need?" If the applicant says he needs software that increases the size of text

on the computer screen, the employer may ask questions such as, "Who makes that software?" "Do you need a particular brand?" or "Is that software compatible with our computers?" However, the employer may not ask questions about the applicant's underlying condition. In addition, the employer may not ask reasonable accommodation questions that are unrelated to job functions such as, "Will you need reasonable accommodation to get to the cafeteria?"

An employer may only ask about reasonable accommodation that is needed now or in the near future. An applicant is not required to disclose reasonable accommodations that may be needed in the more distant future.

- May an employer ask **whether an applicant can meet the employer's attendance requirements?**

Yes. An employer may state its attendance requirements and ask whether an applicant can meet them. An employer also may ask about an applicant's prior attendance record (for example, how many days the applicant was absent from his/her last job). These questions are not likely to elicit information about a disability because there may be many reasons unrelated to disability why someone cannot meet attendance requirements or was frequently absent from a previous job (for example, an applicant may have had day-care problems).

An employer also may ask questions designed to detect whether an applicant abused his/her leave because these questions are not likely to elicit information about a disability.

Example: An employer may ask an applicant, "How many Mondays or Fridays were you absent last year on leave other than approved vacation leave?"

However, at the pre-offer stage, an employer may not ask how many days an applicant was *sick*, because these questions relate directly to the *severity of an individual's impairments*. Therefore, these questions are likely to elicit information about a disability.

THE POST-OFFER STAGE

After giving a job offer to an applicant, an employer may ask disability-related questions and perform medical examinations. The job offer may be conditioned on the results of post-offer disability-related questions or medical examinations.

At the "post-offer" stage, an employer may ask about an individual's workers' compensation history, prior sick leave usage, illnesses/diseases/impairments, and general physical and mental health. Disability-related questions and medical examinations at the post-offer stage do not have to be related to the job.

If an employer asks post-offer disability-related questions, or requires post-offer medical examinations, it must make sure that it follows certain procedures:

- all entering employees in the same job category must be subjected to the examination/inquiry, regardless of disability, and
- medical information obtained must be kept confidential.

Below are some commonly asked questions about the post-offer stage.

- What is considered a *real* job offer?

Since an employer can ask disability-related questions and require medical examinations after a job offer, it is important that the job offer be *real*. A job offer is real if the employer has evaluated all relevant non-medical information which it reasonably could have obtained and analyzed prior to giving the offer. Of course, there are times when an employer cannot reasonably obtain and evaluate *all* non-medical information at the pre-offer stage. If an employer can show that is the case, the offer would still be considered a real offer.

Example: It may be too costly for a law enforcement employer wishing to administer a polygraph examination to administer a pre-offer examination asking non-disability-related questions, and a post-offer examination asking disability-related questions. In this case, the employer may be able to demonstrate that it could not reasonably obtain and evaluate the non-medical polygraph information at the pre-offer stage.

Example: An applicant might state that his current employer should not be asked for a reference check until the potential employer makes a confidential job offer. In this case, the potential employer could not reasonably obtain and evaluate the non-medical information from the reference at the pre-offer stage.

- Do offers have to be limited to **current vacancies?**

No. An employer may give offers to fill current vacancies or reasonably anticipated openings. . . .

- After an employer has obtained basic medical information from all individuals who have been given conditional offers in a job category, may it ask **specific individuals for more medical information?**

Yes, if the follow-up examinations or questions are medically related to the previously obtained medical information.

Example: At the post-offer stage, an employer asks new hires whether they have had back injuries, and learns that some of the individuals have had such injuries. The employer may give medical examinations designed to diagnose back impairments to persons who stated that they had prior back injuries, as long as these examinations are medically related to those injuries.

- At the post-offer stage, may an employer ask all individuals **whether they need reasonable accommodation to perform the job?**

Yes.

- If, at the post-offer stage, someone requests **reasonable accommodation to perform the job,** may the employer ask him/her for **documentation of his/her disability?**

Yes. If someone requests reasonable accommodation so s/he will be able to perform a job and the need for the accommodation is not obvious, the employer may require reasonable documentation of the individual's entitlement to reasonable accommodation. So, the employer may require documentation showing that the individual has a *covered disability*, and stating his/her *functional limitations*.

Example: An entering employee states that she will need a 15-minute break every two hours to eat a snack in order to maintain her blood sugar level. The employer may ask her to provide documentation from her doctor showing that: (1) she has an impairment that substantially limits a major life activity; and (2) she actually needs the requested breaks because of the impairment.

CONFIDENTIALITY

An employer must keep any medical information on applicants or employees confidential, with the following limited exceptions:

- supervisors and managers may be told about necessary restrictions on the work or duties of the employee and about necessary accommodations;
- first aid and safety personnel may be told if the disability might require emergency treatment;
- government officials investigating compliance with the ADA must be given relevant information on request;
- employers may give information to state workers' compensation offices, state second injury funds or workers' compensation insurance carriers in accordance with state workers' compensation laws; and
- employers may use the information for insurance purposes.

Below are some commonly asked questions about the ADA's confidentiality requirements.

- May **medical information** be given to **decision-makers involved in the hiring process?**

Yes. Medical information may be given to—and used by—appropriate decision-makers involved in the hiring process so they can make employment decisions consistent with the ADA. In addition, the employer may use the information to determine reasonable accommodations for the individual. For example, the employer may share the information with a third party, such as a health

care professional, to determine whether a reasonable accommodation is possible for a particular individual. The information certainly must be kept confidential.

Of course, the employer may only share the medical information with individuals involved in the hiring process (or in implementing an affirmative action program) who *need to know* the information. For example, in some cases, a number of people may be involved in evaluating an applicant. Some individuals may simply be responsible for evaluating an applicant's references; these individuals may have no need to know an applicant's medical condition and therefore should not have access to the medical information.

- Can an individual **voluntarily disclose his/her own medical information** to persons beyond those to whom an employer can disclose such information?

Yes, as long as it's *really* voluntary. The employer cannot request, persuade, coerce, or otherwise pressure the individual to get him/her to disclose medical information.

- Does the employer's confidentiality obligation extend to **medical information that an individual voluntarily tells the employer?**

Yes. For example, if an applicant voluntarily discloses bipolar disorder and the need for reasonable accommodation, the employer may not disclose the condition or the applicant's need for accommodation to the applicant's references.

- Can **medical information be kept in an employee's regular personnel file?**

No. Medical information must be collected and maintained on separate forms and in separate medical files. An employer should not place any medical-related material in an employee's non-medical personnel file. If an employer wants to put a document in a personnel file, and that document happens to contain some medical information, the employer must simply remove the medical information from the document before putting it in the personnel file.

- Does the **confidentiality obligation end when the person is no longer an applicant or employee?**

No, an employer must keep medical information confidential *even* if someone is no longer an applicant (for example, s/he wasn't hired) or is no longer an employee.

- Is an employer required to **remove from its personnel files medical information obtained before the ADA's effective date?**
No.

Appendix F
Excerpts from the EEOC's Guidance on Psychiatric Disabilities and the ADA, March 25, 1997

INTRODUCTION

The workforce includes many individuals with psychiatric disabilities who face employment discrimination because their disabilities are stigmatized or misunderstood. Congress intended Title I of the Americans with Disabilities Act (ADA)[1] to combat such employment discrimination as well as the myths, fears, and stereotypes upon which it is based.[2]

The Equal Employment Opportunity Commission ("EEOC" or "Commission") receives a large number of charges under the ADA alleging employment discrimination based on psychiatric disability.[3] These charges raise a wide array of legal issues including, for example, whether an individual has a psychiatric disability as defined by the ADA and whether an employer may ask about an individual's psychiatric disability. People with psychiatric disabilities and employers also have posed numerous questions to the EEOC about this topic.

This guidance is designed to:

- facilitate the full enforcement of the ADA with respect to individuals alleging employment discrimination based on psychiatric disability;
- respond to questions and concerns expressed by individuals with psychiatric disabilities regarding the ADA; and
- answer questions posed by employers about how principles of ADA analysis apply in the context of psychiatric disabilities. . . .

2. Are traits or behaviors in themselves mental impairments?

No. Traits or behaviors are not, in themselves, mental impairments. For example, **stress**, in itself, is not automatically a mental impairment. Stress, however, may be shown to be related to a mental or physical impairment. Similarly, traits like **irritability, chronic lateness, and poor judgment** are not, in themselves, mental impairments, although they may be linked to mental impairments.

MAJOR LIFE ACTIVITIES

An impairment must substantially limit one or more **major life activities** to rise to the level of a "disability" under the ADA.

3. What major life activities are limited by mental impairments?

The major life activities limited by mental impairments **differ from person to person.** There is no exhaustive list of major life activities. For some people, mental impairments restrict major life activities such as learning, thinking, concentrating, interacting with others, caring for oneself, speaking, performing manual tasks, or working. Sleeping is also a major life activity that may be limited by mental impairments. . . .

9. When does an impairment substantially limit an individual's ability to interact with others?

An impairment substantially limits an individual's ability to interact with others, if due to the impairment, s/he is **significantly restricted as compared to the average person in the general population.** Some unfriendliness with coworkers or a supervisor would not, standing alone, be sufficient to establish a **substantial limitation** in interacting with others. An individual would be substantially limited, however, if his/her relations with others were characterized **on a regular basis** by **severe** problems, for example, consistently high levels of hostility, social withdrawal, or failure to communicate when necessary.

These limitations must be long-term or potentially long-term, as opposed to temporary, to justify a finding of ADA disability.

Example: An individual diagnosed with schizophrenia now works successfully as a computer programmer for a large company. Before finding an effective medication, however, he stayed in his room at home for several months, usually refusing

---

[1] 42 U.S.C. §§12101–12117, 12201–12213 (1994) (codified as amended).
[2] H. R. Rep. No. 101–485, pt. 3, at 31–32 (1990) [hereinafter House Judiciary Report].
[3] Between July 26, 1992, and September 30, 1996, approximately 12.7% of ADA charges filed with EEOC were based on emotional or psychiatric impairment. These included charges based on anxiety disorders, depression, bipolar disorder (manic depression), schizophrenia, and other psychiatric impairments.

to talk to family and close friends. After finding an effective medication, he was able to return to school, graduate, and start his career. This individual has a mental impairment, schizophrenia, which substantially limits his ability to interact with others when evaluated without medication. Accordingly, he is an individual with a disability as defined by the ADA. . . .

14. When may an employer lawfully ask an individual about a psychiatric disability under the ADA?

An employer may ask for disability-related information, including information about psychiatric disability, only in the following limited circumstances:

- **Application Stage.** Employers are prohibited from asking disability-related questions before making an offer of employment. An exception, however, is if an applicant asks for **reasonable accommodation for the hiring process.** If the need for this accommodation is not obvious, an employer may ask an applicant for **reasonable** documentation about his/her disability. The employer may require the applicant to provide documentation from an appropriate professional concerning his/her disability and functional limitations. A variety of health professionals may provide such documentation regarding psychiatric disabilities including primary health care professionals, psychiatrists, psychologists, psychiatric nurses, and licensed mental health professionals such as licensed clinical social workers and licensed professional counselors.

An employer should make clear to the applicant why it is requesting such information, *i.e.*, to verify the existence of a disability and the need for an accommodation. Furthermore, the employer may request only information necessary to accomplish these limited purposes.

Example A: An applicant for a secretarial job asks to take a typing test in a quiet location rather than in a busy reception area "because of a medical condition." The employer may make disability-related inquiries at this point because the applicant's need for reasonable accommodation under the ADA is not obvious based on the statement that an accommodation is needed "because of a medical condition." Specifically, the employer may ask the applicant to provide documentation showing that she has an impairment that substantially limits a major life activity and that

she needs to take the typing test in a quiet location because of disability-related functional limitations.

Although an employer may not ask an applicant if s/he will need reasonable accommodation **for the job,** there is an exception if the employer could **reasonably believe,** before making a job offer, that the applicant will need accommodation to perform the functions of the job. For an individual with a non-visible disability, this may occur if the individual voluntarily discloses his/her disability or if s/he voluntarily tells the employer that s/he needs reasonable accommodation to perform the job. The employer may then ask certain limited questions, specifically:

- whether the applicant needs reasonable accommodation; and
- what type of reasonable accommodation would be needed to perform the functions of the job.
- **After making an offer of employment, if the employer requires a post-offer, preemployment medical examination or inquiry.** After an employer extends an offer of employment, the employer **may** require a medical examination (including a psychiatric examination) or ask questions related to disability (including questions about psychiatric disability) *if* the employer subjects *all* entering employees in the same job category to the same inquiries or examinations regardless of disability. The inquiries and examinations do not need to be related to the job.
- **During employment, when a disability-related inquiry or medical examination of an employee is "job-related and consistent with business necessity."** This requirement may be met when an employer has a reasonable belief, based on objective evidence, that: (1) an employee's ability to perform essential job functions will be impaired by a medical condition; or (2) an employee will pose a direct threat due to a medical condition. Thus, for example, inquiries or medical examinations are permitted if they follow-up on a request for reasonable accommodation when the need for accommodation is not obvious, or if they address reasonable concerns about whether an individual is fit to perform essential functions of his/her position. In addition, inquiries or examinations are permitted if they are required by another Federal law or regulation. In these situations, the inquiries or examinations **must not exceed the scope of**

the specific medical condition and its effect on the employee's ability, with or without reasonable accommodation, to perform essential job functions or to work without posing a direct threat. . . .

Example D: An employee with depression seeks to return to work after a leave of absence during which she was hospitalized and her medication was adjusted. Her employer may request a fitness-for-duty examination because it has a reasonable belief, based on the employee's hospitalization and medication adjustment, that her ability to perform essential job functions may continue to be impaired by a medical condition. This examination, however, must be limited to the effect of her depression on her ability, with or without reasonable accommodation, to perform essential job functions. Inquiries about her entire psychiatric history or about the details of her therapy sessions would, for example, exceed this limited scope.

15. Do ADA confidentiality requirements apply to information about a psychiatric disability disclosed to an employer?

Yes. Employers must keep all information concerning the medical condition or history of its applicants or employees, including information about psychiatric disability, confidential under the ADA. This includes medical information that an individual voluntarily tells his/her employer. Employers must collect and maintain such information on separate forms and in separate medical files, apart from the usual personnel files. There are limited exceptions to the ADA confidentiality requirements:

- supervisors and managers may be told about necessary restrictions on the work or duties of the employee and about necessary accommodations;
- first aid and safety personnel may be told if the disability might require emergency treatment; and
- government officials investigating compliance with the ADA must be given relevant information on request.

16. How can an employer respond when employees ask questions about a coworker who has a disability?

If employees ask questions about a coworker who has a disability, the employer must not disclose any medical information in response. Apart from the limited exceptions listed in Question 15, the ADA confidentiality provisions prohibit such disclosure.

An employer also may not tell employees whether it is providing a reasonable accommodation for a particular individual. A statement that an individual receives a reasonable accommodation discloses that the individual probably has a disability because only individuals with disabilities are entitled to reasonable accommodation under the ADA. In response to coworker questions, however, the employer may explain that it is acting for legitimate business reasons or in compliance with federal law. . . .

22. May an employer require an employee to go to a health care professional of the employer's (rather than the employee's) choice for purposes of documenting need for accommodation and disability?

The ADA does not prevent an employer from requiring an employee to go to an appropriate health professional of the employer's choice if the employee initially provides insufficient information to substantiate that s/he has an ADA disability and needs a reasonable accommodation. Of course, any examination must be job-related and consistent with business necessity. If an employer requires an employee to go to a health professional of the employer's choice, the employer must pay all costs associated with the visit(s). . . .

28. Is it a reasonable accommodation to make sure that an individual takes medication as prescribed?

No. Medication monitoring is not a reasonable accommodation. Employers have no obligation to monitor medication because doing so does not remove a barrier that is unique to the workplace. When people do not take medication as prescribed, it affects them on and off the job. . . .

CONDUCT

Maintaining satisfactory conduct and performance typically is not a problem for individuals with psychiatric disabilities. Nonetheless, circumstances arise when employers need to discipline individuals with such disabilities for misconduct.

30. May an employer discipline an individual with a disability for violating a workplace conduct standard if the misconduct resulted from a disability?

Yes, provided that the workplace conduct standard is job-related for the position in question and is consistent with business necessity. For example, nothing in the ADA prevents an employer from maintaining a workplace free of violence or threats of violence, or from disciplining an employee who steals or destroys property. Thus, an employer may discipline an employee with a disability for engaging in such misconduct if it would impose the same discipline on an employee without a disability. Other conduct standards, however, may not be job-related for the position in question and consistent with business necessity. If they are not, imposing discipline under them could violate the ADA.

Example A: An employee steals money from his employer. Even if he asserts that his misconduct was caused by a disability, the employer may discipline him consistent with its uniform disciplinary policies because the individual violated a conduct standard—a prohibition against employee theft—that is job-related for the position in question and consistent with business necessity.

Example B: An employee at a clinic tampers with and incapacitates medical equipment. Even if the employee explains that she did this because of her disability, the employer may discipline her consistent with its uniform disciplinary policies because she violated a conduct standard—a rule prohibiting intentional damage to equipment—that is job-related for the position in question and consistent with business necessity. However, if the employer disciplines her even though it has not disciplined people without disabilities for the same misconduct, the employer would be treating her differently because of disability in violation of the ADA.

Example C: An employee with a psychiatric disability works in a warehouse loading boxes onto pallets for shipment. He has no customer contact and does not come into regular contact with other employees. Over the course of several weeks, he has come to work appearing increasingly disheveled. His clothes are ill-fitting and often have tears in them. He also has become increasingly anti-social. Coworkers have complained that when they try to engage him in casual conversation, he walks away or gives a curt reply. When he has to talk to a coworker, he is abrupt and rude. His work, however, has not suffered. The employer's company handbook states that employees should have a neat appearance at all times. The handbook also states that employees should be courteous to each other. When told that he is being disciplined for his appearance and treatment of coworkers, the employee explains that his appearance and demeanor have deteriorated because of his disability which was exacerbated during this time period.

The dress code and coworker courtesy rules are not job-related for the position in question and consistent with business necessity because this employee has no customer contact and does not come into regular contact with other employees. Therefore, rigid application of these rules to this employee would violate the ADA. . . .

34. When can an employer refuse to hire someone based on his/her history of violence or threats of violence?

An employer may refuse to hire someone based on his/her history of violence or threats of violence if it can show that the individual poses a direct threat. A determination of "direct threat" must be based on an individualized assessment of the individual's present ability to safely perform the functions of the job, considering the most current medical knowledge and/or the best available objective evidence. To find that an individual with a psychiatric disability poses a direct threat, the employer must identify the specific behavior on the part of the individual that would pose the direct threat. This includes an assessment of the likelihood and imminence of future violence.

Example: An individual applies for a position with Employer X. When Employer X checks his employment background, she learns that he was terminated two weeks ago by Employer Y, after he told a coworker that he would get a gun and "get his supervisor if he tries anything again." Employer X also learns that these statements followed three months of escalating incidents in which this individual had had several altercations in the workplace, including one in which he had to be restrained from fighting with a coworker. He then revealed his disability to Employer Y. After being given time off for medical treatment, he continued to have trouble controlling his temper and was seen punching the wall outside his supervisor's office. Finally, he made the threat against the supervisor and was terminated. Employer X learns that since then, he has not received any further medical treatment.

Employer X does not hire him, stating that this history indicates that he poses a direct threat.

This individual poses a direct threat as a result of his disability because his recent overt acts and statements (including an attempted fight with a coworker, punching the wall, and making a threatening statement about the supervisor) support the conclusion that he poses a "significant risk of substantial harm." Furthermore, his prior treatment had no effect on his behavior, he had received no subsequent treatment, and only two weeks had elapsed since his termination, all supporting a finding of direct threat.

Appendix G
Excerpts from the EEOC Enforcement Guidance:
Workers' Compensation and the ADA

INTRODUCTION

This enforcement guidance concerns the interaction between Title I of the Americans with Disabilities Act of 1990 (ADA) and state workers' compensation laws. The purpose of Title I of the ADA is to prohibit employers from discriminating against qualified individuals because of disability in all aspects of employment. On the other hand, the purpose of a workers' compensation law is to provide a system for securing prompt and fair settlement of employees' claims against employers for occupational injury and illness. While the purposes of the two laws are not in conflict, the simultaneous application of the laws has raised questions for EEOC investigators, for employers, and for individuals with disabilities in a number of areas. In this document, the Commission provides guidance concerning the following issues:

- whether a person with an occupational injury has a disability as defined by the ADA;
- disability-related questions and medical examinations relating to occupational injury and workers' compensation claims;
- hiring of persons with a history of occupational injury, return to work of persons with occupational injury, and application of the direct threat standard;
- reasonable accommodation for persons with disability-related occupational injuries;
- light duty issues; and
- exclusive remedy provisions in workers' compensation laws.

REASONABLE ACCOMMODATION

The ADA requires that an employer make reasonable accommodation to the known physical or mental limitations of an otherwise qualified individual with a disability, unless the employer can demonstrate that the accommodation would impose an undue hardship. . . . This section provides specific guidance regarding reasonable accommodation in the context of workers' compensation.

17. Does the ADA require an employer to provide reasonable accommodation for an employee with an occupational injury who does not have a disability as defined by the ADA?

No. The ADA does not require an employer to provide a reasonable accommodation for an employee with an occupational injury who does not have a disability as defined by the ADA.

18. May an employer discharge an employee who is temporarily unable to work because of a disability-related occupational injury?

No. An employer may not discharge an employee who is temporarily unable to work because of a disability-related occupational injury where it would not impose an undue hardship to provide leave as a reasonable accommodation.

19. What are the reinstatement rights of an employee with a disability-related occupational injury?

An employee with a disability-related occupational injury is entitled to return to his/her same position unless the employer demonstrates that holding open the position would impose an undue hardship.

In some instances, an employee may request more leave even after the employer has communicated that it would impose an undue hardship to hold open the employee's position any longer. In this situation, the employer must consider whether it has a vacant, equivalent position for which the employee is qualified and to which the employee can be reassigned without undue hardship to continue his/her leave for a specific period of time. For example, suppose that an employee needs six months to recover from a disability-related occupational injury, but holding his/her original position open for more than four months will impose an undue hardship. The employer must consider whether it has a vacant equivalent position to which the employee can be reassigned for the remaining two months of leave. If an equivalent position is not available, the employer must look for a vacant position at a lower level. Continued leave is not required as a reasonable accommodation if a vacant position at a lower level is also unavailable.

20. Must an employer, as a reasonable accommodation, reallocate job duties of an employee with a disability-related occupational injury?

Yes, if the duties to be reallocated are marginal functions of the position that the employee cannot perform because of the disability. Reasonable accommodation includes restructuring a position by reallocating or redistributing the marginal functions that the employee cannot perform because of the disability. However, an employer need not eliminate essential functions of the position.

21. May an employer unilaterally reassign an employee with a disability-related occupational injury to a different position instead of first trying to accommodate the employee in the position s/he held at the time the injury occurred?

No. An employer must first assess whether the employee can perform the essential functions of his/her original position, with or without a reasonable accommodation. Examples of reasonable accommodation include job restructuring, modification of equipment, or a part-time work schedule. Reassignment should be considered only when accommodation within the employee's original position is not possible or would impose an undue hardship.

22. Must an employer reassign an employee who is no longer able to perform the essential functions of his/her original position, with or without a reasonable accommodation, because of a disability-related occupational injury?

Yes. Where an employee can no longer perform the essential functions of his/her original position, with or without a reasonable accommodation, because of a disability-related occupational injury, an employer must reassign him/her to an equivalent vacant position for which s/he is qualified, absent undue hardship. If no equivalent vacant position (in terms of pay, status, etc.) exists, then the employee must be reassigned to a lower graded position for which s/he is qualified, absent undue hardship.

23. If there is no vacancy for an employee who can no longer perform his/her original position because of a disability-related occupational injury, must an employer create a new position or "bump" another employee from his/her position?

No. The ADA does not require an employer to create a new position or to bump another employee from his/her position in order to reassign an employee who can no longer perform the es-

sential functions of his/her original position, with or without a reasonable accommodation.

24. When an employee requests leave as a reasonable accommodation under the ADA because of a disability-related occupational injury, may an employer provide an accommodation that requires him/her to remain on the job instead?

Yes. An employer need not provide an employee's preferred accommodation as long as the employer provides an effective accommodation—one that is sufficient to meet the employee's job-related needs.

Accordingly, an employer may provide a reasonable accommodation that requires an employee to remain on the job, in lieu of providing leave (e.g., reallocating marginal functions, or providing temporary reassignment).

The employer is obligated, however, to restore the employee's full duties or to return the employee to his/her original position once s/he has recovered sufficiently to perform its essential functions, with or without a reasonable accommodation.

26. May an employer make a workplace modification that is not a required form of reasonable accommodation under the ADA in order to offset workers' compensation costs?

Yes. Nothing in the ADA prohibits an employer from making a workplace modification that is not a required form of reasonable accommodation under the ADA for an employee with an occupational injury in order to offset workers' compensation costs. For example, the ADA does not require employers to lower production standards to accommodate individuals with disabilities. However, an employer is clearly permitted to lower production standards for an occupationally injured employee as a way of returning him/her to work more quickly.

LIGHT DUTY

The term "light duty" has a number of different meanings in the employment setting. Generally, "light duty" refers to temporary or permanent work that is physically or mentally less demanding than normal job duties. Some employers use the term "light duty" to mean simply excusing an employee from performing those job functions that s/he is unable to perform because of an impairment. "Light duty" also may consist of particular positions with duties that are less physically or mentally demanding created specifically for the purpose of providing alternative work for employees who are unable to perform some or all of their normal duties. Further, an employer may refer to any position that is sedentary or is less physically or mentally demanding as "light duty."

In the following questions and answers, the term "light duty" refers only to particular positions created specifically for the purpose of providing work for employees who are unable to perform some or all of their normal duties.

27. Does the ADA prohibit an employer from creating a light duty position for an employee when s/he is injured on the job?

> No, in most instances. An employer may recognize a special obligation arising out of the employment relationship to create a light duty position for an employee when s/he has been injured while performing work for the employer and, as a consequence, is unable to perform his/her regular job duties. Such a policy, on its face, does not treat an individual with a disability less favorably than an individual without a disability; nor does it screen out an individual on the basis of disability.

> Of course, an employer must apply its policy of creating a light duty position for an employee when s/he is occupationally injured on a nondiscriminatory basis. In other words, an employer may not use disability as a reason to refuse to create a light duty position when an employee is occupationally injured.

> An employer need not create a light duty position for a non-occupationally injured employee with a disability as a reasonable accommodation. The principle that the ADA does not require employers to create positions as a form of reasonable accommodation applies equally to the creation of light duty positions. However, an employer must provide other forms of reasonable accommodation required under the ADA. . . .

Example: R creates light duty positions for employees when they are occupationally injured if they are unable to perform one or more of their regular job duties. CP can no longer perform functions of her position because of a disability caused by an off-the-job accident. She requests that R create a light duty position for her as a reasonable accommodation. R denies CP's request because she has not been injured on the job. R has not violated the ADA. However, R must provide another reasonable accommodation, absent undue hardship. If it is determined that the only effective accommodation is to restructure CP's position by redistributing the marginal functions, and the restructured position resembles a light duty position, R must provide the reasonable accommodation unless it can prove that it imposes an undue hardship. . . .

Appendix H
Excerpts from the Presidential Guidelines on Religious Exercise and Expression in the Federal Workplace, August 14, 1997

The following Guidelines, addressing religious exercise and religious expression, shall apply to all civilian executive branch agencies, officials, and employees in the Federal workplace.

These Guidelines principally address employees' religious exercise and religious expression when the employees are acting in their personal capacity within the Federal workplace and the public does not have regular exposure to the workplace. The Guidelines do not comprehensively address whether and when the government and its employees may engage in religious speech directed at the public. They also do not address religious exercise and religious expression by uniformed military personnel, or the conduct of business by chaplains employed by the Federal Government. Nor do the Guidelines define the rights and responsibilities of non-governmental employers—including religious employers—and their employees. Although these Guidelines, including the examples cited in them, should answer the most frequently encountered questions in the Federal workplace, actual cases sometimes will be complicated by additional facts and circumstances that may require a different result from the one the Guidelines indicate.

Section 1. Guidelines for Religious Exercise and Religious Expression in the Federal Workplace.
Executive departments and agencies ("agencies") shall permit personal religious expression by Federal employees to the greatest extent possible, consistent with requirements of law and interests in workplace efficiency as described in this set of Guidelines. Agencies shall not discriminate against employees on the basis of religion, require religious participation or non-participation as a condition of employment, or permit religious harassment. And agencies shall accommodate employees' exercise of their religion in the circumstances specified in these Guidelines. These requirements are but applications of the general principle that agencies shall treat all employees with the same respect and consideration, regardless of their religion (or lack thereof).

A. Religious Expression. As a matter of law, agencies shall not restrict personal religious expression by employees in the Federal workplace except where the employee's interest in the expression is outweighed by the government's interest in the efficient provision of public services or where the expression intrudes upon the legitimate rights of other employees or creates the appearance, to a reasonable observer, of an official endorsement of religion. The examples cited in these Guidelines as permissible forms of religious expression will rarely, if ever, fall within these exceptions.

As a general rule, agencies may not regulate employees' personal religious expression on the basis of its content or viewpoint. In other words, agencies generally may not suppress employees' private religious speech in the workplace while leaving unregulated other private employee speech that has a comparable effect on the efficiency of the workplace—including ideological speech on politics and other topics—because to do so would be to engage in presumptively unlawful content or viewpoint discrimination. Agencies, however, may, in their discretion, reasonably regulate the time, place and manner of all employee speech, provided such regulations do not discriminate on the basis of content or viewpoint.

The Federal Government generally has the authority to regulate an employee's private speech, including religious speech, where the employee's interest in that speech is outweighed by the government's interest in promoting the efficiency of the public services it performs. Agencies should exercise this authority evenhandedly and with restraint, and with regard for the fact that Americans are used to expressions of disagreement on controversial subjects, including religious ones. Agencies are not required, however, to permit employees to use work time to pursue religious or ideological agendas. Federal employees are paid to perform official work, not to engage in personal religious or ideological campaigns during work hours.

(1) **Expression in Private Work Areas.** Employees should be permitted to engage in private religious expression in personal work areas not regularly open to the public to the same extent that they may engage in nonreligious private expression, subject to reasonable content- and viewpoint-neutral standards and restrictions: such religious

expression must be permitted so long as it does not interfere with the agency's carrying out of its official responsibilities.

Examples

(a) An employee may keep a Bible or Koran on her private desk and read it during breaks.

(b) An agency may restrict all posters, or posters of a certain size, in private work areas, or require that such posters be displayed facing the employee, and not on common walls; but the employer typically cannot single out religious or anti-religious posters for harsher or preferential treatment.

(2) Expression Among Fellow Employees. Employees should be permitted to engage in religious expression with fellow employees, to the same extent that they may engage in comparable nonreligious private expression, subject to reasonable and content-neutral standards and restrictions: such expression should not be restricted so long as it does not interfere with workplace efficiency. Though agencies are entitled to regulate such employee speech based on reasonable predictions of disruption, they should not restrict speech based on merely hypothetical concerns, having little basis in fact, that the speech will have a deleterious effect on workplace efficiency.

Examples

(a) In informal settings, such as cafeterias and hallways, employees are entitled to discuss their religious views with one another, subject only to the same rules of order as apply to other employee expression. If an agency permits unrestricted nonreligious expression of a controversial nature, it must likewise permit equally controversial religious expression.

(b) Employees are entitled to display religious messages on items of clothing to the same extent that they are permitted to display other comparable messages. So long as they do not convey any governmental endorsement of religion, religious messages may not typically be singled out for suppression.

(c) Employees generally may wear religious medallions over their clothes or so that they are otherwise visible. Typically, this alone will not affect workplace efficiency, and therefore is protected.

(3) Expression Directed at Fellow Employees. Employees are permitted to engage in religious expression directed at fellow employees, and may even attempt to persuade fellow employees of the correctness of their religious views, to the same extent as those employees may engage in comparable speech not involving religion. Some religions encourage adherents to spread the faith at every opportunity, a duty that can encompass the adherent's workplace. As a general matter, proselytizing is as entitled to constitutional protection as any other form of speech—as long as a reasonable observer would not interpret the expression as government endorsement of religion. Employees may urge a colleague to participate or not to participate in religious activities to the same extent that, consistent with concerns of workplace efficiency, they may urge their colleagues to engage in or refrain from other personal endeavors. But employees must refrain from such expression when a fellow employee asks that it stop or otherwise demonstrates that it is unwelcome. (Such expression by supervisors is subject to special consideration as discussed in Section B(2) of these guidelines.)

Examples

(a) During a coffee break, one employee engages another in a polite discussion of why his faith should be embraced. The other employee disagrees with the first employee's religious exhortations, but does not ask that the conversation stop. Under these circumstances, agencies should not restrict or interfere with such speech.

(b) One employee invites another employee to attend worship services at her church, though she knows that the invitee is a devout adherent of another faith. The invitee is shocked, and asks that the invitation not be repeated. The original invitation is protected, but the employee should honor the request that no further invitations be issued.

(c) In a parking lot, a non-supervisory employee hands another employee a religious tract urging that she convert to another religion lest she be condemned to eternal damnation. The proselytizing employee says nothing further and does not inquire of his colleague whether she followed the pamphlet's urging. This speech typically should not be restricted.

Though personal religious expression such as that described in these examples, standing alone, is protected in the same way, and to the same extent, as other constitutionally valued speech in the Federal workplace, such expression should not be permitted if it is part of a larger pattern of verbal attacks on fellow employees (or a specific employee) not sharing the faith of the speaker. Such speech, by virtue of its excessive or harassing nature, may constitute religious harassment or create a hostile work environment, as described in Part B(3) of these Guidelines, and an agency should not tolerate it. . . .

B. Religious Discrimination. Federal agencies may not discriminate against employees on the basis of their religion, religious beliefs, or views concerning religion . . .

(3) Hostile Work Environment and Harassment. The law against workplace discrimination protects Federal employees from being subjected to a hostile environment, or religious harassment, in the form of religiously discriminatory intimidation, or pervasive or severe religious ridicule or insult, whether by supervisors or fellow workers. Whether particular conduct gives rise to a hostile environment, or constitutes impermissible religious harassment, will usually depend upon its frequency or repetitiveness, as well as its severity. The use of derogatory language in an assaultive manner can constitute statutory religious harassment if it is severe or invoked repeatedly. A single incident, if sufficiently abusive, might also constitute statutory harassment. However, although employees should always be guided by general principles of civility and workplace efficiency, a hostile environment is not created by the bare expression of speech with which some employees might disagree. In a country where freedom of speech and religion are guaranteed, citizens should expect to be exposed to ideas with which they disagree.

The examples below are intended to provide guidance on when conduct or words constitute religious harassment that should not be tolerated in the Federal workplace. In a particular case, the question of employer liability would require consideration of additional factors, including the extent to which the agency was aware of the harassment and the actions the agency took to address it.

Examples

(a) An employee repeatedly makes derogatory remarks to other employees with whom she is assigned to work about their faith or lack of faith. This typically will constitute religious harassment. An agency should not tolerate such conduct.

(b) A group of employees subjects a fellow employee to a barrage of comments about his sex life, knowing that the targeted employee would be discomforted and offended by such comments because of his religious beliefs. This typically will constitute harassment, and an agency should not tolerate it.

(c) A group of employees that share a common faith decides that they want to work exclusively with people who share their views. They engage in a pattern of verbal attacks on other employees who do not share their views, calling them heathens, sinners, and the like. This conduct should not be tolerated.

(d) Two employees have an angry exchange of words. In the heat of the moment, one makes a derogatory comment about the other's religion. When tempers cool, no more is said. Unless the words are sufficiently severe or pervasive to alter the conditions of the insulted employee's employment or create an abusive working environment, this is not statutory religious harassment.

(e) Employees wear religious jewelry and medallions over their clothes or so that they are otherwise visible. Others wear buttons with a generalized religious or anti-religious message. Typically, these expressions are personal and do not alone constitute religious harassment.

(f) In her private work area, a Federal worker keeps a Bible or Koran on her private desk and reads it during breaks. Another employee displays a picture of Jesus and the text of the Lord's Prayer in her private work area. This conduct, without more, is not religious harassment, and does not create an impermissible hostile environment with respect to employees who do not share those religious views, even if they are upset or offended by the conduct.

During lunch, certain employees gather on their own time for prayer and Bible study in an empty conference room that employees are generally free to use on a first-come, first-served basis. Such a gathering does not constitute religious harassment even if other employees with different views on how to pray might feel excluded or ask that the group be disbanded. . . .

Section 2. Guiding Legal Principles. In applying the guidance set forth in section 1 of this order, executive branch departments and agencies should consider the following legal principles.

A. Religious Expression. It is well-established that the Free Speech Clause of the First Amendment protects Government employees in the workplace. This right encompasses a right to speak about religious subjects. The Free Speech Clause also prohibits the Government from singling out religious expression for disfavored treatment: "[P]rivate religious speech, far from being a First Amendment orphan, is as fully protected under the Free Speech Clause as secular private expression," Capitol Sq. Review Bd. v. Pinette, 115 S.Ct. 2448 (1995). Accordingly, in the Government workplace, employee religious expression cannot be regulated because of its religious character, and such religious speech typically cannot be singled out for harsher treatment than other comparable expression.

Many religions strongly encourage their adherents to spread the faith by persuasion and example at every opportunity, a duty that can extend to the adherents' workplace. As a general matter, proselytizing is entitled to the same constitutional protection as any other form of speech. Therefore, in the governmental workplace, proselytizing should not be singled out because of its content for harsher treatment than non-religious expression.

However, it is also well-established that the Government in its role as employer has broader discretion to regulate its employees' speech in the workplace than it does to regulate speech among the public at large. Employees' expression on matters of public concern can be regulated if the employees' interest in the speech is outweighed by the interest of the Government, as an employer, in promoting the efficiency of the public services it performs through its employees. Governmental employers also possess substantial discretion to impose content-neutral and viewpoint-neutral time, place, and manner rules regulating private employee expression in the workplace (though they may not structure or administer such rules to discriminate against particular viewpoints). Furthermore, employee speech can be regulated or discouraged if it impairs discipline by superiors, has a detrimental impact on close working relationships for which personal loyalty and confidence are necessary, impedes the performance of the speaker's duties or interferes with the regular operation of the enterprise, or demonstrates that the employee holds views that could lead his employer or the public reasonably to question whether he can perform his duties adequately.

Consistent with its fully protected character, employee religious speech should be treated, within the Federal workplace, like other expression on issues of public concern: in a particular case, an employer can discipline an employee for engaging in speech if the value of the speech is outweighed by the employer's interest in promoting the efficiency of the public services it performs through its employee. Typically, however, the religious speech cited as permissible in the various examples included in these Guidelines will not unduly impede these interests and should not be regulated. And rules regulating employee speech, like other rules regulating speech, must be carefully drawn to avoid any unnecessary limiting or chilling of protected speech. . . .

D. Hostile Work Environment and Harassment. Employers violate Title VII's ban on discrimination by creating or tolerating a "hostile environment" in which an employee is subject to discriminatory intimidation, ridicule, or insult sufficiently severe or pervasive to alter the conditions of the victim's employment. This statutory standard can be triggered (at the very least) when an employee, because of her or his religion or lack thereof, is exposed to intimidation, ridicule, and insult. The hostile conduct—which may take the form of speech—need not come from supervisors or from the employer. Fellow employees can create a hostile environment through their own words and actions.

The existence of some offensive workplace conduct does not necessarily constitute harassment under Title VII. Occasional and isolated utterances of an epithet that engenders offensive feelings in an employee typically would not affect conditions of employment, and therefore would not in and of itself constitute harassment. A hostile environment, for Title VII purposes, is not created by the bare expression of speech with which one disagrees. For religious harassment to be illegal under Title VII, it must be sufficiently severe or pervasive to alter the conditions of employment and create an abusive working environment. Whether conduct can be the predicate for a finding of religious harassment under Title VII depends on the totality of the circumstances, such as the nature of the verbal or physical conduct at issue and the context in which the alleged incidents occurred. As the Supreme Court has said in an analogous context:

> [W]hether an environment is "hostile" or "abusive" can be determined only by looking at all the circumstances. These may include the frequency of the discriminatory conduct; its severity; whether it is physically threatening or humiliating, or a mere offensive utterance; and whether it unreasonably interferes with an employee's work performance. The effect on the employee's psychological well-being is, of course, relevant to determining whether the plaintiff actually found the environment abusive. *Harris v. Forklift Systems, Inc.*, 510 U.S. 17, 23 (1993).

The use of derogatory language directed at an employee can rise to the level of religious harassment if it is severe or invoked repeatedly. In particular, repeated religious slurs and negative religious stereotypes, or continued disparagement of an employee's religion or ritual practices, or lack thereof, can constitute harassment. It is not necessary that the harassment be explicitly religious in character or that the slurs reference religion: it is sufficient that the harassment is directed at an employee because of the employee's religion or lack thereof. That is to say, Title VII can be violated by employer tolerance of repeated slurs, insults and/or abuse not explicitly religious in nature if that conduct would not have occurred but for the targeted employee's religious belief or lack of religious belief. Finally, although proselytization directed at fellow employees is generally permissible (subject to the special considerations relating to supervisor expression discussed elsewhere in these Guidelines), such activity must stop if the listener asks that it stops or otherwise demonstrates that it is unwelcome.

E. Accommodation of Religious Exercise. Title VII requires employers "to reasonably accommodate an employee's or prospective employee's religious observance or practice" unless such accommodation would impose an "undue hardship on the conduct of the employer's business." 42 U.S.C. § 2000e(j). For example, by statute, if an employee's religious beliefs require her to be absent from work, the Federal Government must grant that employee compensation time for overtime work, to be applied against the time lost, unless to do so would harm the ability of the agency to carry out its mission efficiently. 5 U.S.C. § 5550a.

Though an employer need not incur more than *de minimis* costs in providing an accommodation, the employer hardship nevertheless must be real rather than speculative or hypothetical. Religious accommodation cannot be disfavored relative to other, nonreligious, accommodations. If an employer regularly permits accommodation for nonreligious purposes, it cannot deny comparable religious accommodation: "Such an arrangement would display a discrimination against religious practices that is the antithesis of reasonableness." *Ansonia Bd. of Educ. v. Philbrook,* 479 U.S. 60, 71 (1986).

In the Federal Government workplace, if neutral workplace rules—that is, rules that do not single out religious or religiously motivated conduct for disparate treatment—impose a substantial burden on a particular employee's exercise of religion, the Religious Freedom Restoration Act requires the employer to grant the employee an exemption from that neutral rule, unless the employer has a compelling interest in denying an exemption and there is no less restrictive means of furthering that interest. 42 U.S.C. § 2000bb-1.

F. Establishment of Religion. The Establishment Clause of the First Amendment prohibits the Government—including its employees—from acting in a manner that would lead a reasonable observer to conclude that the Government is sponsoring, endorsing or inhibiting religion generally or favoring or disfavoring a particular religion. For example, where the public has access to the Federal workplace, employee religious expression should be prohibited where the public reasonably would perceive that the employee is acting in an official, rather than a private, capacity, or under circumstances that would lead a reasonable observer to conclude that the Government is endorsing or disparaging religion. The Establishment Clause also forbids Federal employees from using Government funds or resources (other than those facilities generally available to government employees) for private religious uses.

Section 3. General. These Guidelines shall govern the internal management of the civilian executive branch. They are not intended to create any new right, benefit, or trust responsibility, substantive or procedural, enforceable at law or equity by a party against the United States, its agencies, its officers, or any person. Questions regarding interpretations of these Guidelines should be brought to the Office of the General Counsel or Legal Counsel in each department and agency.

Glossary

A

administrative law judge: a government official who presides at hearings of the NLRB or other government agencies. In the absence of objections by a party, the NLRB routinely endorses the administrative law judge's findings of fact and recommendations.

affidavit: a statement of facts set forth in written form and supported by the oath or affirmation of the person making the statement that such facts are true to the person's knowledge, information, and belief. The affidavit is executed before a notary public or other person authorized to administer oaths.

agency: a situation in which one person acts for or represents another by the latter's authority.

agent: one who is acting for an employer or union. An agent's actions may subject a principal to liability with respect to unfair labor practices even in the absence of specific authorization.

amici: a person or organization that has no right to appear in a suit but is allowed to introduce argument, authority, or evidence to protect the individual's or group's interests.

animus: mind or intention. In labor law animus is used as a shortened form of "antiunion animus" or antiunion mind set or intent.

arbitration: the settlement of disputed questions, whether concerning contractual language or fact, by one or more arbitrators by whose decision the parties agreed to be bound308 Increasingly used as a procedure for labor dispute settlement.

B

back pay: wages required to be paid to an employee upon a finding of discharge or layoff of the employee in violation of a contractual or statutory right

burden of proof: the requirement that a certain party to a legal dispute prove a fact or facts in question.

C

case law: the law as laid down in the decisions of the courts as distinct from statutes and other sources of law.

cause of action: the right to damages or other judicial relief when a legally protected right of the plaintiff is violated by an unlawful act of the defendant.

certiorari: an appellate proceeding for reexamination of an action or judgment of a lower court. It usually requires the lower court to certify and return its records to the reviewing court.

charge: a written statement alleging violation of a labor relations statute.

charging party: the person initiating unfair labor practice procedures before the National Labor Relations Board or the person initiating unlawful employment practice procedures before the Equal Employment Opportunity Commission.

civil action: in many states a simplified form of action combining all or many of the former common law actions.

class action suit: an action in which one or more members of a numerous class having a common interest sue on behalf of themselves and all other members of that class.

collective bargaining agreement: a contract governing wages, hours, and conditions of employment between an employer and a union that is the product of the collective bargaining process.

common law: the body of unwritten principles originally based on the usages and customs of the community which were recognized and enforced by the courts.

complaint: the initial pleading filed by the plaintiff in a civil action; also a formal statement by the NLRB, after investigating a charge, that the Board has jurisdiction and *prima facie* evidence that an unfair labor practice exists.

conciliation: process by which a third party acts as intermediary between the parties to a labor dispute, helping them to reach a settlement.

consent decree: an agreement reached by parties to a case after careful negotiation which is then entered as a judgment by a court.

contract: a binding agreement based upon the genuine assent of competent parities, made for a lawful object, in the form required by law, and generally supported by consideration; a collective bargaining agreement.

corporation: an artificial legal person or being created by government grant, which for many purposes is treated as a natural person.

crime: a violation of the law that is punished as an offense against the state or government.

D

damages: a sum of money recovered to redress or make amends for the legal wrong or injury done.

de facto: existing in fact as distinguished from existing by lawful right.

deposition: the testimony of a witness taken out of court before a person authorized to administer oaths.

discrimination: unequal treatment of workers. The National Labor Relations Act prohibits discrimination with respect to hire or tenure of employment as a means of encouraging or discouraging membership in a labor organization.

dismiss, motion to: a procedure to terminate an action by requesting dismissal on the ground that the plaintiff has not pleaded a cause entitling the plaintiff to relief.

due process of law: the guarantee by the Fifth and Fourteenth Amendments of the federal Constitution and of many state constitutions that no person shall be deprived of life, liberty, or property without due process of law. As presently interpreted, this prohibits any law, either state or federal, that sets up an unfair procedure. Due process requires that a defendant be given notice of the charges and an opportunity to defend against the charges.

E

equity: the body of principles that originally developed because of the inadequacy of the rules then applied by the common law courts of England. Equity embodies notions of natural right, justice, ethics, and conscience.

evidence: that which is presented to the trier of fact as the basis on which the trier is to determine what happened.

F

fair employment practice: for hiring, promotion, and tenure of employees without discrimination due to race, color, national origin, religion, or sex.

front pay: an amount of money awarded a victim of discrimination to make the victim whole for the loss of future work opportunities with an employer due to the employer's wrongful discrimination.

G

grievance: a complaint by the union, employer, or employees usually alleging a violation of the collective bargaining agreement.

grievance procedure: a procedure for settling disputes set forth in the collective bargaining agreement. It usually involves several steps, with the aggrieved worker and representative meeting with the supervisor involved, followed by an appeal system with strict time limits, and ultimately ending in binding arbitration.

I

injunction: an order of a court of equity to refrain from doing (negative injunction) or to do (affirmative or mandatory injunction) a specified act. Its use in labor disputes has been greatly restricted by the Norris-LaGuardia Act.

J

judgment: the final sentence, order, or decision entered into at the conclusion of an action which determines the rights of the parties.

N

National Labor Relations Act: the federal statute designed to protect the organization rights of labor and to prevent unfair labor practices by management or labor.

P

picketing: the placing of persons outside of places of employment or distribution so that by words or banners they may inform the public of the existence of a labor dispute.

pleadings: the papers filed by the parties in an action which set forth the facts and the nature of the issues to be tried.

preponderance of evidence: the degree or quantum of evidence in favor of the existence of a certain fact when from a review of all the evidence it appears more probable than not that the fact exists. The margin of probability required is a greater than 50 percent likelihood of the fact's existence.

prima facie: such evidence as by itself would establish the claim or defense of the party if the evidence were believed.

prima facie case: a case that will be sufficient if not contradicted by rebutting evidence.

proof: the probative effect of the evidence; the conclusion drawn from the evidence as to the existence of particular facts.

public policy: certain objectives relating to health, morals, and integrity of government that the law seeks to advance.

punitive damages: damages in excess of those required to compensate the plaintiff for the wrong done, which are imposed in view of the wanton or willful character of the defendant's wrongdoing; also called exemplary damages.

Q

quasi: as if, as though it were, having the characteristics of; a modifier employed to indicate that the subject is to be treated as an analogy to the noun that follows the word *quasi*, as in quasi contract, quasi corporation.

R

recognition: an employer's acknowledgment and acceptance of a union as the exclusive representative of employees in a unit for purposes of collective bargaining.

remedy: the action or procedure that is followed in order to enforce a right or obtain damages for injury to a right.

respondeat superior: let the master answer. This maxim means that an employer is liable in certain cases for the wrongful acts of its employees.

respondent: the party against whom an appeal is taken; the party who must respond and defend against an appeal.

reverse discrimination: preferential treatment with regard to hire or tenure of employment that attempts to remedy past discrimination by means of quotas in hiring or immunity from layoff despite low seniority.

right-to-work law: a state law that prohibits employment arrangements which mandate union membership as a condition of employment.

S

seniority system: a system that grants employees employment preferences according to the employee's length of service.

summons: a writ by which a defendant is notified that an action was commenced against the defendant and must be answered.

U

unfair employment practice: employment discrimination with respect to race, color, religion, sex, or national origin.

unfair labor practices: practices of employers or unions that are prohibited under Section 8 of the National Labor Relations Act or under state labor statutes.

unfair labor practice strike: a strike in protest of an employer's unfair labor practice(s). The employer is required to reinstate such strikers.

V

validation study: a study of a personnel test to determine the test's validity as an accurate predictor of successful work behavior. A method for validating a test is to administer it to all applicants while making selections for hiring without regard to test scores. After an appropriate period of time on the job, work performance can be compared with test scores.

Index of Cases*

---

* Boldface case and page reference indicate case decisions reported in the text.

Index of Subjects

317